Investigating the Sai Baba Movement

INVESTIGATING THE SAI BABA MOVEMENT

A Clarification of Misrepresented Saints and Opportunism

Kevin Shepherd

CITIZEN INITIATIVE

2005

First published 2005
by Citizen Initiative

P.O. Box 5757
Dorchester DT2 7ZX
Dorset
England

ISBN 0 9525089 3 1

British Library Cataloguing in Publication Data.
A catalogue record for this book is available from the
British Library

Printed in Great Britain by
Antony Rowe Ltd., Chippenham, Wiltshire

Contents

Preface

The title of this book was originally conceived as *Gurus Rediscovered – Second Instalment*. The new title does not imply that I believe the phrase "Sai Baba movement" to be the most apt description of the subject matter. Frankly, I do not, and indeed find it objectionable. This phrase has originated with academics who have promoted a misleading context associated with Satya (Sathya) Sai Baba of Puttaparthi. This despite the more plausible theory that the "movement" originated with Sai Baba of Shirdi. At first sight, that theory seems reasonable. Yet there are complexities (including Hazrat Babajan), not least of which is that the figures involved in the proposed "movement" were of a very different orientation to Satya Sai Baba.

The basic situation is that of three ashrams and/or shrine centres which are in rivalry, competing for subscribers. There are actually three "movements" which have emerged in this respect. Yet these three are fundamentally related in terms of underlying events which are so often obscured by devotional interpretations. An exploitative intruder is Satya Sai Baba, who is bracketed with the other three figures by some of his partisans, the latter contingent having been deceived by his claims to be the reincarnation of Shirdi Sai Baba. Thus, the phrase "Sai Baba movement" is a deception, and requires clarification in the face of academic and popular confusions.

Partisans of Satya Sai reserve the main attention for the two Sais, with Upasni Maharaj and Meher Baba gaining lesser profile, especially the lastmentioned. The belief that Satya Sai is a reincarnation of Shirdi Sai has clearly influenced assessments. Meher Baba is often viewed as a rival, and Upasni Maharaj as an interesting but minor figure attaching to the Sai wonder. One will look in vain for an equality of treatment in "Sai Baba movement" writings, and miracles are a preferred feature of the scenario.

The pro-Satya Sai rubric effectively misrepresents the three saints in prospect, and a more equalising presentation of these three figures is necessary. A critical attitude to miracle lore is surely called for in this endeavour. There are also other misrepresentations discernible in sectarian portrayals, as in the controversial issue of the Muslim background of Shirdi Sai having received Hinduizing glosses.

The increasing critical reaction to Satya Sai Baba, both in his native land and abroad, is substantial. Despite the adulation he has gained,

Satya Sai has also evoked much opposition. Reports of his misdemeanours and deceits are dramatically escalating (see the Appendices). His purported miracles have been exposed as charlatanism; only the gullible will take such "miracles" seriously. Yet an American University Press has published a book that clearly evidences a support for Satya Sai in a treatment of his namesake Shirdi Sai Baba. Satya Sai pirated the fame of Shirdi Sai by his sensational claims. The State University of New York (SUNY) Press committed a serious error in that respect, an error made more obvious by recent disclosures about Satya Sai contributed by ex-devotees. In his book *The Life and Teachings of Sai Baba of Shirdi* (SUNY, 1993), Dr. Antonio Rigopoulos has implied his belief that Satya Sai is substantially compatible with Shirdi Sai. The academic response should instead surely be an attempt to disprove the claims of Satya Sai, not to sponsor those claims. Rigopoulos is in clear support of the miracle mentality, a reversion to medieval standards of assessment which do not enhance the intellectual superiority assumed by the academic population. The patronage of a pro-Satya book by SUNY Press has implied the legitimacy of the claims made by Satya Sai Baba, and has also implied that other versions of the "Sai Baba movement" must be wrong. The position of Satya Sai Baba is now morally indefensible. Satya Sai Baba now has so many counts against him that SUNY Press should seriously consider a public disclaimer of their sanction.

The present work amounts to a revised and extended version of my *Gurus Rediscovered* (Cambridge, 1986), which needed re-writing and a change of accent. The amplification was originally conceived as part of *Minds and Sociocultures Vol. 2*, but grew too lengthy when I decided that it was relevant to include Meher Baba – because of his statements about Shirdi Sai Baba, his close connections with Upasni Maharaj, and his inclusion by SUNY Press under the rubric of "Sai Baba movement." These three saints or charismatic gurus exhibit various eccentricities and extravagances. Shirdi Sai became almost legendary in some respects; Upasni Maharaj is more factual, but still subject to devotional distortions. The case history of Meher Baba has much factual detail, though again, sectarian interests have distorted some elements. The literature on these figures is often misleading, and requires correction in the light of more total findings.

The present writer is not a devotee of any of the three saints/gurus analysed here. In my youth I did have some involvement with the Meher Baba sect, and as a consequence was in receipt of information not always easy to acquire. I am very much at loggerheads with the sect promoting the name of Meher Baba. I believe that it is possible to present data on a cult figure without sharing in the devotee psychology.

The first draft of this book was written in Scotland in 1996–7. Several years later I read the proofs and added Appendix One. Subsequently, I revised and amplified some sections of the text and some of the notes, and also added Appendix Two and Appendix Three.

Kevin R. D. Shepherd

August 2004

Dorset

Guide to Contents

SAI BABA OF SHIRDI (SHIRDI SAI BABA)

Mistakenly associated with Satya Sai Baba, 2. *Guru Busters* tv documentary exposed Satya Sai in 1990s, 2–3. SUNY Press promote the "miracle guru" conflation, 4. The belief that Shirdi Sai was born at Jerusalem is not necessarily less valid than other versions, 4–5. Uncertain chronology for Shirdi Sai leaves questions and complexities, 9. Shirdi Sai revealed as Muslim *faqir* in relevant sources. The Hinduized version of Shirdi Sai does not hold up to detailed analysis, 6–7. His date of birth unknown, 9. Akalkot Maharaj, 10–11. The elusive Roshan Shah Mian has implied a Sufi mentor to Hindu scholarship, 11–12. Comparisons between Shirdi Sai and Shah Waris Ali, a liberal Indian Sufi, 13ff. Sai devotionalism has been a source of confusion and miracle lore. The Hindu commentator H. S. Dixit resorted to a theory of supernatural origins, 16. Both Arthur Osborne and Marvin Harper were misled by Hinduizing sources, 16–18. Living in a dilapidated mosque, Shirdi Sai was regarded as a Muslim ascetic by the local villagers, and was debarred from Hindu temples, 27–8. His gradual assimilation by Hindus created an image of him as a miracle-worker, 20–1. Many devotees in his last years were *brahmans* from Bombay. So-called public miracles. 30, 31. His allusive speech, which facilitated conversation with Hindus, 30, 38. His simple lifestyle of renunciation entailed a daily begging round, 23. An Urdu document written by a Muslim disciple reveals him as a Muslim Sufi, 26, 45ff. His commemoration by a Hindu via the Muslim *urs* festival at Shirdi in 1897 confirms his Islamic background, 26–7. The Hindu worship in later years tended to camouflage such actions of the saint as performing the Islamic sacrificial rite known as *takkya*, 31. The image of Shirdi Sai as a vegetarian was preferred by Hindus. His requests for *dakshina*, 35ff. His lavish redistribution of funds by nightfall. His death spurred the Hinduizing depiction, and the minority of Muslim followers were eclipsed, 40ff. The Hinduizing feat of Narasimhaswami and *avatar* claims, 42ff. The *brahman* devotees from Bombay, 44. Theory of *brahman* parentage, 9, 44. Muslim and Sufi identity of Shirdi Sai, 45ff. The Urdu notebook of Abdul Baba, 45ff. Shirdi Sai's indictment of false Sufis, 46–7. Comparison with the *majazib* phenomenon and critique of orthodox Sufis, 47ff. Tajuddin Baba of Nagpur, 53–4. Hazrat Babajan of Poona, 54–5. Meher Baba criticized the miracle instinct of Narasimhaswami, 65. The Chishti saint Zar Zari Zar-bakhsh, 56. Abdul Baba as displaced *pirzada*, 56–7. Shirdi becomes a shrine centre of ritual worship which alienated Muslim *faqirs*, 57. A wrong interpretation of the Veda, 58.

UPASNI MAHARAJ OF SAKORI

A *brahman* taught by an ascetic pundit, 59–60. Disposition for *sadhana*. Forced into child marriage, 61. Second forced marriage, 61–2. Crisis at Bhorgad mountain, 62–3. Third marriage and sojourn at Sangli, 63. As physician and estate landlord, 64. His breathing problem induced by *pranayama*, 64–6. Visits Narayan Maharaj, 66. Becomes reconciled to Sai Baba at Shirdi, 67. The phase at Khandoba's temple and different interpretations, 67ff. Friction with local devotees. Moves to Shinde and Kharagpur, 72ff. His affinity with untouchables, 74–6. Return to Shirdi and first visit of Merwan Irani, 76. Upasni settles at Sakori, 77. His reputation for paradox, 78. Visit to Benares in 1919 and friction with priests, 78–80. Gulmai Irani becomes his disciple, 80ff. Upasni stays at Sarosh Manzil in Ahmednagar and refers to Merwan as Zarathushtra, 85–6. Tending lepers at public feasts, 86. Favours the isolated *jhopri* (hut) at Sakori and sessions with Merwan, 87. Sakori *brahmans* resent Merwan, 88–9. Early biographies of Upasni, 89. Interactions between Upasni and Meher Baba, 89ff. Confinement in the bamboo cage (*pinjra*), 91ff. Discourses of Upasni, 91ff. Visited by Mahatma Gandhi, 93. Gandhi and Dr. Ambedkar, 94–6. Upasni creates the Kanya Kumari Sthan at Sakori, 96ff. His disciple Godavri Mataji, 97ff. Upasni suffers calumny from insular *brahmans*, 98. Further distortion by American crazy wisdom trend, 99. The jealousy of Durgabai Karmakar, 99–100. Upasni's death at Sakori, 101. Godavri Mataji and the *kanyas*, 101ff. [Living on a monotonous diet of bread and chutney, Upasni was a six foot strong man who shocked Gandhi with his retort against social celebrity. Though world-renouncing, he was not the typical Hindu guru. Explosive in temperament, he acted like a bulldog protector to the community of nuns he nurtured, and on whose account he reaped much opposition and scandal from his brahmanical caste.]

MEHER BABA (MERWAN S. IRANI)

His link with Hazrat Babajan of Poona, 82. Visits to Sakori ashram, 76, 81ff. His complex relationship with Upasni Maharaj, 86ff. First ashram at Manzil-e-Meem in Bombay, 105. Derelict site near Ahmednagar becomes Meherabad ashram, 105ff. Colony phase at Meherabad in 1925–6, 106ff. Commences permanent silence in 1925, 106. Promotes the cause of untouchables, 106ff. Discourses of inter-religious complexion, 108–9. His humanitarian activity, 106, 122. His practise of tending lepers, 106, 141, 144. Known to Muslims as Hazrat Qibla, 113. Discouraged beliefs in miracles, 110. Restricts scope for *arati* worship, 110. His validation of prayers and eschewing of initiation rites, 110–11. Strong sense of moral

SATYA SAI BABA OF PUTTAPARTHI

Gurus Rediscovered – Second Instalment
Shirdi Sai Baba, Upasni Maharaj, and Meher Baba

The subject of twentieth century gurus in India is a variegated one calling for some attention to differences. Due analysis of the phenomenon is still fairly rare. A common tendency in the West is to lump all of these gurus together as exploiters, which some or many undoubtedly were, though close analysis would deem that verdict unfair in other cases. Even some materialists are prepared to concede the differences in behaviour and emphasis between Bhagwan Shree Rajneesh, and, for instance, Ramana Maharshi. The private life of Muktananda fares badly in comparison with Aurobindo, and the commercial tactics of the Maharishi Mahesh Yogi are not representative of all other Indian gurus. There are yet other forms of contrast which might usefully be studied. One sector of the guru phenomenon has been described in terms of the "Sai Baba movement," a phrase that may be challenged for certain reasons. The present writer contributed a relatively insignificant work entitled *Gurus Rediscovered*, published in 1986, which has proved controversial. It was intended as an introduction to two figures, and not as a definitive description. In my own view, the style of that work bears the influence too strongly of the first draft (written in my youth), which was immature. I will attempt to improve upon the contents here. This second instalment will first treat Shirdi Sai Baba and then his disciple Upasni Maharaj. A third figure is also treated because of his strong connections with Upasni.

1. Sai Baba of Shirdi (d. 1918)

This figure has become identified in many minds with his namesake Satya Sai Baba of Puttaparthi, who has claimed to be his reincarnation and who has derived considerable fame from the association. Though Satya Sai Baba has gained many admirers in India, he has aroused strong antipathy from other Indians who view his claims of miracle-working in a very critical light.

A 1990s television programme entitled *Guru Busters*, broadcast in the West, provocatively highlighted basic issues concerning Satya Sai Baba. Formerly, writers like myself had warned of the consumerist partiality for "miracles." Now the redoubtable B. Premanand and his assistants tangibly demonstrated the superficial value of presumed supernatural feats.

Guru Busters commenced by profiling the situation of Indian academics and politicians who believe in Satya Sai Baba's purported miracles of materializing jewellery from thin air. The distinguished careers of these partisans tend to impart a flavour of prestige and infallibility to the supposedly miraculous events. Indian critics affirm that the jewellery is produced by sleight of hand, and that failure to recognize this amounts to superstition. A film exists of an incident in which Satya Sai Baba discernibly cheated, producing a necklace in a very dubious manner, deftly acquiring this object by stealth and not by any miraculous means. This film was shown in the television programme under discussion, and has served to weight the criticisms.

Indian critics have been able to observe that Satya Sai Baba gives "miracle" jewellery to the rich who do not actually need it, but gives only sacred ashes to the poor. He does not materialize food for the poor. Instead he caters to an elite of influential people who are led to associate the "miracles" with spiritual status. Satya Sai Baba claims to be an *avatar* or divine incarnation, and the reincarnation of Shirdi Sai Baba who supposedly performed miracles.

India is a country where illiteracy and poverty are still widespread. Religion is often coloured by superstition. Yet it is not merely rural areas that are in question here, but also urban dispositions which too often treat the miraculous as a significator of holiness. There is also the factor that Satya Sai has gained many Western devotees. The authentic attributes of Indian spirituality seem elusive on the media. During the 1960s, Hindus were puzzled and indignant at the assumptions of Western hippies that in India virtually everyone took drugs and that meditation could not be accomplished successfully without drugs. Since that time, other misconceptions have abounded. It is doubtful whether genuine saints would wish to be profiled in the public spotlight which confers celebrity upon opportunists like Bhagwan Shree Rajneesh.

The contingent known as the Indian Rationalists have conducted a campaign against religious superstitions and miracle ruses. That party includes undergraduates, schoolteachers, and young scientists; they take their cue from scientific data and tend to strongly reject Hinduism. Their campaign has attempted to expose the superstitions in evidence at temples and amongst holy men and healers. They complain that many "magical tricks" are in evidence at religious festivals where *sadhus* and others exhibit feats such as swallowing fire and piercing their cheeks with skewers. The Rationalists are also able to perform these feats, and have demonstrated that walking on burning coals is possible to an atheist and involves no supernatural ability. They also expose medical quackery and faith-healing which uses "magical" effects, especially in rural areas. It is popularly believed that healers chanting *mantras* can cure snakebite, a confusion aided by the fact that about ninety per cent of snakebites are harmless. The Rationalists recognize that some ailments are psychosomatic, but their complaint is that many ailments with physical causes go untreated with disastrous results. This sort of problem can also occur with the alternative medicine popular in Western countries.

Satya Sai Baba is assessed as a major deceit by Rationalists. They have publicly duplicated his trick of producing ash, which is achieved by using a sachet held in the palm. The ash is known as *udi* and is considered to be sacred; *udi* is believed by Satya Sai devotees to have healing qualities. This trick is regarded as a miracle by believers, and even some well educated Western academics have been prepared to subscribe to such beliefs. The present writer once received a disapproving letter from a European academic (a partisan of Satya Sai) which strongly queried my "non-miracle" treatment of Shirdi Sai in my early work *Gurus Rediscovered*.[1] He clearly felt that the miracles of Satya Sai proved that Shirdi Sai had been a miracleworker, a form of logic I believe to be acutely deficient. In contrast, I take the view that Shirdi Sai needs to be seen in due perspective, and that the differences between him and Satya Sai are sufficiently marked to merit a clear distinction between the two.[2] Some academics seem to be as primitive in their thinking as rural illiterates where religious matters are concerned.

An academic work published by SUNY Press, and presented as an authoritative version of Shirdi Sai, is very notably sympathetic to Satya Sai. The author writes: "My thoughts turn with deep reverence to the *Svamin* Satya Sai Baba who, through his touch, blessed the package containing all my tapes, casting a benign glance upon me."[3] The references to Satya Sai are non-critical and include the final assessment that "the worldwide fame of the living saint Satya Sai Baba of Puttaparthi is, in itself, an amazing religious phenomenon: the total number of his devotees, in constant expansion, is currently estimated to be as high as ten million."[4] Readers might get the impression that large numbers prove authenticity, which is a very questionable perspective.

Yet perhaps the most dubious feature of the enlarged doctoral thesis under discussion is the suggested relevance of Satya Sai's version of Shirdi Sai, strongly associated with the claim of the former to be the reincarnation of the latter. Satya Sai's report is deemed to be "so informative and evocative of the atmosphere of Indian village life, it seems useful to review it in detail."[5] The narrations of Satya Sai take up several pages. Antonio Rigopoulos does refer to "the hagiographic character of the narration," and observes that the version of Satya Sai minimizes the Muslim and Sufi elements in Shirdi Sai.[6] That is actually an understatement, as the first and longer narrative carried no reference to anything Muslim or Sufi and presented Shirdi Sai as an *avatar* of Shiva.

Although Dr. Rigopoulos appears to have reservations about the Satya Sai version of Shirdi Sai, he affirms that it "bears more interest"[7] than the version associated with Shri Mittha Lakshmi Narasaiyya, a lawyer of Hyderabad. Others can easily disagree, without regarding the alternative as infallible. The version that is supposedly of lesser interest states that Shirdi Sai was born at Jerusalem in 1836, his parents being Vaishnava *brahmans* of Gujarat named Nandlal and Jamunabai. They had associated with a Muslim *faqir* who took them to Mecca, where they visited all the holy places. They returned to India and lived for a time at Pathri village in the district of Aurangabad. Rigopoulos observes that no explanation is offered about the sources of this report, which "clearly aims at the brahmanization of (Sai) Baba's origins, while at the same time framing it within the sacred geography of Islam."[8] The same writer also comments that this report "is quite disconcerting, and can hardly be applicable to the habits of the brahmanic caste in last-century India."[9]

It can here be asked as to whether the "disconcerting" nature of the less popular report actually contains an element of truth beneath the varnish of brahmanization. What if the parents of Shirdi Sai were not *brahmans* within the geography of Islam that is depicted? What if they were Muslim converts? These questions may logically be asked.

The report of the Meccan pilgrimage and the birth in Jerusalem has now also appeared in a variant which seems to derive from an earlier date than some writers assume. An Indian writer has recently drawn attention to a Hindu version which gives somewhat different dates. The names of the parents are the same; this couple are said to have gone on a pilgrimage to all the sacred places in India, at one of which they met a Muslim saint who offered to take them to Mecca. Their pilgrimage to Mecca occurred in 1852, after which they proceeded to Jerusalem, where their son was born in 1858. The child was named Sai by the Muslim saint. They returned to India in 1862, after which the Muslim saint parted from them. The father is said to have died in 1863, and his wife shortly after.[10]

The different dates given should be sufficient to raise eyebrows. The chronology for the early life of Shirdi Sai Baba is uncertain, and has been variously formulated. The report of a birth in Jerusalem can hardly be dismissed merely because some find it "disconcerting." One could very easily infer that an Indian couple who spent ten years in the Near East were not Hindus but Muslims, whether or not they were converts from Hinduism. Their allegiance to the obscure Muslim saint must have been very strong to make such a sojourn tenable. The report was conceivably glossed in transmission amongst Hindus. The origin of the boy's name is not an easy matter to resolve. While this little known report claims that the boy was named Sai by a Muslim saint, the more popular and "orthodox" version has it that the Shirdi saint received his name from a Hindu when he arrived in Shirdi. The objective must be to separate hagiology from possible truth.

Sai Baba of Shirdi has been described as a Muslim *faqir* in some published works. This does not necessarily mean that the subject could not have been a Hindu by birth; the issue is complex, and far more so than is implied by the orthodox version which depicts the subject as a Hindu, or as being in an indeterminate category of religious identity. One recent Indian writer has referred to Shirdi Sai as a Muslim saint,[11] while also giving deference to a well known Hindu report which states that the subject once referred to his parents as *brahmans* of Pathri.[12] This latter report has been the more influential, being compatible with Satya Sai's version of events, and having been promoted by B. V. Narasimhaswami, a major Hinduizing source whose books[13] (along with that of Gunaji) have dominated and moulded the popular image of the Shirdi saint. Suspicion attaches to Narasimhaswami's interpretation because of his tendency to emphasize miracles of the saint.

An objection is in order against the blanket term of "the Sai Baba movement" which has been applied to a group of saints and avataric figures in Maharashtra.[14] That description tends to be employed by admirers of Satya Sai Baba who are satisfied with the association of names, despite the fact that other figures like Upasni Maharaj and Meher Baba (also represented in the supposed "movement") were not miraclemongers. A much more complex and duly differentiated terminology needs to be used in the description of such saintly and bogus phenomena.

What is it about the Hinduized version of Shirdi Sai Baba that is suspicious to critics of that presentation, quite apart from the issue of his religious identity? The major promoter B. V. Narasimhaswami produced a three volume work published at Madras in 1942 entitled *Devotees' Experiences of Sai Baba*. An academic assessor has described this work in terms of "a detailed presentation of alleged miraculous phenomena witnessed and experienced by Sai Baba's devotees, while the saint was living, as well as after his death."[15] Considerable caution is therefore required in relation to Narasimhaswami, whatever latitude for miracles some academics may have entertained. That caution is surely doubly necessary when the reader learns that "the intent of the work (abovementioned) is clearly hagiographic, aiming at the expansion of Sai Baba's popularity among the public at large."[16] This is so often what happened to the profile of both Hindu and Muslim saints, and anyone concerned with history must stand back from devotional and hagiological preoccupations.

A South Indian *brahman,* Narasimhaswami was a former admirer of Ramana Maharshi, at whose ashram he had lived. He had reacted to Advaita Vedanta as being unsuitable for his temperament. He had moved on to contact other saints, namely Meher Baba and Upasni Maharaj. The former deflected him, and the latter proved unacceptable to him. Narasimhaswami moved on to Shirdi, attracted by the growing tomb cult of Sai Baba. In 1936 he interviewed numerous dev-

6

otees of the Shirdi saint, the majority of whom were urban *brahmans* of Bombay. Not having met Sai Baba himself, Narasimhaswami was dependent upon the devotee memory tank as this had formed nearly two decades after the saint's death. The brahmanical glosses strongly favoured Hindu gods. Most of his informants had encountered Sai Baba only in the latter's fading years, at the time of the urban influx from Bombay. The scarcity of Muslim informants was excused by Narasimhaswami on the grounds that he had been unable to find Muslim followers having a sufficient spiritual link with the saint. Though he was prepared to acknowledge Sai Baba as a Muslim *faqir*, the assessment of Narasimhaswami was discrepantly weighted by the views of *brahman* devotees, whose inclination for miracle anecdotes further obscured the contour of events. Though he was an industrious writer, one may conclude that Narasimhaswami was confused in his sense of priorities.

Influential in South India as a popularizer, Narasimhaswami promoted a tomb cult and the attendant miracle lore. He was correct enough in stating that "the mass of Hindus regarded him [Sai Baba] as a Muslim but worshipped him as a Hindu god" (*Life of Sai Baba Vol. 3*, cited by M. Warren, *Unravelling the Enigma*, p. 356). This trend resulted in the saint's shrine becoming totally Hinduized after his death. Although Narasimhaswami shows an awareness that Sai Baba was linked to Sufism, the Hindu writer "admits to knowing little about Sufism, preferring the *bhakti* path of Hinduism and thus wrote about Sai Baba in that vein" (Warren, *op. cit.*, p. 356). Therefore, if the enquirer wants to know about the Sufism of Sai Baba, the major Hindu commentator has to be negotiated.

Some devotees regard the *Shri Sai Satcharita* as the most important text on Shirdi Sai. This was written by Govindrao R. Dabholkar, also known as Hemadpant, a Hindu devotee who knew the saint at Shirdi during his last years. Despite the early date of the text, which has become very popular,[17] it is strongly coloured by hagiographic flourishes. These include a miracle version of the saint's origin supplied in a foreword by H. S. Dixit, who evidently wished to avoid a Muslim identity. Shirdi Sai is here said not to have been born of a human mother. Yet Hemadpant did retain testimonies to the Muslim background of Shirdi Sai, e.g., reporting that he was circumcised and relaying his statement that "I belong to the Muslim caste." Such details were omitted from the English redaction by N. V. Gunaji, a Hindu devotee of Shirdi Sai. *Caveat* serious readers.

"Sai Baba, from his very first appearance in the village of Shirdi and throughout his life, was commonly identified as a Muslim."[18] This salient fact, so strongly attested, was a problem factor to hagiologists writing with the devotional lore of Hinduism uppermost in their minds. The pressing identity cannot fairly be ignored by non-hagiologists.

One of the earliest published reports of Sai Baba came from a British writer. Charles B. Purdom described him as Hazrat Sai Baba, employing a designation applied to Muslim holy men.[19] "Thousands of his devotees were Hindus, and, though he was a Mahommedan, they performed the ceremony of arti in his honour."[20] By the end of his life, the majority of Sai Baba's followers were Hindus, whatever their precise number. His habit of saying *"Allah Malik"* (God is the ruler) could not easily be confused with Hinduism, though writers like Gunaji were tempted in this direction.

"When and where Sai Baba was born, who were his parents, how he passed his boyhood days, are not known."[21] This early assessment of C. B. Purdom is still relevant today,[22] though some materials permit strong inferences upsetting to the majority line on this figure. One early account (and verse) by a Hindu devotee of Sai Baba has been controversially linked with a Muslim identity,[23] though the Hinduizing endeavour of Das Ganu[24] was to connect the subject with a Hindu guru called Gopalrao Deshmukh, who lived at Selu,[25] near the village of Pathri in the vicinity of Aurangabad. The setting was at least partially hagiographical, and depicted Sai as the reincarnation of Kabir. This version has been viewed by some Hindu scholars as unreliable,[26] which has disadvantages also for the version of Narasimhaswami, who adopted a modified form of Das Ganu's account in his Hinduizing *Life of Sai Baba*, where the hero is presented as a *brahman* boy who was adopted by a Muslim *faqir* and his wife.

"The description of Sai Baba's *brahman* origin and subsequent tutelage by a Muslim couple, follows a traditional hagiographic pattern that aims at the Hinduization of the *faqir*."[27] Kabir himself, though born a Muslim weaver, was transformed into the son of a *brahman* widow by legendizers, who also wanted to believe that the medieval saint had no human father and that he was found by a Muslim *julaha* couple who became his foster parents.[28] Some Hindus have associated Sai Baba's birthplace with Pathri,[29] a village fifteen miles from Selu, and located in the Parbhani district of Hyderabad State. However, one might equally choose nearby Manwat, associated with the

Muslim *faqir*. The cue for Pathri is derived from a statement attributed to Sai Baba in a conversation with Mahalsapati, a Hindu devotee favoured in the *bhakta*-oriented reports. The major source for this conversation is Narasimhaswami, who undermined the Muslim identity of Sai Baba and promoted details of Das Ganu's report consonant with Hinduization. Sai Baba is supposed to have said that his parents were *brahmans* of Pathri. However, his use of the word *brahman* has been queried in any factual sense, as his various references to himself as a *brahman* (if these are credited as accurate) have been deemed symbolic by some writers. A case in point are his references to the mosque in which he lived as a "*brahman* mosque." It has been concluded in this regard that he "did not necessarily mean 'Hindu' since he used the word 'Brahmin' in its correct sense of 'spiritual elect.' "[30] Thus, if he had spiritually elect parents (e.g., a *faqir* and his wife), this did not necessarily mean that they were Hindus. There was nothing of the caste system in Sai Baba's attitudes.

Strong questions apply to the accuracy of the Hinduized reports, as the two major sources give different dates for the most tangible event in the subject's early career. His "second" arrival at Shirdi is dated by Hemadpant to 1858, and by Narasimhaswami to 1872. The difference is substantial enough to merit due caution. His date of birth has been variously placed between 1838 and 1858. The present writer opted for *circa* 1850 as a prudent compromise,[31] as it seems inadvisable to support any specific date on the basis of the skeletal and diverging reports available. However, it would be equally plausible to opt for *c.* 1840 in the present state of approximate knowledge and opinion. Or even *c.* 1835. Some writers have been over-definitive in this direction of birth chronology, being influenced by the early dateline associated with Satya Sai's version of events. The year in question here is 1838, merely amounting to a preference. A report gleaned from a Professor of Sanskrit alleges that Shirdi Sai was present at the Indian Mutiny in 1857. It is impossible to substantiate this detail, and too much has been made of the matter by tendencies to avataric hagiology (see Warren, *Unravelling the Enigma*, pp. 391ff.). Even if Sai Baba took a temporary role in the British army when a young man, such an event does not establish his date of birth.

"Sai Baba's devotees are divided on the issue of whether he was born a Hindu or a Muslim."[32] Some say that his ears were pierced, a common Hindu custom, though one not prevalent among Muslims. The matter of whether he was circumcised also lacks definitive evidence. He definitely dressed like a Muslim *faqir* and lived in a ruined mosque. He was notably non-brahmanical in his eating habits, and is said to have consumed meat and fish in the company of *faqirs* who visited him. "The name of *Allah Malik* was constantly on the tip of his tongue."[33] He is reported to have recited the first chapter of the *Quran* in the company of Muslims, though he was also credited with an intimate knowledge of the *Bhagavad-Gita* after a conversation with a *brahman* devotee. He permitted his Hindu and Muslim followers to observe their respective religious customs. Even Hindu writers who favour theories of a brahmanical origin concede that "in many ways Sai Baba was like the Sufis of old."[34]

He was very like some latter day Indian Sufis in his apparel, which comprised a long white robe or *kafni* and a white cloth worn around the head, "a style of dress typical of Muslim ascetics."[35] In the early years at Shirdi, his language was Persian or Arabic (and Deccani Urdu), not Hindi or Marathi. He would habitually refer to himself as a *faqir*, a term commonly designating Muslim ascetics and mendicants. The present writer linked him to the *majazib* tradition of the Deccan, an unorthodox Sufi movement of very varied manifestations, and very much in the *qalandar* mould of eccentricity. That Sufi movement was active in the seventeenth and eighteenth centuries, though kindred spirits in the nineteenth century require to be envisaged.[36] To a man of the temperament denoted, unfettered by considerations of religious orthodoxy, it did not matter what religion was professed by others, and thus the gap between Hinduism and Islam was effectively breached by the *qalandar* type (not always presenting the image of a shaven head or a naked mendicant).

One Western scholar who has been inclined to support the *brahman* identity promoted by Narasimhaswami has nevertheless cast strong doubts upon the chronological framework supplied by the Hindu writer. The latter thought that Sai Baba's sojourn with the Muslim *faqir* and his wife (adapted from Das Ganu) did not last for more than five years. "That such a short estimate could be correct seems quite improbable, however."[37] More revealingly, Rigopoulos adds: "Sai Baba must have remained under direct Sufi influence for a longer period of time, perhaps ten years or even more."[38] That period could have been substantially longer than ten years, depending upon the weight given to various theories about his teachers.

Many Hindu devotees believed that Sai Baba was the spiritual successor of Akalkot Maharaj (sometimes known as the Swami of

Akalkot). It is very difficult to ascertain the truth of this. Akalkot Maharaj was an eccentric Hindu holy man who died in 1878. His outlook was unorthodox, being liberal towards Muslims; he is credited with a complete aversion to caste bias. Although it is very possible that Sai Baba met this entity during his early travels, any such contact may have been elaborated by the disciples of Akalkot Maharaj. One of these disciples, Bidkar Maharaj, is reported to have met Sai Baba at Shirdi in 1873,[39] an encounter which might have provided the origin of the beliefs about spiritual successorship. At the time of his death, the Swami is said to have told one of his followers to "Go to Shirdi in the district of Ahmednagar where there is my incarnation."[40] Several years later, in 1885, another disciple of the Swami, namely Anandnath Maharaj, visited Shirdi and told the villagers that Sai Baba was "a genuine diamond lying on a dung heap."[41] Anandnath Maharaj is also "quoted as having said that anybody who kept away from (Sai) Baba on the theory that he was mad, besides being a Muslim, was the real loser."[42] That statement does realistically reflect the popular aversion to Sai Baba during his early Shirdi phase (which lasted many years), when he was generally believed to be a crazed and eccentric *faqir* who had the additional disadvantage of being a Muslim amongst a Hindu majority. The real story of his life is in large part one of adaptation to the Hindu milieu in which he was situated.

A Gujarati source is Swami Sai Sharan Anand, who, like Narasimhaswami, was a *sannyasin*. (See *Shri Sai Baba*, trans. V. B. Kher, New Delhi, 1997.) Unlike Narasimhaswami, this man did actually meet Sai Baba, in 1911. He reported that the Shirdi *faqir* named his teacher as Roshan Shah Mian. The name is Muslim, and has aroused a mood of rejection in some commentators who argue that it is not mentioned in the major sources (as these are Hinduizing sources, nobody really need wonder at the absence of Roshan Shah). Certain writers have suggested a purely symbolic context for the name of the intrusive mentor, as Sai Baba is said to have frequently mentioned the term *Roshan* in his allegorical tales and parables.[43] Yet Swami Sai Sharan Anand, though a Hindu renunciate, was sufficiently impressed to credit that Roshan Shah was a flesh and blood entity whom Sai Baba served wholeheartedly for over twelve years. When the teacher died, Sai Baba buried him near a *neem* tree.

On the subject of Roshan Shah, a Hindu writer has commented: "The fact that Sai Baba's guru was a Sufi is not a matter of surprise."[44] A very logical reasoning is here followed: the dominion of the Nizam was at that time heavily under Muslim influence (the circumstances have since changed, Hyderabad State being dissolved in 1948; some non-historians have had difficulty in assessing the general situation). What is additionally significant is that the concession to the factor of a Sufi mentor is made in the face of a report from Professor Narke (who taught geology in Poona) that he heard Sai Baba say: "My guru is a *brahman*" (*maza guru brahman ahe*).[45] In other words, Sai Baba's references to the word *brahman* take on a rather enigmatic nuance which it is not advisable to interpret literally; he is known to have been in the habit of allusive and symbolic speech, and to an extreme degree. To assume that he had a *brahman* guru and *brahman* parents in the literal sense is not a convincing historical argument.

The identity of Sai Baba's guru (or *murshid*) has been a question for several decades, there being no data regarded as concrete. According to the *Shri Sai Satcharita* (of Hemadpant), he said that he stayed with his guru for twelve years, and that the guru "was a great *aulia*,"[46] this word being a Muslim term for a saint. (In classical Sufi parlance, the term *awliya* is the plural for *wali*). Yet Das Ganu identified the elusive Venkusha of Sailu (said to have been mentioned by Sai Baba as his guru) with both a Hindu deity and a Hindu mentor of Sailu. Narasimhaswami has likewise come under criticism in this respect. "Based on this information, Narasimhaswami imagines from the obscure and uncertain replies which Baba gave to a first class magistrate in a theft case that he had stated the name of his guru as Venkusha."[47] A Hindu researcher has since queried that assumption; "Venkusha" is a distraction, it would seem. Some continue to uphold the validity of statements about Venkusha reported by Narasimhaswami and others, but even if these are accurate, there is no guarantee whatever that "Venkusha" was a Hindu guru.

A leading Hindu researcher on Sai Baba concludes that Das Ganu was incorrect in the inference that Gopalrao Keshavrao Deshmukh was the guru in question, the latter being earlier in time and dating to 1715–1802 in terms of lifespan. That researcher had earlier expressed the view that it is doubtful whether such a person as Roshan Shah Mian ever existed. This left the issue of a guru in a nebulous limbo, the matter instead being interpreted in terms of a direct perception of the divine. However, the same researcher, Vishwas B. Kher, has more recently stated: "I have revised my earlier opinion and finally come to the conclusion that a Sufi divine was the guru of Sai Baba."[48] One may applaud this honesty in analysis, and one must respect the accompanying consideration that the name of the elusive Sufi is not known (Roshan Shah being considered an abstract wordplay).

Another Indian writer has supplied a controversial theory. The Sufi entity known as Haji Shah Waris Ali (alias Haji Saheb or Waris Ali Shah) has been nominated as the teacher of Sai Baba. He was born at Deva Sharif in North India in 1819. His father Qurban Ali Shah was a religious scholar and owned much landed property. The boy became a *hafiz*, meaning one who has learned the *Quran* by heart. He moved to Lucknow to stay with a guardian who had the reputation of a mystic. At the age of eleven he acquired a Sufi mantle and is said to have begun initiating disciples. He remained celibate, refusing to marry when his family tried to pressurize him. He was not interested in acquiring property like his father, and often stayed in the humble dwellings of poor followers. The ritualism of his early years is said to have become much modified with the passing of time; formal Sufism placed much stress upon rules and customs of etiquette associated with the *dervish* orders. Shah Waris Ali began to travel widely during his teens, and undertook his first pilgrimage (*hajj*) to Mecca at the age of fourteen. He is said to have performed the *hajj* no less than seventeen times, though only seven of these expeditions started from India, as he travelled in Islamic countries further afield for twelve years. Shah Waris Ali favoured three day fasts and seven day fasts. He is also reported to have visited Russia and Europe. Before starting his travels he distributed all his wealth to the poor "and had given up his title to all property and thus owned nothing whatever."[49] Many Hindus are said to have received initiation at his hands,[50] a liberal gesture which received criticism from fundamentalist Muslims. The orthodox also criticized him for not observing the prescribed ritual prayers, though he was able to convince an accusing *mulla* that he was too God-intoxicated to need a separate prayer ritual apart from his contemplations and ecstasies.[51] "He never referred to his own name in speech or writing."[52] This liberal Sufi died in 1905, but did not believe in nominating any successor. This was because "his methods were uniquely related to his personality and could not be reduced to any set formulae."[53]

A newspaper report at the time of his death stated that Shah Waris Ali "was an emblem of broad universal compassion with no trace of any dualism and considered one as all and all as one," breaking the barriers dividing races and creeds.[54] He does appear to have been distinctive in his tolerance towards Hindus. The commentator Khwaja

Hasan Nizami of Delhi wrote in 1909 that he had personally witnessed the impact made on several Hindu followers of Shah Waris Ali, and that "some were inwardly converted to Islam while outwardly continuing in their original faith."[55]

A comparison has been made between Shah Waris Ali and Sai Baba. They both "had a disdain for amassing worldly wealth and belongings." The former relinquished the title to his inheritance, while the latter possessed nothing more than a patched robe, a stick, and a pair of sandals.[56] Both men were sparing with words, and were inclined to give practical demonstrations rather than lengthy explanations, considering book knowledge an inadequate vehicle to reach the spiritual objective. Both of them permitted their followers to remain within the social parameters of their own native religion and to observe the relevant codes. Yet those who wanted to traverse the mystical path "were exhorted by them to go beyond the ritual."[57] Furthermore, "both considered the path of knowledge to be difficult for all to practise."[58] They did not have any special method of initiation, which is a fantasy subject. Many people in India expected initiation from saints, and the number of these who approached Shah Waris Ali are said to have been so large that he resorted to unconventional means to cater for them.[59]

In general, the popular desire for initiation gained very stereotyped responses from numerous holy men in both Hinduism and Islam; the initiators frequently adopted ritual paraphernalia to meet the demand. Such a desire is capable of being manipulated, and the phenomenon duly requires critical appraisal. Sai Baba is notable for not dispensing any formal initiation.

Shah Waris Ali is described as giving brief and cryptic replies to complicated questions. He did not propound new doctrines and wrote no books. There were no sermons from him, and no cultic insignia.[60] Such similarities with Sai Baba do not prove any contact between them, however. B. K. Narayan urges that Shah Waris Ali was the Muslim saint who took the parents of Sai Baba on pilgrimage to the Near East. Three of his pilgrimages from India to Mecca were undertaken on foot, and such a *haji* might indeed have taken Muslim converts to Mecca, or even perhaps Hindus who had become partly or mainly Islamized. Yet firm evidence for the proposed link is lacking. The only evidence that is supplied concerns Major General Enayeth Habibullah, a family patron of the shrine of Shah Waris Ali at Deva Sharif. He wrote to B. K. Narayan stating that one of his friends, who had been a devotee of Shirdi Sai Baba, told him that Sai Baba had been a *murid* (disciple) of the Sufi saint.[61]

One can easily believe that some liberal Sufi entity like Shah Waris Ali was the elusive mentor of Sai Baba during his obscure pre-Shirdi period. Whether the latter had more than one Sufi teacher is entirely conjectural. The probability looms that the early years of Sai Baba were dominated by Muslim Sufi influences of a liberal complexion, whether his birth occurred at Jerusalem or Pathri or elsewhere. It is very difficult not to believe that hagiology altered the factual indications to a Hinduizing contour, emphasizing that aspect of Sai Baba which expressed itself in interchanges with Hindu devotees in his later years. The present state of research does not permit one to definitively rule out a Hindu parentage for Sai Baba, but it does allow the conclusion that, if not born a Muslim, he became affiliated to Sufism at an early age, and was effectively Islamized. He can certainly be described as a Sufi without any insult to Hindu beliefs, as the liberal Sufi undercurrents in India were not censorious of Hindus (unlike the orthodox Sufism). Thus, he may have been born a Muslim,[62] or he may have been born a Hindu, though he became a Sufi of a distinctively liberal type to whom religious differences meant nothing. The fact that he tried to blot out his personal history in a predominantly Hindu environment could easily suggest that he was attempting to minimize his Muslim background. However, that consideration is not necessarily total, as the tendency in genuine ascetics is sometimes one of forgetting birthdays. It does seem reasonable to conclude that the bizarre language of Sai Baba was so cryptic that it is unwise to base historical factors upon various references that he made to either "Roshan" or *brahman* pedigrees.

Some scholars have invoked a comparison in the figure of Chand Bodhale, a sixteenth century Sufi of the Deccan who was a Hindu by birth. This "Sufi divine was the spiritual preceptor of Janardan Swami, who was in charge of the Daulatabad Fort."[63] Chand Bodhale dressed as a Muslim *faqir* and was affiliated to the Qadiri order. Janardan Swami (1504–75) was the Hindu guru of Eknath (1533–99), a famous *bhakti* poet of Maharashtra. A Muslim disciple of Chand Bodhale was Shaikh Mahammad, who wrote the Marathi work *Yogasangrama*, expounding aspects of Hinduism.[64] The point in any comparison between Sai Baba and Chand Bodhale is surely that the former should also be described as a Sufi, even if his family might have been Hindu. Yet that description has very rarely been applied, and to such an extent that the present writer adopted the discreet expedient of a small s for Sufi in *Gurus Rediscovered*, that work being considered so provocative and unprecedentedly bold.[65]

From this perspective, the Hinduizing commentators, since the time of Gunaji, have been minimizing Sai Baba's achievements by not acknowledging the gulf that he spanned between different religious frameworks. To triumph in a Hindu milieu when one is actually a Muslim Sufi is a feat requiring a due appreciation of the subtleties involved. To present the subject as a *brahman* from his birth until his death is a devaluation that gives no idea of his actual range. In Narasimhaswami's influential *Life*, the *faqir* who appeared in the subject's boyhood is implied as a Sufi but only as Sai's first guru, and one who departed the scene after only a few years to make way for brahmanical influences in the shape of Gopalrao Deshmukh, an event which some Hindu analysts now say was a chronological impossibility.

In one well known biography, an Indian writer relegated important considerations in preference for hagiographic information presented in the *Shri Sai Satcharita* of Hemadpant, who was described as a learned author. H. S. Dixit's theory of a supernatural origin for Sai Baba was championed in preference to other data. This method of interpretation dispensed with all probes into the pre-Shirdi phase, and instead asserted that "the saint's own utterances about his origin were pregnant with innuendoes hinting at his supernatural emergence into the world."[66] In such accounts one looks in vain for the word Sufi, and instead finds Sai devotionalism and miracle stories. There is, however, the reflection: "No one knew whether he was a Hindu or a Muslim,"[67] which seems fictitious by comparison with the prevalent belief in Shirdi that Sai was a Muslim (at least until 1918 or even later).

Better than some other accounts was the version of Arthur Osborne, which nevertheless exhibited some bare areas. "It is fairly certain that he (Sai Baba) was born of a middle-class Brahmin family in a small town in Hyderabad State."[68] That assertion certainly hangs very much in the balance. Osborne followed the Narasimhaswami trend in stating that the subject left home "to follow a Muslim fakir," who died a few years later, to be replaced by a Hindu guru whom Sai Baba supposedly referred to as Venkusha.[69] There is no mention of the word Sufi. Venkusha has since been deemed an invention of Narasimhaswami, who was motivated by a dependence upon the Hinduizing beliefs of Das Ganu and others.

Osborne observed that Sai Baba did not fully conform to either Hinduism or Islam, and taught both Hindu and Muslim followers in the terms of their own religion.[70] Being more familiar with Vedanta, Osborne tended to provide Hinduizing touches to his portrait, though he grasped that there was an ambivalence. He observed that Sai Baba "generally used the Islamic name for God, and when he was heard to repeat mantras or sacred phrases they were Islamic, not Hindu; however, he very seldom said the ritualistic Islamic daily prayers."[71] Yet the fact that he is reported to have performed *namaz* on special occasions or on Saturdays is indicative of a degree of Islamization quite foreign to Vedantists.

With regard to beliefs that the man who has realized his true Self is fit to be worshipped, Arthur Osborne comments that: "All this is understood by the Sufis, who are the spiritual elect of Islam....they teach in secret what the Hindus teach openly."[72] That statement may conceal complexities of what is openly distorted and misrepresented, as has perhaps occurred in the case of Sai Baba; Osborne does not identify him as a Sufi, and the impression tends to be given that the subject was an exceptional Hindu openly teaching secrets. Why then did he so often use enigmatic language that caused puzzlement and mind-searching? His locutions were anything but the standard fare of brahmanical punditry and Vedantic exegesis.

A subsequent Western writer was heavily dependent upon Osborne and Gunaji for his version of Sai Baba, which was very noticeably Hinduized. Marvin Henry Harper was a sympathetic American who identified the Shirdi saint with Hinduism. He affirmed of the saint's first appearance at Shirdi that "he wore the garb of a fakir (a 'Muslim holy man'), but his language and teachings were largely Hindu."[73] That error should be compared with the more thorough analysis of Antonio Rigopoulos. "The main reasons for Sai's identification as a Muslim ascetic, at least in the beginning, were two: his dress style and the few words he uttered, which were not Hindi or Marathi but apparently Persian or Arabic."[74]

Harper goes on to tell the reader that the saint's fame was enhanced by the various miracles he performed. He would keep a fire burning in his mosque, and would distribute *udi* or ash to those who asked for it. Harper does not fill in the relevant details, but relays that the fire is reported to have produced many cures. Since the saint's death, the fire has been kept burning and the sacred ash distributed to devotees in many parts of India,[75] being credited with healing properties.

"Sai Baba's teachings were in harmony with the traditional Vedanta as reflected in the *Bhagavad-Gita*."[76] Harper says nothing about Sufi affinities, having been misled by his sources.He relied heavily upon Gunaji's English adaptation of Hemadpant's Marathi work *Shri Sai Satcharita*, which interposed Hinduizing material not found in the original. Gunaji was fond of giving explanations in a Vedantic idiom, and moreover, he omitted many passages of Hemadpant which he disliked, including those referring to Muslim ingredients of the biography. The truth is that Hemadpant did acknowledge Sai Baba's identity as a Muslim *faqir*.[77]

One is left in no doubt that the reductionist contributions are misleading. For instance, the situation of friction between Sai Baba's Hindu and Muslim followers grew marked over the years at Shirdi. "Baba pointed out that if the Hindus wished to please themselves by worshipping him (identified by all as a Muslim) inside a mosque, this was no loss to Islam but only to Hinduism."[78] One may construe the situation in terms of an unusual Muslim who was very socially adroit in maintaining a balance between two rival religious contingents in his following. That situation betokens far more than a harmony with Vedanta.

When Sai Baba settled at Shirdi c. 1870,[79] it was an obscure village in the Ahmednagar district, predominantly a farming community, the Muslims comprising perhaps a tenth of the population and working mainly as artisans or field labourers.[80] The other ninety per cent were a problem for him. "The presence of a Muslim in their midst did not thrill the local people."[81] His white robe and turban remained his permanent attire until the end of his life, and his appearance as a Muslim ascetic need not be understated and should not be ignored. He was called Sai ("saint"), a name evocative of Muslim holy men, and usually considered a term of Persian origin (though the term also came to be applied to some Hindu ascetics).

In an oft-cited conversation of his later years, he was asked what his creed or religion was. The one word reply was "Kabir." This has led to surmisals that he was connected with the sect of Kabirpanthis, the followers of the fifteenth century saint who was a Muslim weaver transformed by later hagiology into a *brahman*. Narasimhaswami even reports Sai Baba as saying "I was Kabir and used to spin yarn," a reference which has been deemed to mean that he was a reincarnation of Kabir.[82] Although there was a Muslim branch of the Kabir-panthis which early separated from the Hindu contingent, it is more convincing to credit that Sai Baba was referring to his liberal inter-religious approach when he asserted his "Kabir" religion, Kabir being a poet ambivalently identified with both Hindu and Muslim traditions. There was a complete absence of sectarian characteristics in the case of Sai Baba.

Because of his references to "Kabir," some writers have stretched the connotations in order to suggest that Sai Baba might have been connected with the Nath yogis, a monastic sect who have existed for centuries in Maharashtra and other regions. It has even been claimed that the fire (*dhuni*) which he kept burning at the Shirdi mosque is indication of a Nath influence. This is offset by the consideration that such sacred fires were also favoured by Muslim *faqirs*.[83] Furthermore, although Nathism did assimilate some Muslim *faqirs*,[84] Sai Baba was not typical of Nath attitudes. One commentator concluded that Yoga and Tantra have to be discounted in the analysis of which path the saint advocated. It is evident that Sai Baba did not want his followers to become renunciates or mendicants, and he warned against the practice of *pranayama* (breath control),[85] which is favoured amongst the Naths.

The exotic text *Shri Sai Satcharita* depicts Sai Baba as practising extreme Yogic exercises. He is said to have vomited up his intestines, cleaned them, and placed them on a tree branch for drying. He is also said to have severed his limbs from his body and strewn them about in different parts of his mosque. This practice is described as *khanda yoga*. He is said to have practised Yoga since his infancy, a detail which should be regarded as suspect in a work which promoted such hagiological components, despite the enthusiasms of Gunaji, and in resistance to H. S. Dixit's conception of a miraculous birth. Yet Rigop-oulos seems to take the narrative seriously in that it "does not diminish the general impression of an assiduous practice of *hatha-yoga* on Baba's part, reproposing the hypothesis of a training in which Natha influences might have played a role."[86] Doctoral theses which do not sufficiently discriminate against hagiological flourishes do not have to be regarded as authoritative texts even if they are published by a pres-tigious university press. The present amateur prefers to remain an analyst "underplaying the miraculous element present in the sourc-es,"[87] to use one accusation made against me by an overplayer.

According to Narasimhaswami's *Life*, the young Sai approached the

Khandoba temple just outside Shirdi but was turned away by the custodian Mahalsapati on the grounds that no Muslim would be allowed to step inside the precincts. He afterwards took up residence in a dilapidated mosque which remained his abode for the rest of his life.[88] Most of the local people regarded him as a strange and bizarre entity, and even as a madman. In their eyes, he was a "mad" Muslim ascetic who had taken his proper place in the local mosque instead of defiling Hindu temples.

There is no date available for his settling at the mosque. It is thought that he may first have approached the Khandoba temple because there was a tradition of Muslim devotion to Khandoba in the Deccan, a tradition reflected in some temple art.[89] He was taciturn and usually spoke only when questioned. He was sometimes heard muttering to himself and chanting. His favoured phrase was *Allah Malik* (God is the Ruler). There were other Islamic sacred phrases on his lips, and sometimes in Urdu rather than Arabic it would seem. Narasimhaswami's *Life* reports one of his statements as "*Maim Allah hum*" (I am God).[90] How such Sufi features could have been overlooked by some writers is difficult to fathom, though Narasimhaswami Hinduized the implications. Yet "such total identification with *Allah* is a feature of some extreme forms of Sufism."[91] The monistic tendencies of Sai Baba were fairly pronounced, as several of his *shathiyat* (sayings) attest. According to Rigopoulos, the saint's identification with the Absolute "was one of the reasons why he was envisioned by Hindus as an *avatara.*"[92]

Several years appear to have elapsed after his arrival at Shirdi before he settled in the mosque. He is thought to have initially stayed on the outskirts of Shirdi in a forest for about two and a half years, and then under a *neem* tree for four to five years. During that lengthy period he apparently had an irregular supply of food, though he eventually developed a habit of going to certain houses every morning for alms. There were two *sadhus* in residence at Shirdi, and a visiting Vaishnava holy man acknowledged his worth.[93]

By 1878 a few Hindus like Mahalsapati (the temple *pujari* or ritualist) had accepted him as their guru.[94] They were in the vanguard of a local revaluation that endowed him with a new reputation as a saint possessing occult powers (*siddhis*), a popular subject of fantasy. The chronology involved is very obscure. Eventually, Hindus attributed to his contact or *darshan* (meeting) the power to grant offspring to childless couples. Ironically, his characteristic Islamic phrases like

Allah karega (*Allah* will accomplish) became feted for this ability in Hindu sectors of popular demand. He only had to touch someone, and Hindu devotees would begin to think that boons were in the offing.[95] Slowly at first, such beliefs developed into the "miracle" mentality that stamped the much later testimonies assembled by Narasimhaswami in 1936. There is reason to believe that Sai Baba himself depreciated this mentality, as certain of his reported statements do acutely devalue the attitude in question.

In 1885 Anandnath Maharaj visited Sai Baba. This disciple of the deceased Akalkot Maharaj extolled Sai to the villagers as a spiritual diamond on a dung heap (i.e., the village of Shirdi, which had in general relegated his status to that of the "mad *faqir*," a Muslim outcaste). This may have been the trigger which caused the villagers to ply Sai Baba "with trifling health problems like fever or a stomach ache in the belief that he could cure them."[96] He was no longer held in contempt. At first he gave them herbal remedies, but eventually resorted to the less time-consuming expedient of gifting *udi* (ash) from his *dhuni*. The recipients credited this ash with a healing power. How far he himself was responsible for the popular beliefs attached to his ash is not entirely clear, and the situation can be differently interpreted. He appears to have regarded ash as a symbol of the transitory; ash certainly has various symbolic connotations amongst Hindu ascetics, who often daub their bodies with it.

A Western commentator urges that "Baba often recommended drinking the *udi* in water daily, assuring that diseases and pain would be healed."[97] The prescription has been confused with strategies of Satya Sai Baba, who copied the supposed precedent on a much larger scale and with significant variations conferring commercial dividends. A definite fact is that Shirdi Sai was not a sleight of hand artiste. The ash always came from his *dhuni*, and he was too poor to "miraculously" produce jewellery from apparent thin air.

There was no medical doctor at Shirdi, and nor even a traditional Ayurvedic practitioner. Sai Baba apparently improvised simple herbal remedies. The date at which he resorted to *udi* is uncertain. Ashes have no medicinal properties. One report says that he stopped giving herbal medicines after one of his patients died, though the explanation is that the sufferer had not followed his prescription. His supporters have denied any element of faith-healing in the bestowal of ash. It is said that he did not encourage credulity, and this seems attested by his habit at the mosque of feigning anger in order to keep visitors away.[98] He seems to have been very partial to a secluded life with a few disciples in attendance. The significance attached to ash by devotees appears to have arisen from his habit of applying *udi* to the foreheads of visitors as they departed from his company. This gesture may have been intended as a blessing, but the ash became credited with miraculous properties, and retained this confusing status after his death.

These developments appear to have been closely related to his emerging liaison with a Hindu following that rapidly outnumbered his Muslim followers. A sense of rivalry emerged between these two factions, modified and held in check by various tactics of the saint. The Muslims were insistent that he was one of them and identified him as a *wali* or *aulia*, meaning saintly person. The Hindus began to view him as one of their own, and not as an outcaste as they had formerly done. The barrier of caste was a looming factor in such a rural environment totally dominated by brahmanical taboos. Hindus received encouragement from his benign references to their deities, customs, and scriptures. He himself adopted a neutral position with regard to his religious identity, though with complexities; he was so well known as a Muslim that he became adroit in giving Hindus the impression of a reconciling saint. He succeeded in mollifying *brahman* scruples; he could converse with Hindus without fear of alienation recurring. His increasingly enigmatic and allusive speech facilitated the lack of division that he fostered. A number of Hindu visitors in later years (including Swami Sai Sharan Anand)[99] were anxious about his reputation as a Muslim saint, though a few were disarmed by his oblique references to himself or his guru as a *brahman*. The mosque allusively became a "*brahman* mosque," with all the subtleties that such a phrase entails. Such strategies made it easier for Hindus to overcome qualms about entering forbidden territory that was considered contaminating for *brahmans*.

There were times when he became annoyed at the probes into his religious background. "When pressed on whether he was Hindu or Muslim, he would often get very angry and abuse people."[100] His basic point seems to have been that he was above religious distinctions; his stance can be read as implying that many Hindus were biased against the "mad *faqir*" because he was a strongly reputed Muslim. His religious tolerance is beyond question, as he also gained Zoroastrian and Christian followers in his later years. What annoyed him was discernibly the worries of high caste Hindus that he was an alien, an outcaste (as all non-Hindus were in orthodox estimation). He seems also to have been annoyed that many visitors asked him for blessings of a purely physical kind, such as the coveted progeny and cures for illness.

He made his food available to the poor and ensured that unfortunates had easy access to his mosque, a latitude which extended to Hindu outcastes, lepers, and stray dogs. He seems to have enjoyed the company of untouchables, with whom he evidently felt in deep sympathy, though they are in low profile in the sources. A leper known as Bhagoji Shinde became his devotee, and the saint favoured him by keeping him in his proximity. It is not surprising that his mosque came to be known in Shirdi by the Hindu name of Dwarakamai, meaning the "many-gated mother." He is said to have named the edifice as Dwarakamai Masjid, thus applying an Islamic inflection.

A major problem arose when "a few Hindus began offering him some kind of worship inside the *masjid* (mosque), though Sai Baba strongly disapproved."[101] The Muslims of the village reacted in protest, as this was idolatry in their eyes. The event has been dated to 1894. Some Shirdi Muslims summoned the *qazi* (Islamic magistrate) of Sangamner and attempted to obstruct the Hindus going inside the mosque. They were prepared to resort to violence, arming themselves with cudgels. It appears that Sai Baba was further annoyed by their intervention, and called in Mahalsapati to proceed with his *puja* or rite of worship.[102] Mahalsapati had apparently been given permission to smear the saint's forehead with sandal paste, a privilege which appears to have been restricted for many years. Other Hindus felt encouraged to worship him, but this *puja* "remained nonsystematic and silent and was generally opposed by Baba."[103] He appears to have been ingenious in smoothing over the irregularities, and maintained to the Muslims that he was only a devotee of *Allah*, an emphasis which surfaces in the sayings collected by Narasimhaswami.

During the 1890s, his fame spread from a limited rural area to cities like Bombay. The growth of his following was slow and not dramatic, and even at maximum, there was nothing resembling the vast numbers who have flocked around Satya Sai Baba of Puttaparthi. Through all the changes Shirdi Sai remained a beggar, going out from the mosque on begging rounds three times a day, and sometimes more. He would redistribute part of the food at the mosque, and put the remainder in an earthen pot which he kept outside the building for the benefit of any hungry passer-by, dogs included. The extreme simplicity of his lifestyle requires emphasis.

An event which occurred in 1886 later achieved celebrity in the devotional annals, though it is important to understand that Sai Baba did not explain the episode. He is reported to have effectively expired for three days, apparently in an attempt to overcome a severe bout of asthma, an ailment to which he was prone. Mahalsapati guarded his body, stopping the police from interfering until his breathing recommenced. This does not appear to have been any kind of stunt such as Indian holy men often indulge in to prove their abilities in *siddhis* (a common practice of *sadhus* is to bury their head in sand, deceiving onlookers into believing that they are deprived of breath, when in fact they can breathe through the sand). However, the event may well have created further interest in his supernatural abilities. Narasimhaswami's *Life* definitely awarded this episode a more exotic interpretation than overcoming asthma, envisaging a divine mission which remained uncompleted unless the saint came back to life.[104]

Amongst the new wave of devotees who emerged in the 1890s was Narayan Govind (Nanasaheb) Chandorkar, who is thought to have met Sai Baba as early as 1891.[105] He was a *brahman* from Ahmednagar, having graduated in philosophy at university and with a reputation for knowledge of Vedantic scriptures. It was this man to whom the saint imparted an explanation of a verse in the *Bhagavad Gita*. The relevant conversation was considered to prove that the saint had a deep knowledge of Sanskrit and has been feted accordingly. The date of the conversation is uncertain. A verbatim report was preserved by Narasimhaswami[106] and others. Recent scholarship has urged that the dialogue does not in fact prove that Sai Baba knew the *Gita* or even Sanskrit, his emphasis being Sufistic (M. Warren, *Unravelling the Enigma*, pp. 356ff.).

It has been possible to confuse Nanasaheb Chandorkar with Nanasaheb Nimonkar.[107] The latter was another Sanskrit-speaking pupil, and one who met Sai Baba at about the same time, in 1890. Nimonkar gained an expertise in Sanskrit, being well known as an exponent of both the *Gita* and the *Jnaneshwari*, to the extent that other scholars of Sanskrit would consult his opinion on matters of exegesis. Yet this fluency was accompanied by a growing conceit in his prowess, and the saint told him to desist from his expositions.[108] Nimonkar (alias Shankar Rao Raghunath Deshpande) had evidently fallen prey to the vanity involved in punditry. Sufis have often pointed out the problem of scholarly pride, and I have heard it said that the true Sufi will make an error in diction rather than claim an expertise which exalts himself. Sai Baba was generally content to be considered a virtually illiterate man, an uncouth rural *faqir*, and he definitely did not pose as an expert on hallowed texts. In his later years he sometimes advised Hindu devotees to study various sacred texts, though not usually for the purpose of expounding them. "For the most part he discouraged them from reading,"[109] concluded Osborne, who reported Sai Baba's statement that "people hope to find Brahma in these books, but it is brahma (confusion) not Brahma (God) that they find there."[110]

One report is significant for a number of reasons. About 1890 a Muslim *faqir* named Javhar Ali arrived at Shirdi and lived in the mosque with Sai Baba. This man is depicted as being an impressive talker who demonstrated his learning. He could repeat the entire *Quran*, and had already made an impression at the nearby village of Rahata through his construction of an *idgah* or place of prayer, a project which had brought upon him the accusation of having polluted a Hindu temple. This was apparently the reason for his move to Shirdi. He began to regard himself as the teacher of Sai Baba, and the latter appears to have been in agreement. For some reason they both moved to nearby Rahata, but the Hindu devotees at Shirdi tried to retrieve their saint. Sai Baba was at first reluctant to return, but soon after, both *faqirs* returned to Shirdi. After a few days, the learned Javhar Ali is said to have been worsted in debate by a local Hindu ascetic named Devidas, as a consequence of which he departed. The interpretation associated with Hemadpant is that through this episode, Sai Baba demonstrated how a disciple should overcome egoism. (Javhar Ali is reported to have returned many years later and prostrated at the feet of the Shirdi saint.)

The version of Narasimhaswami, in the *Life*, gives the impression that Sai Baba went to Rahata for the purpose of some religious education, Javhar Ali being a *maulana* (a term which has the connotation of a professional religious scholar, though it may have been loosely applied). The *maulana* was sceptical of the Hindus who venerated the saint at the mosque, and asked him if he knew the *Quran* and the *shariat* (Islamic religious law). The saint is said to have replied that he had not learned these subjects.[111] A feasible claim is that Sai Baba humbled the pride of Javhar Ali, who may have believed that his orthodox knowledge was superior to the insight of the saint. Javhar Ali prided himself upon being able to recite the *Quran*; he had a group of disciples, and would seem to fit an "orthodox Sufi" role. Yet other dimensions of interpretation are also possible. These Hindu reports of the episode cannot conceal the basic factor that Sai Baba must have been a Muslim in order to fit into the situation at Rahata, where Javhar Ali had been in friction with Hindu temple officials owing to his creation of a place for Islamic prayer. Sai Baba performed menial tasks for Javhar Ali, conceivably serving to honour his colleague's reputation and to vindicate the controversial action. Sai's admission of ignorance has to be regarded with caution. If the saint was really "tutoring" a proud scholar, then he would not necessarily have advertised any knowledge he possessed.

The report of a Muslim writer is relevant in this respect. The Urdu notebook of the *faqir* known as Abdul Baba (1871–1954) represents the minority of Muslim followers who were eclipsed in the popular sources by the Hindu contingent. Abdul Baba was about eighteen years old when he came to Shirdi in 1889. He was the attendant of a Muslim *faqir* at Nanded called Amiruddin. The latter is said to have had a dream of Sai Baba, which made him send Abdul to Shirdi. Under his new teacher, Abdul lived in a stable near the mosque. He gained the reputation of being one of the saint's closest devotees, and although he outlived Sai Baba, until recently he gained only slight coverage by comparison with some of the Hindu followers.[112] He often read the *Quran* aloud at the mosque, because the saint would sometimes open the *Quran* and request Abdul to recite passages from it. A recent Hindu researcher, V. B. Kher, has established that: "From Abdul's unpublished works in Urdu, it is clear that (Sai) Baba had a profound knowledge of Islam, *Sira* (the life of the prophet Muhammad), *sunna* (his code of conduct), *hadith* (traditions), the *fakah*,[113] *shariat*, and the *tarikat*[114]....He was equally at ease with all the Muslim religious works and traditions, including the writings of Sufi shaikhs or orders like Kadaria,[115] Chistia,[116] Suhrawardiya and Nakshabandhi."[117]

The first festival performed in Sai Baba's honour was significantly that of the *urs*, in 1897. The *urs* is a Muslim festival, and usually commemorates the anniversary of a saint's death, though in this instance it celebrated a living saint who was being honoured by a Hindu, Gopalrao Gund of Kopergaon, who attributed to Sai the birth of his son. The Muslim background of the saint was so obvious that Gund had to honour him in Islamic terms. The Shirdi *urs* fair honouring Sai Baba continued for fifteen years. Then, in 1912, Hindus wanted this *urs* festival to be conducted on the same day as their *Rama-Navami* festival. These events serve to confirm the Muslim and Sufi background of the saint. The combined festival became an annual fixture, the Muslims and Hindus undertaking separate processions that were amicably related.[118]

The Muslim devotees of Sai Baba have been estimated to comprise ten per cent of his following,[119] an approximation which can pass muster here. Against the backdrop of an increasing Hindu majority must be viewed his exclamations of identity with various Hindu gods like Vithoba, Mahalakshmi, Ganapati, Maruti, and the *avatar* Krishna. Narasimhaswami reported these affirmations in his *Charters and Sayings*. The saint was portrayed in the influential *Shri Sai Satcharita* as an incarnation of Dattatreya, often depicted as an *avatar* of Vishnu in the rather lavish mythology attendant. Yet Sai Baba himself did not make this identification, "which was attached to him by his devoted *bhaktas*, particularly after his death."[120] However, he is reported to have said that his parents had dedicated him to the god Maruti, which some take as further "proof" of his Hindu origins. A Maruti temple was situated not far from his mosque, and was thus a prominent landmark, although he would not visit the building. A complexity in the saint's disclosure is that it was employed by him as confirmation that he was the "brother" of Maruti; the interpretation can therefore be that this was yet another of his tactics in affirming equality with the Hindu pantheon. The human teacher was the god who could best guard against evils, he may have been emphasizing.[121] (Maruti, alias Hanuman, is the monkey-faced god believed in Maharashtra to guard the village against evils).

In 1908 the Hindu devotees were successful in establishing a regular ceremony of *arati* at the mosque, during which the saint was worshipped.[122] This congregational worship involved the singing of devotional verses known as *arati*. Formerly he had only allowed individual singing, but now this became a communal event. A *pujari* or ritual officiant named Megha Shyam was called in by a Hindu devotee. This *pujari* was inevitably a *brahman*, and more specifically, he was a Shaiva. Yet at first he did not want to participate, having heard that Sai Baba was a Muslim. The saint's established religious identity was often too much for high caste Hindus who had not become his devotees. After initial problems and delays, Megha Shyam began to conduct the worship and opted to recognize Sai as Shiva. This indicates the way in which Hindu devotees transformed him into an ideal of

Hindu preference.

"Sai Baba never encouraged his own worship, though in the last years he gave up resistance and accepted the cult which the Hindus tributed to him, often in a quite ostentatious form."[123] The rapidly increasing ostentation was a consequence of the *bhakta* (devotee) determination to revere him as the equivalent of a *maharaja*, a title which was actually conferred upon him by the enthusiastic devotees. They introduced an array of fans, silver umbrellas, and ritual paraphernalia. Decorations were set up around the mosque, giving the place a festive appearance. In 1909 they acquired an elaborate palanquin drawn by a horse, which they used in processions to and from the mosque. Sai Baba refused this accessory. Yet the "mad *faqir*" had become the virtual king of Shirdi.

He is said to have remained indifferent to the show of pomp that was thrust upon him, and "seemed to be more annoyed than pleased about it."[124] He continued to beg his food and to wear the same old white *kafni* and turban. The devotional chant of "*Sadguru Sainath Maharaj ki jai*" was employed during the daily processions to the *chavadi* (a place where he slept). *Ki jai* means "hail," or "homage to." The Hinduization of his career was now well underway, though not yet complete, as it was still generally recognized that the saint was a Muslim.

The reactions of the Muslim minority are largely unclear. He asked them to be tolerant and avoid violence, and frictions appear to have been minimized, perhaps because the minority were so heavily outnumbered by this time. Some of them managed to join in the spirit of things fostered by the majority, and nicknamed the caparisoned procession horse as "Shamsuddin," which is a Muslim name. Yet a band of musicians played as the name of Hari was chanted alongside the *jai* acknowledging the saint as Sainath, which was a Hindu extension of his name.

It would seem that he consistently avoided entering the Hindu temples in Shirdi, continuing to respect the scruple of the *brahman* ritualists that he was a polluted non-Hindu, a scruple exemplified by his having been refused admission to the Khandoba temple. Narasimhaswami reported him to have said (to his Hindu followers): "There is no difference between a Hindu and a Mohammedan. Mosque and temple are the same. Yet I will respect your susceptibilities, and not enter the temple. Look at Chokamela's life."[125] In other words, although he was the "brother" of Maruti, he was technically unable to

28

enter the Maruti temple or other temples, being an effective outcaste. The reference to Chokamela is very significant; he was a Hindu untouchable or *mahar*, a fourteenth century Vaishnava who protested against the caste bias which snubbed untouchables as polluted outcastes.[126] As a Muslim "untouchable," Sai Baba demonstrated that his mosque was open to Hindus, even though the fastidious *brahmans* regarded him as a defiler of temples. The irony of this situation was glossed by Narasimhaswami and obscured by other commentators like Gunaji, who instead preferred to believe that the subject was a Hindu *brahman* and *avatar*.

The influx of urban visitors (predominantly Hindu) substantially swelled the ranks of his following during the last decade of the saint's life. Most of the devotee reports date from the period beginning *c.* 1910, with only a relatively small number applying to the preceding period. These reports vary somewhat in character, though many of them are partial to miraculous elements and also stress the saint's omniscience. He emerges as a complex figure, exhibiting unpredictable moods and eccentric behaviour, frequently using bizarre speech. He is credited with the ability to help his devotees at a distance, quite independently of his physical presence. He was said to appear in dreams and visions. Although he had moods of anger, it was his compassion that was viewed as the determining feature in events. His methods did not coincide with the typical tactics of holy men. One prominent Hindu devotee, Hari Vinayak Sathe, is reported as saying: "Baba never gave *upadesha* or initiation to anyone, so I did not ask him."[127] Sathe is also reported to have been blessed by the saint with the promise of a son in case he chose to marry. That was in 1905. A number of devotees were preoccupied with progeny, and the saint's blessing was supposed to guarantee this. The expectation of "miracles" may occasionally have become extreme. Fantasy about the supernatural can become a habit in those disposed to it. Sai Baba appears to have thought so when he broke into pieces a certain plank which had become an undue focus of attention. He had suspended this plank from the ceiling of the mosque with old rags, and liked to sleep on it. The plank was six or seven feet from the floor, and he placed lamps upon it. Devotees wondered how he got on and off it, though he was a tall man apparently six feet high and might be credited as athletic when asthma did not overtake him. Crowds are said to have gathered in hope of seeing him in the act, believing the supports to be too frail, but he dispensed with the amusement. The nocturnal resort to a plank was regarded as a miracle by Gunaji, and that belief has continued.[128]

Too much was made of an episode ascribed by some to the early 1890s. Narasimhaswami included this in his *Life*, and described it as the first public miracle performed by the saint. Sai Baba is said to have changed water into oil on an occasion when he was denied oil for his mosque lamps by the local oil vendors, who were in a mood for mocking the mad *faqir*.[129] Did he resort to a magical trick, did he have an emergency supply of oil, or was the episode a product of the hagiological imagination? Such stories do not prove spirituality and nor any adult appreciation of saints.

The increasing devotionalism, pageant, and esteem for miracles may have caused Sai Baba to alter his mode of speech. According to a Hindu researcher, the year 1910 marked a change in this respect. Formerly the saint had used "simple, direct language" but "began to speak in parables and symbology from 1910 as the number of his visitors began to grow in volume."[130] This seems difficult to thoroughly substantiate, and would mean that all the symbolic references would date from the last decade of his life. However, it is very feasible that he increasingly resorted to parables and symbolism during his last years in order to counteract the popular demands upon his time. He is known to have complained in 1910 that he had been ill for two years, having to reduce his diet to bread and water, suffering stringworm, and getting no rest because of the horde of visitors. His intestinal troubles and his asthma might have exacerbated his constant knowledge that devotees inadvertently tired him, particularly when they expected mundane benefits. Thus, he might have decided to make the situation a little bit harder to prize open with a *ki jai*.

In 1912 there appeared on the scene Vaman Prangovind Patel, who later became known as Swami Sai Sharan Anand after he became a *sannyasin*. He was in his early twenties when he came to Shirdi, and began to think that he ought to have brought along his father, who was suffering from dropsy, in order to be cured by the saint. Yet he was perturbed, knowing that his *brahman* parent would be resistant to visiting a holy man who looked like a Muslim *faqir* and who had the reputation of being one. Sai Baba is reported to have soothed his dilemma with the question: "Am I not a *brahman*?"[131] To Vaman Patel, that was the solution. Sai Baba could only be a *brahman*, which meant that he was acceptable to prospective patients. Yet the saint also posed to him the problem of the guru Roshan Shah, a Muslim topic which was adroitly related to parabolic utterances in a climate where saints had to be so careful what they said to the onrush of devotees who preferred *arati* to Quranic recitals.

"I give people what they want in the hope that they will begin to want what I want to give them." This well known saying of the Shirdi saint (imitated and abused by Satya Sai Baba) underlines that what devotees wanted was not what he had in mind. There is a difficulty evident in separating the two layers of attitude, a difficulty attested by a number of writers who effectively place Sai Baba on the same level as the wishes of devotees (frequently amounting to cures, progeny, processions, and devotional ritual). The present author made an attempt not to do that in *Gurus Rediscovered*, and that contribution was deemed too strong a dose of anti-miracle. A pedantic academic has accused me of not citing Narasimhaswami's *Life*, which is one of the confusing and influential promotions of public miracles like changing water into oil.[132]

It would be presumptuous to state exactly what the saint wished to give, as that x factor appears to have been locked up in fairly numerous bizarre episodes and cryptic communications. One can only hope to dwell here upon some of the more obvious features and discrepancies of largely unplumbed events.

The supposed *brahman* exiled in the mosque of Shirdi was definitely not an adherent of brahmanical codes about food purity. He "sometimes ridiculed his devotees" for following the taboos about food that are so inflexibly applied in many ashrams. He made some of his *brahman* devotees eat the forbidden onions in an attempt to make their outlook less rigid. He is also on record as having instructed an orthodox Hindu to buy meat, a tactic considered by some to be a test rather than a condition of eating meat.[133] Although some writers have stated that Sai Baba was a vegetarian, he is reported to have eaten meat and fish in the company of fellow *faqirs*. More specifically, he would often prepare meat for his Muslim followers to consume, though he would prepare vegetarian food for Hindus. Hemadpant reports that the saint occasionally performed the Islamic sacrificial ritual known as *takkya,* involving a goat. Such a practice was abhorrent to high caste Hindus, who clearly preferred the vegetarian myth in a number of cases.[134]

By 1900, the saint's habit of smoking his earthen tobacco pipe (*chilim*) with his devotees seems to have become established at the mosque. When in a good mood, he would pass the pipe around so

that everyone present could take a puff. In 1901 a young Hindu devotee, Vasudev Janardhan, happened to be the sole non-smoker in the
assembly one day. The saint only offered the pipe to this man, and he
hesitated. Nanasaheb Chandorkar then prodded the reluctant one to
smoke, believing that something positive would happen to him as a
consequence. Afterwards, Janardhan is said to have obtained all the
promotions he desired in his career as a census clerk, and this good
fortune he attributed to the saint.[135] This type of belief was prominent
at Shirdi, though not necessarily contributing to insight in all cases.

Though Sai Baba did make some explicit statements about his abilities,[136] in many events it was attribution that seems to have governed
interpretations of what was occurring. A case in point appears to have
been the episode which inspired Hemadpant, alias Govindrao R. Dabholkar (d. 1929), to write a biography of the saint. This Hindu devotee arrived at Shirdi in 1910, and during a subsequent visit not long
after, he witnessed an event at the mosque which puzzled him. He
found the *faqir* preparing to grind a large quantity of wheat on a
hand-operated flour mill. He wondered if Sai was going to store up
flour while living on alms. Yet it was the habit of the saint to give
away any surplus. Four women assumed that the flour was a free gift
to anyone who assisted, and they actually pushed the old saint aside
in order to operate the mill. He was annoyed, but seemed placated by
their devotional songs, which nominally bespoke their love and regard
for him. Perhaps he was testing them, who knows, in such a laconic
situation. The women anticipated that the saint would distribute the
flour in his usual generous manner, and so when they had finished
grinding, they greedily divided the product amongst themselves, and
then began to take away their respective shares. Devotion indeed. Sai
expressed further annoyance, and then told the miscreants to sprin-
kle the flour along the village boundaries. Feeling embarrassed, they
did as he told them, but only after whispering amongst themselves,
which may mean that they doubted whether this was really the best
thing to do. Dabholkar (whom Sai called "Hemadpant") resorted to a
local interpretation of this occurrence. He questioned several villagers,
and was told that there was a cholera epidemic in Shirdi and that Sai
Baba's antidote to this was to place the flour on the village boundaries. Dabholkar enthusiastically took up this version, and concluded
that it was not the grains of wheat but cholera which had been
crushed by the saint. Although he regarded this connection as inexpli-
cable, "that was when I first thought of writing about Sai Baba's life

and his many miracles."[137]

More recently, an academic writer has stated that "Baba's act of grinding grain, symbolically representing the cholera epidemic, is intended to magically destroy the *shakti* of the grain, that is, of cholera."[138] Thus, the *faqir* becomes the magician creating a magic circle of grain along the village boundaries. Yet what about the four women who actually did most of the grinding in a rather hypocritical manner glossed by their devotional songs? Were they magicians as well, caught in the magical circle of superficial devotion? When combined with superstition or ulterior motives, devotion is a very questionable factor. Academic endorsement of superstitions is another problem.

Hemadpant's Marathi work *Shri Sai Satcharita* extolled Sai Baba as a miracle-working saint, and was embellished by H. S. Dixit and altered for the worse by Gunaji. Hemadpant had completed only two or three chapters of his hagiography by the time of the saint's death, having in 1916 gained Sai Baba's consent to write. Narasimhaswami's account of this in the *Life* is a glowing one, suggesting that Sai was the virtual author of the *Satcharita*, though the saint is said to have warned against Hemadpant expressing his own view and refuting other views. That may well have referred to the Hindu-Muslim division of opinion. The composition of the *Satcharita* continued throughout the 1920s until the author's death, growing to over fifty chapters, and was early serialized in a monthly magazine published at Shirdi. It became regarded as a sacred text by the devotional movement which developed after the saint's death. Though the *Satcharita* contains many interesting details, the mode of presentation is frequently questionable and merits due caution.

"No one listens to me or my wisdom"[139] was a complaint of Sai Baba that surely merits heed. In this vein of lament, he said that he had an open treasury, and that he told people to dig out the treasure and take it away by the cartload. Yet nobody would take such pains, nobody brought carts, was his refrain.

He evidently had a problem. Even some of the more committed people who came to him were conditioned to traditional ideas of spiritual methodology such as taking an initiation involving the chanting of a *mantra*. Sai Baba consistently disowned this approach, evidently regarding it as a misleading formality. One Hindu woman who came to his mosque was even prepared to take the extremist step of fasting to death in order to obtain the desired initiation believed to be in the offing. He reasoned with her and said that his own teacher (unnamed in Narasimhaswami's *Charters and Sayings*, where this episode is reported) had never given him any *mantra*. Instead of a formal *sadhana* (discipline), he advocated a dedicated rapport with himself. He even said that the four *margas* (including *bhakti*) and the six schools of philosophy (including Yoga and Vedanta)[140] were unnecessary. Trust in the teacher was enough. There the problem recurs, because trust in the guru is usually interpreted in the sense of devotional surrender and lack of any special effort, putting to sleep faculties which may become totally buried treasure under the manipulative supervision of those gurus who delight in the lack of autonomy of any robot-like "disciples."

In general, Sai Baba did not advocate the practices associated with *sadhana*, especially *pranayama*. About 1910 one Hindu visitor arrived who had contracted breathing trouble during the practice of Yoga, causing him to leave home in search of a remedy. Sai Baba told him to stay in the nearby temple of Khandoba, where his brother Balakrishna is said to have found him cured of his ailment.[141] This report surely relates to Upasni Maharaj, who appeared on the scene at that time, and who had developed a serious breathing ailment through his practice of *pranayama*. He was instructed to stay at Khandoba's temple, and with far more dramatic results than a respiratory alteration. "Whoever proceeds by means of *pranayama* will have to come to me ultimately for further progress."[142] That statement of Sai Baba does seem to have some justification in the case of Upasni Maharaj. A great deal of ignorance prevails about breathing exercises, for some reason imagined to be beneficial by many people unsuited to the stress involved.

Although Sai Baba is known to have instructed several of his more serious Hindu visitors to stay in seclusion at one of the local temples, it is obvious that he drew a sharp dividing line between those who were suited to this kind of sojourn and those who were not. He encouraged most of his followers to retain their mundane role in life and not to renounce the world; he did not wish them to jettison their families or their secular careers and become *sannyasins* or *sadhus* or *faqirs*. In a few cases he explicitly advised against the renunciate vocation, knowing the difficulties that could result. He counselled against extreme asceticism and fasting. He was not known for any fasting habit, unlike his disciple Upasni, and advocated eating in moderation (he himself is said to have eaten little food). According to Narasimhaswami's *Charters and Sayings*, Sai advised against the relinquishment of food and physical exercise. "Do not get over-ascetic by giving up all food, play, and exercise."

Special liaisons with the more introverted individuals like Kashinath Govindrao, alias Upasni Maharaj, were set against the backdrop of Sai Baba's more public image during his last years. At the time when the formal Hindu *puja* began at the mosque,[143] in 1908 the saint began his distinctive habit of requesting *dakshina*, a word of Sanskrit origin denoting a sacrificial fee levied by the *brahmans*. In the case of Sai Baba, use of this word appears to have amounted to a pun on an improvised habit of taxing the urban inflow of devotees, many of whom were *brahmans*. The word usually denotes money or gifts given to *brahmans*. Formerly, the saint had maintained that he was a *faqir* and had kept to a principle of not asking for money. If any devotee had left money at the mosque, Sai would not touch it, and someone else had to take charge of the gift. Yet now, in the changing atmosphere induced by Hindu ritual, he evidently considered that his following needed demands made upon them to complement their continual demands upon him. Or so one might reason on the basis of the details available. He began to ask many visitors for money, though in a very distinctive manner that deserves careful attention.

Narasimhaswami's explanation of this development, in his *Life*, is marked by his reference to Sai Maharaja and his *durbar*. This represents the Hinduizing approach in describing the last years of Sai Baba's life in terms of a *maharaja* (great king) with his court or *durbar*, meaning the assembly of devotees. One reason for this peculiarity was that various types who attended real aristocratic courts also visited the Shirdi mosque and the attendant processional activities. Those types included musicians, acrobats, wrestlers, dancing girls, storytellers, and pundits or religious scholars. The devotional events afforded these people a livelihood in that the saint gained funds to pay them all through requesting *dakshina*. He was effectively their employer. He also had a number of dependants, poor devotees who now stayed in the village and who received his donation. He was also very considerate about beggars and holy men.

The amounts requested by Sai Baba varied between 5 rupees and 250 rupees. Most people he asked for *dakshina* would comply. Many are said to have sent contributions of their own accord, a wealthy donor once paying the large amount of six thousand rupees. So every evening the saint would redistribute the money he had collected, an amount which varied substantially. Some beneficiaries received a fixed amount daily. He kept none of the money himself, remaining a beggar until his death.

Hundreds of people were sometimes in evidence at the processions in Shirdi. Many participants offered gifts of food, and this made it possible to feed two hundred beggars on a daily basis. Poor people definitely did benefit from the redistribution, though so also did some persons who appeared to be mere hangers-on. There were some rare occasions when a visitor was left penniless, though there were other occasions when Sai Baba returned the *dakshina* to the donor. Furthermore, he would not always accept an offering of money made without being requested. The secular authorities attempted to levy income tax on the *dakshina*, but this was impossible to achieve, as he never kept any of it. The incoming funds amounted to the income of a provincial governor. Yet at his death, he had only sixteen rupees in his possession.

His requests for *dakshina* were a controversial matter, many Hindus deeming this scandalous, as the traditional ideal of the *sannyasin* militates against asking for money, and especially on the scale associated with Sai Baba. This might help to explain why Narasimhaswami, himself a *sannyasin*, opted to describe his subject as a *maharaja*. The saint's own description of his role was different. He attributed his requests for *dakshina* to the will of *Allah*. "I ask only those whom the *Faqir* points out" (he had a habit of referring to God as the *Faqir*).

It is said that Sai promised a higher reward to his donors. He had to give them back ten times as much, though this obligation was obviously not intended in terms of money. Devotees believed that future gains would compensate the donor, and some of them probably anticipated an economic windfall. The saint would sometimes explain his requests in terms of a settlement of karmic debts, which meant that he could not always accept gifted money (i.e., money that he did not ask for). When asking for small amounts (ten rupees or less), he frequently applied a form of numerical symbolism, e.g., two rupees meant cultivating faith and patience. Yet sometimes sums larger than ten rupees were given an allusive signification, implying that he was not in fact asking for money but qualities of learning (as in the case of Professor Narke, who literally had no money during his sojourn in Shirdi for many months in 1914, and whose requested *dakshina* of fifteen rupees was said to mean deriving lessons from a religious text he was reading). It is said that he never became angry with those who did not meet his request for any reason. He would never accept *dak-*

shina after nightfall, i.e., after his redistribution.[144]

In 1916 a family party of four Ramadasis (devotees of Rama) from Madras were on pilgrimage to Benares and heard of Sai Baba's distributions among the poor. They stayed at Shirdi for two days and were able to confirm the reports. Three of them became greedy and decided to extend their stay, feeling that if they ingratiated themselves to the saint, they would profit rather well. So they sang plaintive *bhajans* every day in his presence, their devotion a mere mask for cupidity. Only one woman denied herself in this respect, and she is said to have gained a vision of Rama which brought her to tears. This happened at the mosque just after the *arati* ceremony. Her husband afterwards ridiculed her, but that night he had a dream in which he capitulated to the saint and admitted that he had believed Sai to be a Muslim who was trying to convert Hindus to Islam.[145] This report smacks of realism in various details; many Hindus were indeed suspicious of the Islamic environment, and devotion could prove very superficial. The head of the pilgrim family had deemed it expedient to derive money from a Muslim saint whom he otherwise resented.

A *brahman* called Mule Shastri arrived from Nasik to visit a friend of his, Gopalrao Buti, who was a wealthy devotee of the Shirdi saint. This visitor was learned in the six *darshanas*, and was also considered an expert in astrology and palmistry. He was offput by the Muslim identity of Sai Baba, and had strong scruples about pollution by touch from anyone outside the higher castes of Hinduism. Nevertheless, his curiosity to read the palm of the saint got the better of him, and he consented to visit the mosque. He tried to take hold of the saint's hand, but the latter foiled this move by giving him some bananas. Disappointed, the *brahman* returned to his quarters, took his ritual bath, donned a silk *dhoti*, and then sat down to perform the *agnihotra* ritual, a fire sacrifice deriving from the Vedic era. Meanwhile, Sai Baba remarked that he would have to wear an ochre-coloured robe that day. Those around him could not understand what the saint was referring to, as his standard attire was a white *kafni*. Ochre is the colour of the *gerua* robe of Hindu holy men. When it was time for the noon *arati* ceremony at the mosque, one of the devotees invited Mule Shastri to witness the congregational rite. The visitor now expressed caste pride and fear of pollution, and declined to leave his *agnihotra* rite. Afterwards Sai Baba sent Gopalrao Buti to the *brahman* with a request for *dakshina*. Mule Shastri was preoccupied, but as Buti was his friend, he agreed to go to the mosque with his *dakshina*. Yet this time he would not go inside the mosque, fearing pollution from the Islamic edifice and the inmate saint, especially as he (Mule Shastri) had been conducting a sacred priestly ritual. So he remained at a discreet distance in the courtyard. He is then reported to have seen his own ochre-robed guru in the place where Sai Baba was sitting; that guru had died several years earlier. The aloof *brahman* suddenly rushed up the steps of the mosque to embrace the feet of his guru and to join in the *arati* singing. He reportedly saw his deceased guru sitting there until the *arati* was over, when he cognized that it was Sai Baba asking him for *dakshina*. He now prostrated himself before the Muslim saint. We are told that he afterwards recounted this episode repeatedly to whoever was interested.[146] Whatever readers might make of the religious emotions occurring in such situations, it is apparent that a change of colour made all the difference.

The Mule Shastri episode was considered a miracle of sorts. It has been denied that Sai Baba resorted to wearing a *gerua* robe, which does make sense. His mood of independence consistently defended his "untouchable" white *kafni* in the face of nearby temple activity and the pollution complex. The brother of Maruti was a Muslim outcaste; only in elliptical speech could he come a *brahman*.

In 1915 Sai Baba had a severe attack of asthma, and during the last few years of his life he became very frail. He frequently needed help in moving about, though he usually refused to desist from his daily begging rounds.[147] It is impressive that he maintained *faqiri* in an environment which worshipped him. Nana Nimonkar became a close personal attendant during the saint's last two years, and during the evening round of begging, Nimonkar and Gopalrao Buti would sometimes carry him.[148]

On *Vijaya Dasami* day in October 1916, he was in an angry mood and tore off his clothes, going naked for about two hours. What caused this rage is not clear, but it was evidently related to his exclamation that onlookers should decide for themselves if he was a Muslim or a Hindu. Narasimhaswami recounts this episode in his *Charters and Sayings*, and the report is discernibly skeletal. The exclamation apparently pertained to the issue of circumcision, but Narasimhaswami is silent about this, merely stating that after two hours, the leper companion Bhagoji Shinde clothed Sai with a *langoti*.[149]

One of the most suspicious entries in the *Charters and Sayings* is the account of how in 1917, the young son of a Bombay devotee was sitting with the saint at the mosque. A terrible female figure is said to have appeared, with dishevelled hair and a begrimed face, and complete with a long protruding tongue. Jumping over the compound wall, she made for the boy and pulled at him, it is said, until the angry saint kicked her and she ran away. Sai Baba is said to have declared that this was a visit from the terrible cholera goddess,[150] known as Mari. Cholera afflicted Shirdi soon after, and it seems logical to believe that the associations of this tragedy were inserted into a story about the saint. Some stories attest the belief that he spread flour on the village boundaries in order to stop evil spirits or the malignant goddess Devi from entering the community. This cause became associated with his frequent resort to the grinding mill, and Ramalingaswami attributes to him a declaration of his abilities in this respect.[151] Perhaps he was superstitious, or perhaps some of his followers were, believing that he thought like them in the face of epidemics. Hagiology so often reflects the beliefs of the hagiologists rather than the nominal subject.

We may believe in the accuracy of the diary entry which described the visit to Shirdi of the nationalist leader Bal Ganghadar Tilak (1856–1920), the politician of Maharashtra. The date was May 19th, 1917. He paid his respects to the saint at the mosque, who is said to have looked very pleased that day. Tilak was not exempt from a request for *dakshina*. When the party left, the saint gave them his typical gift of *udi*, probably no more than a symbol of renunciation or blessing in such instances. Tilak was not seeking any cure; his views on the meeting are not known, though it has been surmised that he was interested in witnessing the tolerant atmosphere of conciliation between Hindus and Muslims that was attributed to Sai Baba's influence.[152]

It would seem that the Shirdi saint already had imitators during his final years, supposed holy men who copied his name, apparently with an intention to gain fame. These namesakes appeared in Nagpur, Bandra, and Kopergaon.[153] That situation has continued with a more commercial edge.

During the last year of his life he complained that people were pestering him for money; his role as the "maharaja" was now a target for cupidity. Others believed that his blessings could miraculously grant them well-paid jobs. A few months before his death, a new edifice was completed. This had been built in Shirdi by the wealthy Hindu devotee Gopalrao Buti from Nagpur. It was known as *Buti wada*, and was intended as a hostel for visitors. This building was to gain importance in Hindu accounts. Buti proposed a temple and an image of Krishna on the ground floor, and Sai Baba is said to have welcomed this addition, which was not part of the original plan he endorsed.[154]

Four months before his death, he called a Muslim known as Kasim, the son of Bade Baba. The latter was a *faqir* who has reaped relative obscurity, though reputed to have a very close early link with Sai Baba.[155] Kasim was given 250 rupees and sent to Aurangabad on a special mission to contact a *faqir* known as Shamsuddin Mian and arrange for the distribution of food in his vicinity. Sai also gave Kasim a garland of flowers and instructed him to take this gift to a Sufi known as Banne Mian and give him a message: "The light that *Allah* lit, He is taking away."

Kasim and his friend Chhota Khan went to the Aurangabad home of Banne Mian (Banemiyan). This man had Arab attendants, and was reputed to be in a strange state of abstraction from the world. They found him standing with one arm raised in the air; the Arab attendants warned the visitors not to approach too close, fearing that Banemiyan would be angry with them for interrupting his mood. They waited for an hour, during which the Sufi does not appear to have moved. Chhota Khan then plucked up courage, and put the garland of flowers around the neck of Banne Mian. The latter then lowered his arm, and Chhota Khan repeated the message which Sai Baba had conveyed. Banne Mian gazed at the sky with tears streaming from his eyes.[156]

In late September 1918, Sai Baba suffered from a fever which lasted a few days. Afterwards he would not eat, and despite his begging rounds (which apparently continued), is said to have gone for seventeen days with no food until the hour of his death.[157] During the last two or three days of his life, he was too weak to leave the mosque. He was reclining on his bed when he died, attended by several Hindu devotees.

His death occurred on October 15th, 1918. His last words have been differently reported. To the small group of Hindus who were present, he said "Take me to the *wada*; I would feel better there."[158] Yet Narasimhaswami's version in *Charters and Sayings* records the last words as: "I am going. Place me in the *wada*. Brahmins will reside near me."[159] A curious variant of this is: "All Brahmins will be near me."[160] Rigopoulos has deduced that this indicates Sai's "awareness of the future presence of *brahman* temple priests."[161] It is more certain that the Hindu section of his following interpreted the very elastic reference to *brahmans* as a confirmation of the saint's ultimate identity as a Hindu.

According to Osborne, the last words were: "Only Brahmins will be near me."[162] The same writer concluded that "Sai Baba was here using the word 'Brahmin' in its true meaning of 'spiritually inclined person.' "[163] This more allusive context is no proof of a Hindu identity.

There was definitely a marked Hinduizing tendency at work soon after his decease. The Hindus agreed with the Muslims that he should be buried (ascetics not needing cremation), but in other respects a strong conflict arose. The Muslims said that Sai Baba was a Muslim, and the Hindus said that he was a Hindu. The Hindus claimed that he had specified the *Buti wada* as his place of burial, while the Muslims wanted to bury him in a new tomb of the *dargah* type associated with Sufis. The domed *dargah* was well known in the Maharashtra zone. It was eventually decided to call in a revenue officer from Ahmednagar to resolve the dispute. The officer decided that the devotees and villagers should vote on this matter; that recourse inevitably favoured the Hindu majority. The *Buti wada* was strongly identified with the Hindu temple that had been planned there, and thus the vote was interpreted as a sign of Hindu victory. A recent commentator has deduced that this event "brought to completion the process of Hinduization of the saint,"[164] although other analysts say that the endpoint had not been reached.

The biases of the arbitrating revenue officer were another influential factor. The saint's corpse wore a *langoti*, an undergarment worn by both Hindus and Muslims. The officer decided that Sai Baba could only be a Hindu on the basis of this apparel. He also decided that the saint's mode of departing the world was that of a *brahman* saint: sending away most of his devotees, and dying in serene composure. (Sai Baba had actually sent away devotees to go for a meal, just as he usually did as a matter of routine). It has been observed that these deliberations were misleading. The *langoti* garment does not prove Hindu identity, being a common item of clothing amongst all Indians, and known to have been worn by Sufis. Furthermore, Sai Baba's display of placid composure is not exclusive to *brahmans*, but is an attitude common to all ascetics.[165]

Thus, Sai Baba's identity as a Hindu had been established on the basis of a greater number of Hindus in his following and some extremely loaded logic that can be faulted. The disputes are said to have gradually waned after the majority triumph. The minority view, based on more historical considerations, has rarely been welcome. The saint's tomb was thereafter known as Shri Samadhi Mandir, and the mosque became feted as Shri Dwarakamayi. The village of Shirdi eventually became transformed into a major pilgrimage site for Hindus. Meanwhile, Hindu views about Sai Baba's religious identity varied in expression, some writers like Hemadpant acknowledging the Muslim background.

"A major factor in the growth of Baba's fame can be ascribed to the success obtained by Narasimhaswami's publications, which presented Sai Baba as a great miracle worker."[166] As the scholar who wrote this reflection has also opted to criticize me for deeming Narasimhaswami's contribution to be hagiographic,[167] the matter should be duly accented in the interests of public education. The Shirdi revival promoted by Narasimhaswami was gaining momentum during the 1940s, and his works have gained several reprints. Though his multi-volume *Life of Sai Baba* does furnish many interesting and useful details, it is also confusing, and was accompanied by the assumption that the subject was both a Sufi and a Hindu *bhagavata* (adept). The Hinduizing glosses tend very much to overshadow the deference to a Sufi role, which is virtually eclipsed. One may credit that the author of the *Life* made attempts to avoid what could be considered crude hagiology, and did actually believe that he had produced a serious historical account. Although a "Sai Baba movement" partisan has described Narasimhaswami's *Life* as "the most important contribution to an understanding of the Shirdi saint,"[168] this is misleading if the extent of the Hinduizing interpretation is not duly stressed. The first volume deals with the biography of the saint, volumes two and three with the lives of his prominent devotees (mainly Hindus), while volume four offers an interpretation of his teachings and the devotional movement in his name. The work as a whole minimizes the Muslim components, and furthers the belief that miraculous phenomena emanating from the saint have continued after his death, a belief promoted very strongly in Narasimhaswami's earlier work *Devotees' Experiences of Sai Baba*. The investigator approaching Narasimhaswami's books requires to exercise an attitude of due caution. He attributed such statements to Sai Baba as "I shall be active and vigorous from the tomb also." Shirdi emerged as the focus for a tomb cult, one from which Narasimhaswami derived a fair amount of prestige, which may even be one of the reasons why he argued in his *Life* against viewing Upasni Maharaj as the successor of Sai Baba.[169] A living successor would have meant a diminution of the saint's miraculous activity after his death, an activity vested in the tomb cult and writers like Narasimhaswami.

The fact that Sai Baba did not establish any ashram did not prevent Shirdi from becoming a centre of tomb veneration. The devotional belief was that veneration of his tomb was sufficient, and that miraculous phenomena would continue to be exercised by the deceased. Influenced by Narasimhaswami's presentation, Arthur Osborne wrote: "There was no change in Sai Baba's guidance of devotees, his answering of prayers and his protection in time of trouble."[170] We may be sure that a change had occurred in that Narasimhaswami became the President of the All India Sai Samaj, an organization based at Madras and founded in 1939.

In his *Life*, Narasimhaswami promoted the theme of Sai Baba as an *avatar*, and referred to his reincarnations as a series of *avatars*. This theme developed from oblique references arising in conversations with devotees that were enthusiastically interpreted in accordance with beliefs of devotional Hinduism. The saint was supposed to have mentioned his many births in the past, and to have said that he would be born again and again to help his devotees. These beliefs were systematically fashioned upon the basis of such statements as "we shall meet again and again." There developed a new expectation that he would reincarnate soon. Narasimhaswami also underlined a report from H. S. Dixit (a Hindu devotee), who "seems to have said" that Sai Baba predicted his sudden reappearance as a boy of eight.[171] This need not be taken too seriously in view of the need for stenographic accuracy in such reports. Also, the interpolations of Dixit should be notorious in view of his preference to believe that Shirdi Sai had enjoyed a miraculous birth without the need for a mother. Critics have noted that Satya Sai Baba declared in 1961 that what Shirdi Sai really told Dixit was that he would reappear again as a boy in eight years, meaning in 1926, the date of Satya's birth.[172]

Amongst the claims of various entities to be *avatars* of Shirdi Sai, the claim of Satya Sai has met with by far the greatest celebrity. The latter did not have Muslim connections, and his version of the saint was of the Hinduizing variety which became popular. In 1943, when he was sixteen years old, Ratnakaram Satyanarayana Raju declared that he was Sai Baba. This Hindu boy of Puttaparthi village had learned the knack of manifesting candy from apparent thin air, a feat deemed to be sleight of hand by his father. Presumed identity with a departed saint gradually gained him the limelight, and he assumed the name of Sai Baba as his own. When he gained more wealth, he produced jewellery instead of candy, although Shirdi Sai had never resorted to sleight of hand tricks. Though Satya gained millions of supporters, the majority of Shirdi Sai devotees did not believe in his claim.[173] One can only hope that improved education and critical acumen will recognize basic differences, and that the blanket term of "Sai Baba movement" imposed by undiscerning Western academics will be discarded.[174]

Some Hindus depicted Shirdi Sai as an *avatar* of Dattatreya, a complex deity favoured in Maharashtra. The cult of Dattatreya has ascetic auspices, and is associated with the word *avadhuta*, which refers to a type of holy man believed to transcend caste distinctions. Some Hindu *avadhutas* were depicted as being in affinity with Sufis. The status of a Dattatreya incarnation was applied to fairly numerous holy men in nineteenth century Maharashtra.

The Muslim identity of Shirdi Sai Baba became increasingly obscured by the urban wave of *brahman* devotees from Bombay which occurred from 1910 onwards. "The majority of the visitors during the eight year period after 1910 were generally householders and Hindus who were both literate and vocal" (Warren, *Unravelling the Enigma*, p. 360). This situation contrasts strongly with the earlier one in which visitors to Shirdi were frequently itinerant Muslim *faqirs* who "true to their renunciate goal, shunned any worldly contact and in general were neither vocal nor literate" (*ibid.*). All the biographies were written by Hindus. Many miracle anecdotes were supplied by the urban wave of householder devotees, and celebrated in the output of the Hindu renunciate Narasimhaswami. The preoccupation with such matters as progeny and career prospects are householder susceptibilities, not renunciate traits.

The Sufi background of Shirdi Sai links with the Muslim population of the Deccan plateau, part of Maharashtra. Here the dominions of the Nizam of Hyderabad were independent from British rule during the nineteenth century. The Nizam was a Muslim ruler, though his subjects were mainly Hindus. In some places like Pathri, a stronger concentration of Muslims existed. At Pathri "even today sixty per cent of the population is Muslim" (*ibid.*, p. 87), a fact which afflicts the theory of Sai Baba's *brahman* parentage. The Nizams ruled from 1724 until 1948, and their administrative language was Deccani Urdu, a Muslim tongue deriving from Arabic and Persian and admixed with some Marathi elements. This language was spoken by Sai Baba, as is attested by Hemadpant, though the saint had to speak in Marathi to the urban wave of Hindu devotees who came to Shirdi in his last years. Many tombs of Sufis, the now ruined *dargahs*, feature in the landscape of Maharashtra, especially at places like Khuldabad. The Muslim devotees naturally wished to add one more *dargah* to the horizon at Shirdi, though a Hindu shrine was the outcome of the majority preference. Sai Baba's reputed birthplace of Pathri was in the Nizam's dominions, though Shirdi was located in the Bombay Presidency, the area of Maharashtra ruled by the British Raj.

Although the *Shri Sai Satcharita* of Hemadpant affords significant testimony to the Muslim background of the Shirdi saint, that devotional work preferred a context in the Hindu *bhakti* tradition of Maharashtra. Hemadpant was also concerned to popularize the new shrine as a place of pilgrimage in association with the *bhakti* tradition. Turning to Abdul Baba's recently exhumed notebook in Urdu, we find much more of the Sufi environment in "pre-urban" Shirdi. However, some embellishments are discernible. Abdul includes a laudatory devotional song which refers to the saint's power of granting progeny (*ibid.*, p. 288). After Sai Baba's death, Abdul Baba (d. 1954) used this notebook as a "book of oracles" in a manner well known to popular Sufism (*ibid.*, p. 264). In such usage, the pages are opened at random for a prediction assumed to be in the offing. The same fate befell the poetry of Hafiz and other works. In such respects, the *baraka* (power, ability, blessing) of the Sufi saint remains elusive and is a factor of superstition. *Baraka* was popularly believed to be present in Sufi tombs, though very much at issue is what precisely occurred during the lifetimes of the very diverse saints comprising Sufism. Hagiology reduces the value of many extant records of Sufis found in Persian and other languages. Medieval Hindu saints are even more encumbered by legend.

The Urdu notebook of Abdul Baba is a curious mixture of utterances, stanzas, lists, alphabets, and incantations. There is a lack of organisation in the format, and the jottings have a fragmentary complexion. These notes were written down while (or after) listening to expositions of Sai Baba on the *Quran*, the Sufi hierarchy, and other matters. No sectarian affiliation is discernible, as various Sufi orders are mentioned impartially. Though the document is deficient, it does confirm the Sufi identity of Sai Baba. He was fond of quoting Rumi.

"Sai Baba openly admitted to being a Muslim" (*ibid.*, p. 384). The *murid* or disciple known as Abdul Baba was not constrained by brahmanical fears of pollution from outcastes. Yet Abdul appears to be representative of "popular Sufism" in some respects, which may not reflect the full perspective of his teacher. His notebook includes conciliatory verbal gestures to Hindu themes, testifying to the fact that Sai Baba was not insular. It is evident that Sai Baba was basically concerned with *marifat* or gnosis, and he is reported to have uttered many daring affirmations of his own identity with the divine. Yet he "was also aware of the dangers of giving sacred information to the ignorant" (*ibid.*, p. 327). He stressed austere discipline as a prerequisite.

In the Urdu notebook, the Shirdi gnostic criticizes the *mullas* and *alims* (religious scholars), and also the legalists with such roles as *qazi* (judge). These categories are accused of being corrupt in accepting bribes (*ibid.*, p. 306). False Sufis are also denounced. Some reputed *faqirs* and *pirs* (Sufi adepts) were so impure as to be described in terms of "Satans in human form" (*ibid.*, p. 300). Notably strong in tone are such accusations as:

"Some *faqirs* are so wicked that we feel like taking away their *kafni* (robe) and consigning them to the fire" (*ibid.*).

Pretence and lax lifestyle are implicated here. What Shirdi Sai would have said about his namesake Satya Sai might severely contradict the numerous eulogies written during the last thirty years and more by persons measuring spirituality in terms of miracles and wealthy display. Shirdi Sai lived as a beggar in exacting *faqiri* ("poverty") until his death. He was therefore well qualified to hit at the tactic of the false Sufi who displays skills "in order to fill his coffers and amass wealth" (*ibid.*, p. 306).

Instead of dwelling on miracles, Sai Baba here advocates "severe renunciation and celibacy" (*ibid.*, p. 299). That is not a householder ethic. He says that in order to realize God, the prerequisite of "divine insight" is necessary (*ibid.*, p. 298). Those lacking this "can never have self-realization" (*ibid.*). Metaphorically, he adds that "those who have not tasted, or who have lost their power of taste, will not know" (*ibid.*). Honey and wax are the same to people in whom the power of taste is damaged, he pointed out. Tastelessness is a distinguishing feature of the New Age created in America and Europe, where the word gnostic currently signifies bonehead, in succession from Aleister Crowley.

There is a complexity too easily overlooked. Shirdi Sai states that the fake *pirs* "pretend to be orthodox, to fast" (*ibid.*, p. 306), assuming the guise of austerity for the wrong ends. Obviously, those without taste will be liable to chew the cud provided by dubious "orthodox Sufis," who included in their ranks many insularists of Indian Sufism who militated against Hindus with an almost fundamentalist zeal. In this, they were not so very different from *brahmans* who feared pollution from outcastes (who include Muslims).

The indictment of false Sufis is wide-ranging. Not only does Shirdi Sai criticize those who mistake "the dance and song of the prostitute" for Sufi practice (*ibid.*, p. 301), but he also reflects adversely upon those who boast about being *sayeds* or *pirzadas* or *shaikhs* (*ibid.*). *Sayed* means a descendant of the prophet Muhammad, while *pirzada* was a term often used to denote family descendants of Sufi *pirs*. A number of *pirzadas* had roles as custodians of Sufi tombs, roles in which the concept of *baraka* was easily exploited as a means of gaining gullible disciples (*Gurus Rediscovered*, p. 18).

The gnostic utterances of Shirdi Sai are reported to have included his identity with *Allah*, *Parvardigar*, and other transcendent matters. The statements *Ana'l-Haqq* (I am the Truth) and *Mai Allah hum* were both represented (Warren, *op. cit.*, p. 326). Yet he described himself as the slave of *Allah* when in his "ordinary" moods. Although familiar with various features of Islamic exegesis, Shirdi Sai departed from the role of orthodox Sufi, and may be compared with liberal Sufi radicals in earlier times. That consideration should include the *majazib* associated with Bijapur, who comprised a trend which opposed the urban and landed Sufis. The latter were so frequently theologians militating against religious toleration. The *majazib* were a diffuse phenomenon operating at many levels in eighteenth century Deccani counterculture, which included degenerates. Designations like *majzub* seem rarely to have been used with any sense of technical precision, and were merely popular blanket terms of association.

If Sai Baba had lived several generations earlier at Bijapur, he would have been considered a "madman" by orthodox Sufis. The "mad *faqir*" in the dilapidated Shirdi mosque was an outsider to the dominance of the *ulama* (theologians), whose preaching so often castigated Hindus and who so often assumed a knowledge of Sufism. The gnostic *faqir* pointedly asks why *namaz* (Islamic prayer) should be performed five times a day "if all the time we are engrossed in devotion to God" (*ibid.*, p. 302). Preferring a due absorption in *Allah*, Shirdi Sai asks "what need is there to go to the *masjid* (mosque), the

47

dargah (tomb shrine), or listen to the Qutba" (*ibid.*). Yet Shirdi became the site of a tomb cult apprehending the gnostic *faqir* as a Hindu *avatar*.

It has been deduced that Muslim Sai shunned all rituals for the first fifty or more years of his life in Shirdi (*ibid.*, p. 29). However, *namaz* was performed intermittently in his mosque along with other rituals at the time of Muslim festivals (*ibid.*). He occasionally recited the *fatiha* or opening chapter of the *Quran*. No Hindu deities were ever worshipped in his mosque, though he was known to donate money for the repair of local Hindu temples (*ibid.*) One may conclude that Shirdi Sai was both within and without the orthodox Islamic law, and was effectively criticizing negative aspects of both the well known polarities of *ba-shar* (inside the law) and *bi-shar* (outside the law). These polarities are crudely simplified even by scholars, who frequently opt to distort *bi-shar*. The latter term "popularly refers to numerous subgroupings affiliated to dervish orders, who at their worst were antinomian addicts of alcohol or hemp" (*Gurus Rediscovered*, p. 15).

In the sense of demonstrating advanced dimensions of *bi-shar* (and liberalism), Shirdi Sai Baba was discernibly more outside than inside the law. Cf. Warren, *op. cit.*, pp. 111–112, for some discrepant exegesis amounting to misrepresentation, in which the terminology of Meher Baba is confused with research references to the *majazib*, and in which *masts* (God-intoxicated) are confused with the very rare category of *majzubs*, thus contradicting the same terminology (of Meher Baba) that is mistakenly interposed. Liberal Sufis also followed the "strict Sufi path" which Dr. Warren denies to *majazib*, which means that orthodox and landed Sufis are glorified by myopic scholarship that is anomalously desperate to snub criticism of Satya Sai Baba, who is one of the more lawless and unprincipled pretenders to spirituality.

The argument which Dr. Warren was here misrepresenting had pointed out that the "orthodox Sufis" (including hereditary descendants, theologians, landed gentry, and religious insularists) had caricatured unorthodox (or liberal) Sufis of the Deccan as "madmen" (*majazib*). Some orthodox Sufis urged *jihad* against the infidel. The liberal Sufis did not despise Hindus, and did not patronize a corrupt monarchy. It is a mistake to subvert such details with "states of consciousness" talk that misses the social crux to a pronounced degree, and while supporting an impostor like Satya Sai as a divine incarnation. Cf. the misread page 19 of *Gurus Rediscovered*, cited in such an erroneous context by a Satya partisan. Misinformed readers should be told that in Meher Baba's version of the "spiritual hierarchy" of seven thousand members, only three are *majzubs* in the exacting sense he applied to that term. There is therefore no possible association with the extensive *majazib* tradition of the Deccan, only in academic misconstruction. As the recipient of such misconstruction, I do not feel obliged to accept all aspects of a Ph.D. thesis which exhibits serious lapses in accuracy of citation and due context. "Perfected Master" talk and Sufi honorifics are no acceptable substitute for the onus of what really happened in historical and social affairs.

The current standards of the Ph.D. thesis permit facile assumptions like the following. Because Meher Baba and some of his followers referred to Shirdi Sai as Hazrat Sai Baba (Warren, *op. cit.*, p. 112), then any associations of Sai Baba with the term *majzub* (plural *majazib*) are taboo. Dogmatic scholarship will hopefully one day understand that the popular usage of such terms as *majzub* was not the same as that proposed by Meher Baba. Dr. Warren also imagines that Meher Baba's work with *masts* in India during the 1940s was equivalent to working with the *majazib* of the Deccan (*ibid.*, p. 111), an error that could be grave in implication for contemporary academic research. The *majazib* of Bijapur are known only partially from the sources, but it is clear that they do not equate with *masts* (even allowing for a few exceptions possible).

In view of the misrepresentation from an academic quarter, it is necessary to make the following points:

1) Dr. Warren narrows down the historical and sociological perspective in *Gurus Rediscovered* (chapter one) to her attribution of a spiritual state, in the process discarding my entire argument about differences amongst Sufis. If that is Ph.D. scholarship, then the standards need to be increased in order to accommodate what is really being said in alternative research.

2) My reflections upon Sai Baba's affinities and discrepancies with *majazib* of Bijapur (living several generations earlier) require to be seen in due perspective according to the information I presented, not in accordance with the academic misconstruction of Meher Baba which was arbitrarily imposed. My comments about *majazib* were not made in relation to persons failing "to return to normal worldly consciousness" (Warren, *op. cit.*, p. 111), but to other persons who included the (Islamized) Jewish Sufi Sarmad, whom I described as "a highly literate *majzub*" (*Gurus Rediscovered*, p. 21). Sarmad was known as

a *majzub* and was well aware of his hostile surroundings, which were so fatal as to cause his execution in 1660–1 at Delhi. The title phrase of my book *From Oppression to Freedom* was a direct reference to Sarmad's premature end (*Oppression*, p. 134). That book was not mentioned by Rigopoulos or Warren, an indication of the lapses in Ph.D. prowess. Jewish Sufis, literate *majazib*, and social dichotomies are unknown and obscured in some Ph.D. dissertations which can tend to substitute caricature that is perhaps not far removed from the hagiographic contractions written about the *majazib* of Bijapur. Those *majazib* can be viewed as one local manifestation of a somewhat larger trend to liberal Sufism that gained varying characteristics in India during the Mughal era and after.

3)   The *majazib* of Bijapur are only very partially known, which is an understatement. In a misrepresented book I stated that "the *majzubs* are described in hagiographies that frequently amount to a caricature of the subject; typical entries on them merely state the name, place of origin, and some aspect of behaviour that 'seemed particularly bizarre to the biographer,' to borrow an apt phrase of Eaton" (*Gurus Rediscovered*, p. 20). Dr. Eaton was less apt in making conflations about *majazib* and drug experiences, as the evidence in that direction is not convincing in the case of so many obscure *majazib*. We may assume that there were some or many lapses amongst copyists, which is a different subject.

4)   Many *majazib* of Bijapur appear to have nurtured monistic beliefs which were heretical to Islamic orthodoxy and to the Sufi establishment vested in prestigious dervish orders. Such beliefs had precedents in figures like Hallaj, though some manifestations are not well known.

5)   The monism and eccentric behaviour of Sai Baba do tally with features relating to the *majazib* of Bijapur. Sai Baba even criticizes (in Abdul's Urdu notebook) some of the status roles that were obnoxious to the *majazib*.

6)   Unlike some of the *majazib*, Sai Baba did not go naked. It is not known how many of the *majazib* adopted this Hindu custom. Nudity is not a crime in India, being a characteristic of some Hindu holy men known as *naga sadhus*. The gesture of nakedness on the part of *faqirs* betokened an affinity with Hindu renunciation in the face of the oppressive contempt for Hindus expressed by many orthodox Sufis, who sometimes invoked *jihad* against the hapless infidels. During the seventeenth century, a trend towards religious tolerance

was furthered by the Sultan of Bijapur, and which resulted in a new wave of Sufi types converging upon that city of the Deccan. Yet many of these incoming Sufis were orthodox in outlook, "particularly those who were members of the Qadiri and Shattari orders," and those zealots "opposed the toleration as being religiously aberrant" (*Gurus*, p. 17). Dr. Eaton described them as "glorified *ulama*." They incited the court of Bijapur to *jihad* while acquiring government land grants. This trend to a "Sufi petty gentry" thrived on hereditary descent. In contrast, the liberal Sufis opted for an independence from the trappings associated with theological zeal. Some of the *majazib* came from noble families, and some were the sons of orthodox Sufis. "They had renounced their privileged lifestyles, and in general were practically indistinguishable from commoners" (*Gurus*, p. 19).

7) Sai Baba was not a *bhang*-drinker, unlike some of the less discerning persons classified under the conglomerate label of *majazib*. *Bhang* is a form of cannabis favoured by aberrant *sadhus*. Eaton's generalizations about *majazib* and *bhang* may be strongly questioned owing to the paucity of reliable documentation. Mediocre *faqirs* did resort to cannabis. While there are many *sadhus* and *yogis* who resort to cannabis, there are many who do not. Pseudomonism is a perennial problem induced by drug experiences.

8) The Chishti order of *dervishes* gained a reputation for being the most liberal Sufi order. Many of the *majazib* appear to have possessed Chishti affiliations. Their order prohibited drugs and alcohol, and there is no proof that the majority of them broke those particular rules. What they were concerned about deserves a more flexible description than some orthodox Sufis were prepared to give from the "petty gentry" platform. There is no proof that Sai Baba was affiliated to the Chishti order.

9) The present writer did not equate Bijapur *majazib* with the definition of *majzubiyat* expressed by Meher Baba. I have been familiar with the latter definition for many years, but this does not answer to various usages of the words under discussion in traditional sources, which opted for generalized meanings that were frequently of popular association. So I preferred instead to follow the scholarly rule that later schemas or definitions should not be imposed upon earlier linguistic classifications. That rule has been flouted by at least one Ph.D. dissertation, which accuses me of an error in associating Sai Baba with *majazib*. The accusation is curiously pedantic and very misleading. Dr. Warren describes a *majzub* as one "overcome with a mystical

51

experience as a gift of Grace" (*Unravelling the Enigma*, p. 111), and cites *Gurus Rediscovered*, which does not use any such phrase or explanation. Nor does her definition reflect the exegesis of Meher Baba, whom she seems to invoke as a support. I am supposed to have described Sai Baba in this sense as a *majzub*, which I definitely did not. What I really said was:

"The literal meaning of the Arabic word *majzub* varies in different glossaries, but in general it signifies a sufi saint who becomes absorbed in Allah. In the Bijapur tradition, it referred to those who forsook Islamic orthodoxy in favour of an ascetic life in which states of consciousness (and not rites and customs) were the paramount consideration. The plural term *majazib* has appropriately been translated as 'illuminati.'" (*Gurus*, p. 22.)

The word *majzub* was often applied indiscriminately to anyone who could be considered a "madman," as being unorthodox, as being heretical, as being extremist, as being Hinduized. That word did not connote any specific spiritual state in such usage. Sai Baba can legitimately be compared with *majazib*, with due qualifications, as many in that amorphous category were more kindred to him than to proscribing orthodox Sufis with a canny eye on their coffers.

Dr. Warren attributes to *Gurus* the accompanying description of a *majzub* as one who "fails to return to normal worldly consciousness" (*Unravelling the Enigma*, p. 111). That description cannot be found in my book. I am supposed to have depicted Sai Baba as a person in that disabled category. The inaccuracy of such misrepresentation may be gauged from the fact that I attributed to the Shirdi *faqir* "a due equilibrium in *baqa* involving the 'normalization' of his consciousness in relation to the external world" (*Gurus*, p. 24). Such terminology and nuance is clearly not understood by some scholars.

One possible reason for such misrepresentation is "Satya Sai" bias, a problem caused by the cultic estimation of the miraculous. In *Gurus* I made such statements as: "If the public are indoctrinated with concepts of *siddhis* (occult powers), then they are open to deception at every moment" (*Gurus*, p. 22). The fact that Satya Sai miracles have been condoned in doctoral dissertations is proof to the public that academic errors are potentially dangerous and a partner to deception.

10)   Shirdi Sai was not an orthodox Sufi as known in Indian Sufism. He was instead an "Hallajian" type of monist critical of status roles, and in this sense comparisons with Bijapur *majazib* are valid. His conversations in Marathi with Hindu devotees, in which he re-

52

ferred amenably (if cryptically) to their gods and avatars, are not the stamp of an orthodox Sufi, and this point would only need labouring to tunnel vision.

11)   Despite the *Quran* recitals he evoked from his disciple Abdul, Sai Baba "had no external connection with orthodox Islam or the Muslim *shariat*" (Warren, *op. cit.*, p. 368). The devotional literature includes a report from Das Ganu that the saint was occasionally in conflict with local Muslims "as very often his acts and ideas did not agree with their orthodoxy" (*ibid.*, p. 110). Despite the fact that Das Ganu was a Hindu, his statement in this respect may be credited as accurate. Sai Baba refused to go to an urban locale in order to perform Friday prayers (*ibid.*). It is also evident that he believed in reincarnation (*ibid.*, pp. 368–9), though some of his references to that subject were oblique. Reincarnation is not an orthodox Islamic belief, though this topic (sometimes known as *tanasukh*) was in currency amongst dissident Muslims over the centuries. It was regarded by the orthodox as being outside the law, and treated by fanatics as being a punishable offence.

12)   In his early years at Shirdi, Sai Baba was considered a "madman" (*pagal*) by the local Hindus. This stigma was apparently derived from his rather intense demeanour, which varied from being taciturn to explosive. He had kept aloof, was heard muttering to himself, and when angered, could rant at intruders. He had a habit of throwing stones at people whom he considered to be intruders, or as possessing deficient attitudes. He was definitely not seeking company or limelight. Devotees were sometimes puzzled by his sense of aversion. Some of his traits are strongly reminiscent of *majazib* characteristics; it is possible that unsociable behaviour became a copyist convention in some sectors of the Bijapur phenomenon, but the sources are conflatory. Eventually, the retiring and eccentric *faqir* gained a large number of devotees. In his later years he was not a decorous greybeard but someone far more unpredictable. His mood varied from being gentle to verbally aggressive. However, the extreme of reaction to the intrusions of devotees was exhibited by his contemporary known as Tajuddin Baba (d. 1925), a Sufi of Nagpur. When he became famous, Tajuddin was beset with unwanted visitors who requested his blessings and supposed miracle powers. He wanted to escape what he felt was an oppressive predicament caused by saintly fame. So he resorted to an extreme tactic. He went naked to a tennis court where some representatives of the British Raj were playing one

of their favoured games. He is said to have acted like a madman on that occasion, intent upon gaining the acute disapproval of the tennis club. His exhibition outraged the presiding powers, who apparently included memsahibs of genteel upbringing. He was submitted to a local lunatic asylum, where he stayed happily for many years, gaining a welcome degree of quiet and insulation against the horde of miracle seekers. Yet eventually a new wave of admirers began to visit him in the asylum. (Shepherd, *Hazrat Tajuddin Baba*, unpublished paper; cf. Warren, *op. cit.*, pp. 196ff.)

Tajuddin did nothing wrong save to cause disapproval. Native nakedness was not understood by the British, and was unwelcome on tennis courts. He acted like a madman for a purpose that was subsequently recognized. Bizarre though the episode does sound, it is a striking tangent to the careers of gurus like Satya Sai Baba who cultivate public spotlight with such zeal and manipulative ability. The perspective provided by Sufi "madmen" might even be described as a form of "crazy wisdom," though one needing due qualifications in view of the confusion caused by the Tantric versions in America. Unlike Daism (the sect of Adi Da) and decadent Vajrayana, moral codes were not flouted. Devotees were not sexually abused, but perceived as having a rudimentary intelligence that imposed restrictions upon a Sufi vocation. Another sector of rudimentary intelligence are drug addicts, who are frequently confused with mysticism by people who do not understand the difference between a spiritual development and an artificial experience that damages the scope for growth.

13)   A discrepant statement of Dr. Warren relates to "the female saint Hazrat Babajan, who is today viewed as one of the most famous Sufi *majzubs* of Maharashtra, with striking points of similarity with Sai Baba in terms of lifestyle and miraculous powers" (*Unravelling the Enigma*, p. 200). Note that Hazrat Babajan (d. 1931) of Poona is here described in taboo parlance as a *majzub*. The miraculous element is overstated. Babajan was an exceptional entity, and one of the most distinctive unorthodox Sufis of her time. Miracle stories have been elaborated in relation to her, though certain of these need firm critical treatment. A kernel of reliable and semi-reliable data remains after such sifting. An attempt was made by the present writer in that direction, an effort notably ignored by Dr. Warren, who does not cite the first non-devotee biography of Hazrat Babajan, published in Cambridge in the English language. Academic one-upmanship is a disconcerting factor. Cf. Shepherd, *A Sufi Matriarch: Hazrat Babajan*

(Cambridge 1986). Dr. Warren instead preferred to cite a booklet published by the Avatar Meher Baba Poona Centre which incorporated a chapter entitled "Miracles of Babajan" (K. K. Ramakrishnan and M. R. Kantak, eds., *Hazrat Babajan: The Emperor of Spiritual Realm of her time*, Poona 1981, pp. 47–58). A brief but relevant biography by Dr. Ghani (whose vocational name was Munsiff) was also included (*ibid.*, pp. 23–34). I restricted my own biographical effort to 78 pages in view of the paucity of reliable information. Unlike the Poona booklet, *Sufi Matriarch* was annotated, with reference to scholars like Schimmel, Rizvi, Kopruluzade, and Eliade. One may add here that Dr. Warren's book on Sai Baba has substantially helped to flesh out the Muslim and Sufi background of the subject, and accordingly deserves due citation. She has made a number of useful criticisms of the devotee literature on Sai Baba. There are, however, flaws of emphasis and also of reporting in relation to non-devotee contributions. Those flaws could imply an undue bias towards the miracle appetite fostered by Satya Sai Baba. That appetite is also evident in the SUNY Press book by Dr. Rigopoulos. Dr. Warren emphasizes miracles of Shirdi Sai, Satya Sai, diverse Sufis, and even miracles popularly attaching to Sufi tombs. In contrast, the present writer does not make such emphases, and I am not persuaded that I have to be misrepresented and underpresented as a consequence of such a critical standpoint.

Due critical assessment will point out that the AMB Poona Centre booklet on Babajan attributed the varied contents to Meher Baba and Dr. Ghani. In fact, articles of Ghani comprise much of the contents, including the chapter enticingly edited under the rubric of miracles. That chapter contains anecdotes which are not always classifiable as miracle lore. Dr. Warren was evidently confused by the editing, and inaccurately states that "Meher Baba did record a few [miracles]" of Babajan (Warren, *op. cit.*, p. 201). That error was a specific reference to the chapter on miracles. Meher Baba was not in any way the author, or part author, of that contribution by Ghani. This is an instance of how the appetite for miracles can distort the record in basic respects, leading to potentially serious problems for later researchers.

Dr. Warren is rather free with references to Meher Baba in her book, but does not relay some of his basic emphases. In contrast, the booklet on Babajan did convey Meher Baba's emphasis that "*siddhis* are therefore rightly regarded as obstacles to the attainment of realization" (*Hazrat Babajan*, p. 40). Instead of dwelling upon the implications here, Dr. Warren instead attributed to Meher Baba her own

55

limitation of recording miracle stories. *Siddhis* denote occult powers and the ability to perform supposed miracles, which have been the stock in trade of Satya Sai Baba, and affording a lucrative front for his sexual abuse. The word *siddhis* should be sufficient to provoke nausea in rational people.

Because some academics have got their priorities wrong, they ignore the reasons why Meher Baba criticized the miracle instinct of Narasimhaswami, and instead accuse critics of that instinct as being opinionated. The standards of Ph.D. thinking are not always beyond reproach.

14)   The difficulty of sifting the historical truth from Sufi legend and hagiography is attested by two recent reports relating to the Chishti saint Zar Zari Zar-bakhsh (d. 1309), one of the early Sufis active in the Deccan, and whose tomb is at Khuldabad. According to Rigopoulos, his community "developed remarkably liberal and even pro-Hindu tendencies, bringing about a peculiar blend of Islamic features and *advaita-bhakti* teachings" (*Life and Teachings of Sai Baba of Shirdi*, p. 6). Zar Zari is a legendary figure. The Khuldabad Chishtis of the fourteenth century made firm rules against accepting gifts that might compromise their independence. Subsequently the Sufi shrines acquired a political role. Some of the Chishti *shaikhs* had rather orthodox characteristics, and it is difficult to imagine *advaita-bhakti* affinities in some cases. The Chishti exegete Gesu Daraz (d. 1422) was orthodox enough to repudiate the teachings of Ibn al-Arabi and even Rumi (*Gurus Rediscovered*, pp. 13–14). One could hope that Zar Zari Zar-bakhsh was more liberal. Yet in the eighteenth century Persian work *Sawanih*, composed by Sabzawari, the legendary Chishti saint is described as being "the eliminator of infidelity and innovative influences, and he was the knower and defender of the faith of Islam" (C. W. Ernst, *Eternal Garden*, SUNY Press, 1992, p. 164). Liberal or orthodox? Will Shirdi Sai one day be described as an advocate of *jihad* or as a *bhang*-drinker, depending upon distorted preferences?

15)   Sai Baba's Muslim disciple Abdul Baba became custodian of the Shirdi tomb at the saint's decease. Abdul was thus a *pirzada*, though a very rural one differing from the officious hereditary ambience which had accompanied famous Sufi tombs elsewhere in the Deccan. In his earlier years at Shirdi, Abdul had been committed to the *faqir* lifestyle of self-denial and poverty, though later he married and had a family. His tendency to the oracular use of his Urdu notebook situates him in popular Sufism. He seems to have assimilated

56

some of the devotional mood which gained ascendancy. Amongst his apparent interpolations in the Urdu notebook is the phrase stating that "the present Kaliyuga *avatar* is Sai Baba" (Warren, *op. cit.*, p. 287). However, between ten and twenty avatars are here said to be living at the same time. Such statements did not appear in orthodox Sufi canons of expression.

For a few years after his teacher's death, Abdul seems to have been regarded as the leading local devotee of Shirdi. The appurtenances of the tomb were still very simple, and retained the mood of a *dargah*. In 1922 came the intervention of H. S. Dixit, an influential Hindu who decided that the tomb needed to be supervised in a Hindu manner. There was an argument between Dixit and Abdul. Attempting to take over the tomb, Dixit created a Public Trust (Sansthan) that was deemed illegal by Abdul. Dixit was a solicitor and used his career skills to eliminate the custodianship of Abdul. The Muslim underdog lost his counter-suit in the law courts. The Hindus had now taken control of the saint's tomb. Abdul was forced to leave, though in later years, when he was no longer considered a threat, he was permitted further participation in maintaining the shrine.

Abdul was one of the devotees later interviewed by Narasimhaswami, whose industry failed to set the situation in due context. Dixit was one of the *brahman* devotees who Hinduized Sai Baba; it was he who fabricated the belief that the saint had not been born of a human mother. That was an obvious attempt to negate Muslim associations, and renders more suspicious the belief that Sai Baba declared himself to have been born of *brahman* parents. By the 1940s, the strongly Hinduizing interpretation of Gunaji was widely confused with the real Sai Baba. The rugged Muslim *faqir* became the Hindu *avadhuta* and the celebrated *avatar*.

Under the auspices of Dixit's Hindu organization known as the Shri Sai Baba Sansthan, the tomb at Shirdi became increasingly ornate, culminating in 1952 with the installation of a large marble statue of Sai Baba near the tomb precincts. That statue was worshipped in a manner accorded to Hindu deities, and this innovation is reported to have deterred visits from *faqirs* thereafter (*ibid.*, pp. 269–70). Muslims will not accept anthropomorphic representation in religious worship. The statue was life-size, and was frequently garlanded. It was seated on a silver throne.

Ten years later appeared a book by the *brahman* Swami known as Sai Sharan Anand. He had become a devotee of the saint in 1911, and had much later become a *sannyasin* in 1953. Sharan Anand himself became credited with supernatural powers and he fostered the "superman" image of the Shirdi saint. His book included the statement that high caste Hindu devotees believed Shirdi Sai to have worn Muslim garb and to have entertained Muslim habits "for the purpose of killing or removing the wrong interpretation of the Veda and drawing attention to the truth that everything – all without exception – is Brahman" (*ibid.*, p. 34, citing S. S. Anand, *Shri Sai the Superman*, Bombay 1962). In other words, everything is Brahman only if it is Hindu. The wrong interpretation of the Veda was here being identified with Islam. Despite his emphasis on the elusive Roshan Shah Mian, the Hinduizing bias of Sharan Anand seems to have been somewhat stronger than that of Narasimhaswami. Yet the worst distortions adhered to the reincarnatory claim of Satya Sai, whose career of abuse has surely amounted to a wrong interpretation of the Veda.

2. Upasni Maharaj of Sakori (d. 1941)

The well known disciple of Sai Baba was definitely a *brahman* by birth; there is no dilemma concerning origins in his case. However, various other details of Upasni's biography have given rise to different interpretations, and some details are very little known. The most popular version of his life has been deemed unreliable in part.[175]

The subject was born on 15th May 1870 at the village of Satana in the district of Nasik. His *brahman* ancestors had officiated as priests. He was named Kashinath Govind Upasni Shastri. For convenience, I will refer to him throughout as Upasni, the name by which he was commonly known in his later years. He was the second of five brothers, but differed from the others. When he was seven, his father and grandfather decided to send him to school, but his religious instincts caused him to dislike the curriculum. Friction occurred between he and his teacher, and this grew so acute that he was allowed to leave. Instead he received instruction from his grandfather Gopala Shastri, a learned pundit with the disposition of an ascetic. Gopala had served at the court of the Maharaja of Baroda, at whose death he had lost his position and income, the family becoming poor. The boy's father, Govind Shastri, did not become a priest or pundit, but instead took the role of a clerk attached to the legal profession; he moved from Satana, leaving Upasni to live with his grandfather. At some uncertain date, the learned Gopala became a *sannyasin* and renounced his family. He seems to have regarded it as his duty to teach the young Upasni, who showed strong affinities with ascetic ideals and who was considered a problem case by his parents.

Gopala Shastri taught his grandson the Vedas and related scriptures. The boy was evidently very partial to Vedantic teachings, and is said to have been averse to lessons from temple priests.[176] It was *sadhana* (spiritual discipline), not ritual matters, which interested him. He was impressed by the tales of austerities undertaken by sages profiled in the *Puranas* and the Epics. "Applying the traditional teaching that the body is the prison of the Self, he looked upon his body as an enemy."[177] The boy began a habit of fasting, a form of self-denial in which he appears to have excelled. However, he seems to have gone to extremes and to have neglected "natural activities of youth that would develop his body."[178] The ascetic streak in our subject was very strong, and this was apparently what endeared him to his grandfather, who disliked the secularizing influence at work in Hindu lifestyles. The old man encouraged the boy to take an interest in Yoga, and Upasni eagerly practised posture (*asana*) and breath control (*pranayama*). He would do this both at home and at a nearby cremation ground, the traditional setting for ascetic practices. His preoccupation with *pranayama* was to endure for many years, though with drastic consequences. Had he known of what problems he would encounter, he would surely have desisted from that deceptive exercise in which risk to lung function can occur.

The young enthusiast also took up *mantra japa*, which means the repetition of *mantras*, usually scriptural phrases deemed to have a supernatural effect, though devotional *mantras* also abound. This practice tends to be very stereotyped and can encourage a mood of dependence upon repetitious formulae. The boy's level of introversion was acute, and some onlookers were very critical, deeming him to be an extremist. His parents took this attitude, and it is said that in some moods Upasni despaired at being so economically useless to his kin. He had apparently left school by the time he was ten, and yet did not earn anything for the family. His uncle Damodar is said to have sympathized with him, along with his grandfather.

The old pundit was not solely responsible for Upasni's orientation in a lifestyle of *sadhana*. The second inspirer emerged in his life at a time when he was critically ill. In his childhood he suffered from acute stomach aches, apparently related to poor digestion. Doctors diagnosed him as incurable when his health broke down. His family then consented to him being taken to a local woman who had the reputation of being a healer. This elderly Hindu was an eccentric widow who refused to conform to customs of mourning by removing personal adornments after the death of her husband. She continued to wear her bangles, and was ridiculed by some as a witch. Upasni himself had formerly taunted her, along with other children, and she at first refused to help him. He subsequently visited her every day and followed her instructions, reassessing her as a true *bhakta* or lover of God. She was evidently not one of those presumed healers who encourage superstitions, e.g., the category who believe they can cure a deadly snake bite by chanting *mantras*. It is said that Upasni was freed of his critical ailment through his association with her, and this apparently increased his desire to leave school.[179] It is possible that his partiality for fasting was conceived as an antidote to digestive troubles.

For reasons that are not entirely clear, Upasni moved to Dhulia to stay with his parents. It seems that they fostered the idea that he was a financial burden to them, which made him feel depressed. He also felt that the only way he could resolve the situation was to become a mendicant ascetic and leave home. However, the senior members of his family decided that he should be married, and despite his protests, they arranged his marriage with a girl of eight named Durga. Child marriage was one of the worst features of the caste system, and one which reformers were even then attempting to combat. This unwanted match is said to have occurred when Upasni was fourteen; reports differ as to whether he left home before or after the marriage.[180] Some writers state that in desperation he left his wife after some months and fled to Nasik, taking refuge at the home of an acquaintance of his grandfather, though continuing to beg his food. His father instigated a ruse to get him back by sending a message saying that his mother was seriously ill. This was an untruthful story, but succeeded in making the youth return.[181]

Upasni was a victim of tensions involved in the situation of family demands versus ascetic retirement. Paternal wishes were considered paramount in the caste system; renunciation could wait for the fading years of life (or never) in many minds, whatever sufferings were involved for the odd one out. The evils of child marriage had the blessing of caste approval, and even the boy's grandfather appears to have sanctioned the paternal arrangement.

The deep-rooted persistence of child marriage may be gleaned from the fact that the reformer Keshab Chandra Sen (1838–84), despite his campaign for legislation against this custom, had his daughter married when she was still a child. It was only *sati*, the burning of widows, that was prohibited by the British government. Child marriages are still quite common in India, and "there is a dramatic rise in the instances of young women burnt to death by their husbands or their husbands' relations in order to obtain dowry."[182]

Within two years of their marriage, Upasni's girl wife Durga(bai) died from illness, a victim to the high mortality rate in India. The youth daily requested his parents to give their permission for him to adopt *sannyas* and enter the fourth stage (*ashrama*) of life. They were adamant that he should remain in the householder (*grihastya*) stage, and uncompromisingly arranged a second marriage for him. The bride was only nine, again a victim of the system that left no choices. The bridegroom is said to have given her little attention, and after about a year, he again left home, leaving the girl with his relatives. He apparently secured his flight only by going for a walk on the pretext of obtaining a medical book for study. Another version says that his parents at last complied with his wishes and gave him permission to leave, fearing that he would grieve himself to death. Whatever the truth here, it was recognized that marriage had in fact made no difference to his disposition for the renunciate life.

Upasni made his way south to Poona, where he stopped at a temple on the outskirts of the city. It was the haunt of beggars living in a grim condition of semi-starvation. He begged from house to house, sharing his alms with the beggars. Disappointed with events, he moved west to Kalyan; he found difficulty in obtaining food, meeting with rebuffs until an old Maratha woman took pity upon his starvation. She is said to have recited to him a verse in Marathi which he later repeated many times. This began with the injunction to "maintain life even on water, if you get nothing else."[183] There is little doubt that he had the ability to endure starvation.

He journeyed through a jungle near Nasik. He apparently thought of returning home, but was filled with despair at the prospect of such a dead-end. He came to the mountain known as Bhorgad, and sighted a cave high up on the steep slopes. He now contracted a death-wish, deciding to kill himself by undertaking *prayopavesha*, fasting to death, a drastic recourse sometimes adopted by Hindus in moods of crisis, though often in the hope of having a prayer granted. Upasni appears to have had no such hope; he merely believed that the grim recourse was the easiest way out of his psychological turmoil, perhaps exacerbated by his realization that the ascetic life was not giving him any fulfilment. His idea was simple – he would sit in the lonely cave without food and drink until he expired, thus terminating his sufferings. It was evidently not fasting that worried him, but acute frustration. After two days in the cave, he began a silent repetition of *mantras*. He did not sleep and eventually lost consciousness. He had a vision of someone pulling the skin off his body, and afterwards regained normal consciousness. He found himself in an extreme predicament. He suffered from intense thirst, and his body was so stiff that he was unable to move. Only his right forearm was capable of movement. He was surely now in a worse situation than he had been as a mendicant worrying over his family connections and his lack of sublime bliss.

Very weakened, Upasni soon slipped back into unconsciousness (some Indian accounts confusingly refer to this as *samadhi,* evidencing the general uselessness of such vocabulary). He was awakened by a thunderstorm, and the ensuing rain created a small pool in the cave that saved his life. His plight shook him out of his death-wish, and with his functioning hand he scooped water to drink. He slowly massaged his body and restored sensation to his devitalized limbs. After a few days, still starved of food, he experienced a vision of a Hindu and a Muslim who pulled away his skin to disclose a divine essence; they told him that they would not allow him to die. This vision caused him to feel that he had a special destiny, and gave him sufficient determination to leave the cave. This proved a very arduous endeavour; he was so weak from starvation that he had to slide and crawl down the hill. His body had become a living skeleton of skin and bones, and he grasped that he had been in the cave for months. At the foot of Bhorgad mountain was the small village of Gawalwadi, the home of an aboriginal tribe. They gave him food and nursed him back to health.

The period he spent in the cave is variously said to have been many months, nine months, and one year. That seems to exaggerate the critical condition of long duration in which he lacked food and water. If the standard dating can be relied upon, then he was twenty years of age at that time.[184] He had to stay in Gawalwadi for three months in order to recuperate, and his psychological attitude changed as a result of the ordeal. He decided to return on foot to Dhulia to rejoin his family. Upasni was now acclaimed as a *tapasvin,* one who undertakes an austerity, as a consequence of his lengthy fast.

Within a short time his father died and his grandfather became seriously ill. Upasni prepared medicines for the dying old man, and to this has been traced his subsequent interest in a medical career. His wife also passed away. He is said to have left home in order to foil a plan of his mother and uncle to force upon him a third marriage. For some reason, he agreed to this match about six months later. The bride was apparently in some affinity with his own aspirations. He took his new wife to Poona, where he lived at the home of his brother Balakrishna, who was a college Professor. Yet he went alone to Sangli, where he chose to stay in the Shri Dattaguru temple, "leading the life of a devout monk for two and a half years."[185] He resumed an ascetic diet, restricting himself mainly to the leaves of trees, supplementing these with grains and fruits. Some say that his purpose in this sojourn was to study Ayurvedic medicine, a traditional branch of learning which has been put to varied uses. He decided to become a physician and started a dispensary at Amraoti,[186] near Nagpur, apparently in 1896. During the next several years Upasni became very successful and ended up a wealthy man. For three years he edited a monthly journal in Marathi devoted to Ayurveda, and was much esteemed in the relevant brahmanical circles. Though he gave free treatment to the poor, his professional standing attracted a solid income. He was concerned to provide for his wife, to whom he seems to have become deeply attached; she bore him a son who died after only a few months. It is said that he was subject to moods of abstraction which made him restless, aware that he had become a rich householder whose lifestyle was now at variance with his ascetic ideals.

As time passed, his attention lapsed from his medical work, and he thought that the most productive course would be to acquire land. In 1906 Upasni decided to invest his money in a large tract of land near Gwalior which included a number of villages. He became an estate landlord, and is said to have paid thousands of rupees for this property, which encompassed hundreds of acres. The purpose was to farm uncultivated land, though he also expected to increase his wealth by collecting rents on the land. He became much preoccupied with this venture, moving from Amraoti. There was a setback when tenants refused to pay their rents, while government taxes exerted a heavy toll. Within two years he was embroiled in a number of lawsuits. As a consequence, he lost his lands and his money. His reputation also suffered, as he had gained the social profile of a professional man who never made mistakes. The pressures reacted adversely upon his health. Now bankrupt, Upasni returned to Amraoti in 1908.[187] He still had his dispensary and attempted to revive his medical practice. Yet he was too disillusioned by the train of events and had lost incentive and ambition. It seemed to him that the lifestyle of the householder and the role of the professional man led nowhere; he had to return to his renunciate roots, to avoid entanglement in earning more and desiring security. Being careful not to upset his wife, he gained her consent in his new resolve and closed his dispensary in April 1910. He and his wife left together for places of pilgrimage.

They went to Ujjain and Omkareshwar, where Upasni undertook an intensive schedule of meditation which absorbed most of his time. At Omkareshwar he underwent a critical experience which caused him much suffering. Different accounts have attributed this problem to intensive meditation[188] and to *pranayama*,[189] and it would seem that both of these practices are realistically to blame. Upasni had indeed reverted to his old extremism, and had unwisely revived the *pranayama* exercises which his grandfather had taught him when he was a boy.

His wife found him lying unconscious one day. He seemed not to be breathing, as if he were dead. She desperately threw water into his face. He regained consciousness, but not normal breathing. Upasni was now in a very grim predicament, the normal functioning of his lungs having been disrupted. He could only breathe by applying an artificial movement to his stomach. His despair was acute. His *sadhana* had gone wrong, had left him in a seemingly hopeless mess. He was now dependent upon his wife to get him to Nagpur, where they sought professional treatment for the problem. Alas, the medicine did not work, and no cure was in the offing. He was constantly gasping for breath.

His wife was so distraught that she came to believe that her husband's malady was a consequence of her evil *karma* incurred in a former life. As a penance, she is said to have walked 125,000 times around a sacred fig tree, which must have been exhausting. It is more convincing to believe that the cause here lay in Upasni's adoption of breathing exercises as advocated by brahmanical expositors of Patanjali Yoga, the effects of which were exacerbated by deep meditation or "samadhi" in which awareness is distracted from the body, leaving the practitioner less able to diagnose what is happening. *Pranayama* exercises create a preoccupation with breathing processes, and can alter the breathing pattern best suited to individual physical needs. All such considerations are obscured by obsessive meditation, which is not equivalent to insight.

Moving to Dhulia to stay with his brother, Upasni's breathing problem became so painful and laborious that in sheer desperation he set out alone in search of a yogi who might cure him. He felt that otherwise he would have to commit suicide. In April 1911 he made his way to Rahuri, near Ahmednagar, to visit a yogi known as Kulkarni Maharaj. This man was only able to massage him and administer a relaxing hot water bath, which was not a cure. Kulkarni Maharaj attributed the ailment to intensive yogic practices and advised a visit to Sai Baba, whom he described by the Muslim term of *aulia*. Upasni reacted to this advice, being thoroughly averse to the prospect of visiting a Muslim for guidance.[190] Instead he preferred to go into a nearby jungle, sick with despair, in the attempt to achieve *samadhi*,[191] as the yogis describe a state of "stopping the mind," perhaps an experience as problematic as disrupted breathing processes. The sole tangible gain he seems to have derived from this period was the advice from an old country physician to drink only hot water, advice which he is said to have found beneficial and which he apparently followed thereafter.

His resistance to visiting a Muslim saint can easily be explained in terms of his conditioning to a Hindu milieu. He had been tutored by a brahman pundit, had followed Hindu codes of asceticism, and had been immersed in a phase of professional and economic success in caste society lasting for over ten years or so. He reflected the full weight of caste bias in his religious perspective, though he did not actually deem himself to be in need of a guru, which is a Hindu concept. He reacted to Sai Baba merely because of the latter's Muslim background, as did a number of other *brahmans*.

Rather than visit Shirdi, Upasni travelled to Bombay in order to see Narayan Maharaj (d. 1945), whom he had encountered once before. This *brahman* holy man had an ashram at Kedgaon, near Poona, where he had built an ornate temple consecrated to Dattatreya, in which he would daily perform *puja*. Though he had been a rigorous ascetic in his early days, Narayan Maharaj had been gifted with much wealth and his ashram had an air of opulence reflected in his attire, which has been compared to that of a *maharaja*. It is said that he purchased a new automobile every year.[192] He lived in a small palace at the ashram, where he would give *darshan* (meeting) while seated upon an elaborate throne.[193] An underground room was built alongside this palace, and there he would retire daily into seclusion for several hours, which seems more fitting. When Upasni met him at Bombay in June 1911, the regal saint made some allusive remarks and said there was no further need for any contact between them. Upasni departed in frustration, and made his way back to the yogi Kulkarni Maharaj at Rahuri.

The yogi again urged him to meet Sai Baba. Seeking to overcome his visitor's religious bias against Muslims, Kulkarni Maharaj proffered his conclusion that Sai Baba was above creed and caste, and that Sai was in no way inferior to Narayan Maharaj. This time Upasni set aside his prejudices and proceeded to Shirdi in late June 1911. Yet he did not like the situation involving a mosque, although he participated in the *arati* ceremony which attracted Hindus. He talked with local Hindus who eulogized the saint, but it was too obvious that Sai Baba was a Muslim, and Upasni was not prepared to follow him. He quickly moved on to visit a Hindu guru at Kopergaon, who, to his dismay, advised him to return to Shirdi. After a week he was induced to go back, and became reconciled to Sai's request that he should stay in the vicinity. Upasni decided to attend the *arati* ceremony daily and to see Sai Baba as often as possible. It is said that he learned to understand the cryptic language of the saint, who showed an acquaintance with his past history, though in oblique terms.

Having initially rebelled at following Sai Baba's instructions, Upasni became convinced that the old *faqir* was an omniscient entity who held the key to enlightenment. The ensuing phase has received differing interpretations, and a number of episodes are bizarre.

After some hesitation, Upasni gave all the money he had with him to Sai Baba, and as a consequence, he found himself living as one of the beneficiaries of the saint's bounty. He did not like being dependent in this way, however, especially as the situation involved charity from local people. After a few months he wanted to leave. Sai was adamant that he had to stay, and told a devotee named Madhavrao Deshpande that Upasni would have to stay for four years. The saint told Deshpande to take Upasni to Khandoba's temple, where he was required to live in undisturbed solitude. Sai Baba strongly hinted that Upasni had a great future, and that he was unique amongst the disciples. Upasni did not feel at peace over the issue of staying until he had a personal encounter with the saint in which the latter said of him: "I have given everything to him.... I am entirely responsible for him."[194]

Upasni's associations with Shiva apparently commenced with his sojourn at the Khandoba temple on the outskirts of Shirdi. Khandoba (or Mahalsapati) is a much venerated divinity in Maharashtra, being considered an *avatar* of Shiva, in addition to other interpretations. The temple at Shirdi was one of hundreds in that area of India. This was not a large building, and was disused and dilapidated, being extremely uncommodious by that time. The squalid interior was open to snakes and scorpions, who were to be Upasni's most regular companions. There is little wonder that he was at first disquieted about what was happening. He told his brother Balakrishna that he did not understand what Sai Baba was doing to him. At first he was worried that his breathing problem would interfere with events, but the saint waved this matter aside, indicating that Upasni would not die but instead would transcend death. The disciple had apparently continued with the hot water treatment, inconvenient though that must have been on a hot day. However, the indications are that his breathing ceased to bother him.

Sai Baba had not given any prescriptions for a *sadhana*, to use a word to which Upasni was accustomed. There was only the injunction to live quietly, doing nothing. There was no Yoga, no programme of *tapas*, no formal tuition. Yoga was not desired; it was not meditation that was required, but a rapport with the saint. Narasimhaswami and other writers have nevertheless interpreted the phase at Khandoba's temple as a *sadhana*.

Upasni at first found difficulty in discarding his habit of *mantra-japa*, which he had favoured since boyhood. This appears to have been one of the major targets of Sai Baba's insistence that he was not to do anything but stay quiet. Eventually Upasni grasped that his former conditioning was not compatible with what his teacher wanted.

The new occupant at first left the Khandoba temple daily to attend Sai's *arati* ceremony. At some uncertain date, the saint told him to stop coming to the mosque – he did not belong with the devotees, his course was different. Some of the other Hindus were becoming jealous of him, as Sai Baba often emphasized his value and potential, elevating him to the level of an *avadhuta*, a holy man who had renounced all links with the world. Despite Sai's praise, a powerful mood of resentment seems to have spread throughout the village. Upasni was deemed by many to be aloof and peculiar, as indeed he might have seemed in following the saint's instruction to keep quiet and do nothing. There seems to have been little connection between popular sentiments and the actual wishes and designs of Sai Baba; the gap was very wide in the case of Upasni.

News arrived at Shirdi that Upasni's wife died in February 1912. Some say that he expressed no remorse, while another report says that he asked Sai Baba to ensure that the deceased spouse was in a sublime state. It is also said that he was often depressed and even contemplated suicide during his first months of retreat. A change came over him, and his brother Balakrishna could not understand what had happened. On one of the last occasions when Upasni visited the mosque, Sai had remarked to him: "Wherever you see, there is none but me."[195]

At first Upasni went for food daily to a hospice run by H. S. Dixit, a prominent Hindu devotee of Sai Baba who was happy to give him free meals. Some problem arose in this arrangement by July 1912. Upasni was then no longer welcome, and seems to have decided to keep away from devotees as much as possible. He began fasting in a severe manner, indifferent to solid food. He was apparently still willing to participate in a devotional ceremony occurring on August 15th, when an emblem of Sai Baba (the *padukas*) was installed under a *neem* tree closely associated with him. Upasni composed a verse for that event, being considered an erudite pundit, though some devotees were jealous of this distinction. His learning had become evident in former months when he had joined religious tutorials undertaken by G. S. Khaparde, the literate colleague of B. G. Tilak. For some reason, Sai Baba sent Khaparde to the Khandoba temple (in early 1912) in order to read aloud the *Pancadashi* to the occupant. Khaparde (also known as Dada Saheb) may have overdone this license to preach, as Upasni seemed disinterested and indrawn, and the readings accordingly ceased. Khaparde was one of the more intelligent devotees of Sai Baba, and this episode may have provided one of the tests which Sai occasionally set for the learned. Khaparde was accustomed to giving daily lectures on the *Pancadashi* and other religious texts throughout his stay at Shirdi in 1911–12, and Upasni's disinterest may have been better medicine than pride.[196]

Upasni's fasting continued for a long time, though apparently with brief intervals of respite. The nature of his "sadhana" has sometimes puzzled investigators. There are two basic interpretations, that following the orthodox version of Narasimhaswami, and the unorthodox interpretation associated with Upasni's disciple Meher Baba. The orthodox version presents the subject as a suffering saint who was primarily in despair at the privations he encountered.[197] The alternative version presents him as having achieved *nirvikalpa samadhi* after the initial phase, followed by the less well known process sometimes defined as *sahaj samadhi*. As the present writer has already attempted coverage of the alternative,[198] so widely neglected and ignored in the conventional reports, I here dwell on some of the details that have caused difficulties.

The "suffering saint" version attributes to the subject's severe fast of one year various spiritual experiences. "As a result, he not only became emaciated but passed through his *bhramishtavasta* and *unmathavasta*, that is, states resembling insanity, in which he saw visions, and external objects took on unusual and fantastic forms."[199] His body acquired a skeletal appearance, and this has conveyed to some a sense of suffering, especially as certain remarks he made to (unwanted) visitors seemed to emphasize his imminent "death." One academic commentator has stated: "He was always sad."[200] Other versions mention his radiance. "Upasni's countenance was always fresh and bright."[201]

Upasni's introversion was accompanied by an abusive attitude towards visitors, whom he seemed to regard as intruders. He is said to have thrown stones at anyone who approached.[202] Even his brother and his mother found difficulty in conversing with him. Some people brought him food, but he would leave this for dogs and crows. He seemed oblivious to scorpions and snakes. These creatures bit him and crawled over his body. There may be some truth in the (unorthodox) belief that "he had to be unconscious of his body to survive such conditions."[203] We do not appear to be discussing a man who was merely enduring hardships because Sai Baba had told him to stay quietly in the squalid temple. His behaviour was somewhat in excess of that consideration.

He had become a naked temple-dweller. Yet, after a while, he would sometimes leave the temple and wander about in the rural locale, apparently wearing a piece of sack cloth. He seemed to feel an affinity with the untouchables, and would help them to clean the streets and sewers, which was the menial vocation imposed upon them by caste society. He seemed intent upon accomplishing hard manual labour, often on his own. He drew water, broke stones, milled sugar cane, and is even said to have dragged a plough over fields of a local farmer, like a human bullock. Those habits are explainable in terms of the recognition that he had to normalize his responses, which had become abnormal. He did not take a bath, and was covered in a layer of dirt, made worse by an eccentric habit of lying in mud and filth. He had apparently contracted a disconcerting tendency to drink his own urine. On one occasion he lay down on the ground and embraced a dead horse even while vultures were devouring the carcase. At one period he bathed a leper who was in an advanced stage of disease; Upasni would drink the bathing water after the pus had collected in it from the crippled fingers of the sufferer.

Years later he described some of his experiences in a rather elliptical manner which emphasized his addiction to pain and his aversion to pleasure.[204] This is a theme often associated with Tantra; in Upasni's version, pain had become a source of bliss. This is not a straightforward theme to understand, as his fragmentary reminiscences of his

Shirdi period included a reference to the opening of the *brahma-randhra*, a term associated with Tantric yoga and which means "Brahma's orifice," located at the crown of the head, and popularly believed to represent the point at which the soul escapes the body at death. Yet in the sense in which Upasni employed this term, the meaning is that of a "death" while still living, a liberation in which "the inner and outer Brahma became one,"[205] he said. By Hindu standards therefore, the inference of a spiritual realization is valid. Moreover, he strongly implied that his experience had been one of perceiving the whole universe[206] as a result of this "opening." Sai Baba apparently regulated this obscure process via certain instructions.[207] However, it is now difficult to discuss such matters, as the subject has been obscured by devotees and academics who do not understand them.

Upasni became a weird and emaciated entity who was capable of galvanic physical exertion, who disliked visitors, and who was liable to say or do almost anything if annoyed. People formed their own opinions of him. A few thought he had become a saint, while others thought he had gone crazy. There were also intermediate views, e.g., he was preoccupied with death and fasting, and was trying to achieve *samadhi*, the stopped state of mind. Perhaps in truth he had achieved *samadhi* of an intense kind, and was now trying to get out of it. Traditional doctrines do not always encompass realistic eventualities.

Many devotees of Sai Baba were puzzled and annoyed when the old man declared Upasni to be a great guru, and said that Upasni should be worshipped in the same way that he himself was worshipped. This occurred on July 18th, 1913, on the day known to Hindus as *Guru-purnima*, a time for the devotee to venerate his guru. Sai sent one of his female devotees, named as Chandrabai Borkar, to the Khandoba temple with instructions to worship the occupant in a formal manner. Predictably enough, Upasni was annoyed at the intrusion. The visitor persisted and performed the *arati* ceremony before him (this usually involves waving a lighted oil lamp on a tray and singing a hymn of praise). It is said that from this event originated his name of Upasni Maharaj or Upasni Baba. The name Upasni (Upasani) is less of a name than an honorific in this context, and signified his talents in fasting and worship.

It became evident that Sai Baba wished Upasni's *arati* to be regularly conducted. Upasni was totally uninterested in this new development, and at first resisted the attempts made by a small group of devotees with scruple. Eventually he gave in and permitted the worship, though the chronology is obscure. The fact is that many people in Shirdi opposed this worship of Upasni, even though it was performed at Sai Baba's behest. The most extreme case of objection was in the shape of a *brahman* ascetic named Nanavali, who himself had the reputation of a madman (*pagal*). He would interrupt the *puja* at the Khandoba temple by throwing mud at Upasni and taunting him. Nanavali appears to have been jealous of both Sai and his disciple. According to Narasimhaswami, this rival even went to the extreme on one occasion of tying Upasni with ropes. The latter was weakened by fasting, and Nanavali was thus able to drag him to the mosque, reviling him before spectators.

In November 1913, Sai Baba prodded a *brahman* devotee known as Bapusaheb (Sakharam Hari) Jog to take food to Upasni, who had been fasting.[208] Upasni was typically gruff and told the visitor to give the food to dogs and birds and to leave. He said further that he was not different to crows and dogs, and that to feed those creatures would be to feed him. Jog said that he could not understand this "high philosophy," and so he would take the food away if Upasni did not eat it. This caused annoyance, and in a rage Upasni flung a literal brickbat at the visitor, drawing blood from his arm. It was now Jog's turn to get angry, and he asked some villagers to tie Upasni with ropes and carry him to the mosque.[209] It is clear that Jog's intention was to expose to Sai Baba what he considered to be a grave breach of etiquette on the part of the high philosopher. When the latter was brought before Sai as a captive, the mosque saint merely ordered the saint of Khandoba's temple to be untied. According to Narasimhaswami, Sai remarked: "He is a man of God; let none trouble him." Sai reiterated to Upasni the injunction to sit quietly in his temple.[210]

On the basis of Narasimhaswami, some have thought that Upasni could not understand the attitude of Sai Baba towards him.[211] Yet one may conclude that Narasimhaswami and many Shirdi devotees did not understand the contour of these events. Bapusaheb Jog was thwarted in his mood of retaliation; he later became an admirer of Upasni, being one of those who perceived that myopia had enveloped the events under discussion.

The major reason why some people thought that Upasni was not in affinity with Sai Baba was because of his secretive nocturnal departure from Shirdi. He left at midnight for the town of Shinde, accompanied by a medical doctor. Another doctor (Chidambaram Pillai) who remained in Shirdi would not disclose the new location, being a loyal admirer of Upasni and having become a personal attendant. Upasni wanted his whereabouts kept a secret. The date of this exit is given by most writers as July 25th 1914, though Charles Purdom gave the impression that it was later.[212] I will here accept the earlier date and proceed on that assumption.

The orthodox devotional interpretation still current at Shirdi has been stated in the following words: "(Sai) Baba advised him, much against Upasni's own wish, to stay in Shirdi for four years doing *tapas* but he fled away after three years, it is said much to his detriment."[213] Thus, Upasni is presented as having been told to perform conventional Hindu penance, not just sitting quietly and doing nothing (which is what Sai Baba actually said). He was in error to leave, and suffered for it; that is the impression conveyed by sectarians. This curt version may be described as suffering from bias against imagined rivals to the guru. Eliminating any successor to Sai Baba, devotees at Shirdi were able to sustain their belief that the deceased saint remained in miraculous contact with them, so that it made no difference whether he was dead or alive.

The alternatives to this bias must be fairly considered by those capable of doing so, and the material is not without interest from a sociological point of view.

The most obvious reason for Upasni's departure was to escape the increasing hostility of the local villagers, whose ideas were influenced by the jealousy surfacing amongst Sai's devotees and holy men like Nanavali. A minority were sad that he had gone, however, especially a woman named Durgabai Karmakar, who is said to have taken meals to him daily. Early in the year he had started taking liquid food, but eventually started to take solid food, perhaps at the insistence of the doctors in contact with him (Dr. Pillai had been very concerned at his low heart beat the previous year). Durgabai was at first a devotee of Sai Baba; she was a widow who had come to stay in Shirdi with her young son. Sai Baba gave her the task of looking after Upasni at the temple; the date of this development is obscure. She was the only person from whom he would accept food, even though he was at first abusive towards her. He later referred to her as his "spiritual mother," it would seem.[214] Soon after departing, Upasni sent for her to join him at Shinde, where she prepared meals for him. Dr. Pillai also went to live at Shinde.

The doctors attending Upasni seem to have been very concerned about his physical condition. He had recently begun to take solid food instead of liquid food, and this transition caused major problems. His digestive system was chaotic, and he had developed severe haemorrhoids. His dire need for an operation upon the latter ailment appears to have been the major reason for his move to Shinde. Here he lived at the home of Dr. Ganapatrao, who was thus able to give him proper medical attention and to engage the services of a surgeon to perform the necessary operation. The patient refused to take any chloroform, a gesture which astounded the surgeon, and which made the operation a very painful matter. Upasni's detachment from pain seems to have been the trigger for stories about his reputed *siddhis*. The doctors afterwards tried to coax him into ordinary habits, but to little avail. He would not wear any conventional attire, and nor even a robe, but instead adopted the expedient of wrapping a gunny cloth around his waist. This mode of attire was maintained until his death.

He was invited by Dr. Pillai to stay at the latter's home in Nagpur. Upasni refused to eat the food provided for him there, and instead begged for food daily in the city streets. People started to come for his *darshan*, a word which denotes a meeting with a holy man in the traditional manner of reverence. His first discourses are traced to this period. However, he was basically averse to crowds and wanted to move on. He was invited to Kharagpur, and consented on condition that his identity was kept a secret. He arrived there in October 1914, and despite the efforts made by his host, people began to flock around him. This seems to have been largely due to his distinctive mode of living. He still looked dazed and abstracted, and did not appear normal. He would lie down in the most impossible places, including a local mosque, and was completely indifferent to his own comfort. He would beg for food with an earthen pot that gradually became broken, though he would not change it. Some Anglo-Indian boys once found him in a dazed state lying on the ground. They thought he was a madman and mischievously placed a garland of old shoes around his neck.

For days Upasni wandered around the town with this cumbrous necklace, resisting attempts to remove it. This kind of "crazy" behaviour was accompanied by an insistence that God was in everything – in the beautiful and the ugly, the clean and the unclean. He began to patronize the local untouchables, and the consequence was that they virtually adopted him as their saint, to the acute dismay of *brahmans*.

He became venerated as a *sat-purusha*, an enlightened soul. Yet he would undertake manual labour with the untouchables, helping road-workers, sweepers, corn-grinders, cobblers, and blacksmiths. He cleaned streets and hovels in the manner of a *bhangi*, the term applied to scavenger outcastes who were allowed only the most menial tasks by caste Hindus, who regarded them as defiling. These unfortunates lived by scavenging rubbish and unwanted items. Even to be touched by the shadow of an outcaste was believed to be contamination for a *brahman*. That was the social code which had been in process since the Vedic era. There were now about fifty million untouchables in India, uneducated and living in acute squalor. Upasni chose to side with them even before Dr. Ambedkar began (in the 1920s) his campaign to free the untouchables. As Dr. Ambedkar was himself an untouchable (though educated in America), it is the more remarkable that Upasni was a *brahman*, a former pundit prior to his transformation at the hands of a Muslim saint.

Gandhi called the untouchables *harijans* or "children of God" (they often called themselves *dalits*). They were outcaste, excluded from the four social classes or *varnas*. Even the *shudras* were within this framework, though forbidden to hear the Veda. The *Code of Manu* directed untouchables to live outside the villages; they were enjoined to use broken dishes for food, to keep out of villages and towns at night. They were delegated tasks as corpse-bearers and executioners, and were permitted to take the clothing and ornaments of the executed.[215] They could only perform polluting tasks such as working with leather and sweeping excrement from the village. "The untouchable classes almost certainly go back into the first millennium B.C."[216] Some scholars think that both *brahmans* and untouchables were established at the same time. The untouchables still form about a fifth of the Indian population, some scholars have estimated. The *Code of Manu* typically condemned inter-caste marriages. The term caste (*jati*) is more complex than class (*varna*). According to *Manu*, the untouchables (*chandalas*) are a caste born from sexual misconduct between different classes.[217] *Manu* contemptuously calls them by the rhetorical word "dog-cookers," deeming them to be highly polluting, though the term *asprishta* (untouched) is not much used in Sanskrit sources. They were technically only one of the outcaste groups (e.g., carpenters).[218]

In February 1915, Upasni moved from the home of his well bred host Chinnaswami to live in the untouchable quarter of Kharagpur. He chose a cow stable adjoining the hovel of an untouchable couple named Namdeo Mahar and Bhagubai. Caste Hindus would not normally set foot in the untouchable precincts for fear of contamination. His high caste devotees were now placed in the dilemma of not seeing him or else entering the abode of the dreaded outcaste. Yet there was no mistaking his message – God was in the untouchables also. A steady trickle of rich caste Hindus began to visit him in his new abode. His favourite tactic was to place in front of them some item belonging to his host Namdeo, with the injunction to worship the item because God is in everything. This was a very bitter pill for *brahmans* to swallow, and some could not or would not take it. A hostile group of *brahmans* plotted together in an attempt to harm him. A miracle story formed around this episode; Upasni is said to have made himself invisible to his opponents. To these caste Hindus, Upasni was a lethal threat to their social standards of prestige, even though he was a holy man and theoretically beyond caste. It may have been this ruthless opposition which caused him to leave Kharagpur suddenly on August 4th, 1915. He had spent ten months in support of the untouchables, and had aroused hatred amongst some *brahmans*. He left for Nagpur without informing anyone; devotees in Kharagpur are said to have wept. He sent a comforting telegram to them from Nagpur.[219]

After a short stay in Nagpur he returned to Shirdi, again making his abode at the Khandoba temple. This time some differences were discernible. He was much less of a "madman" than formerly, and less subject to the dazed states of ecstasy for which he was noted. Despite local opposition, a number of Sai Baba's followers would go to take the *darshan* of Upasni, and he became increasingly feted for his discourses. Unlike Sai Baba he was clear in his idiom and spoke to Hindus in a language that they could easily understand. This had the effect of cementing his own local following. He had also gained interest from a smaller number of Muslims during his stay at Kharagpur.[220] His link with Zoroastrians is well attested.

In December 1915 the most famous of his Zoroastrian disciples came to him for the first time. After encountering Sai Baba in Shirdi,[221] Merwan S. Irani went to the Khandoba temple and was hit by a stone which Upasni threw at him in a complex saintly mood. "Upasni Maharaj had again been fasting and was reduced to a skeleton."[222] That report is perhaps puzzling, but indicates the spartan nature of Upasni's lifestyle. According to the reminiscences of Merwan Irani (alias Meher Baba), the impact of the stone commenced his own "return to normality" after a spiritual realization, part of a process which took a further six years under Upasni's guidance.

A contingent of Sai Baba's devotees grew so jealous of Upasni that they tried to harass him, while extremists amongst them "plotted to murder"[223] him. To avoid these problems, he asked Sai's permission (through an intermediary) to move to Miraj for a second operation for haemorrhoids. A surgeon lived at Miraj and the operation was successful. Upasni is known to have travelled to several other places also. It is said that he returned to Shirdi afterwards, when the hostile situation had abated. When he settled at Sakori on a permanent basis in July 1917, some Shirdi devotees of Sai Baba were pleased to see him go. The mood of "only one guru here" later influenced even a writer like Arthur Osborne, whose well known book *The Incredible Sai Baba* contained no reference to Upasni,[224] although Osborne viewed Ramana Maharshi with such manifest approval.

Sakori was a small village situated a few miles south of Shirdi, and about nine miles from the railway station at Chitali. Upasni was invited there by a group of farmers who revered him. He chose to live at the edge of a cremation ground on the outskirts of Sakori, and here the farmers led by Shankar Patel constructed for him a small mud hut. Nearby stood a large banyan tree, beneath which he would often sit and sometimes discourse. A core of regular visitors gradually emerged, only some of them *brahmans*. During the 1920s, the number of *brahman* devotees increased, and miracle stories developed in train – various diseases were said to have been healed by Upasni, and financial troubles were believed to be solved. However, some materials permit a much deeper insight into events than the popular overlay which accumulated.

For some years Upasni Maharaj would not accept money from anyone, and nor would he ask for money in any circumstance. Nevertheless, various adroit donations enabled a small *ashram* to form around him during 1919–20. Sai Baba had not established any ashram, despite his requests for *dakshina*. The ashram is a community living in their own independent buildings, generally associated with Hindus, though the word is loosely used. Upasni may have felt that the new situation gave him some protection against critics. He was no longer a public spectacle, but guarded by devotees. One of these was the *brahman* Bapusaheb Jog, formerly a critic but now completely won over by Upasni's magnetism and teachings. After the death of Sai Baba, Jog settled at Sakori, but was at first frustrated in his desire to perform an *arati* ceremony before Upasni, just as he had done with

Sai Baba. He frequently requested this ceremony, but Upasni persistently refused to allow it, except on the occasion of religious festivals. Upasni did permit a small temple to be erected near his hut in honour of Sai Baba, and as a concession to devotional appetites, he allowed his own photograph to be placed in that makeshift shrine along with a photograph of Sai Baba. This temple was at first associated with Zoroastrian followers, but was taken over by Jog and other Hindus. In later years several more temples were built by Hindus when the ashram expanded from very simple roots. Upasni at first kept the disposition for ritualism on a firm leash, but this proved more difficult as time passed.

At the end of 1919 he began to travel intermittently to various places, mainly in Western and Central India. His first major expedition was to Benares, the leading centre for *brahman* priests, where he sanctioned the reading of Sanskrit texts by forty learned pundits, a gesture which enhanced his prestige amongst caste Hindus, though the event as a whole proved controversial. When he returned to Sakori, his devotees begged him to accept some service from them. He said characteristically that he wanted nothing – he retained an extremely simple lifestyle until his death, and was averse to ostentation. He would not wear ochre robes or finery, but only his gunny cloth, and still liked to sit or recline in places of filth and desolation. However, he did give permission for his followers to erect a rest-house for the accommodation of visitors. He made this into an unusual project, having caste Hindus work alongside untouchables and Zoroastrians, and also including women.

Although untouchables were included among his followers, the high caste Hindus were basically averse to his egalitarian tendencies and in later years presented him in a modified light. They interpreted Upasni to mean that he endorsed the stigma of untouchability, a belief which should be treated with caution. "Upasni supported the need for social reforms, but revealed his traditionalism by discouraging the removal of the ban on widow remarriage and by supporting the practice of 'untouchability.' "[225] He has thus gained a reputation for being paradoxical.[226] One might place him in the same category as Sai Baba, who was "more than once deliberately misleading his devotees by paradoxical gestures and teachings."[227] The biases at work amongst devotees of caste persuasions were very strong, and perhaps paradox was a reaction to those biases.

A closer investigation of the visit to Benares is relevant. This occurred in November 1919, when Upasni stayed at a Shaiva temple in the sacred city, accompanied by a Hindu devotee and his Zoroastrian disciple Merwan Irani (who became known as Meher Baba the following year). The awaited event was a *maha-yajna*, a sacrificial fire ritual performed by over a hundred *brahmans*. It is said that seven hundred followers of Upasni were in attendance, probably an exaggerated number for that date. Yet they were outnumbered by "thousands" of devotees of Sai Baba who had arrived from various parts of India (this number also seems to be inflated). The meals were specially prepared by *brahmans*, but Upasni wanted the Zoroastrian Merwan Irani and his Poona comrade Sadashiv Patel to oversee the food arrangements. This was not conventional conduct.

In the centre of the tent (*pandal*) erected for the ritual, a large painting of Sai Baba was displayed. The ritual fire burned for eleven days, and on the twelfth day a feast in honour of the *brahman* officiants was held. By that time over ten thousand *brahmans* had assembled (that number is credible). When they sat down for their meal and saw the painting of Sai Baba, some of them caused a disturbance by insisting that the Shirdi saint was a Muslim and therefore they could not join in a feast which had been dedicated to a Muslim figurehead. For two hours Upasni tried to reason with the objectors, urging them to forget their religious prejudices. He did not deny that Sai Baba was a Muslim, but maintained that the deceased saint was above religious distinctions, existing as much for *brahmans* as for Muslims. His audience would not accept the argument, and the officiating ritual priests joined the protest. He offered to increase their *dakshina* (payment) to fifteen rupees instead of five, but still they refused to eat the food provided. They insisted that the detested painting must be removed.

Upasni refused to displace the picture of Sai Baba, and in disgust he told his followers to go to the banks of the Ganges and summon the poor by banging drums. Led by Merwan Irani and Sadashiv Patel, the devotees served the food to the poor who soon appeared on the scene with eager hands. It is said that nearly 15,000 poor people were fed, and yet still a considerable amount of food remained. Upasni ordered the surplus to be thrown into the river. The priests looked on with shock as buckets of food were flung into the waters, at last realizing that they were losing both extra monies and their meal. They began to apologize, begging Upasni not to waste the food, which they would now condescend to eat. He was angry with them and refused to comply. He detested their insular attitude to Sai Baba, and derided them, saying that there was no food left, and that Sai Baba was the real pundit (religious expert), not those who liked to call themselves the pundits of Kashi (Benares). In a mood of annoyance, he broke up the assembly of priests and said farewell to his followers, returning to Sakori.[228]

This event tells us a great deal about Upasni Maharaj, who, like Sai Baba, became substantially obscured by orthodox views imposed by *brahman* religionists. There were other occasions when he confronted priestly biases, but events were not always so clearly reported.

One of the early followers of Upasni at Sakori was a Zoroastrian woman named Gulbai Irani (whom he renamed Gulmai, which became her most familiar designation). She was born in poverty in 1882, her family living in a single tenement room in Parel, Bombay. Her parents were both Irani Zoroastrians, being emigrants from Iran. Her father had been a master carpenter in the employ of the Qajar monarch; he had forsaken the financial reward for a lavish door he had made for a regal castle at Tehran upon learning that the Shah had unjustly imprisoned the Prime Minister. The carpenter had departed for India to safeguard his integrity, but there met with bitter poverty. Gulbai was his fourth child, and she had to assist her overworked mother in the drudgery of household work. Her delicate health was undermined, and she had to be taken to Ahmednagar to stay with her aunt. She was denied the opportunities and social life of Parsi girls in well-to-do families who were then beginning to reap the benefits of the measures furthered by the Parsi reformists. The prospect of her marriage was discussed when she was only ten years old. She had no say in the matter, like so many Hindu and Irani girls who were at the mercy of priestly patterns of protocol established over many centuries. Although some of her relatives were not in agreement, she was married in 1896 at the age of fourteen. Her youthful husband, Kaikhushru Sarosh Irani, was still at school. In conformity with the conventional practice, she lived with the family of her husband at Ahmednagar. Her own family were hoping for some financial advantage in the match, and were exasperated when the business of Kaikhushru's father failed. Her husband drew a pittance from his service with the Cursetji family of Ahmednagar, and she gave birth to four children. Kaikhushru allowed his overbearing mother to take charge of the housekeeping, which caused additional pressures for his wife, as the matriarch diverted money to her large number of relatives.

80

Gulmai's inability to provide her children with immediate needs caused her much anguish. Prone to fatigue and ill-health, her mental torture made her seek solace in meditation. She developed a love of solitude, and would often lock herself in a room for prayers and contemplation, seeking to escape the large communal family in which she had been unwillingly placed. Her husband was eventually sympathetic, and even read her some poems of Kabir, which aroused in her the desire to meet a guru like Kabir. Yet her other relatives were alarmed by her unorthodox tangent, and led by her mother-in-law, they enlisted the services of four Parsi priests, who are described in the source report as *dasturs*. She did not want their attention, but had no choice in the matter. They performed elaborate and superstitious ceremonies intended to help Gulmai regain identity as a "this worldly" Zoroastrian fighting Ahriman. She was horrified by their dogmatism and lack of insight, and wondered at how such men had been leading the Zoroastrian community for so many centuries.

In 1919 she heard of Upasni Maharaj when her sister-in-law Gulnar visited him at Sakori. Gulnar was enthusiastic, but Gulmai was deterred at the prospect of meeting a *brahman* guru, especially as she felt that her husband would object. Instead she preferred to meet a Muslim saint of Ahmednagar called Hazrat Maulana Gilori Shah, whom her husband respected. This saint struck her as very genuine and non-dogmatic. In August her sister Soona and the latter's husband came to Ahmednagar for a holiday; they broached the prospect of a visit to Upasni, who had gained some Parsi followers. Soona's husband Kaikhushru Masa had met Sai Baba at Shirdi, and had formerly visited Upasni, who had made a deep impression upon him. Gulmai declined to go with them, and so they accompanied her sister-in-law to Sakori. This trio told Upasni of Gulmai's domestic travail and requested his blessing for her. He is said to have remarked: "Don't worry, she will have to come and the whole family will come to me."

A fortnight later, after constant persuasion, Gulmai agreed to accompany her brother-in-law Kaikhushru Masa and three other Iranis from Poona on a visit to Sakori. One of her companions was Rustom, the uncle of Merwan Irani. They were approaching Upasni's mud hut when she noticed two young Iranis sitting beneath a tree. These were Merwan Irani and his comrade Behramji Irani. She had already heard of Merwan, often known respectfully as Merwanji (or Merwan Seth). Gulmai knew of his frequent visits to Upasni, and had learned that he was reputed to be in a state of exalted consciousness. Yet she was puzzled because she had also heard that he had become insane, which was a theme spread abroad in Parsi sectors by his mother, who could not understand the effects of his association with Hazrat Babajan of Poona, the latter being an aged female saint of Sufi reputation. Merwan's father Sheriar was actually a relative of Gulmai's own father, and had attended her wedding. The men in her party now started a conversation with Merwanji. He seemed to be quite unaffected by his growing celebrity; he talked about Upasni and Hazrat Babajan, not about himself.

Afterwards Gulmai's party went inside the hut of Upasni. She recognized the occupant to be the same person she had seen in a recent dream which had made a deep impact upon her. Previously she had entertained a number of set ideas as to how the Hindu sage would act and speak; this was partly the reason why she had at first declined to see him, apparently imagining a decorous pundit giving dogmatic discourses on the Vedas and performing pompous rituals. She now found that Upasni did not answer to any of her conjectures, and that he was the last thing she had expected. He was entirely informal and successfully bridged the gulf with a visitor who was not merely a Zoroastrian but also a woman. She felt a greater impact than that afforded by her contact with Maulana Gilori Shah, and her reserve crumbled. Upasni did give one short discourse concerning the spiritual path, to which she listened intently. She felt no offence when he said that family life was inferior to a life of spiritual striving, as she felt this to be true from the suffering she had known. Upasni made it clear to the visitors that they could not expect family benefits from him, but only what he had. His manner of speaking was very forthright at times.

After lunch the visitors gained a second meeting with Upasni, this time one by one. Gulmai grew worried as to how she might best unburden her mind to him. Nearing the door of the hut, Merwan then came up to her and told her to tell Upasni honestly and unreservedly about the matters which were troubling her. These words had a calming effect, and when she again entered the hut she had the strong impression that she was meeting someone she had known for a very long time and who was very important to her. Under the impact of this feeling, her words merged into tears. Upasni told her that he was closely linked with Zoroastrians, and that she could see him often, but that her domestic situation meant that she could not stay at Sakori as

82

she now desired. Gulmai was worried about her social alienation, and also about a rash of pustules which had developed on her body. Upasni indicated that her affliction was psychosomatic, being due to her unhappiness. He told her not to worry, and also extended his previous statement on family life. He said that although *sannyasins* performed *puja* and *sadhana*, the highest form of worship was to be in the world and to remain untouched by it through balancing a longing for God with the observance of mundane duties. Upasni tends to emerge as a sophisticated guru who was prepared to modify and adapt his emphases in accord with individuals and not as general rules. He did not promise miraculous cures, and could communicate very successfully with non-Hindus.

Gulmai emerged from the hut to find Merwan recounting episodes about Sai Baba and Babajan. Her party participated in the *arati* ceremony at the nearby temple which feted the photographs of Upasni and Sai. Her Zoroastrian party left Sakori by horse *tonga* in the evening, proceeding to the railway station. Merwan and Behramji accompanied them in a bullock cart, a rougher mode of travel.

At home Gulmai found new depth in her meditations, and no longer felt inclined to repeat the external prayers she had practised so often. She was a frequent visitor to Sakori thereafter, and often encountered Merwan on these occasions. It was only in response to her questioning that he would speak of his own inner experiences and sufferings. As a consequence, she became certain that Merwan had achieved the celebrated state of *nirvikalpa samadhi* of which the *brahmans* spoke, and believed that he was the disciple who most understood Upasni. Merwan Irani is said to have stood out in every respect from the others at Sakori. He exhibited a complete indifference towards physical comforts; his clothes were often ragged, though he had never assumed any renunciate garb or robe (he wore a common jacket, shirt, and trousers like other Iranis and Parsis). He was observed to inaugurate and finance a number of public feasts at Sakori for the benefit of the poor amongst the Hindus. Sometimes he was silent, and at other times he sang religious songs when the mood took him. He sometimes appeared to be dazed. Upasni gave him much attention, often sitting alone with him, though some of the *brahmans* became jealous when the guru praised the young Zoroastrian, who was still only in his twenties.

After some weeks Gulmai again visited Sakori. This time Upasni told her something of the situation around him. He said that after Sai

Baba's death, both Muslim and Hindu devotees had been transferred to him. These people expected his attention, and so at times he reprimanded them (a measure for which Sai Baba had set a precedent). The explanation sounds strange to Westerners. Upasni tended to be confrontational with obstinate and egoistic men when he was in a mood of anger; however, his explanation was that they needed the reprimand and tough treatment. He also told Gulmai that many Zoroastrians came to him, and that those from Poona had created the small temple nearby (Merwan had funded this building, apparently earlier that year of 1919).

Contact with Upasni gradually transformed Gulmai. Her new serenity was eventually acknowledged by her family, though not without some initial frictions. She kept a photo of Upasni in her "prayer room," which she used as a focus for meditation. Her husband was influenced by adverse criticism of Upasni started by Zoroastrian bigots. He stealthily removed the photo, but found that his deed of sabotage made no difference. Later, he himself became an admirer of the Hindu sage.

In December 1919, Gulmai stayed at Sakori for two weeks. She was accompanied by her second son, Adi K. Irani, who was then sixteen. His mother persuaded him to make the journey, though he was conventionally biased against meeting a Hindu holy man. Yet Adi's scepticism evaporated at first sight of Upasni. The two visitors were housed for the night in a goat stable; such primitive accommodation was all that existed during these early days at Sakori before new buildings appeared. Rain fell heavily during the night, and the roof leaked in several places. They only had gunny cloth as bedding, and had to rely upon an umbrella as protection from the rain. When they approached Upasni next morning, he remarked: "Last night my hut was drenched with water." Yet it was plainly evident that his hut was perfectly dry; Gulmai knew that he had been referring to the goat stable. This kind of "concealed" speech was fairly typical of Upasni's informal communications, and though not so allusive as the symbolic speech of Sai Baba, such references could easily confuse those intent upon literal meanings.

Adi departed from Sakori as formerly agreed, Upasni having given permission for him to stay only one day. Gulmai did not want to leave, despite the uncongenial conditions. She cheerfully endured the discomforts of the primitive stable. There was no hotel fare, and her meals consisted solely of bread and chutney. She slept upon grass, took open air baths in the cold, and ceased to worry about the black scorpions which fell from the roof in the pitch darkness. There were no torches or electricity in such a rural place. She passed twelve days in this manner unscathed, and experienced a heightened state of consciousness in which she was aware only of the attribute of being. She later said that she did not know whether she was asleep, awake, or dead, and that she forgot all questions of where, why, and how. Becoming absorbed in this state, she ceased to eat food; she refused to eat even when Upasni ordered her to do so. She eventually yielded to his wishes only when he threatened to go without food for her sake. Upasni is said to have slapped her when trying to make her extrovert the necessary attention upon food. As a consequence, she felt that she understood something of his sojourn at the Khandoba temple; he had not wanted to eat because of an inner state of expansion, which was nothing to do with any programme of austerities such as devotees were inclined to imagine.

Shortly before she departed from Sakori, Upasni remarked that people usually liked holy places where large and imposing temples stood, thus attracting influential and prestigious persons. Yet Sakori was a very different prospect involving a barren rural landscape and a complete lack of pomp. He expressed to her a low opinion of pilgrimage, saying that the only real pilgrimage was to the living human *sadguru*.

On subsequent visits Gulmai made to Sakori, Merwan described her sojourn in the goat stable as a test devised by Upasni; according to Merwan, she was the first woman amongst Upasni's followers to have been placed in such a privileged situation. Merwan's communications gave her comfort at a critical juncture, as her relatives were now trying to restrict her movements, stung by sour gossip. Local Parsis in Ahmednagar spread rumours of a Hindu influence being allowed to enter a Zoroastrian household, attributing this breach to a lack of control on the part of family elders. Her husband Kaikhushru eventually came to regard this gossip as religious intolerance, a decision facilitated by his respect for the Muslim saint Maulana Gilori Shah.

In 1921 Upasni was invited to Ahmednagar by Gulmai. The occasion that prompted this was an opening ceremony for her new abode in the Shani Galli locality. This building, newly constructed by her husband, was called Sarosh Manzil. After initial reluctance, Kaikhushru agreed to let Upasni perform the ribbon-cutting ceremony; he was thus standing against the local Zoroastrian community, a faction approximately two hundred strong. Upasni accepted the invitation, and he was transported from Sakori in a car driven by Gulmai's sons Rustom and Adi. He stayed at the new house for over a week; hundreds came to visit him, including people from other cities like Poona and Bombay. Different religions and social classes were represented. Bigoted Parsis criticized the event, as did members of the host family who feared public opinion. Gulmai's mother-in-law had sternly opposed the idea of sheltering Upasni in view of orthodox Zoroastrian disfavour, but she was outvoted by her son, and unobtrusively took the *darshan* of the saint.

Upasni had insisted that Merwan should be present that week, and so the latter stayed at Sarosh Manzil as an honoured guest. He arrived from Poona accompanied by Gustadji Hansotia, a Parsi who had been in close contact with Sai Baba at Shirdi but who had since been transferred to Upasni with the emphasis from Sai that: "There is no spiritual difference between him and me." Upasni had encouraged Gustadji to cultivate Merwan's company as often as possible. Merwan sometimes referred to Gustadji as his "shadow," which was an acknowledgement of their frequent proximity. A man like Gustadji had learnt how different saints were basically interconnected, even though their activities seemed to vary.

Kaikhushru Irani looked on with a mixture of fascination and anxiety, the latter emotion caused by the local Parsi criticism of his sponsoring Upasni. The Hindu visitor made a deep impression upon him, and he personally took the saint back to Sakori by car. He was very surprised at Upasni's disclosure to his family just before getting into the automobile: "Your prophet Zarathushtra will be manifested when I supply an engine to Merwanji, who will carry in the attached carriages to various stations all those people who are prepared to go." When he said this, Upasni pointed to Merwan, who was standing nearby.

In contrast to his earlier poverty, Kaikhushru Irani was now making his name as a merchant. His increasing affluence helped his wife to support varied activities at Sakori. Upasni asked her to participate at public feasts there; on such occasions he would feed and bathe lepers, a gesture seldom made by gurus. Merwan suggested a special Zoroastrian celebration of Upasni's birthday, and was instrumental in making the plan for a rest-house (*dharamshala*) at Sakori for the benefit of visitors in the rural backwater. At his suggestion, Kaikhushru agreed to donate several thousand rupees for the construction of the rest-house and an ashram compound during 1920. Upasni gave his permission for the building work. A mason was hired, and the general labour was undertaken by the devotees. Upasni himself assisted the mason with the finishing touches, and Merwan is said to have participated. Durgabai Karmakar drove a bullock cart, while other women were allowed to carry stones and earth along with the men. Gulmai stayed with Durgabai and assisted in various ways.[229]

On January 14th 1921, the Hindu holiday of *Makara Sankranti* was celebrated at Sakori. Upasni allowed devotees to perform *puja* before him on this occasion, but the main event was a feast given for the benefit of many poor people from the neighbouring villages. Upasni distributed clothing to them, and afterwards several of the poorest people were bathed, including lepers. Merwan notably helped Upasni to bathe these unfortunates,[230] who were shunned by all societies, and who were desperately in need of improved hygiene.

In addition to the new rest-house, the temple was rebuilt when the flimsy original was blown down in a gale. This edifice became a Dattatreya temple, quite different to the idea underlying the precedent, which was that of a shrine to Sai Baba. The only structural addition that Upasni himself requested was a new hut some distance from the building operations. He seemed intent on isolation. This new hut (*jhopri*) was a rudimentary construction which was speedily erected within the cremation ground, at an uninviting spot overgrown with pear cactuses and thorns, and inhabited by snakes. This was the stuff of Shaiva ascetics, not ritual *bhaktas*. He offput visitors by pelting them with stones; when he wanted to see the devotees, he would return to the original hut.

The only person whom Upasni allowed to approach him in the second hut was Merwan. This became conspicuous when Merwan came to stay at Sakori in July 1921 for six months. He had almost no possessions and was for the most part introverted. He stayed during the day in an improvised room near the temple, but at night he would go to the secluded *jhopri* in the cremation ground. He would sit alone in the hut with Upasni, nobody else being allowed near. These sessions involved no speech or tuition, and were generally over by two a.m. Merwan would then return to his own room, but did not sleep. A Hindu named Yeshwantrao Bhorawke was delegated by Upasni to be the personal attendant of the Irani visitor, and this man regarded Merwan as a saint. Yeshwantrao found that Merwan did not sleep and rarely ate, but would instead frequently ask for *pan*, a popular masticatory.

At the end of his stay, Merwan normalized and began to take food regularly.[231]

It is discernible from various details involved that Merwan's normalization paralleled the experiential process undergone by Upasni at the Khandoba temple. One difference is that Merwan's experiential process took longer and his temperament was less difficult than that of Upasni. Since January 1914, as a result of his contact with Hazrat Babajan, Merwan Irani had been in a strange state of inward fixity which had only gradually become compatible with his physical surroundings.[232] Few people had understood him, and he had sometimes been tagged as the "mad Irani" by extroverts. As such states are still not generally understood, it is difficult to be more descriptive, even if one were capable of describing abstruse matters elusive to both scholars and devotees. Such gnostic matters were indeed a closed book to many devotees in the environs of Shirdi and Sakori, as the data attests.

The Zoroastrian participation (and also the Muslim element) at Sakori was subsequently eclipsed by the activity of brahman devotees. The latter contingent became resentful of Merwan's prominence. Upasni was known to say that Merwan had become malik (ruler) of the universe,[233] a disclosure which inflamed the hostility of brahman devotees. Their mentation imposed the question: "How could a Zoroastrian become the chief disciple of a Hindu sadguru?"[234] Merwan made his exit from the Sakori scene early in 1922, and undertook his own career at Poona, Bombay, and Ahmednagar. He was regarded as a rival by the brahmans of Sakori. Shortly after Merwan's departure, Upasni allowed resident devotees and others to visit him freely at the second hut. The eccentric explanation he gave for this new latitude was that the evil spirits which had inhabited the cremation ground were now exorcised from the spot.[235] This was doubtless much more acceptable to biased brahmans than a disclosure that the interval with Merwan had been more important than anything else at that time.

Merwan (alias Meher Baba) later stated of the jealous brahmans: "They were so fanatical that if they could, they would have killed me, but myself and Yeshwantrao remained unaffected by the atmosphere."[236] The acute envy may have been the reason for his nocturnal visits to Upasni, thereby maintaining more secrecy. Murder appears to have been envisaged very tangibly by some fanatics. At some elusive date, Upasni himself was administered poison, the blame for

88

this being put on Durgabai by the miscreants. The dose of poison is said to have been lethal, but Upasni recovered after a period of feeling numb.[237]

Gulmai Irani was also neglected in the official Sakori annals, though she remained in close contact with Upasni until his death. Her dual role in following both he and Meher Baba conflicted with devotional mono-guru obsessions.[238] She often relayed messages between Upasni and Meher Baba, who only met once after 1922.[239] Although Upasni Maharaj was held in esteem at the ashrams of Meher Baba, *brahman* devotees at Sakori were disdainful of Meher Baba, and Gulmai was inevitably reminded of the situation at Shirdi which had eliminated Upasni from the reckoning. Sectarian versions of history are not always comprehensive, and seem to prefer lacunae.

During 1922–3, Meher Baba stayed with a large group of male disciples at a house called Manzil-e-Meem in Bombay. While there, he instigated the publication of three biographies of Upasni, representing three languages aimed respectively at Muslims, Hindus, and Zoroastrians. Some of his group were formed into a publishing committee, and it was they who produced the books. One of his Muslim disciples wrote an Urdu biography entitled *Garibonka Asara* (*Protector of the Poor*).[240] An introduction was specially commissioned for this book from the pen of Khwaja Hasan Nizami, a well known Muslim scholar.[241] A Marathi version was initially prepared by Sadashiv Patel, to whom Upasni had dictated some material; the first draft was given to the well known Marathi writer Madhav Nath.[242] A Gujarati version was written by one of Meher Baba's Zoroastrian followers, and subsequently edited by Sohrabji Desai, a Parsi scholar and poet who lived at Navsari.[243] These works were the first to make Upasni known to the reading public, and confirmed his link with Meher Baba. There were hostile reactions from orthodox Parsis.

Certain features of this phase have caused puzzlement. While publishing works which celebrated the life of Upasni Maharaj, his disciple Meher Baba simultaneously sent him a letter which stated that there was no further connection between them. Meher Baba also disowned any further connection with the devotees at Sakori. Upasni responded in February 1923 by making very critical remarks about Meher Baba, whom he continued to refer to as Merwanji.[244] In contrast, the latter did not disparage his teacher, but instead asserted his independence.

The last visit of Meher Baba to Sakori had occurred in October

1922, a visit that was never repeated during Upasni's lifetime. On that occasion, Upasni had openly declared that the Zoroastrian was a great spiritual master, and he had even instructed all those present in Sakori to touch the feet of Meher Baba in homage.[245]

At this period Upasni told some of Meher Baba's disciples: "Even though the whole world and myself included were on the other side, you should stay on his side."[246] Upasni had therefore given fair warning of what he might do, and the outcome was predicted by Meher Baba.

When Gulmai visited Upasni early in 1923, he asked her why the books about him had been published by Merwanji. He said that the biographies would create trouble for him, and that he did not want people to know of him. Though it is true that Upasni Maharaj possessed a retiring nature, it is also true that he had earlier agreed to his biography being published.[247] The "paradoxical" strategy was evidently in process here.

On March 1st 1923, Gulmai's son Rustom K. Irani was sent to Sakori by Meher Baba. He was rebuked by Upasni, who began speaking against Baba and his disciples. Upasni said that Merwanji was not a saint, and that he (Upasni) was no longer responsible for him in any way. However, it was obvious that the Hindu sage was in an extreme mood. He ordered Rustom to break the bars of the bamboo cage in which he had interned himself. The visitor (a sturdy young man) complied, managing to break one of the bamboo bars. Upasni then appeared more angry than before and reviled Rustom. He asked the visitor why he had damaged the cage. Rustom then said that the saint himself had requested this. Upasni did not disagree, and then told him to bring a large stone and hit him on the head with it. Rustom became worried at this command and could not oblige. Upasni then began to verbally abuse Baba and some of his men.[248] Rustom had to leave, feeling that the situation was impossible.[249]

In such moods of displeasure, Upasni resembled some of the antics of Sai Baba, who was known to flare up in situations that taxed the ingenuity of onlookers. In those moods, Upasni was liable to use coarse language and to appear ferocious. His followers took an indulgent view of these moods, in which he could make statements that contradicted others he uttered. Whatever his motives were, the "anti-Merwanji" statements pleased some of the *brahman* devotees, and served to cement his increasingly brahmanical following at Sakori. Most of the Zoroastrians went with Meher Baba (though the latter also gained many Hindu devotees from elsewhere and a significant number of Muslim adherents).

The bamboo cage in which Upasni had confined himself requires comment. In late December 1922,[250] he told a carpenter to construct this curiosity from bamboo poles. It was installed at his hut when devotees were absent, and they arrived to find him locked inside the cage, the carpenter fitting the last bars after he had gone within. The bamboo poles were about five feet high, and enclosed three sides, the fourth side being an existing wall. He could not stand up inside this cage (*pinjra*), though he could recline at full length. He was clearly visible to visitors through the bars and refused to come out. Food and other necessities had to be passed to him through the bars. He was plied with questions as to why he had imprisoned himself, and apparently said that he had to atone for the errors of his devotees. He is reported to have said that the gods and saints of all religions were present with him in the cage. The belief developed that whoever died thinking of the cage would attain liberation (*mukti*), a belief which is difficult to credit. The cage became a venerated symbol of atonement and divine bliss. The occupant does not appear to have fasted, but to have maintained a simple diet of bread and chutney.

Bapusaheb Jog and other *brahmans* commenced the habit of performing the *arati* ceremony before the cage during Upasni's confinement. In early 1923, in a conversation with Gulmai Irani, the saint complained about the ritualism, saying: "Tell them to stop performing *arati* before me; I do not want to be worshipped."[251] He also remarked that he was planning to die in the cage, which was a paradox for popular interpretations. Feeling distressed, Gulmai asked the purpose of his confinement. In a mood of anger, he said that his actions were "on account of the whole world"[252] and "when I am unable to do anything for the good of the world, I have to do *this*,"[253] meaning to live in the cage. These rather cryptic remarks again evidence a paradox, though it is reasonably certain that *arati* observances were imposed upon him by the wishes of *brahmans*. Upasni had consistently refused the finery such as silk cushions which devotees had attempted to gift him with, and perhaps he even considered himself to be a prisoner of their mentality.

When his fifty-third birthday was celebrated in May 1923, he asked Gulmai to lead the *arati* routine instead of the men. He obligingly put his legs through the cage bars so that devotees could touch his feet in the *darshan* routine. This was one of their demands that his internment disrupted, being otherwise a daily occurrence. Touching the head to holy feet is a Hindu custom. Owing to the sheer volume of visitors that day, for the first time Upasni came out of the cage, but the crowd became uncontrollable and the police had to be summoned to regulate the *darshan* queues. A palanquin procession circled around him for hours, and perhaps he was dizzy by the time he got back into the cage. The next day he would not come out, and although devotees wanted to bathe him, he told them to bathe a leper instead, saying that this would amount to bathing himself. His sister found that she saw his face reflected in the leper, and bowed down to the sufferer instead, much to the saint's approval. At his instigation, *puja* (worship) was performed before the leper. On that day also, Upasni was happy when visiting disciples of Meher Baba gathered around his cage; this time no abusive remarks were in evidence. He even told Gulmai to maintain her attitude that these men belonged to both himself and Merwanji.[254] The paradox had moved full circle.

Some devotees later made much of a statement attributed to Upasni that salvation was assured if the various fasts, feasts, and ceremonies of the Hindu calendar were observed.[255] It is perhaps more accurate to deduce that he endorsed observances of his native religion in relation to instructions from the guru, a factor which may modify ceremonies considerably. This might explain why he created such a mood of veneration for the bamboo cage as being representative of liberation. Yet devotees were so anxious to secure his "release" from the cage that a non-stop *saptah* or service of worship was maintained until he stepped out of confinement in February 1924. Veneration for the cage as a holy relic persisted for the rest of his life, encouraged by his own regular salute to this feature of the Sakori landscape. In 1928 rich Hindu devotees replaced the bamboo poles with silver bars, an extravagance which he lamented. Upasni insisted that some of the original poles be restored to the relic, perhaps feeling that a false liberation was in danger of occurring. He is said to have undergone other confinements after 1924.

Wealthy devotees gradually transformed the simple ashram into a shrine centre. In addition to the Dattatreya temple, smaller shrines eventually appeared here that were dedicated to Shiva, Khandoba, and Ganapati.

In 1923 some of his discourses began to be published in a Marathi journal called *Sai Vak Sudha*, and these were later published as a separate book.[256] Numerous discourses were translated from Marathi into English. Many of the discourses converge with themes in traditional Hinduism,[257] though there are some "independent" gnostic reflections such as: "I am the Ancient One. I am in the Beyond-State, beyond duality and non-duality. I am in the world but not of it. Because I have to behave like a man of the world, do not misunderstand me."[258] It seems that in his eyes, to live as an informed holy man in a brahmanical ashram, was a secondary thing of the world. Upasni was definitely not a worldly man as most people envisage that category. He claimed to simultaneously experience the state of *maya* and the state of divine existence. That *sahaja* is not open to verification.

Though many devotees tried to fit him into the category of a *satpurusha* who endorsed traditional Hinduism, Upasni remained one of the most unpredictable figures in *brahman* ranks. His moods of anger could shatter expectations of the moment.[259] A remarkable instance of this is afforded by the visit to Sakori of Mahatma Gandhi. This visit occurred during the 1920s.[260] In 1924 Meher Baba had told Rustom K. Irani to send Gandhi a copy of the newly published Gujarati biography of Upasni. Gandhi appears to have been impressed by the contents, and afterwards went to Sakori to investigate. At most Hindu ashrams Gandhi would have been ceremoniously greeted as a great celebrity and given red carpet treatment, his patronage being deemed a blessing. Gandhi probably expected this sort of reception at Sakori. Instead, Upasni exhibited great annoyance, and expressed abusive language towards his visitor. The gist of his remarks was: "Who says you are a *mahatma* (great soul)? You may be a great man, but what is that to me? Why are you bothering me?" It was a demolition of pride and formality, but worst of all in Gandhi's eyes, Upasni made a gesture which the politician deemed audacious. Upasni was wearing his gunny cloth when Gandhi arrived, but he removed this and went stark naked. This was apparently a tendency of his in some situations, particularly when annoyed by the demands of social etiquette imposed by caste Hinduism. The category of *sadhus* known as *naga* favour nakedness, and are considered beyond caste rules. The gesture was too much for Gandhi, who preferred loin-cloth saints of gentle demeanour. He departed with a negative impression.

In 1931 Gandhi found Meher Baba much more acceptable as a spiritual personage, the latter always being fully dressed and possessing an amiable disposition respectful of visitors. They seem to have been on very good terms for a while, though not always in agreement.[261] Meher Baba's private remarks about Gandhi were often respectful, though sometimes critical.²⁶² He tended to defend Upasni's hostile behaviour, saying that the latter was a *sadguru*, though Gandhi was unwilling to alter his unfavourable impression.

It would seem possible that Upasni Maharaj identified Gandhi as a deficient representative of caste Hinduism, a subject which gained a paradoxical flavour at Sakori ashram. Upasni wanted the Dattatreya temple there to be kept open to untouchables, though some of his high caste followers were resistant to such considerations.²⁶³ He is said to have preferred the coarse speech of the commoner, which became accentuated in his angry moods. Yet this "commoner" orientation of Upasni is typically ambiguous in relation to the content of his more formal discourses that were prepared for publication. It is definite that Gandhi's thinking underwent a pronounced change between 1921 and the early 1930s. Although he looked benignly upon outcastes, Gandhi defended the four Hindu castes to such an extent that he wrote in 1921 that the Hindu "prohibition against intermarriage and interdining is essential for the rapid evolution of the soul."²⁶⁴ Gandhi's subsequent experiences and reflections led him to annul this orthodox belief in November 1932, when he described the same two prohibitions as "weakening Hindu society."²⁶⁵ Upasni had broken interdining taboos long before Gandhi visited him, and as the disciple of a Muslim, he had incurred orthodox displeasure similar to the disdain reserved for inter-caste marriages. Upasni was probably annoyed that the Shirdi devotees were transforming his teacher into a Hindu (instead of an "untouchable" Muslim), a factor confirming the bias with which he had to perpetually contend.

A person who dealt with bias in a different manner was Dr. B. R. Ambedkar. Educated in America, where he gained his doctorate, during the 1920s Dr. Ambedkar commenced his campaign of freeing some fifty or sixty million untouchables from what was effectively slavery. In addition to their plight as scavengers, they were denied water rights by caste Hindus and were prohibited from entering temples. In order to escape their plight, some of the untouchables gained a new identity as Muslims or Christians; in Hinduism, their status was less than that of cattle. When Ambedkar revolted against this situation in a social demonstration, his followers were brutally beaten by British law-enforcers and caste Hindus. Ambedkar disliked Gandhi's Congress party, deeming them to be caste Hindus who cared nothing about the depressed classes. They labelled him a traitor for going to the British Commission in an attempt to represent his cause.

94

Ambedkar collided with Gandhi, who was unusually sympathetic to the untouchables for a caste Hindu, but who said that he would campaign for them entering the temples only after India gained independence. Views of the differences between these two men have differed substantially. It is definite that Gandhi did not want divisions in Indian politics, fearing that these would undermine hopes for independence. Supporters of Dr. Ambedkar have said that, despite Gandhi's liberalism towards the people he called Harijans ("children of God"), Gandhi basically took a traditional standpoint in caste matters, believing that untouchables would get reborn as caste Hindus. The orthodox conception of reincarnation is indeed backward. At the Round Table Conference held in London in 1931, Gandhi wanted to eliminate a separate vote for untouchables, an attempt which was discarded by the British government. Gandhi afterwards declared that he would fast to death to prevent separate electorates for untouchables and caste Hindus. The British then retreated from their humanistic stance, leaving Ambedkar on his own to deal with the crisis. Gandhi had won the support of high caste Hindus, and it is said that Ambedkar had to back down during Gandhi's fast at Yeravda jail. It has been argued that Ambedkar feared being stigmatized as the killer of Gandhi, which would have meant the killing of untouchables. Some also say that Ambedkar lost his opportunity to free the untouchables as a result of his conciliation with caste Hinduism.[266] Yet such arguments seem unfair to Gandhi, who fasted in order to banish untouchability by ensuring cooperation between caste Hindus and outcastes. As a consequence of his fasting in September 1932, many temples removed the ban on untouchables, and there were various gestures made in the direction of ceasing discrimination. A spirit of reform fleetingly emerged, but segregation did not end when Gandhi broke his fast. Yet orthodox caste Hindus signed the Yeravda Pact which stated that nobody would be regarded as untouchable by reason of birth. Gandhi afterwards made a point of attending marriages between Harijans and Hindus. In February 1933, while still in prison, Gandhi started a society to help Harijans.

It is undeniable that Gandhi was liberal towards untouchables. He even adopted one of them as his daughter, and at his ashram accomplished the menial task of cleaning lavatories, a task generally reserved for scavengers. Dogmatic Hindus did not forgive his tangent, but thousands of high caste Hindus visited his ashram over the years, his influence facilitating liberal attitudes. Gandhians began to employ untouchables in their households, breaking ancient taboos.[267] Yet critics emphasize that Gandhi did not abolish caste, the factor which underpins the stigmas prevalent in Indian religion. "Gandhi fought for their rights, especially the right to enter Hindu temples.... but even he wanted to maintain the caste structure."[268]

Modern India retained the caste system, and as a consequence the untouchable cause received a setback, many Hindus not sharing Gandhi's unusual liberalism. Though untouchability was officially abolished, the stigma effectively remained in force, especially in the villages, where the victims continued to live in much the same way. In 1956 Dr. Ambedkar embraced Buddhism, renouncing Hinduism. Millions of untouchables are said to have followed him in this conversion, shortly before his death that same year. He has been accused of idealizing the role of Buddhism in the history of untouchability to an extent unjustified by the evidence.[269] Be that as it may, injustices and atrocities against Hindu Harijans have since been reported, the accusation being made in 1968 that "the law against untouchability is almost inoperative because of the indifferent attitude of the so-called upper caste Hindus holding key positions."[270]

Upasni Maharaj would not involve himself in political matters, though he expressed approval of the struggle for independence and is said to have advised some of his followers to become participants. However, his basic view was that political freedom would be of minimal use without a spiritual regeneration. A problem exists for his extant reflections in that he did not articulate anti-caste themes which certain aspects of his lifestyle support. Like Gandhi perhaps, he wanted social reforms but did not systematically undermine caste. His elliptical patronage of the *brahmans* was not geared to matters which politicians were discussing. Yet he definitely was progressive in his emphasis upon the education of women, whose low status he regarded as deplorable. He did not advocate any secular model of "liberation," but instead a religious education rooted in Hindu ideals of the home.[271]

The major feature of Upasni's later years is generally acknowledged to have been the creation of what was apparently a unique institution. This is sometimes described as a women's ashram, though more specifically, a community of nuns (*kanyas*). It became known as the Upasni Kanya Kumari Sthan. The word *kanya* is sometimes translated as "virgin." The word *kumari* means a young woman. The word *sthan* means "abode." The meaning that Upasni himself gave to the phrase *kanya kumari* was that of a virgin or nun who destroys untruth and leads others to God. The ideals involved were diametrically opposed to that of the promiscuous woman who figured in left hand Tantra (both Hindu and Buddhist varieties), currently celebrated in Western sectors with an atrophied appetite.

The leader of the *kanya kumari* nuns was Godavri Vasudev Hata-valikar, better known as Godavri Mataji (Mai). She was born at She-gaon in 1914, and was only ten years old when she first visited Sako-ri. That was in 1924.[272] She came with her mother, both of them being sent by her father Vasudev, who had received favourable reports about Upasni. The saint told Godavri that the ashram belonged to her, a disclosure which puzzled his followers. Shortly after, she was married to a young man named Vishnupant, apparently with Upasni's full approval. It is said that she did not live with her husband even for one day, as he immediately departed to finish his studies at Bombay. She was left in the ashram as a resident. Four years later, in 1928, Vishnupant visited Upasni in consternation, saying that he wanted to renounce the world and to dedicate his unwanted wife to God. At first the saint demurred, but then said that the girl (now fifteen) could have her marriage annulled by being dedicated to the god Shiva, after which she could be dedicated to him (Upasni) in a spiritual marriage. The Sanskrit term for "spiritual marriage" is *Brahma vivaha*, and runs the risk of being misunderstood by Westerners.[273]

It seems that the tradition of dedicating a young woman in "marriage" to a deity is an ancient practice in India. The theme of "marriage" to a saint or *sat-purusha* is more controversial, largely because Upasni used this concept to elevate the status of celibate women in caste society, which traditionally reduced female privileges and options. While he made concessions to orthodox ideas about married women which derive from the *Code of Manu*, he was remarkably bold in his establishment of the Kanya Kumari Sthan for unmarried women who were consecrated to a deity and to himself as their guru. His emphasis was basically that, via association with a God-realized *sat-purusha*, a *kanya* can acquire union with God. This association should ideally be of her own choice, or else decided by her parents. Thus, the "spiritual marriage" amounts to the instruction of the celibate *kanya* by the guru and is believed to lead to God-realization. In this context, the *kanya* is sometimes referred to as a *Brahma vivaha*, an idiom stressing her importance. Through the guidance of the *sat-purusha*, the *kanya* may lead others (including men) to God, and is credited with the ability to save the souls of all those who take her *darshan*, including men. This was not a teaching welcome to many caste Hindus, especially *brahmans*, whose male prerogative in ritual and textual recitation was considered supreme and unchallenged.

The first man to prostrate himself at the feet of Godavri was her husband, who acknowledged her as a manifestation of the Divine Mother, to use terminology associated with (right hand) Shaktism. This was after her new celibate marriage to Shiva and Upasni, which was in full accord with her own wishes, as she desired to be a renunciate. Vishnupant departed permanently, and Godavri dedicated herself to the service of her guru. In July 1928, on the day of *Gurupurnima* (celebrating the worship of the guru), Upasni made a special gesture to his female disciple. He took from his neck a rosary which had originally belonged to Sai Baba and placed this around the neck of Godavri. He spoke briefly of her future role of prominence and worshipped her as the Divine Mother, conducting some simple rites and ordering the assembled devotees to perform an *arati* in her honour. He told them not to bow to him but to her, as she was the supreme *shakti*. She is said to have made rapid progress in her *sadhana*, though she aroused jealousy. She had never attended school, but possessed a very retentive memory which gained her familiarity with teachings and texts.

Another girl, an eleven year old named Prema, was also given to Upasni as *kanyadan* (gift of a *kanya*) by her father. She was followed by three others who were offered to him in the same religious manner. It was now his responsibility to teach them. Although Shaiva auspices had been involved in the "marriages," in 1932 a strong Vaishnava complexion was conferred when the five *kanyas* were "united to Shri Krishna," an event which became controversial. The underlying strategy of Upasni was to negotiate a major taboo of caste Hinduism. The orthodox pundits rigorously maintained that only the three higher castes could read and recite the scriptures. Along with *shudras* and untouchables, women were denied this privilege. Defying that prohibition, Upasni argued that a *kanya* who had committed herself to *Brahma vivaha*, and was theoretically capable of saving many souls, was entitled to read and recite the Vedas. He ignored priestly protests and ensured that the *kanyas* in the new *kumari sthan* were taught Sanskrit and the professional brahmanical methods of reciting Vedic texts. This innovation met with resistance, and he became the target of criticisms and calumnies from insular *brahmans*.

Afterwards, another girl also became a *kanya*. Upasni "had the intuition to recognize the innate chastity of the woman" and his tactic in this respect was "to select virgin girls at a tender age and to train them rigorously to achieve the unfettered state of spiritual enlightenment."[274] Those Daist and Tantric writers who have mistakenly implied that Upasni was a representative of bohemian crazy wisdom merely reflect the devolutionizing trend in American socioculture which is incapable of chastity and instead degrades human potential according to the lusts of an exploiter like Da Free John (Adi Da).

The standards of discipline Upasni set for the *kanyas* was very high, involving an arduous programme of study and contemplation. One may credit that "the Sthan achieved a triumphant revival of the old Vedic atmosphere where women took a leading part in the spiritual regeneration of the country."[275] The Upanishadic figure of Gargi[276] had argued on equal terms with the male thinkers, before the legalists had imposed the accumulating strictures. Upasni tried to undo those strictures, though in accord with traditional ideals of celibacy that preserved discipline, unlike the mood of "liberation" in Western countries whose god is orgasm.

Far from being a Tantric sensualist like Da Free John, Upasni was "a rigid disciplinarian; he was exacting, uncompromisingly strict, and almost harsh to all faults of omission and laziness."[277] In common with his contemporary Shri Aurobindo, he disliked left hand Tantrics, while his "passion for austerities led him to impose fantastic restraints on his disciples, particularly on the *kanyas*."[278]

The nature of his relationship with the *kanyas* was seriously distorted by rumours which percolated from the ashram. The major figure in this setback was Durgabai Karmakar, the woman who had followed Upasni to Sakori from Shirdi with her young son Raghunath. She became the unofficial manager of Sakori ashram in the early years, seeing to the needs of visitors. When Godavri arrived upon the scene, Durgabai began to feel jealous. Upasni seemed to single out Godavri for special attention, and referred to her later role as leader of the ashram. During the late 1920s and early 1930s, this situation of jealousy boiled over when Upasni gave an increasing amount of attention to the group of *kanyas* that he formed. Durgabai's jealousy was aggravated by the most orthodox contingent amongst the male devotees, who were now shocked and annoyed that Upasni encouraged women to perform sacrosanct Vedic rites. These *brahmans* opposed the *kanyas*, and took advantage of Durgabai's jealousy by telling her stories which made her completely hostile to Godavri. Durgabai is said to have possessed a very trusting nature, and did not query the reliability of what she was told. The goad caused her to use her position as ashram manager to make Godavri's life very difficult in various ways. She was greatly annoyed by the spiritual marriages that occurred, and opted to interpret these celibate events as an indication that Upasni had become the victim of lust. She sent a message to Meher Baba at distant Meherabad via her son Raghunath. Unlike the *brahmans* at Sakori, Durgabai still had great respect for Meher Baba and requested him to visit Sakori in order to investigate the *kanya* issue. Meher Baba sent back a reply that she was completely wrong in her assessment of the situation, and that there was no need for him to visit Sakori.[279]

In a confused state of mind, Durgabai left Sakori in 1933 to reside at Sholapur. She had not been able to prevent the ascendancy of the *kanyas*, whom Upasni made the pivot of his activities. Her misinformed version of events was exploited by "some orthodox Hindu scholars who wanted to repudiate Maharaj's spiritual status."[280] Her former prominent position in the ashram and her lengthy acquaintance with Upasni was treated by this hostile faction as justification for their accusations. They created a scandal by writing articles in Marathi journals. Legal charges were contrived against Upasni, and a lawsuit was pressed, eventually requiring his appearance at a court in Ahmednagar.[281] The opposition was repulsed. His critics failed to prevent the young nuns from living at Sakori and performing the Vedic rituals elsewhere claimed to be a male prerogative.

Several years after her departure from Sakori, Durgabai "realized her mistake and repented deeply."[282] She was now frail and unwell. She made a reconciliation with Upasni, who forgave her for the problem she had caused, and also made special arrangements for her wellbeing. He ensured that she had medical care and obtained her a monthly allowance. She died not long after in May 1939.

Meanwhile, the small *kanya* community had established itself as a major feature of the Sakori ashram (which became known as Upasni Nagar). The nuns adopted a distinctive garb. A training in Sanskrit and recitation preceded an initiation of the novice into full *kanya* credentials. Upasni is said to have instigated the ritual for this event, which became extended into a three day event after his death, when the young nuns were initiated by Godavri. The "marriage" of the *kanya* to Deity was then viewed as being vested in Godavri Mataji (or

Mata). During his last years Upasni increasingly delegated to this woman the responsibility for leadership of the ashram. There were marked differences in their temperament, she being far more moderate than him. To no other person would he give such latitude for change. His lifestyle was one of an unremitting austerity, epitomized by his gunny cloth and simple diet.[283] Living a disciplined life, she nevertheless modified his exacting regime, and he did not protest, though he is reported to have ruefully predicted: "It is no use, this Mother (Mataji) will sweep away all my old-fashioned and orthodox restrictions with her indulgence."[284]

Upasni did not like the new temples at the ashram and the devotional desires for aesthetic display. Yet he gave permission for a temple dedicated to the goddess Kanya Kumari, in which the *kanya* became a symbolic icon. He may have observed a severe fast at the end of his life,[285] though he remained active. In October 1941 he obtained a rather secretive meeting with Meher Baba in an obscure hut at Dahigaon.[286] In November 1941 he visited Hyderabad as a guest of a wealthy devotee. In December he visited Poona, but refused to allow anybody to take his *darshan*, substituting a coconut instead. He kept muttering that he was tired and would close up matters very soon. He returned to Sakori on December 19th, where he did give *darshan* for two days, though he complained of a pain in his chest. On December 22nd he departed for Satana, where a temple had been constructed over his former home in honour of his birth there; upon request, he installed some *jyotilingas* in this temple, but said cryptically that the sun was setting. After a restless night, he arrived back at Sakori on December 23rd, in a state of exhaustion. Upasni did not follow his usual habit of bowing to the bamboo cage, his favourite edifice at Sakori, but instead went directly to his hut. Early the next day, December 24th, he complained of a severe pain in his heart, and died peacefully shortly after. His body was buried near the cage, and a tomb (or *samadhi*) later erected. A statue of him was put in the cage, which was preserved as a relic, and a large hall (the Sabha Mandap) was built around the cage and tomb.

Godavri Mataji was believed to be his successor, and the Kanya Kumari Sthan gained new inmates, numbering about twenty or more by 1954. The nuns were occasionally invited to recite the Vedas at religious festivals in various places.[287] Godavri gave the other nuns guidance in their *sadhanas*, and moulded the general routine. She favoured rituals, though she considered *nama-japa* (repetition of a divine name) to be more efficacious. As her reputation grew, she was credited with miraculous powers. Unlike Upasni, she was not subject to moods of anger, and a "sweetness and light" was considered to be her distinguishing hallmark.[288] "In contrast to the other saints whom we met personally, she appears somewhat shy and retiring,"[289] wrote an American visitor to Sakori. Some devotees believed her to be an incarnation of the goddess Durga. She was not eccentric in manner, and did not give discourses in the way that Upasni did. Godavri did not advocate withdrawal from the world, and unlike her teacher's emphasis upon the value of suffering, she affirmed a joyous attitude to life.

While Upasni possessed many elements of an austere *jnani* disposition, Godavri was noted for her affinities with *bhakti*, often translated as devotion. "She advocates the practice of God-adoration in any way suitable to the temperament and calibre of the aspirant."[290] According to a well known Indian writer, Godavri emphasized the power of *mantras*, and would initiate *sadhakas* with sacred names or phrases. A great reliance is often vested in this traditional recourse at Indian ashrams. However, Godavri Mataji did not neglect to stress the gradual purification of thoughts, motives, and actions, and also the necessity for persistent efforts in *sadhana*.[291]

"She has ushered in an era of gracious living," wrote Mani Sahukar, a reference to "the courage and the vision to reject all formal manifestations of austerities."[292] This was a departure from Godavri's early ashram background of ascetic living cultivated by Upasni, who was incompatible with comfort to the very end. Sahukar, who graduated from the Elphinstone College in Bombay, clearly found Godavri's approach very appealing. "To look well-groomed and attractive, and to live with beauty, without getting attached in *moha*,[293] is Godavari Mataji's way of life."[294] It needs to be added that good grooming was not here intended in the sense of salon glamour. Godavri and other graduate nuns dressed in yellow *saris*, while the novices dressed in white. She was considered to have met the challenge of modernism in her anti-ascetic emphases, in which renunciation applied to thoughts and desires rather than to an emaciated body. "To live with beauty" seems in part to have referred to her patronage of *kanya* ritualism, which encouraged the performance of traditional *puja* (worship), an avenue of devotional expression which adorned statues of gods with flowers, jewels, and sandal paste.

Rituals favoured in the Kanya Kumari Sthan were primarily the *kanya* initiation, the *arati* ceremony, and the *yajna*. The *arati* was performed four times a day, when the nuns sang hymns praising Upasni and Godavri, waving the sacred tray of lighted incense and oil lamps before Godavri and the image of Upasni which had been placed in the venerated bamboo cage. The *yajna* is more difficult for non-ritualists (both Indian and Western) to appreciate, being an elaborate form of Vedic sacrifice designed to propitiate deities. The *kanya* version of this ritual was performed in the *Yajna mandir*, a temple located underground and visible to spectators through a grid in the roof. Here stood a fire pit in which oblations and butter (*ghee*) were offered to Agni, the god of fire, though the climax was a processional walk around the ashram. One visitor commented that "the *yajna* creates a climate for Divine visitation, and devotees report visions of deities emerging from the flames to receive the offerings."[295] Critics said that the Sthan did nothing in the way of social service.[296] The real problem appears to be that the *brahman* caste had shirked social service for many centuries, expecting to be served by the lower castes and outcastes. Hindu nuns cannot be blamed for problems established by a patriarchal society; it seems that Upasni adroitly encouraged feminine competition with the priests as a first step towards outmanoeuvring the stranglehold of caste conditioning.

The concept of service in the world achieved orthodox celebration in the *Bhagavad Gita*,[297] a much quoted Vedantic text that is associated with Krishna. This work advocates social responsibilities in accordance with the system of caste, and does not recognize social problems that became aggravated over a long period of time. Those problems included outcastes, the subjection of women to barbarities like *sati*, and child marriage.

As a former child bride who had been rescued from problems by spiritual marriage with Upasni (as Krishna), Godavri Mataji appears to have given deference to the counsel of Krishna in the *Gita* to Arjuna, the emblem of *kshatriya-dharma*. Hindu thinkers as varied as Swami Vivekananda, B. G. Tilak, Mahatma Gandhi, and Shri Aurobindo had done the same, if in different ways. Unlike Tilak and Gandhi, Godavri was not a politician, and unlike Vivekananda and Aurobindo, she had not received a Western education. Neither of these qualifications were necessary to perceive, as she did, that men in general "act like bears," which was a reference she made in relation to the assassination of President Kennedy in America.[298] She felt that men should become real men, not beasts – a consideration which will be respected here. She believed that science could improve physical conditions, though she taught that periods of retirement from worldly life were necessary for a spiritual renewal.[299] Thus an element of abnegation was proposed, a factor which perhaps remains the key to basic events at Sakori.

3. Meher Baba of Ahmednagar (d. 1969)

Though some writers on Sakori have made little or no reference to Meher Baba, this measure seems inadmissible on the basis of materials to hand. Many devotees who came to Upasni after 1921 had never set eyes upon Meher Baba, formerly known as Merwan Irani. The orthodox version of events in vogue at Sakori tended to be that he had set himself up as a rival to Upasni Maharaj, and was merely a Zoroastrian disciple of Hazrat Babajan who could safely be ignored. Even Godavri Mataji did not meet him until almost thirty years after her arrival at Sakori. One might usefully attempt to broaden the picture here, to ascertain more of what was occurring in that area of India.

After leaving Sakori in January 1922, Meher Baba gathered around him an inter-religious following composed of Zoroastrians, Muslims, and Hindus. At first he stayed alone in a hut (*jhopdi*) at Poona for a few months, and then moved to Bombay, where at a large house known as Manzil-e-Meem, he lived with over forty male disciples for some ten months. That phase has been described by some writers in terms of his first ashram, though it did not bear any close resemblance to the conventional Hindu ashram. Many of the men involved had to attend ordinary jobs in the city, although discipline was very strict. There were twelve Muslims included. Baba's first permanent ashram did not come into being until a couple of years later, at a place which became known as Meherabad.

Meher Baba first arrived at Meherabad in May 1923. The site was a disused military camp of the British army, situated in a famine area five miles south of Ahmednagar. It was very inhospitable, being a barren place infested with snakes and scorpions. Nearby was the agricultural village of Arangaon, whose population included many untouchables. The derelict site was not considered very desirable, and was eventually gifted to him by Kaikhushru Irani, the husband of Gulmai who had recently met with economic success, and who had purchased the property at auction. The British had left a disused stone water tank on a small hill, which became known as Meherabad Hill. In the lower part, across the railway track, was a well. At first Baba did not stay long, preferring to travel, but during April and May 1924 a period of temporary settlement occurred. His companions had to perform hard manual labour in restoring the camp, and referred to their lifestyle as one of "*ghamela* Yoga," which was an improvised pun phrase deriving from the pan (*ghamela*) used by labourers to move earth and stones.

Even when Meher Baba settled at Meherabad on a more permanent basis in early 1925, his disciples did not exhibit the characteristics of "austerity, meditation, and yoga practise" that are generally associated with Indian ashrams. The emphasis was upon manual labour, humanitarian activity, and obeying specific orders given to different individuals. He permitted a colony to develop, and established a dispensary and hospital, a school, a leper asylum, and quarters for the destitute and disabled. It is said that during 1925–6, some five hundred patients were treated in the hospital and that nearly seven thousand people were treated in the dispensary. The Hazrat Babajan School is said to have accommodated nearly two hundred children, mostly from Arangaon. Meher Baba directly participated in these activities. He personally tended lepers and the destitute in a manner reminiscent of Upasni Maharaj, though he took such matters further than Upasni did. These activities were rare amongst Indian gurus.

Resident disciples and devotees at Meherabad became known by the term *mandali*, a Marathi word signifying a group or family, and which was not in standard ashram usage. Meher Baba commenced his distinctive silence on July 10th, 1925, a restraint which he was to maintain unbroken until his death. Baba afterwards communicated by means of an alphabet board, ceasing to write after 1926. At the end of 1926 he closed down the colony, stating that the purpose had been served.

A notable feature of Meherabad was the inter-religious complexion, differing radically from most other ashrams in India. Though Meher Baba permitted Hindus their own form of worship, he would not allow caste stigmas, and systematically broke down brahmanical taboos in the dining arrangements. He was a social leveller, and promoted the cause of the untouchables at an early date, giving much attention to the local *mahars* of Arangaon.[300] This grouping were an untouchable contingent whose hereditary occupation was to remove dead cattle from villages and to sweep the streets of filth. They were often reduced to eating rotting carcases, and were considered defiled meat-eaters by the *brahmans*. They lived in a state of acute poverty, superstition, squalor, and lack of hygiene. Nobody usually raised a finger to help them. High caste Hindus justified this state of affairs by invoking reincarnation as a rationale. Meher Baba also taught reincarnation, but in a completely different form to the superstitious version which buttressed caste orthodoxy. He was concerned to educate the *mahars* and to break their dependence upon the menial tasks allotted to them by caste society.

He started a school in March 1925 (known as the Hazrat Babajan School), which substantially included untouchable children. This amounted to a programme for educating the parents also, as Baba gradually eroded the social divisions which custom tried to perpetuate. Even the untouchables had preserved a set of social divisions amongst themselves, on the basis of occupation, thus exhibiting their own "caste system." When working with the poor and distributing food to them, he would not tolerate caste qualms amongst his Hindu followers. Unlike Upasni Maharaj, he was not paradoxical about his objectives. Meher Baba is known to have stated that his intention was to destroy caste prejudices root and branch. This was too much for some bigoted Hindus. Others were in a dilemma over how to respond to such a "guru."

Untouchables were customarily denied access to the wells of caste Hindus. Hygiene was high on the list of priorities in Baba's school at Meherabad, where he frequently bathed the *mahar* boys, who seem to have numbered about thirty by the summer of 1925. A group of *brahmans* visited him on one such occasion that summer, eager for the encounter traditionally known as *darshan*. They bowed before him, but he is reported to have greeted their veneration with scepticism, saying: "It is no use having *darshan* like this unless you are prepared to do the work I do." They were averse to going near the untouchable boys, and felt the sting of his words. It is said that they joined him and his assistants in the task at hand, though similar instances involved acute reluctance and non-compliance.[301] Meher Baba deemed *darshan* of this nature to be an act of hypocrisy, and was frequently averse to becoming involved in the procedure of *darshan* (too often a rigmarole in which the visitor expects some benefit imagined to be in the offing). "The only God here is these children whom I worship,"[302] he would say to shocked caste visitors.

Some of his *brahman* devotees were very anxious when in 1925 he demolished caste divisions between the untouchable boys and the *brahman* boys at mealtimes. The *brahman* boys willingly obeyed, but an elderly *brahman* devotee became so indignant that his face grew flushed. Meher Baba asked one of his Parsi devotees whether the annoyed man wished him to respect "the prejudices and arrogance of the *brahmans*." Baba himself then exhibited annoyance, and "with fire in his eyes and giving a slight blow to his own body," he declared: "I have put on this body with a view to destroying the entire fabric of the caste system, and destroy it I will, despite the opposition of the bigoted *brahmans*. The caste system is as absurd as it is tyrannous; it has nothing to do with religion in the true sense of the word."303

Unlike Upasni Maharaj, Meher Baba did not permit any permanent religious edifice at his ashrams. In 1925 he permitted two makeshift Hindu temples made of bamboo matting, one for the untouchables and another for *brahmans*. That situation soon dissolved, and there were no temples or mosques,304 only plain and simple buildings for habitation. The two exceptions to practical utility were a *dhuni* fire and his future tomb (constructed on Meherabad Hill in 1938, and bearing the symbols of world religions).305 The *dhuni* improvisation did not follow any specific religious formula, and remained ambivalent in terms of religious identity. The *dhuni* was situated at Lower Meherabad, and was generally lighted on a monthly basis. Some might see a Zoroastrian complexion here, while others might sense a resemblance to Sai Baba of Shirdi. However, there was no distribution of ash (*udi*), and Meher Baba disclaimed the importance of miraculous phenomena.306

Some orthodox Zoroastrians, and also secular Zoroastrians who had lost their faith, accused Meher Baba of being a fraud. The orthodox priests saw him as a rival, as a mystic who undermined the importance of rituals and conservative customs. A general problem amongst all religious parties was that of how to classify him. Muslim adherents called him Hazrat Meher Baba, seeing in him a Sufi, while the Hindus just as enthusiastically called him Sadguru Meher Baba. This left the Parsis and Iranis with a dilemma, as he was not an orthodox Zoroastrian. Many of his Zoroastrian followers opted for the simple Indian title of *Shri*, a term of veneration shared by numerous holy men and respected persons. This became the normative title for him in correspondence and public relations, and continued well into the 1950s. The title of *avatar* was a much later innovation of the mid-1950s,307 adopted during a phase which obscured many details of earlier decades.

Meher Baba made an extensive use of both Vedantic and Sufi terminologies, and seems to have had no parallel in this respect amongst mystics of modern times. His discourses were distinctive from the start, and are strikingly original. He was obviously not a Vedantist in

108

his background, save by association with Upasni Maharaj. (Not all of Meher Baba's Sanskrit-oriented terminology is Vedantic, but is also drawn from other forms of Hinduism). He did not present himself as a Sufi, and there is nothing in his presentation that resembles the paraphernalia of the *dervish* orders, with which Sufism is generally associated. He is known to have referred to "half-baked Sufis," and had no affinity with the doctrinaire format of "orthodox Sufism." He respected the heritage of classical Sufism, more especially the type represented by Bistami, Hallaj, and Rumi. In terms of Indian Sufism, he expressed an esteem for Khwaja Saheb Muinuddin Chishti of Ajmer, whose tomb he visited. Yet Meher Baba was not Islamic, and it is only possible to directly compare him with Zoroastrian antecedents, namely the Kaivani (Sipasi) trend of Mughal times.[308] Such a comparison amounts to an approximation only, there being a complete absence of doctrinal *ishraq* in his teachings.

He did not emphasize religious texts, and his manner was not that of a pundit or religious scholar. He implied that mystical texts were anachronistic, giving traditional exegetes fuel to create and maintain religious divisions. He preferred poetry to discursive expositions in referring to past formulae. He was very partial to quoting Kabir and Hafiz. His wide religious sympathies extended to Mahavira the Jain,[309] Francis of Assisi,[310] Tukaram,[311] Guru Nanak,[312] and the Bab.[313]

The Hindus at Sakori, or rather most of them, were unable to come to terms with the Irani (and Iranian) dimensions of Meher Baba. His intercultural disposition and affinity with Sufism were too much for the brahmanical devotees there to assimilate. They chose to think of him as a rival to Upasni, and as one who opposed the caste system which they held dear.

His undertaking permanent silence did not resemble the case of Shri Aurobindo (1872–1950), who is generally depicted as having retired into a routine of meditation and writing. In contrast, Meher Baba remained exceptionally active, undertaking numerous journeys both in India and abroad, and frequently in an incognito capacity which escaped the press. His ministrations to the poor continued for many years.

His followers were surprised when he commenced silence, as he was noted for his fine singing voice, which is said to have moved listeners to tears. He apparently regarded this loss as a trifling consideration, and conveyed that his restraint was for the purpose of what he called his "work." His remarks about this factor often sound fantastic, similar to his later claims of being the *avatar*. However, by the 1950s he was in competition with Hindu *avatars* who sometimes flouted rules of basic deportment in their miracle-mongering. Meher Baba was not a miracleworker or miracle vendor, and far more than Upasni Maharaj, he openly discouraged belief in miracles, disclaiming all miraculous achievements. This is an impressive aspect of his career, and renders academic usage of the gloss phrase "Sai Baba movement" a rank misnomer for reasons that should not be difficult to detect. His attitude was consistent in this respect until his death, and the biographical literature on Meher Baba, whatever flaws it may contain, is relatively free of the hagiological tendency to emphasize miraculous deeds[314] of the saint or master wielding *siddhis*.

In 1954 he stated: "Many miracles have been attributed to me, but I do not perform miracles. I do not attach importance to miracles. When people think that miracles have been performed, their faith has done it."[315] He did say that he would perform only one miracle, but this reflection has a very mystical slant. "I have said that my miracle will be not to raise the dead, but to make one dead to himself to live to God. I have repeatedly said I will not give sight to the blind, but I will make them (people) blind to the world in order to see God."[316] This mystical "miracle" thus emphasized transformation of the self, which preoccupation with vulgar miracles does not achieve.

Meher Baba often referred to the breaking of his silence, the date for which was continually postponed over the years. The apparent prediction about his renewed speaking caused speculation amongst those who took him literally. He was also known to make statements like, "If my silence cannot be heard, of what avail words?" The element of contradiction was perhaps part of a method which aimed at defeating crude expectations.

During the 1920s at Meherabad, Meher Baba often allowed Hindu devotees to perform *arati* in his presence, though he discouraged other rituals. Afterwards he terminated this latitude for *arati*, which ceased at the ashram; that ceremony thereafter appeared only at festivals or public functions in which Hindus participated. He was far more partial to the recitation of special prayers which he dictated in his later years. Two of these prayers became well known amongst his followers, namely the Prayer of Repentance and the Universal Prayer.[317] The latter demonstrates his intercultural use of technical religious terms. There were many solemn occasions during the 1950s when he participated in prayer sessions he arranged for the *manda-li*, including those in which a Zoroastrian prayer, a Muslim prayer, a Hindu prayer, a Sikh prayer, and a Christian prayer were recited by different men.[318] There is no doubt that Meher Baba supported and validated the use of prayer, contrary to the example of antinomian mystics. He would bow down in an act of worship during the prayer sessions. He did not, however, support the use of initiation rites, which he never undertook and which he disclaimed as a superfluous adjunct, quite unlike the custom in most Indian ashrams.

In the matter of diet he fasted often, and was a vegetarian. He was generally strict about imposing a vegetarian diet at his ashrams, though followers who lived elsewhere were free to eat what suited them. Alcohol was strictly prohibited at his ashrams, and during the 1960s he made his stance against the use of drugs like LSD so outstandingly clear that he became the Eastern figurehead for opposing God in a Pill.[319] His sense of moral values was marked, and his followers were left in no doubt that promiscuity was frowned upon by him. If they could not lead a celibate life like him, then they were to get married in a respectable manner. He was the polar opposite to Bhagwan Shree Rajneesh, who in 1974 established a notorious ashram in Meher Baba's home town of Poona. That was five years after the death of the latter. Rajneesh sometimes referred to Meher Baba without any comprehension of what the deceased entity had been doing.[320] Rajneesh was a subversive pseudo-gnostic, not a genuine mystic; he created a licentious commune which attracted many hedonists from the West who were recruits for a bizarre version of *sannyasa* sometimes dubbed Rajneesh Neo-Tantra.

Although Meher Baba himself lived a strict celibate life and regarded this as the highest ideal for lifestyle, he did not impose that ideal upon everybody else. He made no attempt to found a monastic order or sect, and his followers were free to marry (save in a few instances where he advised against this). He advocated the theme of "Be in the world but not of it," a theme of Sufi affinities, and frequently warned against the dangers of complacency in the vocation of "external renunciation." His meaning was that formal renunciation of the world does not guarantee any purification, much less any enlightenment. The large number of holy men who have provided discrepant and confusing advice is surely some proof of his contention.

He did not wear the ochre robe of the Hindu holy man, but a thin white robe known as *sadra*. This was not the white *kafni* of Muslim ascetics, but an alternative related to the Zoroastrian garment or sacred shirt that is worn with the *kusti* or girdle. Meher Baba did not wear any *kusti*, though he is known to have honoured the *kusti* ceremony of Zoroastrianism (and also associated Zoroastrian prayers). His white trousers were as much Persian as anything Indian. Unlike Sai Baba and Upasni Maharaj, he did not go barefoot but wore sandals. During the 1920s he wore a battered jacket made of rough blanket material (known as the *kamli* coat), originally brown but subsequently covered with blue and black patches as it wore out. He never resorted to opulent clothing. He wore his hair long, though from the late 1930s he frequently braided his hair; in such features he looked more like a yogi than an Irani, though he was habitually clean-shaven except for a moustache. In the 1920s, Khwaja Hasan Nizami referred to him as "the clean-shaven Zoroastrian," the lack of a beard serving to distinguish him from Muslim Sufis as well as Hindu *rishis* (both Sai Baba and Upasni Maharaj had beards).

During the 1920s, his hair had a strong auburn tinge, not nearly so dark as it generally appears on black and white photographs.[321] This is one indication of his ethnic stock;[322] though he was born in India, his parents were both emigrants from Central Iran. Such people were called Iranis, and are technically distinct from the Parsis, who were domiciled in India for many centuries, and a number of whom had intermarried with the Hindu population, while Hindu conversions to Zoroastrianism had also occurred. The Iranis represent the pure Iranian blood of pre-Islamic Iran, when Zoroastrianism was the national religion of the country. The Aryan communities exhibited tendencies to blonde or auburn hair. Despite his contrasting asceticism, in Meher Baba can be seen some of the characteristics of Irani Zoroastrians from Central Iran. He was industrious, practical, and philanthropic, while even his marked sense of humour may be considered a Zoroastrian trait (Pliny mentions a legend that Zarathushtra was born laughing, which some scholars treat as an indicator of Zoroastrian tendencies to merriment). Meher Baba's humour was abundantly transmitted even through silence, and this trait is attested in films of him. His emphasis on telling the truth may be equated with a basic tenet of Zoroastrian religion. To these attributes he added an affinity with Sufism and a flair for seclusion and acute spiritual moods which are perhaps best likened to the mysticism of Azar Kaivan (d. 1618) and his circle of Zoroastrians who infiltrated other religious sectors in India. At least, there is no other obvious source of comparisons in terms of ethnographic data. Such matters are overlooked in popular devotional coverages.

His cosmopolitan disposition was emphasized when, in 1927, he established at Meherabad a distinctive school for boys known as the Meher Ashram. This institution dispensed both secular and religious education, and was notable for facilities in teaching Persian, a feature which attracted Muslims, both Sunnis and Shi'is.[323] More specifically, the tuition became mystical when Meher Baba himself began to teach the boys. This school gained over a hundred pupils, and in November 1928 included 20 Muslims (some of them Shi'is), 32 Zoroastrians (mainly Iranis), one Indian Christian, and one Jain. The Hindus were in the majority with forty-eight boys, of whom fifteen were *mahars* (or *mangs*),[324] a significant number at that period when untouchables were customarily excluded from any such privileged curriculum. Another interesting detail is that the *mahars* outnumbered the *brahman* boys, who are listed as being eleven strong.

A number of the boys developed acute mystical interests and symptoms; they were accommodated in a separate curriculum known as the Prem Ashram. Some relatives of Muslim inmates proved difficult, deeming the curriculum too removed from orthodox Islam and fearing ostracism from hostile parties who circulated adverse rumours. The fact is that certain Muslim boys achieved the leading roles in the Prem Ashram, themselves experiencing mystical states that are generally associated with hallowed texts and greybeard saints. It was a very uncommon institution, and the original record of events was written by a Muslim witness who solicited an introduction from the pen of an influential Indian Muslim known as Maulana Mazhar al-Haque, a former President of the All-India Muslim League. The latter was impressed with Hazrat Qibla[325] Meher Baba and his school, and wrote that it was necessary to read the account with the eye of a Sufi.[326]

One of the boys achieving an unusual contemplative focus was a *mahar* named Suryabhan. According to Ramju Abdulla, he was conspicuous for his silence and general indifference to his surroundings. When the time came for him to be sent back to his village, local boys stoned him as a result of his withdrawn demeanour. The molesters may have been caste Hindus. He remained indoors for six days to avoid being harassed, but when he emerged on the seventh day, the same problem occurred. Instead of retaliating, he again retired in his stoical manner. It was nothing unusual for untouchables to be humiliated, though village elders grew annoyed because he was so aloof from the social pattern of the village. The headman (*patel*), who must have been a high caste Hindu, tried to reprogram him to the local disposition of thinking. In his turn, Suryabhan was annoyed at the system of persuasion used in an attempt to alienate him from Meher Baba and the Prem Ashram. More than most, he probably understood the difference between social conditioning and psychological insight, between socially convenient religion and spiritual achievement.[327]

Another untouchable boy who gained a notable sense of independence from oppressive society was Shahu Mahar. This youth became "one of the most thorough contemplatives of the Prem Ashram."[328] When he was sent home, he would not conform to local living standards and instead erected a small hut for himself in a quiet location near his family quarters. In this hut he remained secluded in deep meditation for nearly eighteen hours every day. The *mahar* boy had become a yogi, one may conclude, and one might speculate as to how many of his type had become freed by wise men in former centuries.

However, such unusual instances can give a lop-sided idea of what Meher Baba was doing. He did not usually advocate or permit a lifestyle of intensive meditation; some boys in the Prem Ashram were exceptions to the general rule. His basic educational plan for untouchables was to prepare them for university, but this proved difficult on a number of accounts. The curriculum of the Meher Ashram conformed to university regulations, and there were three language groups tutored in Persian, Marathi, and Gujarati. Many Indian boys found the prestige language of English a daunting prospect, especially untouchables, who generally lacked any prior education. Meherabad was not a wealthy ashram, and could not afford to rehabilitate on a permanent basis.

Meher Baba himself was multi-lingual. His Zoroastrian upbringing had rendered him conversant with Gujarati and Persian. He had also become familiar with the local language of Marathi spoken by the Hindus. In Poona he had attended a Roman Catholic school before graduating to the prestigious Deccan College. He was proficient in English as a consequence. His alphabet board displayed the letters of the English alphabet, and onlookers were often surprised at the fluency of his silent communication, though his sentence structure tended to a degree of abbreviation. His published messages and discourses were edited by different hands. Certain members of the *mandali* became accustomed to reading aloud his words from the board, and translating where necessary.

An early manuscript written by him, probably in 1925, is a brief metaphysical text composed in English and Gujarati, and related to the more obscure book which he wrote at that time. (*Explanations of Spirituality in Meher Baba's Own Hand*, New Jersey 2000.) Afterwards, in January 1927, he gave up writing except for signing his name. His signature was M. S. Irani. Contrary to some misconceptions, he never wrote letters after that date. (At the end of his life he relinquished even the alphabet board and used hand gestures to communicate.)

In September 1929, Meher Baba made a voyage to Iran, typically travelling as a third-class passenger, accompanied by fourteen of his disciples. He had been to that country once before, in 1924, but had not gone beyond the port of Bushire. This time he did make an expedition into the interior. The tour was notable for not having been advertised or promoted, another typical feature of his journeys. He wished to remain aloof from public contact, but as he moved from town to town, an uninvited acclaim occurred. His companions expected a quiet journey, and were amazed at the response which occurred in Central Iran from different sectors of the people. The enthusiasm was shared by many Shi'ite Muslims in addition to welcomes from Irani Zoroastrians.

On October 15th he arrived in Isfahan, the former capital. He took accommodation in a low class hotel, and for a few days sojourned according to plan in peace and quiet. Word leaked out of his presence there via two young Muslim servants, and other Muslims then requested to see him. Eventually he agreed to give audience to these people, and many visitors came. Popular interest was fanned by an incident in which he gave a cardamom spice to a sick boy on the brink of death; the latter recovered, and a rumour spread that a miraculous healing had occurred. Meher Baba's reaction was to express a strong wish to leave. Crowds of Muslims gathered, along with some Zoroastrians; the rush to pay him homage was so great that he retreated from Isfahan the next day, after a week in that city. He moved to the suburb of Djolfa, principally inhabited by Armenian Christians. Yet crowds followed from the city, intent upon seeking his blessing and finding out more about him. The Police Commissioner of Isfahan, a Muslim Sayed, was one of these new admirers. The *mandali* were surprised that some Muslims had pinned lockets to their coats bearing Meher Baba's photograph; this was not an Islamic custom. Baba consented to answer questions, and his radiance is said to have attracted some of the Armenians as well. Yet he soon departed unobtrusively for Yazd, saying that he wanted seclusion. Admirers seldom understood that he liked to travel incognito, a trait not typical of gurus.

Meher Baba and his group left for Yazd on October 22nd. They reached their destination after two days, arriving at night and staying at an inn. Baba is said to have foiled the plan of a prominent Zoroastrian merchant, Arbab Sohrab, to arrange a public welcome for him in Yazd. This city of Central Iran was closely associated with Zoroastrian history in the Islamic era. Here in the surrounding villages, oppressed Irani Zoroastrians had survived for thirteen centuries as a harshly tolerated minority. In that rural area had lived Meher Baba's ancestors. His father had left the Yazd plain several decades before, while his mother similarly originated from the village of Khooramshar (she had been born only a few days after her parents had landed in Bombay).[329] In very recent years a new evaluation of the Zoroastrian heritage had begun to emerge in the progressive milieu furthered by the new Pahlavi dynasty. Having gained political representation and an increased degree of tolerance, the Irani Zoroastrians grew more prosperous when some of them urbanized, principally in mercantile sectors. They were no longer aliens from Yazd as in former times. The Muslim response to Meher Baba at Isfahan is partly explainable in terms of the new cultural atmosphere that had developed, in which Shia Islam was far less insular than before. Now in Yazd, Baba was welcomed with great enthusiasm by Zoroastrian merchants and commoners, though the priestly response to him is a blank. In the wave of reformist tendencies infiltrating from Parsi India, some Irani Zoroastrians felt resentful at the way in which priestly mandates had dominated Zoroastrian life for such a lengthy period.

A wealthy Zoroastrian merchant known as Arbab Rustom Khushrav offered a bungalow to Meher Baba for the duration of his stay. The Irani visitor accepted, but as soon as the public located his abode, they descended upon the bungalow in large numbers. This time he permitted them to see him in an Iranian equivalent of *darshan*, and did not flee the scene. The leading merchant of Yazd was Arbab Sohrab, a Zoroastrian who had gained much influence in government and social circles. It was this man who played the major part in spreading news of Meher Baba's arrival, and in organizing various events that ensued. Those events extended to the participation of many Shi'i Muslims.

The visitor stayed for four days in Yazd, and could only accept some of the many invitations pressed upon him. On the second day, one of his visits was made to the home of a distinguished Zoroastrian known as Arbab Shahriyar (Sheriar), a devout man who regarded him as a prophet. In the afternoon of that same day, Baba attended a reception arranged at the home of Arbab Sohrab, where nearly thirty influential citizens of Yazd expressed their esteem for the visitor. The Arbab delivered a speech eulogizing the philanthropic activity and the sainthood of his silent guest. This was followed by an *extempore* speech from a Muslim, no less a figure than the Inspector of Finance of the Iranian government. He referred to Meher Baba by the title of *Hazrat*, and also in terms of his being a great *buzurg* (saint). This official is reported to have said: "I believe that he can teach us real religion and that he will revolutionize the world."[330]

The climax of the reception was open to all, both rich and poor, and thousands of people are reported to have poured into the grounds of the Arbab Sohrab's residence. Baba managed to make an exit, and went into the city centre, where thousands of inhabitants, mostly Muslims, had gathered to welcome him. His hosts had arranged that he visit places of public importance, and he now complied with this request. At the same time he instigated a search for a place of seclusion he could resort to, but no venue could be found that met his requirements. In the evening he moved out from the Muslim environs to Zoroastrian village precincts in Jafrabad, where the inhabitants welcomed him. He took a hurried meal at the home of his Irani disciple Baidul (R. B. Irani), a member of the *mandali* who had been despatched to Iran for a time. Baba returned afterwards to the city, being transported by car for safety. The streets of Yazd are said to have been packed with townspeople struggling to see him. He was taken to the Zoroastrian Girls' School, an institution in which he expressed a close interest. This school was a significant innovation of recent times, female education in Zoroastrianism having suffered for many centuries prior to the activities of reformists in Parsi India.

The third day of Baba's sojourn at Yazd was similarly busy. His name was by now a subject of conversation all over the city. Not only Muslims and Zoroastrians, but also Bahais and Babis[331] expressed a deference that was surprising to his own companions. Members of both these sects are said to have displayed a marked veneration for him, although it had been feared that they would resent him as a rival celebrity. In the afternoon Baba moved to another village called

117

Mubaraka. Both Muslims and Zoroastrians lived here. A setback occurred at this juncture. One of Meher Baba's travelling party was a young man called Aga Ali, the hero of the Prem Ashram whose Muslim family had become resentful of his tuition under a Zoroastrian mentor. This family now lived at Mubaraka and wanted Aga Ali to stay with them, though they had permitted him to join Baba's party at the port of Mohammerah. Now a special visit was made to their home, but the family elders insisted that the boy must remain with them and not participate further in the tour. Baba was not happy over this, but instructed Ali to remain at Mubaraka. The insular attitude of this boy's relatives may be gauged from the report that one of his uncles wanted to kill Baba, who was regarded as an interfering infidel. The fanatical elder concealed a pistol in his boot, intent upon murder. When he came face to face with Baba, his mood altered and he bowed to the Irani. He afterwards repented of his dire plan, and sent Baba a large basket of peaches as a gift.[332]

From Mubaraka, Meher Baba visited his ancestral village of Khooramshar, the birthplace of his father Sheriar and the home of his grandfather Mundegar the *salar*. He is reported to have been in a very good mood upon arrival. Local Zoroastrians must have deemed it a triumph that one of their own breed could become so feted by the Muslims of Yazd, their hereditary enemies of former generations who had kept them in servile subjection as *dhimmis*, as infidel labourers and fire-worshipping priests.

Several Bahais appeared with their local leader amongst the crowd which assembled at Khooramshar. They came from mere curiosity, their leader being determined not to acknowledge the visiting celebrity in any way. Yet when he came into the presence of Meher Baba, he gradually lost his reservations. To the surprise of his retinue, the Bahai leader first bowed before Baba, then asked his group to follow suit, then asked them to kiss the visitor's hand (a sign of esteem), and finally to prostrate themselves at the visitor's feet. Meher Baba undoubtedly possessed a strong charisma, and the fact that he was silent and did not lecture anyone appears to have left a good impression with Iranians. Some Bahais perhaps felt that they should honour a Zoroastrian *Hazrat*, someone who was quite distinct from the priestly contingent and the Muslim *ulama*.

When Baba returned to Yazd that evening, one of the visitors who approached him was another Bahai, this time an eminent figure of the sect, leader of the Bahais in Shiraz. He had come by aeroplane from his native city with the sole intention of meeting Baba. That intention was sectarian, as he intended to challenge the visitor with theological questions. Yet at the moment of encounter, he fell at Baba's feet exclaiming: "You are God!" This change of heart was perhaps triggered by the perception that Meher Baba was not a rival preacher; Bahais found that he did not fit the stereotype of religious teachers in Iran. When the Bahai leader departed, he moved through the crowd exclaiming "I have seen God!" Onlookers were fascinated, as it was considered a unique sight to see a Bahai preacher acting in this manner. Soon afterwards, this man gave an unorthodox sermon to a large gathering and declared: "If you want to see God, see Hazrat Meher Baba; in Hazrat Meher Baba, God has manifested Himself."[333]

The visitor from India insisted upon leaving at eleven a.m. on the fourth day at Yazd. He had found the city unsuitable for his seclusion purposes. Hundreds converged at his bungalow to bid farewell. They pleaded for photos of him to keep in memory, and his disciples like Kaikhushru Afseri gave away what they had. Even orthodox Shi'i Muslims were asking for photos of a Zoroastrian. In order to continue the journey, Baba had to leave the throng without being able to eat. The next morning his party arrived by car at the city of Kirman. At his command, the cars were driven into a garage, and the party remained behind closed doors. He did not want any visitors, but despite precautions taken, a Zoroastrian merchant known as Rustom Sohrab Irani learned of his arrival. This merchant was leader of the Zoroastrian Anjoman[334] of Kirman, and invited the visitor to his luxurious bungalow. Baba at first refused, but appeared to soften when it was urged that the party could make a secret entry at the abode in prospect. However, this plan evaporated when news of the visitor leaked out to the public. Hundreds gathered in the hope of seeing Baba, but he asked for the garage doors to be kept closed. The police were called to disperse the crowd.

After only a brief halt at Kirman, Baba and his men travelled on to Bam, where he stayed for two days in a quiet house, remaining secluded and inaccessible. He told his companions to deflect all visitors from seeing him, and remained incognito as Arbab Merwan (Arbab is not a name but a title of respect). A visitor who was bold in attempting an entry, and who succeeded, was a General of the Iranian army who arrived in full uniform complete with sabre; he expressed to Baba his belief that the spiritual rebirth of Iran was necessary as distinct from a show of military power. He made a gesture of placing his sword on the floor before Baba as a sign of respect. Another eminent visitor was the police commissioner of Bam, who admitted that he had gained entry to Baba by using a red tape procedure. Meher Baba told this man that he would return to Iran, break his silence, and "manifest," apparently meaning in Iran, or so it was assumed. (He did return in 1931.)

The incognito policy is notable. One of the reasons was evidently a concern to keep out of any political involvement. There had apparently been a rumour in circulation that he was an *imam* or *rasul* (saviour), and reactions were varied. Some of his new admirers had wished to hail him in public and make his name broadcast in all regions to encourage the change leading away from medieval attitudes. Some wished him to meet the Pahlavi monarch Reza Shah and to be publicly acknowledged as a spiritual benefactor of Iran. Influential men offered to arrange a meeting with the monarch, but Meher Baba declined. He would not agree to remaining a public focus of attention for any longer than his brief stay in Yazd; it was said that royalty might have envied the way in which he was so honoured there. Baba had certainly gained more adulation in that city than at any other place upon his travels. Yet his chosen vocation was non-political in orientation, and his journeys were generally undertaken in low profile. One may conclude that he did not exploit the Iranian situation to his advantage, as he chose to leave unobtrusively by taking the difficult overland route from Bam to Duzdab on his way back to India.

His companions expected him to take the easier and safer route by sea, but instead he made them hire a bus and an experienced Muslim driver. Baba insisted upon tackling the overland route to Duzdab, even though this entailed driving through a dangerous desert sector where many caravans had perished. The overland route was not intended for passenger traffic but the transport of goods. Before departing, Baba unexpectedly granted an audience to a number of local people in Bam who wanted to meet him. He left Bam in the afternoon of November 1st 1929, and there followed four arduous days of negotiating sand dunes and steep mountain roads with dangerous bends. Severe privations were encountered, and three men in the party became seriously ill. Arriving at Duzdab, they took the railway train to Quetta and Lahore.

Less than two years later, Meher Baba returned to Iran in June 1931. He went by car from Duzdab to Mashad in total secrecy, accompanied by only a small party. He had specified that he would give no interviews and that seclusion was his sole purpose. He stayed in Mashad for a fortnight, and would frequently walk about the city in disguise. The young Muslim Aga Ali had since rejoined him, and was one of his companions; Ali was now a personal attendant and was dexterous at reading Baba's alphabet board. Baba had a special interest in the shrine of Imam Reza, an important place of pilgrimage for Shi'i Muslims. For several nights he went to this shrine at midnight, remaining in seclusion inside for two hours while the *mandali* stood guard outside. This arrangement was only made with considerable difficulty. Religious orthodoxy prevailed at the shrine, and as Meher Baba was not a Muslim, he was prohibited from the precincts. A leading Shi'i divine, who was in charge of the shrine, made his entry possible by suspending the general rule; this intervention occurred because the cleric had been strongly influenced by a dream in which an important holy man entered Iran. The cleric believed that Meher Baba was the man he had dreamt of, and felt that he had been appointed to ensure the visitor's link with the sacred shrine.[335]

A few months later, in September 1931, Meher Baba made his first voyage to Europe, and in similar circumstances of low profile. He took with him only three disciples, namely Aga Ali, Rustom K. Irani (the son of Gulmai), and his Parsi secretary F. H. Dadachanji. His voyage was further obscured by the publicity devolving upon Mahatma Gandhi, who travelled on the same ship *Rajputana* for the purpose of attending the Round Table Conference in London. Meher Baba quickly moved on from Britain to America, where it was discovered that the New World was not very welcoming. The immigration officer at New York disapproved of Baba's silence and was suspicious of his alphabet board. The official exclaimed contemptuously: "You came to America to teach our people with this board! How foolish!"[336] American democracy had misinterpreted the event, as no teaching mission had been planned. Nobody knew of Baba's arrival except two or three people who had come to the docks to meet him. He stayed in America for a few weeks only, remaining in low profile, giving private interviews which rarely lasted longer than five minutes.

On his second visit to Europe, in the spring of 1932, some of his new English followers tried to publicize his presence. The press thus elaborated a description of him as the "Indian messiah." The journalist James Douglas had prepared a questionnaire with the collaboration of the orientalist scholar Sir Denison Ross. Douglas later wrote that this document was designed to trap the foreign visitor. It is relevant to ask what Sir Denison Ross was doing in his erudite behind the scenes role as the trapper of British Empire subjects. Such scholars, very comfortably established behind Empire desks, were perhaps not the best assessors of what was happening in the contemporary world. It is very doubtful whether Sir Denison had accomplished one tenth as much humanitarian work as Meher Baba; he had not bathed lepers, for instance. He researched texts and penned elegant monographs amongst a handful of literati who never went near untouchables, unlike Meher Baba. Such members of the academic caste invariably travelled and lived in comfortable accommodation, unlike Meher Baba. What did Sir Denison Ross really know about Asiatic mysticism? He was cut off from it, viewing the mystics as aliens and himself as a bastion of knowledge, powered by his august credentials and backed up by his salary. This situation continued until very recent times, and perhaps still continues today in some departments.

James Douglas felt obliged to report in the *Sunday Express* of April 10th, 1932, that Meher Baba had threaded his way through the questionnaire without stumbling. "His mastery of dialectic is consummate; it was quite Socratic in its ease."[337] Very possibly he did not need to try very hard, as the questions were so simplistic that only an orientalist scholar or a journalist might have found them difficult. Baba politely told the interrogation that he was a Persian, and that although he had been born in Poona, his father and mother were both Persians. That ought to have stopped the slang about the Indian messiah, but it could not stop the loaded question: "Are you a pantheist?" (Western scholars often went into intellectual contortions over the word pantheism, this being considered a dire crime by Christian theologians). With a Persian smile, Meher Baba replied no. "When you know God, it is plain; the Self is one with Him at the height of experience."[338] It may be doubted whether preoccupations with pantheism would have enabled scholars and journalists to view alternatives in an enlightened manner. This interchange conceivably spotlights one reason why Meher Baba made such a habit of being incognito, and why he afterwards told his over-enthusiastic British devotees to cease their publicity drive in future.

Some critics could not understand why he afterwards made a visit to Hollywood, and why he participated in what appeared to be "Italian holidays" with a group of middle class British women.[339] Perhaps he considered that when not secluding himself in an Umbrian cave, the society women were an entertainment and less presumptuous in their attitudes[340] than the learned scholars of the Empire. It is evident that he preferred the down to earth tendencies of the Kimco group to the obsessive "esotericism" of people like Meredith Starr and Paul Brunton. Starr insisted upon routine meditation for all at his retreat in Devon, even when Baba was present, and wanted to be the leading disciple in all situations.[341] Brunton had met Baba in India, and was at first an admirer; yet he turned nasty when his expectations were thwarted.[342] Brunton produced a distorting account of events in a bestselling book that was uncritically received by his readers. As an accompaniment to his string of popular books, Brunton improvised the credentials of Ph.D., a very suspect innovation which has been suggested as the consequence of his belief that he studied philosophy at the "Astral University," an elusive institution which he supposedly encountered during his astral travels.[343] The dubious credentials deceived a large general readership who imagined that Brunton was an expert in Eastern religious texts. Instead of conducting Yoga classes with psychologically unbalanced meditators, Meher Baba preferred to visit places like Avila and Assisi and Hollywood. An idiosyncrasy of his was to indicate that he would soon break his silence, an event which was never in any obvious evidence; this device shook off irksome characters like Meredith Starr, and might be regarded in the light of a test set for superfluous expectations.

With regard to Meher Baba's temporary focus upon Hollywood, this does not have to be regarded as the superficial diversion of an entity who was not sufficiently spiritual. He was perhaps being practical in a project of investigating what the cinema might do to inspire the masses. He wanted eligible contacts to make a film incorporating spiritual themes, but the project did not achieve fruition, and he afterwards abandoned the link with movie producers. In his view, the cinema was a medium that should inspire to finer horizons – it sometimes achieved that until America became the permissive society and Hollywood churned out too many four letter word obscenities and other crudities to enrich exploiters of perverted democracy.

Even when Richard Attenborough made his award-winning film about Mahatma Gandhi years after the death of Meher Baba, critics found much to disagree with in the content of the movie version of Indian Independence. To ascertain what really happened in some matters is not straightforward. Strangely enough perhaps, the neglected Meher Baba emerges in the database as one of the "fringe" participants in a key issue of the Indian national drama: untouchability.

Mahatma Gandhi had first met Meher Baba during his voyage to London in September 1931. The press distorted their contact by creating the story that Meher Baba was the spiritual adviser of Gandhi. Their meetings and exchange of correspondence occurred at another level. It is evident that Gandhi was more than a little interested in Meher Baba, and that he was fascinated by aspects of the Irani's activity and teaching. He must have compared the benign Meher Baba, silent and yet so cordially communicative via the alphabet board, with the explosive figure of Upasni Maharaj. Gandhi could not understand why Baba asserted that Upasni was a spiritual giant. Yet he could readily appreciate other matters such as Meher Baba's humanitarian activity, his acute sympathy for the untouchables that was so rare amongst Indian holy men, his cosmopolitan inter-religious following, his seclusions and fasts, his low media profile and incognito journeys. Baba insisted that he would not participate in political issues, which were the primary concern of Gandhi. Yet Gandhi clearly wanted to know the Irani's view of contemporary events. He even urged that Baba should meet Dr. Bhimrao Ramji Ambedkar (1891–1956), leader of the untouchables, who was not on good terms with caste Hindus. Gandhi was subsequently imprisoned by the British government.

On September 6th 1932, Meher Baba sent one of his Hindu disciples, Dr. Nilkanth (alias Nilu) Godse, to visit Dr. Ambedkar. Nilu was still in medical school in Bombay at that time, and Baba was staying at Nasik. Dr. Ambedkar was interested in the Irani mystic, and agreed to see him immediately. Ambedkar had been born in Maharashtra as a *mahar*, and cannot have missed registering Baba's sympathy with the *mahars*. Baba had already met some of the other untouchable leaders earlier in the year.[344] The new meeting was arranged at a venue in Bombay, and Meher Baba went specially to that city to meet Dr. Ambedkar on September 12th. A record was made of the conversation. Both men stated that they had wanted to meet each other for a long time. Meher Baba reiterated that he had no connection with political events, but also made clear that he held the untouchable cause very dear. He described how he had made *brahmans* at his ashram live and eat with untouchables, and how he had made his *brahman* followers bathe untouchable boys against caste scruples. He said that a lengthy meeting had occurred between himself and Gandhi the day before the latter's arrest by the British; Gandhi had asked him to tell the Harijan leaders to accept a joint electorate. Gandhi had promised that if the Harijans would accept this plan, he would meet them and be very sympathetic to their rights, and use his influence to ensure justice. (Yet at that time, Gandhi still needed to make concessions about the reservation of seats for untouchables at government level.)

Meher Baba added his own view to Gandhi's incentive. He advised Ambedkar to accept the proposal of a joint electorate, and also stipulated "a reservation of seats" to represent untouchables. Baba said that the best way to secure the rights of untouchables (he did not refer to Harijans) was to act now. He said that to press for a separate electorate for the depressed classes would be to "run the risk of forever clashing with Hindu society and establishing yourself as a separate class, branded Untouchable forever and least desired."[345] He added that Gandhi was sincere and would keep his word; Gandhi's influence would carry weight with other classes (i.e., *brahman* and *kshatriya*, Gandhi being a *vaishya*). Baba further commented that he (Baba) would inwardly help the cause of the depressed classes. Such statements referred to his "inner work," regarded by some as a saintly eccentricity. Whatever the status of such references, there is no doubt that Meher Baba was sincere in his desire to aid the untouchables, and that he trusted Gandhi's integrity.

Dr. Ambedkar replied that he would like to do as he was advised here, but said that he had to first consult his untouchable colleagues, both at provincial and all-India level. He promised to argue for the new plan. This meeting was omitted from official history, and some readers have been surprised to find that it occurred. Dr. Ambedkar evidently agreed to the meeting and also to present the new proposal because he knew that Meher Baba was sincere and that the Irani was a completely independent entity from caste Hinduism. It may even be that Meher Baba had influenced Gandhi in the direction of including the untouchables more comprehensively by catering to their political requirements of representative seats.

Shortly after Baba's meeting with Dr. Ambedkar, he sent two of his disciples (a Parsi and a Muslim) to visit Gandhi, who was incarcerated at Poona in Yeravda jail. F. H. Dadachanji and Ramju Abdulla arrived for an interview on September 21st, 1932. Their conversation was recorded. Gandhi seems to have been puzzled as to why there was so little news of Meher Baba on the media. "I often enquire of those near me as to why there is no news of Meher Baba."[346] Gandhi thought that Baba had maintained his silence for too long; he could not understand the restraint of the non-politician. He was surprised to hear that Baba had recently been travelling not merely in America, but also in China and Japan (very briefly in Japan, and incognito in both the Oriental countries). The two envoys dutifully told Gandhi about misrepresentations which had appeared in Western newspapers concerning his connection with Baba, and they also relayed a rather enigmatic message from their teacher that he (Baba) wished Gandhi to fast for forty days. Gandhi mildly remonstrated at this message, saying that people were uneasy about his newly commenced fast. Ramju construed that Baba was asking Gandhi to continue; however, there was an appended clause that Gandhi should spend the fortieth night of the proposed fast with Baba, which would win him enlightenment. This clause was in response to a former desire of Gandhi to spend a night of privation with Baba in order to gain the "key."[347]

The immediate context of this message to Gandhi was significant. The Hindu politician had decided to commence a "fast unto death" on September 20th, one purpose being to provoke caste Hindu conscience into appropriate action with regard to the untouchables. Yet Rabindranath Tagore was worried that Gandhi would die of starvation in such a difficult attempt at resolution. It is evident that Meher Baba was encouraging Gandhi to fast, though for a limited period only. During those tense few days, a process of negotiation with Ambedkar was underway while Gandhi's blood pressure grew critical. The Ambedkar-Gandhi convergence resulted in the Yeravda Pact on September 24th, 1932, an event of some importance. On September 25th, Ambedkar gave a speech in Bombay which praised Gandhi's conciliatory attitude over the new political agreement between Hindus and untouchables. Yet he also expressed his regret that Gandhi had not been more agreeable the previous year, when he had opposed the "Harijan reserved seats" that he was now endorsing. Some X factor had modified Gandhi's attitude. The day after Ambedkar's speech, Gandhi broke his fast when the British government approved the Pact.

It is difficult to avoid the implications that Meher Baba was a bridge between the two principal players in this national drama. His role was ignored by the caste Hindus and subsequently overlooked by both Gandhi and Ambedkar. Meanwhile, as a result of Gandhi's fasting, the changing tide of public opinion made many Hindu temples open to untouchables for the first time. Other prohibitions were also relaxed. Dr. Ambedkar will have known that Meher Baba's sanction of the new integrative plan made sense, though he never publicized this feature of the situation (and nor did Meher Baba, who remained incognito). The Yeravda Pact declared that nobody would be regarded as an untouchable by reason of his birth.

Some progress had undoubtedly been made. Yet there was a long way to go. The untouchables eventually fared badly at the hands of caste Hinduism, even though untouchability was officially banned and Dr. Ambedkar was able to draft portions of the new Indian Constitution. In principle the untouchables had a chance to emerge as social equals; in practice they remained underdogs to high caste Hindus who benefited from Gandhi's feats of diplomacy to secure Independence.

Reverting back to Yeravda jail, the episode of the emissaries from Meher Baba is of interest. Chanji and Ramju were made very welcome by Gandhi in a courtyard of the prison, and they conversed with him for several hours that day (September 21st, 1932). Baba's full message was that the settlement of the electorate problem, for which Gandhi had started fasting, would soon be resolved. The request for Gandhi to fast for forty days was qualified by the emissaries in terms of Baba's wish for Gandhi to "keep on fasting, if possible." Gandhi was worried about his bodily stamina, and Ramju told him of Baba's encouragement in this respect, reporting cases amongst the *mandali* who had fasted without physical harm. Gandhi seems to have forgotten his own reference to the "key" in a former conversation with Baba, though his interest in the latter is evident from his disclosure that "almost every day" in the jail there was some reference to the Irani in the conversations of his party. Gandhi was evidently doubtful that a settlement would be "reached and confirmed both here and in London," though he was committed to the theme that "untouchability must disappear."

The "fortieth night" never occurred. The speed and decisiveness of the new agreement embodied in the Yeravda Pact surprised many onlookers, both Indian and international. There was no further meeting between Meher Baba and Gandhi, though in subsequent years there were occasions when Baba sent emissaries to Gandhi with messages. Baba is said to have urged Gandhi to come to him, warning that Gandhi's life was in danger. Some say that Baba wanted Gandhi to give up his political career.[348] It is definite that Gandhi was assassinated by a Hindu extremist.

In one of his communications, Meher Baba stated: "India became depressed with the establishment of the depressed classes. When the depressed classes are raised up, India will find herself to be one of the greatest countries, if not the greatest, in the world."[349]

During the Second World War, Meher Baba opposed Gandhi's stress on pacifism in the face of Hitler and the Japanese aggression, and his emphases again converged with those of Dr. Ambedkar, who was pro-British and who advised untouchables to join the British army in the interests of defence. Meher Baba stated that "the ideal of non-violence, in the face of aggression, is impractical for the masses."[350] When Gandhi was informed of Baba's outlook on this subject, he expressed shock and said that it was "wholly inapplicable." Meher Baba tried through intermediaries to make Gandhi change his mind on that issue, but the politician refused to do so.[351]

There were notable differences in other directions also. In December 1933, Meher Baba made a very critical reflection about Upasni Maharaj and Narayan Maharaj of Kedgaon. He observed that both of these Hindu gurus were allowing the *brahmans* much ceremonial latitude. He accused those ceremonies of being sectarian, and said that it was a waste of the thousands of rupees that were expended in such functions. He said that the two gurus specified were themselves "above and beyond these caste prejudices," and that even Swami Vivekananda, despite his learning, had given his environment a typically Hindu atmosphere. Meher Baba also remarked that he himself was not following any particular religion or endorsing sectarianism (he eludes all categories of doctrinaire Zoroastrianism). He had even stopped allowing *arati* and *puja* on festive occasions, contrary to his earlier years at Meherabad. Some of the *mandali* (ashram staff) were surprised at his sharp criticisms, and he then treated the matter affably, saying that he had been joking about the wasting of funds. Yet there was still a sting in his accompanying remark that sectarian *brahmans* were trying to gain the upper hand at the ashrams of Upasni and Narayan Maharaj, "where caste, creed and ceremonial demonstrations have no place and should have vanished."[352] Although he had muted the critique, he had made his point very strongly against the underlying trend in caste Hinduism. He was accusing the ashrams at Sakori and Kedgaon of being retrogressive. Caste had been eliminated at his own ashram.

It was notably Meher Baba who intervened in the legal proceedings that were instigated against Upasni Maharaj after he had made the *kanyas* his "spiritual wives" in 1932. Some of Upasni's detractors in Rahuri filed a lawsuit against him. Not content with this, the hostile party spread abroad much slander, claiming that Upasni was a polygamist and had seduced young girls into his ashram for illicit purposes. When Meher Baba was acquainted with the details, he asked his disciple Rustom K. Irani to have the legal proceedings transferred to a court in Ahmednagar, and this was done. Afterwards, on September 20th 1934, he sent Adi K. Irani, Vishnu Deorukhkar, and another Hindu disciple[353] to Sakori with a special message for Upasni. Baba said that he was in financial difficulty, and requested repayment of a loan of 15,000 rupees which he had made to Upasni in the early 1920s. If this request was met, he would postpone his next trip to the West and free Upasni from his problem in the law courts with the assistance of influential devotees like Sir Akbar Hyderi.

When Upasni received this message, he gave a reply which was recorded. He complained that his detractors had been successful in off-putting devotees who had formerly visited him and contributed donations to Sakori ashram. He scarcely had enough money to maintain his defence in the court, and his cattle were reduced to a skeletal appearance for lack of fodder. He said that Merwanji[354] (Meher Baba) could have these cattle if he wanted. He requested that Merwanji should move to Sakori and manage things for him. "Tell Merwan that I seek his forgiveness for not being of any use to him; by his own righteous deeds, he has realized God."[355] Upasni had thus again reversed his denial of Baba's spiritual talents, a denial evoked in 1923. Upasni was observed to be weeping (not characteristic of him) as he bowed to the three envoys, saying that he was a beggar with nothing left.

The envoys returned to Meherabad, and two days later, Baba sent a further message to Upasni, saying that he would postpone his journey to the West as a consequence of Upasni's legal problem.[356] Subsequent events in this regard are still partly obscure, though Upasni's position was eventually vindicated, and helped by the apology of the erring Durgabai Karmakar. Sakori ashram began to attract visitors again. This period was not adequately evaluated by Narasimhaswami and other writers on Sakori events, who left out some happenings in ignorance. The slander mounted by detractors during the 1930s was severe, and very offputting to high caste Hindus, who included Narasimhaswami. The basis for the slander was gossip, female jealousy, and the brahmanical demotion of female rights.

On February 16th, 1936, Upasni made a significant visit to the home of Gulmai Irani in Ahmednagar. This event is missing in orthodox annals of Sakori. The date was that of Meher Baba's forty-second birthday according to the Zoroastrian calendar. The venue was the Khushru Quarters, as the building was known, and here Gulmai had been instructed by Meher Baba to stay after spending a lengthy period at his ashram (where she was part of the embryonic women's ashram, though her role in events was later understated in the devotional literature of the Meher Baba sect, which preferred to view his sister Mani as the major figure alongside Mehera J. Irani).[357] Gulmai's son Adi visited her that day, and later penned an account of the event. Baba was absent from Meherabad, being in Mysore, and had stipulated that there was to be no birthday celebration in his honour. Adi and his Zoroastrian colleague Padri (F. N. Driver) were just about to leave Khushru Quarters when Upasni arrived in the rear seat of a car. The visitor was wearing his usual gunny cloth. Upasni walked into a room that had long been reserved for his use during his visits to Ahmednagar. Gulmai used this room for prayers and contemplation, and had lovingly preserved the gunny cloth which Upasni had worn on his first visit to her former abode (*Sarosh Manzil*) in 1921. This cloth was spread on the floor in the shape of a settee, and was referred to as the *gadi* (seat) of Maharaj in accordance with Hindu custom. Facing this was a wooden settee used by Meher Baba, whose photograph was prominently displayed on that item of furniture. Upasni was accompanied by his secretary B. T. Wagh, a Hindu who was very sceptical about rivals to his guru (as he chose to regard them), including Meher Baba. Upasni sent this man away on an errand into the city, leaving himself alone with the Zoroastrians.

Upasni occupied his *gadi*. To be more precise, he stood on the *gadi* in a rapt attitude of prayer, his hands folded. Adi K. Irani was amazed to see him uttering words of prayer as he looked intently at the photograph of Meher Baba. This was an unprecedented event, and continued for a full five minutes. Afterwards Upasni said that he liked the photo, and added: "I like Merwan. He is great. He is unique. I bow before him. Let me pray in his presence. Please convey my salutation to him."[358]

Adi writes that he was puzzled by this demonstration of respect. In Hindu custom, it is the disciple who owes respect and allegiance to his guru, and not vice versa. Adi was even more surprised when Upasni asked Gulmai for a tray and a lamp with which to perform the "*arati* of Merwan." She hastily fetched these objects, and Upasni began waving the tray around Baba's photo while chanting praises. This was quite unprecedented, and would have been strongly resented by some devotees at Sakori. Upasni further asked Gulmai to tell Baba that he had been to Khushru Quarters on his (Baba's) birthday, prayed in front of his picture, and performed his *arati*. The homage was clearly intended as a birthday celebration. Adi K. Irani comments that he had seen Upasni eulogize Meher Baba on many occasions in the past, but never in this manner of homage.[359]

Upasni's new attitude of reverence for Meher Baba was difficult for the *brahmans* at Sakori to assimilate. They managed once again to eschew the facts, even if this was more difficult for them to do while their guru was alive. Upasni kept sending messengers to Meher Baba to request that he take over the management of Sakori ashram. These events were not publicly aired, but were well known to the minority concerned. These requests of Upasni were insistent in 1936 and continued until 1940; Meher Baba's replies were adamant that the Hindu sectarian atmosphere at Sakori would have to end before he could agree to the request. In May 1940 he delegated Adi K. Irani to relay his latest reply to Upasni. His communication firmly set three conditions in the event of his becoming manager of Sakori:

1)   All the Hindu rituals at Sakori would have to stop.
2)   The value of Sakori ashram, now known as Upasni Nagar, was less than 500,000 rupees. This sum would have to be paid by Baba in instalments (as he did not have immediate access to that sort of funding).
3)   Upasni was to execute a gift deed, and in the event of the full amount being paid for the ashram, he should deliver the deed to Meher Baba.

Upasni was more than usually compliant with these demands, and Adi returned to Meherabad with the reply. Meher Baba promptly dictated a finalizing arrangement, saying that he would pay 50,000 rupees on August 1st 1940, and the balance after four months if his requirements were met. He listed three reasons for his decision:
(a)   To create unity between religions by abolishing "the Hindu rituals, ceremonies and customs" that were dominant at Sakori ashram.
(b)   To free Upasni from the responsibility of running the ashram.
(c)   To remove the notoriety wrongly associated with Upasni's "spiritual marriage" to the nuns at Sakori, a notoriety also reflecting unfavourably upon Meher Baba as the disciple of Upasni.[360]

The upshot was that Upasni agreed to all the conditions. Meher

Baba sent a letter to Gulmai Irani, who was then staying with Upasni at Sakori, expressing his satisfaction with the agreement and stating that he would pay a lump sum of 500,000 rupees within six months, as he had many running expenses involved in his different ashrams and in maintaining various devotees and their families.[361]

On May 18th 1940, Yeshwantrao Borawke arrived at Meherabad to see Baba. He was one of Upasni's chief disciples, and had been on close terms with Baba during his visits to Sakori in much earlier years. Yeshwantrao was outstanding for his affinity with Meher Baba in the face of brahmanical resistance at Sakori. The new agreement was like a bombshell to the orthodox contingent. They doubtless applied pressure on that issue. Whatever happened precisely, the new agreement did not reach fruition and Meher Baba did not assume management of Sakori ashram, which remained an outpost of caste Hinduism.

For several years Upasni had been informing Gulmai "I wish to see Merwanji." He wanted Baba to meet him at Sakori. This was not an open disclosure. Gulmai passed on the message to Baba in her rare capacity as joint disciple of these two mystics. Baba said that he would only meet Upasni once more, but not at Sakori, and that he would not be able to speak because he was observing silence. Upasni agreed to abide by these terms, and wanted the meeting to occur at a deserted spot known as Dahigaon, a few miles from Sakori. Here stood a thatched hut in a garden which was chosen as the venue. The meeting took place in secretive conditions with only a very small number of people present outside the hut.

The meeting at Dahigaon was scheduled for October 17th, 1941. The hut was about forty miles north of Meherabad, and Meher Baba was driven there by car with a few of his disciples, including Gulmai, who was the only woman present. When the party arrived from Meherabad, they found Yeshwantrao Borawke waiting for them, Upasni having sent him to unlock and clean out the hut. At 4.30 p.m. Baba despatched Gulmai with Sarosh K. Irani to bring Upasni from Sakori; they were told to bring nobody else but Upasni. At 5.30 p.m. the car returned, and Upasni alighted and walked to the hut, the others having been told to keep outside the compound. The meeting lasted only half an hour, and then Upasni was driven back to Sakori. Baba afterwards gave a brief report of the meeting, which exists in different versions. He said that he bowed to Upasni and then Upasni embraced him and wept; they sat down and Upasni talked about the World

War, Baba's silence, and other matters. Baba motioned that they should leave the hut but Upasni detained him for a further five minutes, saying that the powers of various *sadgurus* were vested in him (Baba) and that "I leave everything to you."[362]

Two months later, Upasni died as recorded above. Meher Baba told those of his followers concerned to cease going to Sakori now that Upasni was dead.[363] He was not interested in being feted as the successor of Upasni, and actually gave an alternative explanation.[364] He cannot be accused of exploiting the situation. The subsequent history of Sakori ashram in relation to Meher Baba is complex. A strong opposition to him continued amongst the male contingent there after the death of Upasni. The favoured version of Upasni's life was Narasimhaswami's *Sage of Sakori*, a problematic work. Many events did not gain due recognition or clarification in that work. In 1954 Meher Baba stated to a small group of Westerners: "The men there (at Sakori) made it appear that I was not the spiritual heir of Maharaj, only of Babajan, and spread the news that Godavri was in charge of the ashram and Maharaj's spiritual heir."[365] Another statement of Baba on record is that the men at Sakori "had spread rumours that I was not spiritual but was an ordinary disciple of Maharaj and therefore Godavri was given the charge of the ashram."[366]

According to Meher Baba's own report, Godavri Mataji kept quiet about him during the 1940s, although she did not agree with views of the male devotees at Sakori. "Godavri loved me in secret," he said, although they had never met. The Sakori *brahmans* became increasingly annoyed that he gained a growing number of followers. Upasni's secretary Wagh had become a major figure of the management at Sakori, and some accounts refer to him as the manager. "He (Wagh) used to spit when anyone spoke of Baba at Sakori."[367] The atmosphere of suppression may be imagined.

However, Godavri overcame this trend of bias. She met Baba at Ahmednagar and invited him to visit Sakori.[368] There were two occasions when he made visits. His visit there on November 14th, 1952, was very brief and occurred at sundown. This was the first time he had set foot in Sakori for thirty years.[369] A more extensive reception occurred on his subsequent trip to Sakori on March 20th, 1954. The event which facilitated this visit was the "housewarming" celebration at the new abode of the faithful Yeshwantrao Borawke, who lived just outside the ashram precincts. There Baba was garlanded, and he continued on to meet a warm reception from Godavri Mataji and the *kanyas*. One of his travelling party has commented: "Godavri Mai, although now the head of the entire ashram, likewise bowed down to Baba without hesitation, the way she used to pay homage to Maharaj."[370]

The mood at Sakori had been divided. The manager Wagh and his supporters were averse to Baba's visit, being worried about Godavri taking his *darshan*, an action which could be interpreted as a gesture of defeat for the opponents, and which would mean that Sakori ashram had irrevocably welcomed Meher Baba as a spiritual celebrity. Godavri's action of bowing down to Baba seriously compromised the position of the opponents.[371]

Many persons present on that occasion had misgivings about what Baba's attitude would be towards them; they also knew that he disapproved of the ritualism and customs of caste Hinduism. Meher Baba proved conciliatory and diplomatic in his statements, though he did not neglect to assert his spiritual status, contrary to the stigma that he was an ordinary disciple. He walked around the temples and other buildings, and then sat down near Upasni's tomb and the cage (*pinjra*). At his side were Godavri and Gulmai Irani, the latter being the only woman in his party. A crowd of perhaps two hundred people were present as he gave a spontaneous "talk" on his alphabet board. He alternated between three languages – Marathi, Gujarati, and English – a by no means uncommon event in his case, and one that made reproduction of his words rather difficult. He covered basic Sakori history very sympathetically, scrupulously refraining from reference to the hostilities which had been meted out to him. He praised Upasni, and referred to the misunderstandings generated by Durgabai (whom he always called Durgamai), the woman who had become jealous of the attention given to the *kanyas*. He allusively described Upasni as having played a "dual role," and neatly explained away Upasni's assertion in the early 1920s that he had "given nothing to Merwan." Baba indicated that Upasni had not told any untruth; there was nothing to give, a gnosis having been evoked in him (Baba). He also recounted an episode occurring in the early 1930s when Durgabai's son Raghunath had come to Meherabad with a message from her which expressed her belief that Upasni had become a victim of lust, won over by young girls, and thus she requested Baba to visit Sakori. He (Baba) had told Raghunath in reply that: "You and your dear mother are completely wrong."[372] Baba had then said that Raghunath could not even begin to fathom the nature of Upasni's "spiritual work"

134

and that there was no need for him (Baba) to visit Sakori. He had given a message for Durgabai not to lose her trust in Upasni.

Baba also told the assembly at Sakori that his visit was made in fulfilment of his promise to Upasni (at their last meeting) to keep an eye on that ashram. He was very tactful over the question of rituals. He addressed the *kanyas* on this point and said that "although God is beyond all ceremonies and rituals," they should obey Upasni's instruction to conduct their worship in the way he had outlined. They should not "perform these ceremonies mechanically with a dry mind, or else they will bind you." The objective was to realize that everything but God is illusion, and "unless and until you experience this, all else is just bunkum."373

Baba's commentary on events seems to have produced a new sense of respect for him amongst some of the audience. He had made it easy for opponents to accept an olive branch. He moved about the ashram with Godavri, who was undoubtedly the most responsive amongst the host contingent, and after lunch gave a discourse. He departed by car that afternoon, and stopped by the side of the road on the journey home. He then conveyed to his companions that he was very pleased with the visit, and that Godavri had made the gesture of requesting him to sit on the swing (*jhula*) used by Upasni, an item of great devotional significance in Krishna worship. He had told her: "Play your part as (Upasni) Maharaj has instructed you, without any doubts."374 He had then asked her whether she would do something if he (and not Maharaj) asked her to. She replied, "If I can do so in this ashram atmosphere." Baba then requested her to accomplish "something that was quite simple but not very easy."375 She agreed, but he would afterwards not divulge any details to others.

Despite his positive assessment of the event, Baba said that he would not again go to Sakori. However, he did relax this consideration later the same year, saying that he should fulfil the prediction of Upasni that Merwanji would bring Westerners to Sakori. He arranged with Godavri to visit Sakori ashram again on September 20th 1954, and took with him a group of sixteen Western male devotees who were staying at Meherabad for a few weeks. The ashram manager Wagh led the reception party at Sakori, and from the gate of the village Baba's car (belonging to Sarosh Irani) was taken in a procession to the ashram with a brass band playing in front. When Baba alighted, Godavri and the *kanyas* performed his *arati*, and afterwards a further routine involving the *jhula* (swing) was engaged upon. It was clear that Godavri wished her companions to worship the visitor, despite her own status in the ashram, and she herself rocked the sacred swing while Baba sat on it. A devotional song was uttered in two separate performances of this rite, after which Baba gave a separate interview to Godavri. He asked all the Westerners to bow down to Upasni's tomb, first bowing himself by way of example. Not all of the visitors were keen to do this, a few knowing comparatively little about the deceased and feeling alienated from Hindu customs. Yet everyone complied. The visit lasted two and a half hours. Two of the Westerners wrote of Baba: "He looked strained and suffering, as he did throughout the visit."[376] This contrasts with reports of his radiance on his earlier visit in March.

Wagh took the Westerners on a tour of the ashram and had interests in showing them literature. An American named Ludwig Dimpfl relates of this occasion that the visiting group encountered some of the followers of Upasni. "Although we did not know it at the time, they regarded Baba as a rival who was competing for loyalties."[377] These people were keen to exchange addresses and had "a number of books by and about Maharaj ready to distribute to us."[378] Dimpfl obtained this literature, but on the way back to Meherabad, Baba took the books away from him and other members of the party, insisting that all the Sakori literature should be relinquished,[379] saying he would give it back later if necessary. He gave a significant explanation for this action the following day, which the Westerners failed to include in their reports, but which was incorporated in a less well known diary written by an Indian devotee of Meher Baba, namely Kishan Singh. This report did not surface for many years in the relevant literature, and has to date been overlooked by theorists of the supposed "Sai Baba movement." It is incumbent here to give some attention to what Meher Baba is reported to have said.

He referred to the subject of miracles, disclaiming any performance of these. He warned against the atmosphere of preoccupation with miracles that existed at Shirdi. This disposition was present to a lesser degree at Sakori. The distractions at both places were due to "one very good soul who made a mess of things because of his ignorance."[380] He then named B. V. Narasimhaswami as the culprit, and gave a brief but graphic account of that individual's career. He said that Narasimhaswami had come to him in Nasik and requested to stay with him and write his biography. This request was declined, and Baba suggested that Narasimhaswami instead go to Sakori and write the biography

136

of Upasni Maharaj. "This dear fellow got very upset,"[381] which may be read as an understatement. The frustrated biographer did go to Sakori, stayed for some while, and wrote the book *Sage of Sakori*. (This book had been salient in the literature given to the Westerners visiting Sakori the day prior to these disclosures). It seems to have been primarily because of this book that Baba had asked for the Sakori literature to be relinquished by his guests. When writing his book about Upasni Maharaj, Narasimhaswami "gave his own interpretations."[382] Meher Baba's description of this book was recorded by Kishan Singh as: "Half of it is good and half absolute nonsense."[383]

According to the same report, Meher Baba said that after writing *Sage of Sakori*, Narasimhaswami "began to doubt Maharaj for keeping young girls and so forth, but this book was already published."[384] No dates are supplied. "He then went to Shirdi to the shrine of Sai Baba,"[385] where he gathered information from the local people and devotees about the miracles of Shirdi Sai. Meher Baba described these supposed miracles as "petty things," and in this context referred to "how Sai Baba blessed women and they got children, how he placed his hand on the head of a poor man and he became rich, and how he lit a lamp with water."[386] Narasimhaswami gave wide publicity to his miracle-filled account and people began to flock to the Shirdi shrine from all over India.

Meher Baba blamed Narasimhaswami for having created the "miracle instinct" at both Shirdi and Sakori. Visitors to Sakori were habitually given *Sage of Sakori* to read, as this fitted management ideas of what Upasni Maharaj did and taught. The mood for miracles dovetailed with ritualism. Baba explained to his guests that he had taken away their literature on Sakori so that they would not be confused about the contents.[387]

Even taking into account any possible errors in transcription, this report amply testifies that Meher Baba's view of the popular presentation of Shirdi Sai and Upasni Maharaj was dismissive, and indeed, was diametrically opposed to the tastes encouraged by Satya Sai, who has relied heavily upon the standard image of the miracleworker at Shirdi. The differing orientations are so marked as to merit an acute criticism of the academic theory that all these diverse figures – Shirdi Sai, Upasni Maharaj, Godavri Mataji, Meher Baba, and Satya Sai – are appropriately brought under the label of "Sai Baba movement." That label is a very dubious conflation used by those who do not properly assess the relevant materials,[388] including Narasimhaswami's

Life of Sai Baba.[389]

Godavri Mataji had furthered the cordial relations with Meher Baba when she attended his mass *darshan* at Wadia Park in Ahmednagar on September 12th, 1954. She was visible on the platform where Baba sat underneath a large *pandal* (tent), and was accompanied by thirteen of her nuns. She had also visited Meherabad on September 14th with the same *kanyas*, again taking Baba's *darshan*.[390] He often praised her, and at the end of September he remarked: "She is a unique female personality and loves me beyond words, and to me she is the dearest of the dear."[391]

Wagh and other senior male devotees at Sakori attended the special gatherings for men held at Meherabad on September 29th–30th. Meher Baba then publicly introduced key men at Sakori, and magnanimously called Wagh "one of the few main pillars of Sakori."[392] Yet despite Godavri's instigation of change in Sakori ashram, and her subsequent contacts with Baba,[393] various men of that institution seem to have perpetuated the old idea of Baba's rivalry with Upasni. Meher Baba's three visits to Sakori in the early 1950s are perhaps reminiscent of Upasni's visits to Shirdi in 1925 and 1936 when much veneration was expressed for the latter, although the official Shirdi view remained one of sectarian division. Too many devotees had imagined that Upasni was a rival of Sai Baba; too many devotees afterwards believed that Meher Baba was a rival of Upasni and an ordinary disciple. So many beliefs created by sectarians pass muster as "history," a deficit which appears to be available in many biographies and hagiographies attached to diverse religious traditions.

The establishment of a women's ashram was very rare in India at that time. The one formed by Meher Baba predated that of Upasni, and followed a different format. The inmates of both ashrams were celibate, but there were no Hindu auspices in the one created at Meherabad in the mid-1920s. Rituals were eschewed, and textual recitation was non-existent. The Zoroastrian core of the Meherabad women's ashram was supplemented in the 1930s by a number of Western women, most of whom departed over the years back to Western countries.[394] There were no initiations or special robes, and the lifestyle, though very simple and sheltered, was not geared to any institutional programme. During the 1940s, the home of the Zoroastrian women moved from Meherabad Hill to the new ashram near the village of Pimpalgaon, about nine miles north of Ahmednagar. This new ashram became known as Meherazad, and the women's quarters were more commodious than the spartan environment of Meherabad. Unlike the Kanya Kumari Sthan, the female contingent at Meher Baba's ashrams did not grow in numbers but became reduced in numbers over the years, leaving only half a dozen members by the 1950s at Meherazad (and one or two at Meherabad). The most celebrated of the women involved was Mehera J. Irani, whose secluded career is notable.[395]

It is clear that Meher Baba did not intend his women's ashram to become an institution. This contrasts with the plan of Upasni Maharaj for his *kanyas*. Indeed, it is also clear that Meher Baba did not intend to create any sect or religion, as he explicitly denied this prospect. In later years, he significantly allowed the number of *mandali* (ashram residents) to dwindle markedly, not replacing them as he easily could have done. His devotees have often repeated that he did not wish to found any religion, though in practice their network of Avatar Meher Baba centres conveys the impression to observers that a dogma and a devotional religion are in the making. Thus, although his ashrams were kept on a leash of very low staff numbers in his last years, devotees have attempted to create officious *avatar* auspices for their own activities of propagating his "message," which they tend to interpret in a very devotional manner. The discrepancies should be duly noted.

Meher Baba definitely did claim to be the *avatar*. An inspection of various statements he made on this subject leaves no room for doubt. He also used the Persian term *saheb-e-zaman*, but that was not popular amongst Hindu devotees. The term *avatar* is variously interpreted in India; Meher Baba employed this Sanskrit word to denote a cosmic spiritual function occurring at cyclical intervals of time. Reactions to this are usually very hostile from religious parties, while his devotees defend the claim rather enthusiastically, sometimes adding things that he never said. It is surely possible to discuss the Irani mystic more rationally, outside the very rigid "believe it/don't believe it" biases attendant upon messianism. The ethnographic, sociological, and mystical material contained in Meher Baba's case history can be studied without becoming a dogmatic spokesman for or against.[396]

The defenders of the *avatar* claim often give a misleading impression of the subject's life prior to 1954, when he first began to publicly state that he was the *avatar*. His career prior to that date was remarkably varied and complex, and included an incognito profile that is very rarely found in guruism. One of his discourses dating to 1938 was entitled "Avatar" but did not include any personal references. Al-

139

though various of his private disclosures, hints, and obscure references were linked to the *avatar* theme prior to 1954, there was a general mood of uncertainty amongst his followers as to the precise status they should attribute to him.[397] This is made abundantly clear in the report of an episode occurring in 1948, when even his ashram *mandali* expressed a variety of views about his status which included lesser rankings than that later promoted.[398] Even a major partisan biographer was in controversy within the movement over his views about Baba's avatarhood.[399]

An activity which was conducted almost exclusively through incognito travels was that of contacting hundreds of Muslim and Hindu entities whom Baba defined as *masts* ("God-intoxicated") and other categories of mystic. This activity dated back to 1936, when he established an ashram for mad people at Rahuri. Here Meher Baba personally ministered to mad and indigent persons as part of the philanthropic projects that he accomplished over many years. Included amongst the inmates of the "mad ashram" were a few *masts*, an abstracted category who often appear to be mad but whom Meher Baba described in terms of a spiritually absorbed type with a completely different psychology to mad people. Such persons, he said, are only found in Eastern countries, and mainly in India and Pakistan. There is no comparable treatment of this subject to be found elsewhere,[400] and some Westerners have since made erratic references to his activity in this respect without duly comprehending the context.[401] Some academic definitions of the word *mast* are unsatisfactory.[402]

The primary feature of Meher Baba's activity in the late 1930s and throughout the 1940s was his work with *masts* and related types. The scope and intensity of his journeys in pursuit of these entities are surely remarkable. There can be no doubt of his sincerity and commitment in the laborious expeditions undertaken all over India and Pakistan. It was a unique project, stretching from the Afghan frontier to Bengal, from the Himalayas and Kashmir to Trivandrum and Ceylon. Specific ashrams for contact with *masts* were established on a temporary basis in a few locations, though in the main, it was he who went to them and not *vice versa*. The overall purpose of the project is obscure, as it was expressly related to his "work," which Dr. Donkin did not attempt to elucidate. The project was carried through with no concessions to publicity; Baba did not want to be seen or recognized on his travels, and only in 1948 did a published record appear, and that was studied only by a small number of readers.

Dr. William Donkin's book *The Wayfarers* (1948) included on the title page an emblem which had been devised at Meher Baba's ashram with his permission. The emblem bore the motto "mastery in servitude" and included icons representing four major religions: Zoroastrianism, Hinduism, Christianity, and Islam. A few years later, the *dharma* wheel of Buddhism was added to the same emblem on the title page of Baba's major treatise, published in 1955. This theme of five world religions being united in a universalistic concept was subsequently imitated in a specifically Hindu context by another party[403] who lived in a very different manner to Meher Baba. The unity of religions is an insipid theme if the servitude is lacking, or if the mastery is confused with, e.g., procuring jewellery for the rich castes.

Meher Baba was still washing the feet of lepers at Meherazad during the 1960s (such occasions were attended by a gift of food and clothing, and sometimes money). That was after he had suffered two motor accidents, the first occurring in 1952 and the second in 1956. The latter was very serious, resulting in an injured hip which hindered his movements for some time thereafter, and which resulted in a much slower and less secure gait and a heavier physical appearance noticeable in films and photographs.[404] The films made of *darshan* occasions, when he was accessible to devotees and/or the public during the 1950s and 1960s,[405] have tended to convey to some viewers the impression of a public spectacle. In actual fact, much of his time was spent in a semi-seclusion in which he saw only a small number of people. There was nothing resembling the daily *darshans* encouraged by other well known gurus.

Very difficult to find in any other contemporary saintly biography are parallels to the phase which Meher Baba called the New Life. In 1949 he terminated his "Old Life" by closing down his ashrams and walking into obscurity with a small group of *mandali*. He insisted that his companions were not to show him any special honour or veneration, a demand which proved difficult for some of them.[406] After a number of vicissitudes, two years later he returned to Ahmednagar and reinhabited the ashrams. Not long after, the "Free Life" of 1952–3 commenced, and he made two *darshan* tours in Andhra Pradesh which gained him many new Hindu followers. By that time the Muslim element in his following was a very small minority, far outnumbered by Zoroastrians and Hindus. There were some Sikhs included, and also the Christians and others in Western countries.

After the abnegation of the New Life, Meher Baba seems to have felt that a public announcement of his credentials was in order. This occurred in September 1954 at a *darshan* in Ahmednagar, and has proved controversial. Meanwhile, the Free Life had climaxed and he had undertaken a *darshan* tour in Andhra during February 1954 that lasted a fortnight. In Andhra he became feted by many Hindus as the *avatar*. He started out by third class rail to this region of India where Satya Sai Baba was to gain much fame in later years. Satya Sai was then promoting his image as a reincarnation of Shirdi Sai, who died eight years before his birth. According to Meher Baba, masters like Shirdi Sai do not reincarnate.[407] Therefore, one of these *avatars* (i.e., Satya Sai or Meher Baba) must be wrong.

On 21st February 1954, Meher Baba visited a Shirdi Sai venue at Guntur in Andhra. He had been invited to visit the Sai Baba Samaj, where an elaborate chair was reserved for him. He sat on the ground instead, but did agree to touch a photograph of Sai Baba and the foundation stone for a proposed temple. He conveyed: "This grand old man (Shirdi Sai) was and is a unique personality in the spiritual world; and he knows, and only a few like him ... know, that I am the Ancient One."[408] The reader will note the dualism; Meher Baba was not an *avatar* of Sai Baba. The contention was that only a few advanced gnostics knew the Ancient One. Therefore, it would logically be impossible for lesser beings to penetrate these issues, so that gnostics must be judged on the basis of their lifestyles and deeds, not on the basis of devotional sentiments or miracle stories.

One of the most graphic of Meher Baba's *avatar* statements is that entitled *Meher Baba's Call*, delivered in September 1954 and much celebrated by devotees. "I continue to come as the Avatar, to be judged time and again by humanity in its ignorance, in order to help man distinguish the Real from the false."[409] Evidently, the purpose of this venture is discrimination between the real and the unreal. A pertinent point to consider is whether the unreal includes mawkish sentiments about avataric events and spreading the avatar's message on the part of devotees unfledged in discrimination.

It is evident that Meher Baba was not captivated by the notion of "Baba centres" spreading his message. He was in fact very critical of contributions in this direction. This issue arose during the Andhra tour in 1954, when he convened a special meeting of devotees at Rajahmundry on March 1st. The official report of this event was much contracted. He told the audience that "for my work it is not necessary to have centres or offices, nor accounts and the collecting of money."[410] He made it clear that "there is no greater 'Baba's Centre' than the heart of my lover; those who truly love me are my centres in the world."[411] He disclaimed responsibility for any formal centres that might be established. "Outwardly, you may establish hundreds of centres for Baba, or none at all; that is your own responsibility."[412] He was presented as not prohibiting the establishment of centres, though making it difficult for any belief that he promoted them; the impression is given that he left the matter to personal disposition, himself having stressed what the real "centre" should be. "I need no propaganda or publicity"[413] is a categorical statement.

The official message that was circulated under the title "What Baba means by Real Work"[414] was a substantial abridgement of his statements made at Rajahmundry. The full facts of the episode go much stronger against Baba Centres. At this meeting with prestigious devotees, he abolished all Baba Centres in Andhra, a dramatic gesture which upset and puzzled some of those present. He dissolved a committee of four eminent "workers" for his presumed cause, men whom he evidently deemed deficient because of their propaganda tactics. He also said that he would have nothing directly to do with any Centre or any literature about him. He dissolved a publications venture known as Meher Publications. Further, he stated that he was going to stop all correspondence, making it very clear that he was unconcerned with all the devotional obsession about Baba Centres and that he wanted to distance himself from the distraction. He reiterated that the true centre was the conscientious "Baba lover" who radiated his message "through living the life of sacrifice, love and honesty for the divine cause."[415] The message was defined in terms of comprising that "God alone is real and everything else is unreal."[416]

In later years a number of devotees persisted in attempts to establish Baba Centres, and some succeeded. During the subject's lifetime, there were very few of these centres in the West. He instigated a search for the centre at Myrtle Beach, South Carolina, though some rather extravagant claims have been made for that place since his death.[417] In India, Meher Baba was believed to have relaxed his earlier strictures by 1959, when he commented that there was no centre in Ahmednagar, the place closest to his ashrams. This was treated as a sign that he wanted a centre in that city, and some local Hindu devotees organized sessions of *bhajan* music at a private house. Eventually a separate building was found and the Ahmednagar Centre was inaugurated in 1962. Baba consented to attend the opening ceremony and gave a message expressing his satisfaction with the venue. Two years later, he also attended the opening ceremony of a similar Centre at Poona. These were the only two such centres that he sponsored in this manner, in the two cities most closely associated with him. His modified standpoint in relation to those centres was: "Though it is true that my real centre is the heart of the individual, it is helpful for my lovers to come together and think and talk about me, to discuss my teachings and messages, compare notes with each other, and cooperatively try to come closer to me in understanding and spirit."[418]

Baba drew the attention of the new Ahmednagar Centre to humanitarian work, generally neglected amongst devotees but which he himself had been furthering since his period at Sakori with Upasni Maharaj. For three successive years Meher Baba instructed the leaders at this centre to bring him one hundred lepers. There were no leper asylums in the vicinity, and so these unfortunates had to be searched for in the city streets. The lepers were taken by bus to Meherazad, where Baba washed their feet, bowed down to them in homage, and gave each a bundle containing clothes, food, and money. In the third year he conducted this charity in a courtyard at the Khushru Quarters, closely adjacent to the new Centre.[419]

Such humanitarian work is not the rule at Baba centres, which have proliferated since his death in Western countries. Those who attend these centres tend to assume that they represent Meher Baba, and can be quite officious at times, even though their only mandate is to talk about him and discuss his teachings. To do much more than that would be liable to create a religion, which he expressly did not want.

At the time of the Free Life, he had made a clear statement of his attitude to religion and founding a religion. "I cannot and will not identify myself with any caste, creed, religion, or political party. From my point of view, all religions are great, but God is greater....I am of no religion. Nor do I seek to establish another religion or add to the numberless illusions that divide man against man."[420]

He added that "no religion was ever intended to be anything more than the gateway to God as Truth," but that every religion had eventually become an obstruction to the unclouded perception of that Truth.[421] "As soon as the Truth of direct inner realization is intellectualized and formulated, it becomes enmeshed in creeds and dogmas" which "have a tendency to bind the soul in the very attempt to emancipate it."[422]

As devotees are people who do not have inner realization, it seems logical to be very cautious of various beliefs which become stereo-typed at Baba Centres, just in case those beliefs are half-way or more to dogmas binding the soul.

Meher Baba's teaching or "message" is sometimes described in terms of "Love and Truth," which is one of the abbreviations found in some of his short dictations. His longer dictations reveal that the catchphrase is inadequate, if convenient for the rhetoric often found at Baba Centres. His *Discourses* had appeared during 1938–42 in a serialized format in a journal, subsequently appearing in bound volumes and undergoing different editorial refinements.[423] More technical was his magnum opus *God Speaks: The Theme of Creation and Its Purpose.* This was published in 1955,[424] and was not read by some devotees owing to the complexity of wording.[425] That volume is definitely not a devotional work, and does not benefit from the glib rubric of Love and Truth preferred in circles lacking a thorough readership. This treatise includes much terminology adapted from Sufism and Vedanta (and some other Hindu traditions), and also includes the Buddhist word *nirvana* (though in an unusual context). Meher Baba's version of Sufi nuances escapes from sectarian dervishism and Islamic dogma, while his version of Vedantic terms is articulated in a very different context from caste Hinduism. His exposition of reincarnation is not comparable to the brahmanical doctrine of rebirth which condemns low castes and outcastes to the fate imposed by the high castes.

A message which Baba gave in Andhra in 1954 spotlights the basic drift of his contentions regarding the distractions of ritualism: "If, instead of performing ceremonies and rituals mechanically as age-old customs, people were to serve their fellow beings with the selflessness of love, taking God to be *equally* residing in one and all, and that by so serving others they are serving God, my work will have been fulfilled."[426] While Dr. B. R. Ambedkar joined the Buddhists in his frustration with the sloth of caste society, Meher Baba reacted in another manner. He did not forget the poor and the lepers in his last years. As a non-Hindu and a non-politician, he knew that he could not perform the miracle of overcoming the caste divide, but he did point to what was necessary for civilization to occur.

He annoyed some Hindu yogis and rival God-men by not glorifying the traditional role of the world-renouncer and the various trappings of *sadhana* and *tapas*. He told many Hindus in Andhra that for many centuries "sadhus and seekers, sages and saints, *munis* and monks, *tapasvis* and *sannyasins,* yogis, sufis, and *talibs*"[427] had been under-going great hardships in the effort to free themselves from "the maze of actions and to realize the Eternal Existence."[428] They had failed because "the more they struggled with their 'self', the firmer the 'self' becomes gripped by life through actions intensified by austerities and penances, by seclusion and pilgrimages, by meditation and concentration, by assertive utterances and silent contemplations, by intense activity and inactivity, by silence and verbosity, by *japs* (*japa*) and *taps* (*tapas*), and by all types of Yogas and *chillas.*"[429]

His point was that neither action nor inaction could unbind the self, quietism being yet another form of action and a form of binding, producing self-deception. An activating agent other than the 'self' was necessary to overcome the pull exerted by that 'self.' The "life of the limited self is sustained by the mind creating impressions."[430] The impressions do not stop in Raja Yoga or external renunciation or *bhakti* (devotion) or routine *sadhana.* According to Meher Baba, the impressions can only stop when the aid of a *sadguru* or *qutub* is sought and acquired[431] (the word *avatar* does not appear in this message). That theme involves the concept of "surrender" of the deceptive self to one whose self is transformed.

The latter theme, repeated in other dictated statements, often meets with resistance on the part of people committed to various exercises and techniques. The appropriation of such themes by Bhagwan Shree Rajneesh and other gurus is clearly distorting, as they replaced the context with an array of bizarre exercises and therapies sufficient to sustain lewd speech and wrong actions for a lengthy period. The deceptions practised in guruism and popular religion are so deep-rooted and pervasive that it might yet be necessary to transcend the four Yogas by becoming a sane humanitarian and rational analyst.

The only "exercise" which Meher Baba taught was the interaction between master and disciple (unless one includes the prayers he dictated). It is logical enough that prescriptions for self-control and transformation can vary greatly with individuals, and cannot wisely be administered on a generalizing basis. Yet the very simplicity of Meher Baba's approach led to banalities in those who could only achieve a devotional focus. The celebratory slogan of "Avatar Meher Baba *ki jai*" began to appear at places like Andhra in 1954,[432] and was thereafter very frequently a popular refrain at *darshans.* The following year Baba stated: "There is no sense in shouting '*Avatar ki jai*' every now and then. If you want to shout, do so within your hearts; let it not be

Sai Baba of Shirdi

Upasni Maharaj, Bombay 1920s

Upasni Maharaj, Bombay 1

Upasni at Sakori, 1930s

Sakori

Upasni Maharaj with the kanyas, Sakori 1930s
(Godavri Mataji top left, pinjra in background)

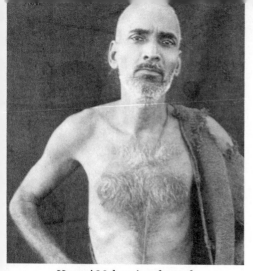

Upasni Maharaj at the end
of his Shirdi phase

Hazrat Babajan of Poon

Sheriar Mundegar
father of Meher

Merwan Irani at the time of his visits to Sakori

Upasni at Sak

Meher Baba, Quetta 1923

Meher Baba, Meherabad 1925

her Baba, Prem Ashram period 1928–9

Meher Baba, Meherabad 1927–8

Bombay 1929

Bombay 1932

Portofino, Italy 1933

London 1931

Meher Baba incognito at Lugano, Switzerland 1932
with Delia DeLeon

East Challacombe, Devon 1931

Halstead, Sevenoaks 1933

Cannes 1937, with F. H. Dadacha

Meher Baba incognito at the
Sphinx of Gizeh, Egypt 1933

Meher Baba and a mast,
Rahuri ashram 1936–7

Some of the mandali in Devon, 1932, l to r F. H. Dadachanji, Baba's brother
Beheram Irani, Dr. Ghani, Baba's brother Adi S. Irani, Adi K. Irani, Kaka Baria

Meher Baba cleaning a toilet area
at Meherabad 1938

New Life phase, Mahabaleshwar 1950

New Life phase, Mahabaleshwar 1950

Bathing a leper, Pandharpur 1954

Tembi Hill, Meherazad 1955

Poona 1957

Poona 1965

Mehera J. Irani, late 1930s   Meherazad, 1960s

Meherazad, 1960s   Meher Baba's tomb, Meherabad Hill 1962.
                    Beryl Williams of New York (inset) is in the doorway

Meherabad Hill, 1962   Mehera's garden, Meherazad 1962

Meherabad Hill, 1954, back gate,
l. to r. Meher Baba's tomb, meditation cells, old hospital building, Baba's cabin

Guruprasad, Poona, 1962   East-West Gathering,
                                           Guruprasad, Poona 1962

Meher Baba's mother Shirin

Merwan Irani (standing) and elder
brother Jamshed, Poona, 1913

: Baba's father Sheriar,
  Shirin, and brother Jal,
  Poona 1920s

Meherabad Hill 1938, at newly finished tomb,
l to r, Shirin, brother Adi, Meher Baba, sister Mani

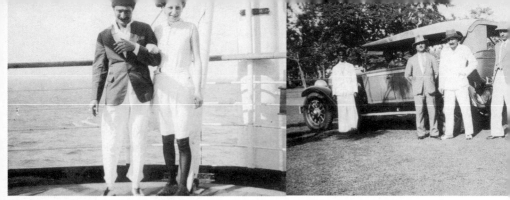

French beret, early 1930s

Early 1930s
l to r Kaka Baria, Meher Baba, Adi S.

Incognito guises, 1930s

St. Mark's Square, Venice, 1932,
with Quentin Tod and Herbert Davy

London, December 1932
l to r Jal Irani, Vishnu Deorukhkar, Enid Corfe,
MB, Norina Matchabelli, Adi S. Irani, Kaka Baria.

Meherabad Hill, 1938

Gulmai Irani and Mehera J. Irani,
Nasik, early 1930s

Mehera J. Irani (b. 1907),
Meherazad, late 1970s

Meherazad 1952, l to r (standing):
Gustadji Hansotia, Baidul, Pendu, Eruch Jessawala

Meherazad, 1962   Outside the Mandali Hall, Meherazad

Mandali Hall, Meherazad 1962   Mandali Hall, 1964

Tembi Hill, Meherazad, late 1960s

heard by others."[433] That caution was not generally heeded in subsequent years.

Contrary to some reported deeds of Shirdi Sai, Meher Baba consistently opposed certain desires in his devotees. In 1955 he conveyed: "I want to warn all who approach me that they should not expect health, wealth, wife, or children from me; I tell you that those who have associated with me through love have suffered complete material pain."[434] It may be concluded that he was not trying to deceive anybody.

He is known to have complained that he did not like being garlanded, as the floral wreaths made him feel cold or soiled his jacket. Yet devotees always garlanded him at *darshans*, sometimes profusely (even a helmet of flowers was pressed upon his head). It can be asked why he did not stop the enthusiasts if he was averse to that sort of celebration. A verifiable fact is that *darshans* had been scarce during the 1930s and 1940s, and that even during the 1950s (the peak period for this enthusiasm) he was frequently not approachable. *Darshans* became medically unwise for him by 1965, when he was afflicted with severe neck pains that required a cervical collar. His last mass *darshan* at Poona in 1965 entailed much personal pain, and he required help when standing. *Darshan* occasions were the only time when large numbers of devotees saw him, entailing the traditional bowing at the feet that is commemorated by Hindus. Most of the people who attended *darshans* were Hindus; in contrast, most of his ashram staff were Zoroastrians during the last two decades of his life.

In October 1954 he relinquished the alphabet board and thereafter resorted entirely to a distinctive language of hand gestures. The films taken of him portray an animated man with a very mobile face capable of swiftly changing expressions. The sense of humour frequently comes across, though there is also a more abstracted visage represented. Only a few of the *mandali* were intimately familiar with the gestures, and his major interpreter was Eruch B. Jessawala, a Parsi. The relinquishment of the alphabet board would seem to underline Meher Baba's aversion for the spoken and written word, despite his contribution of a technical book. He is well known for asserting: "I have come not to teach but to awaken."

During the 1950s and after, he referred to his devotees as "lovers," and this description (perhaps of Sufi origin) many of them took up as an identifying label by the late 1960s.[435] From this developed a habit of calling him "the Beloved," an idiom favoured in the newsletters (known as the Family letters) for Western devotees penned by his sister Mani. Though often lavishly praised by devotees, these letters (more specifically, the later specimens) have also received some criticism.[436]

During the 1950s, Meher Baba made three visits to the West, which were to be his last. In 1952 he went to America and Europe. He stayed for the first time at the new Meher Center-on-the-Lakes at Myrtle Beach.[437] He arrived there on April 22nd, and consented to give a schedule of interviews. Some black Americans like Beryl Williams and Edward James notably infiltrated the majority of whites, braving the segregation practised in the southern states. Baba successfully drew them out, and always stood up when receiving black Americans. Edward James was a Negro pupil of Ivy Duce, who was projecting an American form of Sufism called Sufism Reoriented. James was a keen reader of books on spiritual subjects, and Baba humorously asked: "Tell me in exactly five words what you have learned from all these books." James was stumped by this request, and Baba then spelled out on the board the answer he had wanted: "I have not learned anything."[438] It has often been Sufi practise to admit the limitations of learning; those who do not do this can deceive themselves acutely.

Only a small number of people saw him regularly at Myrtle Beach. He left the Centre on May 21st en route to California, but suffered a motor accident on May 24th, in which his nose and two limbs were injured. Nevertheless, the effects were mild by comparison with his second motor accident which occurred in India four years later. He himself never drove a car, always being chauffeured.

In July–August 1956 he undertook a "world tour," involving a speedy itinerary that lasted only a few weeks. Moving on from Europe, he stayed for a week in New York, but "all this time he was in semi-seclusion; he was also very tired." Yet "he gave the appearance of full strength and vitality, being his humorous, lively, attentive, patient self, with no signs of exhaustion."[439] He gave interviews and continued on to the Myrtle Beach Centre, where he spent six days. He moved quickly on to California, and on the route homewards, stopped for several days in Australia, his first visit to that country. He landed at Sydney airport on August 9th and departed on the 14th, though many of the people who were invited to meet him did not pursue any further contact with him,[440] their inclination being of a casual nature.

In May 1958, Meher Baba went to Myrtle Beach for two weeks to participate in what he called a *sahavas*,[441] a term to which he gave the meaning of an intimate companionship or an intimacy of love. This was not conceived as a didactic or teaching event, though some discourses were dictated for the occasion. He explained that discourses and messages were mere words in the absence of appropriate responses, and that what he wanted was "love and obedience." Some of the concepts involved have an affinity with Sufi ideals of "companionship" (*suhba*), which basically relates to discipleship, though the subject has been interpreted in many variants, frequently of an institutionalized nature. The Sufi novice was supposed to undergo a phase of discipleship in which he surrendered his ego to the *murshid* or *shaikh*.[442] Baba also stressed surrender as an outcome. This theory often sounds extreme to Western critics, and was perhaps over-generalized by devotees. It is obvious enough that a fortnight was only preparatory; Baba exhibited strong changes of mood from humour to deep abstraction. In the traditional Sufi sense, this would have signified that the companions should transfer from one mood to another likewise, though some found a transition difficult to achieve.

He continued on to spend a few days in Australia in the first week of June. He went from Brisbane to a property about sixty-five miles north at Kiel Mountain. This was a property of eighty acres on top of a small mountain, which had been purchased earlier in the year by an Australian devotee named Francis Brabazon. Over fifty people arrived to welcome him. Brabazon tried to press ownership of the property upon him, but Baba declined, "saying that he now held neither goods nor property."[443] It was observed that on "this second visit to Australia Baba was serious, at times unsmiling and withdrawn, and certainly more stern than he had been on his first visit."[444] A prestigious devotee[445] writes that Baba "was less inclined to humour our moods"[446] on that visit to Queensland.[447] He pressed the issue of obedience,[448] a topic which was often presented dogmatically by some devotees without regard for context.

Most Western devotees rarely saw him after 1958. At a *darshan* event known as the East-West Gathering, occurring at Poona in November 1962, Western devotees were invited to attend along with Eastern followers. The event lasted only four days (November 1st–4th), and only those with sufficient funds could meet the occasion. A total of 137 Westerners attended, and approximately 3,000 devotees from India and Pakistan (and a few from Iran).[449] Afterwards, only a very few Westerners saw Meher Baba again.

149

Commencing in late 1965, he gave a string of warnings about the use of LSD and other drugs. He told an American visitor that many *sadhus* in India smoked hashish, which gave them a temporary elation comprising a "false experience" that leads away from spiritual reality. He said that indulgence in drugs like LSD was harmful physically, mentally, and spiritually, and that repeated use of LSD leads to a disability which might prove incurable. He strongly warned against extensive damage that could be created by LSD amongst the undergraduate population in the West. He contested the theories of drug exponents like Dr. Timothy Leary and Dr. Richard Alpert (Ram Dass), and hammered out a counter-message of "No Drugs." Alpert wrote to him on the matter, and in reply Baba said that no drug could help to attain the spiritual goal, and that all drugs, LSD in particular, give only a semblance of true spiritual experiences, their effect amounting to "a glimpse of the false reality."[450] Many people in America were unwilling to credit the validity of these statements and disregarded them as an interference with so-called "progressive" thinking. Not all of these people lived for very long. In addition, a large number of patients from various medical institutions have testified to long-term effects of an unpleasant nature as a consequence of being administered psychedelic drugs under inexpert professional care.

Meher Baba spent his last years moving between Meherazad and Poona (Pune), staying at the latter place during the summer in a palatial bungalow (known as Guruprasad) that was owned by a Maharani (the summers were cool in Poona compared to the Ahmednagar area). Most of the year was spent at the ashram, a quiet place where simple living standards prevailed. He continually stressed that he wanted no letters or interruptions from devotees. Correspondence was allowed in emergency. Yet there were some breaks in the prohibition on visitors.

In February 1967 an Australian visitor who was invited to Meherazad observed that Baba's appearance was one of suffering. He now wore a neck brace and sat "physically tortured and helpless with the aftermath of two severe accidents and a lifetime of fasting, sleeplessness, and service."[451] His stomach was said to be "ruined by a lifetime of fasts and neglect."[452] He kept moving in his chair to ease the pain in his body. The contrast with his demeanour in 1956 was acute, at a time when he had still been so vibrantly active. He had to be carried in a chair from his living quarters to the hall where the men *mandali* congregated with him twice daily. There were only a small number of the men left, predominantly old men. There were seven men and six women *mandali* at Meherazad, and "the average age more than sixty years."453 It is evident that Meher Baba was not attempting any expansion, but rather closing down his ashram setting. Many Western devotees had difficulty in assessing what was happening; they could not believe that he would die without them all seeing him again. Many believed that he would start to speak in the physical sense. A *darshan* for the Westerners scheduled for 1965 had been cancelled due to his poor health; only the Eastern devotees had gained a *darshan* that year. Many Westerners waited in anticipation, expecting to be called to India, and to descend *en masse* upon the man who clearly preferred privacy in his frail condition. Mani's newsletters tended to encourage a romantic and sentimental picture of events, though the suffering of Baba was mentioned in those documents. The doctors could not alleviate his cervical pain.

In July 1968 he stated that his "work" in seclusion was completed one hundred per cent to his satisfaction. Yet still he would not see devotees because of the strain on his health. Apart from other problems, his walking days were finished.454 Devotees were insistently requesting that he give *darshan* now that his seclusion "work" was over; he responded in October with the message that he would give *darshan* the following year, during the summer at Poona. However, in late December 1968 his health seriously deteriorated. He became subject to muscular spasms, and after 12th January he never left his room at Meherazad and was confined to a surgical bed. On January 30th, 1969, his body was subject to many severe spasms. He told one of his doctors "My time has come." The next day, January 31st, he expired at mid-day while sitting on his bed after further severe spasms. Eruch Jessawala attempted a mouth to mouth resuscitation for nearly thirty minutes, and he was relieved for a short while in this effort by Francis Brabazon and Bhau Kalchuri. Dr. Goher, one of the women *mandali*, gave the inert body of Meher Baba several injections in a desperate attempt to revive him. The *mandali* at first could not believe that he had died. Dr. Donkin and two specially summoned medics were more objective, and stated that Baba was now deceased. The women *mandali* were very shocked, but Dr. Ram Ginde of Bombay wrote out the death certificate and asked the men *mandali* not to be sentimental but to become practical. The women *mandali* wanted to keep the corpse at Meherazad, and Baba's sister Mani Irani argued with Dr. Ginde that Baba had once told her that if he went into a coma he would revive after seven days. Dr. Ginde duly explained that what had happened was not coma, as a person in coma still has a beating heart. Yet Mani would not agree with the medical verdict. Dr. Donkin had been the first of the *mandali* to display a practical attitude, and the second appears to have been Eruch Jessawala, who grasped that the doctors were right and that the corpse must now be duly removed to the tomb at Meherabad. Only Eruch's attitude could persuade the women.[455] Just a few days earlier, Mani had sent a newsletter to the West giving the information that a *darshan* would be held in Poona in the summer. All expectations were now shattered.

Meher Baba's mouth remained tightly closed at his death. His sufferings were endured in unbroken silence. Sceptics have considered this reticence a proof that he was a hoaxer. Against that allegation must be set fairly numerous statements of his that strongly indicate a mystical perspective on "speaking." One of his well known references was "I speak continuously with my heart." That statement appeared on the front cover of *The Awakener* journal in 1963. A similar statement was: "I am never silent, I speak eternally in the human heart."[456] It therefore becomes rather more difficult to affirm that he had contrived a hoax in predicting that he would break his silence and speak the "Word." There were various intricacies in his statements. In his "final Declaration" of 1954 he stated that he would not utter spiritual lectures but instead "speak only One Word, and this Word will penetrate the hearts of all men." Critics say that even if it be conceded that he did not mean a physical speech act, then he was surely being optimistic in the claim. Difficulties for partisan exegesis exist in that Meher Baba gave a subsequent clarification of the relevant message in which he said that the reference to his uttering the One Word of Words "was said in my own 'language' and simultaneously in yours, because when I utter that Word, it will be an audible word to you" (Purdom and Schloss, *Three Incredible Weeks*, p. 84. Cf. Purdom, *The God-Man*, p. 278). Critics say that he must have meant a physically audible word, or was merely designing a hoax, while defenders of the theme say that the strongly accented emphasis on the factor of his own "language" means that there is scope for metaphysical subtleties. His own "language" was defined by him as being incomprehensible to devotees in respect of the underlying meaning. The sociologist must retire on these points, and settle for the observation that Meher Baba was employing jargon that could be variously interpreted, and which was viewed in a rather vague semi-literal manner by many devotees.

152

The observer is here obliged to point out the partisan contention that Meher Baba must be considered correct in having predicted in 1954 that a "strange disease" would attack his body, clarifying that this prediction was expressed in ordinary language. The implication is that he had foreseen the damaging effects of his second motor accident in 1956, which ramified into cervical problems and acute muscular spasms. Thus, the prognostication issue has some difficulties for the pro-hoax argument, and this must logically be conceded.

The *mandali* and a number of devotees were not concerned about the absence of any clearly audible word. Yet some devotees had apparently expected a tangible and clearly audible speech act, or perhaps even some form of miraculous event. An uncertain number of people are said to have forsaken their allegiance on this account. It seems that some of the disappointed persons were not categorical followers but interested parties or fringe enthusiasts. In the West, the category of "Baba lover" was sometimes ambiguous – cases were known of young people who were unable to throw off drug influences completely. New devotees were often an unstable factor in the late 1960s. Yet there is reason to believe that some long established devotees were disappointed at the lack of any sensational element in Meher Baba's decease. The only sensation was that he had died without telling them, and the shock wave was strong. Conversely, some say that he had in fact given cryptic warning of his death in various statements that were not assimilated very well during the last few months of his life, probably because of the obsessions with a *darshan* event. Yet quite apart from such issues as the breaking of silence or the fact of unexpected decease, some reactions had already set in against other features of the movement. Pete Townshend is on record for stating that the pop star Melanie (who was at first very interested in Meher Baba) had become offput by over-gushing devotees who talked about love but who squabbled among themselves and assembled in Centres like ministers of the church (Giuliano, *Behind Blue Eyes: A Life of Pete Townshend*, p. 119). However, devotees generally subscribed to the belief that no religion was in process. Soon after Meher Baba's death, an elaborate argument emanated from the Myrtle Beach Centre that their community of Baba lovers was not even a sect in point of accurate classification. That now seems rather an optimistic assessment in view of the total data.

While there were various explanations and confusions pertaining to the issue of an apparently unbroken silence, there was probably more

153

upset over the fact that the much anticipated *darshan* in the summer had suddenly evaporated. Western devotional expectations had been very high, as over six years had elapsed since the last opportunity of seeing Baba for most of those concerned. The *mandali* had contributed to the expectations, especially Mani. Yet during January 1969 there had been considerable consternation and uncertainty at Meherazad as to how the scheduled *darshan* would actually occur, in view of Baba's critical state of health. This uncertainty was expressed in Mani's newsletter dated January 26th, 1969, though with the accompanying emphasis that *darshan* would somehow take place.

In addition to the official line about *darshan* in the summer at Poona, a strange trend had occurred in Meher Baba's statements. He had made some rather cryptic remarks about a *darshan*. He said that the event would be easy in accomplishment and that he would be under no strain and would give *darshan* in a reclining position. He is also reported to have said that it would be different from all previous *darshans* he had given, and that it would be the last *darshan* given in silence. Furthermore, he said that his work would then be finished and he would be in exaltation. However, there was a mingled note of foreboding. He implied that the end of his work would cause his collapse, and yet this would amount to his "glory." The *mandali* issued an official report of these statements in February, 1969, including his allusive assertion that: "A very poor man winning a rich lottery can become so excited over his fortune that he collapses and dies" (Le Page, *The Turning of the Key*, p. 224). Baba explained this metaphor in terms of his "fortune" amounting to the completion of his work. These remarks caused puzzlement at the ashram from October 1968 onwards. The "last *darshan*" was assumed to be the forthcoming summer event at Poona.

The *mandali* later recognized that the prediction about appearing in a reclining position answered exactly to the period when Baba's corpse was laid to rest in his tomb at Meherabad and remained on view for a week to the many visitors who arrived to pay their respects. That event occurred in the first week of February 1969, and was at first referred to as the last *darshan*; a report by Dr. Bharucha describes the event as the "last *sahavas*." Only a very small number of Western devotees had been able to make the trip to India at such short notice. The *mandali* subsequently interpreted events to mean that the "last *darshan*" would occur at Poona for two months from April 10th to June 10th, thus keeping to the original schedule which had been planned. This official decision involved no living Baba and no corpse. There was to be no sitting or reclining Baba, but instead an empty chair at Guruprasad.

When the medical doctors Ginde, Brieseman, and Donkin asserted the fact of decease on January 31st, they may have wondered why resisting sentiment was in such strong evidence at the ashram about an obvious event. The *mandali*, though more especially the tearful women, could not believe that Meher Baba had died. The fact of expiry soon became accepted, but some beliefs that persisted are very questionable. Immediately after Baba's coffin had been buried at the Meherabad tomb, Adi K. Irani sent out a message on February 8th which attested the decision of the *mandali* to further the former plan which was now a cause of embarrassment. "Despite Baba's physical absence those lovers who desire to visit Guruprasad Poona to honour Baba's invitation for darshan up to tenth June can still come" (Davy, *Love Alone Prevails*, p. 676). The last *darshan* at the tomb in February became overshadowed by the improvised last *darshan* in Poona, but that anomaly has been ignored in the movement under discussion. The Poona event became known as the Great Darshan.

Many Eastern and Western devotees travelled to Guruprasad (the Maharani's large bungalow in Poona) for the strange event presented by the surviving *mandali*. The visitors had come to believe that this event was Baba's wish for them. Most of the Westerners had not been present at the "last *darshan*" in February. Encouraged by the *mandali*, the visitors believed that Meher Baba was incorporeally present to receive them at Guruprasad. As a consequence, devotional beliefs became very confused over the subject of the last *darshan*. The influential British devotee Delia De Leon has stated of the Poona event in her memoirs that "Baba had always said he would take this *darshan* lying down and all those lucky enough to attend said they felt his presence very strongly."[457] On the same page, De Leon states that the *mandali* were carrying out Baba's instructions in organizing this "Great Darshan" (*The Ocean of Love*, p. 207). The fact that De Leon attended the event at the Meherabad tomb in February tends to underline the confusion in exegesis that was emerging. The belief that the *mandali* were carrying out Baba's instructions is no more convincing than Mani's refusal to believe Dr. Ram Ginde when he wrote out the death certificate.

Outsiders to the movement have observed that while Meher Baba's remarks about reclining at a "last *darshan*" can be reasonably construed as referring to the week of corpse exposure at his tomb, it is not logically possible to credit the devotional system of belief which transposed that event to the summer occurrences at Poona the same year. Thousands of Indian devotees are said to have attended the Great Darshan, and nearly seven hundred from other countries; the *mandali* were catering in Poona for a much larger number of Westerners than the small minority of Americans who had been able to view the reclining corpse. Had the new religion already begun? It is definite that Meher Baba's after-death presence was being emphasized at Guruprasad not long before that attractive bungalow of the Maharani Shantadevi was demolished to assist the ashram finances. A critic may ask at what point Baba ceased to vacate the premises, as he was not physically present there after the summer of 1968.

Devotees relied heavily upon the surviving *mandali*[458] for an interpretation of events.[459] It was assumed that the *mandali* would inevitably know what was best to do as a result of their long years with Baba. Mehera was often shy and retiring, especially with males, and did not have the disposition of a preacher. The most vocal representatives were Mani, Adi. K. Irani (Baba's secretary who lived at Ahmednagar), and Eruch Jessawala. Their views became accepted as gospel truth, and quickly formed into a vehicle of exegesis regarded as comprehensive and mandatory. They represented familiar authority figures, and their status became enhanced after Baba's death.[460]

Letters from Mani to the Western devotees continued after her brother's demise. In a collective epistle written after the "great *darshan*," she described that questionable event in terms of: "You had the Beloved's *darshan*. And you had his *sahavas*, seated for hours before him in Guruprasad, communing with him (Baba) in silence and in speech....You brought Baba with you and he was already here to receive you, you took him with you and he is as ever with us."[461]

Thus the mood was established that Baba had not really died. The empty chair at Guruprasad was invested with Baba's presence by such reassurances. Mani's eloquence went a long way towards creating the belief that Meher Baba remained at work in the lives of his devotees. Strangely enough, they still needed to visit his tomb on Meherabad Hill, an event of pilgrimage which had the bonus of gaining audience with the surviving *mandali*, whose words were regarded as continuing proof that the situation was just as it should be. The *mandali* emphasized that Meher Baba had no successor,[462] being a unique avataric figure who was all-sufficient against lesser masters, who now became viewed as effective rivals. It is understandable that the *mandali* would have been alarmed at the appearance of the permissive Rajneesh in Poona, and also that they would have resented the inroads in Andhra made by the miracle-mongering Satya Sai. However, their exegesis went far beyond the bounds of commonsense warnings against opportunists unfledged in self-denial. According to the doctrine of the *mandali*, there was nothing else worth investigating because the Avatar held the key to all problems.

A belief that became strongly entrenched is expressed in the following words of supporters: "Baba is perceived as intervening in the unique and particular details of each follower's life history, ministering to each person's distinctive spiritual needs, and aiding in the development of his human and spiritual potential."[463] This is surely a field for the most acute deceptions about life histories and spiritual needs, leading to a potentially massive inflation. Attempts to give due warning in such matters are met with strong resistance from prestigious devotees with set ideas about their spiritual potential in which no problems exist.[464]

During the late 1960s and early 1970s, a number of people emerged from a hippy background in psychedelic drugs and became devotees of Meher Baba. They added to the confusion by using an exotic jargon not formerly in evidence, though Mani's terminology appealed to them. Thus Baba's "love game" became an idiomatic obsession. "Baba's umbrella" was another hip catchphrase. American new wave devotees tended to favour the saying "Don't worry be happy," and as a consequence outsiders to the movement sometimes imagined that this was the extent and purport of Meher Baba's philosophy. This rather banal saying was lifted from a haphazard system of reference supplied by devotional literature. It has become associated with Delia De Leon, a British devotee, who was an early recipient of this consideration.[465] Baba thereafter used the phrase as an aside on some occasions, but it can never accurately be confused with his philosophy. Only the neo-hip wave could reduce the metaphysical teaching in his magnum opus to a trite slogan, though it is true that they had Mani's rhetoric to guide them. The evidence might indicate that Meher Baba did not really want to see Western devotees at the end of his life, but devotional fantasy revised the indications at the so-called Great Darshan.

It is arguable that the Meher Baba movement is now a sect which has taken at least a few steps towards becoming a religion unintended by the putative founder. The belief that he is still intervening in the lives of devotees tends to be furthered by those who create and staff Baba Centres. It is clear that Meher Baba did not intervene at a crucial point in the career of the rock star Pete Townshend who founded such a Centre in London and soon after relapsed into unfortunate habits.[466] Yet another Centre in Britain has recently stated: "Through Baba's will it is the unfortunate role of the Association to request money to do Baba's work."[467] That was over twenty years after the subject's death, and twenty-five years after his work had ceased according to his own statement. The questionable nature of devotee claims is apparent. The history of the Meher Baba Association (or rather the antecedents of that British organization) has been misleadingly presented,[468] and it seems to have been forgotten that one of the reasons why Meher Baba disbanded the Andhra Centres in 1954 was because they collected funds in his name.

The *mandali* claimed to interpret Baba's after-death presence, and in a manner which strikes observers as extreme. He is supposed to be infallibly guiding his devotees. Yet Meher Baba did not undertake to guide people after he died;[469] instead, he said that his tomb would be revered[470] and that his influence would linger.[471] Visitors to the tomb were encouraged by the *mandali* to attend *arati* services and to sing *arati* songs at that spot, and a few wondered when the peace and stillness of Meherabad would end as ritualism increased. The tomb was generally referred to by the Hindu word *samadhi*, and Americans imitated this idiom, although the structure resembles a Sufi *dargah* more than anything Hindu. Some Western visitors were disappointed that Meherabad was so simple, small, and incommodious, testimony to the frugal standards Meher Baba had maintained. He is known to have stated that Muslims would one day visit his tomb in large numbers, a development which has not so far occurred.

The decision of the *mandali* that there was no successor led to some elaborately contrived formulations denying the need to look for a living teacher. One of these disclaimers reads: "Masters of the path and perfect masters, although they retain their Power when they drop the body, they do not have the authority to use that Power. But in the case of the Avatar it is different – God always retains Absolute Power and the Authority to use it, whether he is in the body or not."[472] This argument has logical difficulties and tends to undermine itself. That argument has been used as a justification for attendance at Meherabad and Meherazad, where Baba's presence is said to be felt tangibly enough to discount any other factor. Unlike devotees, Meher

Baba did acknowledge the importance of *sadgurus* ("perfect masters," as he translated that Hindu term), and was at some pains to spell out the function of a "spiritual hierarchy" in his major book. The subject becomes rather amusing when devotees insist that only the Avatar reincarnates, and thus lesser masters are superfluous. This fantastic argument means that for seven hundred years (according to them), they can wait for the next Avatar, who is somehow all the time still present with them. In this religious doctrine, it is the devotees who are the most effective ministers of divine grace, it would seem. One might instead believe that they have miscalculated the situation. Nobody sane needs to charge off looking for gurus (so often a bankrupt endeavour), but a more thorough analysis of sectarian matters is surely called for.

While any successor was vanquished,[473] the *mandali* took the privileges. Mani's counsel was held in high esteem, and Eruch's discourses in the *mandali* hall at Meherazad were received without any question.[474] The *mandali* did not claim any spiritual enlightenment, although their status as close disciples tended to be taken as proof of their wisdom – which was effectively regarded as infallible by visitors to the ashrams. The devotional system of belief they promoted tended to invest them with an exclusive monopoly on the subject of Meher Baba that was extended in a lesser degree to prestigious senior devotees in various countries. It is evident that ashram hierarchies can create sectarian dispositions which require efforts like those made by Godavri Mataji to counteract.

A concept in vogue was that of a "family" of Baba lovers, a description first appearing in Mani's newsletters or "Family Letters." In theory this was an egalitarian concept.[475] By the 1990s, the "family" was gaining certain qualifications in ashram practise. Visitors to the ashrams were segregated in such matters as lodgings on the basis of the number of years they had spent as devotees. Thus, the "old" devotees gained privileges, while the "young" devotees were lower on the scale of priorities.[476] In this way, the "family" became hierarchically stratified according to chronological distinctions. A few may have begun to resent this, but most devotees seem to have accepted the situation uncritically as "Baba's will." There was a tendency for prestigious devotees to be given more attention from the elite *mandali*, especially Mani, who had long been accustomed to this arrangement. The *mandali* stood at the apex of the status pyramid and were effectively avataric in the competition with lesser masters. However, fund-raising is conducted on an equal basis amongst the subscribers.[477]

One could wonder if there were any psychological resemblances to the earlier situation existing at Sakori, when the manager Wagh and his colleagues had screened out an unwanted factor, expressing an emphatic disdain for Meher Baba, who was considered to be a dangerous rival and an ordinary disciple of Upasni Maharaj. Devotional views are not always reliable, and should not be accepted uncritically.

There is the rather strange coincidence that at Shirdi, Sakori,[478] and Meherabad, the deaths of the venerated saints were believed to change nothing for devotees. The venerated deceased entities were somehow still alive.[479] Rivalries between sects continued, one difference being that there was no stress on miracles at Meherabad.

If one is prepared to credit in any way the relevance of Shirdi Sai, Upasni Maharaj, and Meher Baba as mystics, then it is evident that their teachings differed. Their policies differed also. Such details tend to confound the issue of a "perennial philosophy" as popularly promoted by various writers. One possible conclusion afforded is that the underlying impact of the saint/master is circumscribed by audience capacities, and shaped to some extent by their own temperament (e.g., bizarre, aggressive, moderate). Although a figure like Upasni Maharaj did converge with some emphases in traditional Hinduism, there is also something comparatively indefinable about his career which does not fit orthodox religion. Shirdi Sai and Meher Baba definitely did cut across religious boundaries to a radical extent. Followers of such entities discernibly create sects and divisions, and often distort facts in an unintentional manner. Alternative entities seen as a threat to sectarian identity are screened out in various ways, sometimes being suppressed altogether.

It can be difficult, but not impossible, to penetrate the hindsight imposed by some twentieth century sects that are relatively well documented. Yet it is practically impossible to penetrate some earlier records of saints/masters that exist in a far more fragmented state with opaque hagiological coatings. Scholars have the problem of inheriting skeletal sectarian relics that may hold little or no fact. Devotees produce religions full of authority figures who were perhaps far more deficient than is popularly believed. One modern myth created by scholars is the "Sai Baba movement," which stealthily props up the proclaimed talents of Satya Sai Baba, who bears no resemblance to other figures subsumed by this glib label. The phenomenon in question could just as well be called the Upasni Maharaj movement, or even the Hazrat Babajan movement,[480] but that would not be so commercial a prospect for the Satya Sai network.

Notes

1.   Shepherd, *Gurus Rediscovered: Biographies of Sai Baba of Shirdi and Upasni Maharaj of Sakori* (Cambridge: Anthropographia Publications, 1986).

2.   Cf. A. D. Bharvani and V. Malhotra, *Shirdi Sai and Sathya Sai are One and the Same* (Bombay: Sai Sahitya Samithi, 1983); N. Kasturi, *Sathyam Sivam Sundaram: The Life of Bhagavan Sri Sathya Sai Baba* (4 vols, Prasanthi Nilayam: Sri Sathya Sai Books and Publications, 1981); H. Murphet, *Sai Baba: Man of Miracles* (London: Muller, 1971); E. Haraldsson, *Modern Miracles: An Investigative Report on Psychic Phenomena Associated with Sathya Sai Baba* (New York: Fawcett Columbine, 1988). These works, like most others in print on Satya Sai, are partisan and strongly coloured by miracle beliefs. A mildly critical analysis can be found in L. A. Babb, "Sathya Sai Baba's Miracles" (277–92) in T. N. Madan, ed., *Religion in India* (Delhi: Oxford University Press, 1992). I will here follow some of the data afforded in that article. "The strict facts of his personal biography and manner of life are buried beneath layer upon layer of hagiography" (*ibid.*, p. 279), to the extent that Babb could not cite any objective account by a devotee. Satya Sai was born into the Raju caste at (or rather near) the village of Puttaparthi in Andhra Pradesh. In 1943 (miscalculated as 1940), he declared himself to be Sai Baba, and achieved a change of name accordingly, his original name being Satyanarayana. He began to create a sensation by "materializing" sacred ash (*udi* or *vibhuti*), which terminated his attendance at school and made him into a holy man. He gained a large regional following during the 1940s, and in 1950 the construction of his ashram at his native village was completed. He travelled in both South India and the North, and his fame spread during the 1950s. He has visited East Africa but "his constituency is basically Indian" (*ibid.*, p. 282), including many affluent devotees who have "provided his cult with vast resources and unparalleled public visibility" (*ibid.*, p. 278). In 1963 Satya declared that he was the incarnation of Shiva and Shakti, with the attendant clause that Shirdi Sai had only been Shakti (note how the rather macho Shirdi saint is here feminized). Thus his declaration goes much further than being a reincarnation of Shirdi Sai, and amounts to being an *avatar* of Shiva-Shakti. The purpose of his incarnation is to "reestablish Vedic and Shastric religion" (*ibid.*, p. 284). He gained a reputation for materializing large quantities of sacred ash "from his hand inside an inverted pot" (*ibid.*) on the occasion of the *mahashivratri* festival, accompanied by the spectacle of "materializing" *lingas* (emblems of Shiva) "within his body, which he then ejects, with signs of pain and difficulty, from his mouth" (*ibid.*).

163

Critics say that this is a form of blatant showmanship involving considerable deceit. Yet his following is heavily recruited from urban English-educated Indians, with many Western devotees also. He has been described as "the sole trustee of the various trusts" (*ibid.*, p. 286) which function in his sect. "Donations are accepted and property held by a legal entity known as the Central Shri Sathya Sai Trust" (*ibid.*, p. 285), and donations can be made at any branch office of the Canara Bank, which is nationwide. Critics say that he is an accomplished businessman. His organization publishes numerous books about him, the problem for assessors being to determine what is fact as distinct from hagiology. In addition to his ashram at Puttaparthi, Satya Sai has a colony at Whitefield, near Bangalore, and has other residences elsewhere in cities like Madras. Devotees can pay substantial sums to buy "permanent rights in a place to stay during visits to the ashram" (*ibid.*, p. 288). The criterion seems to be money in such matters of receiving devotion. Satya Sai's organization stresses social service and education, which at first sight seems impressive to would-be subscribers. Though Satya definitely does patronize those activities, it seems to be the wealthy devotees who dispense the charities, the figurehead being far more conspicuous for miracles like "materializing" valuables for his urban worshippers. By 1979 there were four Sathya Sai Colleges in India, including those for girls; a *bal vikas* (child development) programme was also promoted, seeking to supplement secular education with religious instruction. This *bal vikas* project is proclaimed as being non-sectarian, though "the symbolism deployed in the classes is distinctly Hindu" (*ibid.*, p. 287). Following a general trend in neo-Hinduism, Satya Sai considers his message to be religiously universal, though in practise this is ambiguous. "What Muslims make of this kind of ecumenism I do not know," writes a sociologist (*ibid.*). The analysis is forthcoming that "even if some concessions are made to other religions in these classes, they are clearly locked into essentially Hindu devotional patterns" (*ibid.*). Indeed, a close investigation of his teachings reveals a basically conservative attitude, involving "a view deeply conditioned by the ideology of caste" (*ibid.*, p. 290). The teaching of Satya Sai Baba "does not advocate the upsetting of existing hierarchies" (*ibid.*), a point underlined by his statement: "The cry of equality now being used as a slogan is a vain and meaningless cry" (*ibid.*, citing Kasturi, ed., *Sathya Sai Speaks Vol. 9*, p. 29). Satya's discourses have appeared in a multi-volume work compiled by his biographer N. Kasturi, published at various venues since the early 1970s. According to the assessment of Babb, there is present in Satya Sai's eclecticism "a persistent note of cultural nationalism of a kind that sometimes verges on nativism" (*ibid.*, p. 289). There is also "a harsh judgment of the Westernization of India" (*ibid.*, p. 290) expressed by Satya Sai Baba, who advocates instead "the folkways that have been preserved by the folk-mind of this land" (*ibid.*, citing *Sathya Sai Speaks Vol. 7*, p. 43). Critics wonder if that means the folk superstitions about miracles which Satya uses to enhance his avataric role. Satya stands in contrast to Swami Vivekananda, who wanted to employ Western science to offset superstitions. According to the sociologist cited above, Satya's "views on the innate characteristics of women are of a piece with his views on caste, and are hardly enlightened, at least from a feminist point of view" (*ibid.*, p. 291). The discourses of Satya Sai advocate that women should not be seen or talked about, and should be invisible partners and inspirers (*ibid.*, citing *Sathya Sai Speaks Vol. 9*, p. 65). Although Satya is associated with the education of women, his ideal is not therefore what Westerners conceive of as emancipation. He has attracted many Western admirers via the New Age media, though a fair number of these have become non-partisans after discovering more about him. Cf. Shepherd, *Minds and Sociocultures Vol. 1* (Cambridge: Philosophical Press, 1995), pp. 714–16, which comments in a critical vein on a holiday brochure produced in Britain about Satya Sai Baba and his Indian centres.

3.   A. Rigopoulos, *The Life and Teachings of Sai Baba of Shirdi* (Albany, New York: State University of New York Press, 1993), p. xix. This book claims to be a "comprehensive monography" based on a Ph.D. thesis of 1987. It became rated as a major work on the subject, but has some marked defects. The interpretation is basically in the Hinduizing mould, though with some acknowledgement of a Muslim and Sufi complexion to the subject. The version of Rigopoulos tends to follow the "orthodox" angle of the Shirdi Sai Baba Sansthan, and is strongly anchored in the miracleworking presentation of Narasimhaswami and Gunaji. There is also a disconcerting deference to the views of Satya Sai Baba. The overall paradigm is that of the "Sai Baba movement," in which are included references to Upasni Maharaj and Meher Baba, though in a subsidiary register which obscures much relevant detail.

4.   *Ibid.*, pp. 376–7.

5.   *Ibid.*, p. 21.

6.   *Ibid.*, pp. 26–7. Of the longer narration, Rigopoulos notes that "the whole perspective is a Hindu one" (*ibid.*, p. 25), while the second and shorter account given in 1990 allows four years of adoption by a Sufi *faqir* in Shirdi Sai's infancy. It is difficult to avoid the conclusion that non-Hindu elements have been relegated in the version of Satya Sai.

7.   *Ibid.*, p. 21.

8.   *Ibid.*

9.   *Ibid.*, p. 20, and citing as the source a booklet entitled *Sri Sai Vani* (July–Aug. 1981). This citation gives the false impression that the report associated with the Hyderabad lawyer is a late one of recent years.

10.   B. K. Narayan, *Saint Shah Waris Ali and Sai Baba* (New Delhi:

Vikas, 1995), p. 16, citing Rajarshi Bala Sanyasi, *Life and Teachings of Sri Sai Baba* (Bangalore: Sri Parasakti Ashram, 1949), pp. 8–13.

11. Narayan, *op. cit.*, p. 101.

12. *Ibid.*, pp. 17, 102, citing Narasimhaswami, *Life of Sai Baba Vol. 1*, p. 30, and Gunaji, *Shri Sai Satcharita*, p. 40. The Hindu view is that Sai Baba told Mahalsapati (a Hindu devotee) that he was a *brahman* of Pathri and was given into the custody of a *faqir* during his infancy.

13. See B. V. Narasimhaswami, *Sri Sai Baba's Charters and Sayings* (Madras: All India Sai Samaj, 1942*); idem, Devotees' Experiences of Sai Baba* (3 vols, Madras: All India Sai Samaj, 1942); *id., Life of Sai Baba* (4 vols, Madras: All India Sai Samaj, 1955–6; third edn, 1980–5). Rigopoulos, *op. cit.*, p. xxvii, has criticized the present writer for not having mentioned Narasimhaswami's *Life* in my *Gurus Rediscovered*. In that book I did indeed express my distrust of Narasimhaswami's hagiographic and Hinduizing tendencies, and did indeed fail to mention one of that writer's influential works, comparatively late in publication by comparison with other sources. The supposedly exhaustive work of Rigopoulos is by no means beyond criticism. Only Vol. 1 of the *Life* is actually biographical, and the work as a whole "presents a Hinduized version of Sai Baba's life, overshadowing the Islamic influence and background" (Rigopoulos, *Life and Teachings of Sai Baba*, p. xxv). Narasimhaswami may be credited with a genuine attempt at serious biography, but some of his major assumptions and theories have been very misleading, and it is arguable that Rigopoulos has fallen prey to some of these. My amateur contribution, not intended as any exhaustive study, was offered as a remedy to the predominant influence of Narasimhaswami's version. *Gurus Rediscovered* was merely an amplified draft (written mainly in 1978) of an earlier work written in my youth and which was part of a larger unpublished manuscript containing other information about Sai Baba and Upasni Maharaj, in addition to some other saints and gurus. In retrospect, I will concede that it was a failing of mine to omit reference to Narasimhaswami's *Life*; however, the context of my sparing references to his books should be duly noted. Those books have served to distort many events and need not be regarded as definitive. Rigopoulos has evidently borrowed and adapted my cues about the Sufi dimensions in the life of Sai Baba, and briefly acknowledges *Gurus* as a ground-breaking work. The way I arrived at that perspective was by screening out the camouflage provided by Narasimhaswami. I might add that Rigopoulos neglected to mention several of my own published books relating to events in Maharashtra, including *Meher Baba, an Iranian Liberal* (Cambridge, 1988), though he specifically included the latter figure in his version of "the Sai Baba movement."

14. Rigopoulos, *The Life and Teachings of Sai Baba of Shirdi,*

p. 249, citing the description of C. S. J. White, and deeming this appropriate. The paperback cover of the SUNY Press volume tends to promote that blanket description with the statement: "A vast and diversified religious movement originating from Sai Baba of Shirdi, is often referred to as 'the Sai Baba movement.' " The very diversity should belie the blanket description, at least in university literature, though standards are falling. In particular, it is very doubtful if Satya Sai Baba does originate from Shirdi Sai, and also questionable that Meher Baba can be brought under this heading with due accuracy. The latter's first mentor was Hazrat Babajan, who has been relatively ignored. Cf. Shepherd, *A Sufi Matriarch: Hazrat Babajan* (Cambridge, 1986), which is missing from the list of sources given in Rigopoulos, *op. cit.*, p. 219 n.174.

15. Rigopoulos, *op. cit.*, p. xxv.

16. *Ibid.* The questionable work *Devotees' Experiences of Sai Baba* was cited in *Gurus Rediscovered*, p. 79 n.70. I maintain that it is healthy for amateurs to be deeply sceptical of the contents, contrary to the gullibilities of academic enthusiasts of the "Sai Baba movement." I also noted that Narasimhaswami's *Charters and Sayings* contained "some interesting material" (*Gurus Rediscovered*, p. 79 n.61). It is, however, doubtful if some of the sayings attributed to Sai Baba are accurate, although these are regarded as gospel by enthusiasts. The "Sai dialogues" are not beyond suspicion of having been moulded by the expectancies and proselytizing aims of the Shirdi revival assisted by Narasimhaswami. Cf. M. Warren, *Unravelling The Enigma: Shirdi Sai Baba in the Light of Sufism* (New Delhi: Sterling Publishers Ltd, 1999), pp. 13ff., 353ff., who observes a number of relevant points about the Hindu biases of Narasimhaswami, but who is unwilling to credit certain other criticisms about that commentator relayed by the present writer from the literature on Meher Baba. Dr. Warren's version of some emphases found in my *Gurus Rediscovered* is distorting, possibly because that work criticized Satya Sai Baba, whom she supports. Her book is unusual for an attempt to evaluate the Sufi background of Shirdi Sai in the face of Hinduization. Cf. the critical remarks in my *Pointed Observations* (Dorchester, Dorset: Citizen Initiative, 2005), pp. 371ff., note 98. Dr. Warren accuses me of of having dismissed Narasimhaswami as "an opportunist, whose only interest was in elevating himself through writing the biographies of holy men" (Warren, *op. cit.*, p. 24 n. 38). That is an undue compression of the details. I was relaying remarks of Meher Baba, who strongly criticized the miracle instinct of Narasimhaswami, which also found expression in the latter's biography of Upasni Maharaj. Also, I was pointing out that when Narasimhaswami went to Shirdi in the 1930s, he did not have any mentor to correct the devotional distortions that were occurring, and which he furthered (*Gurus Rediscovered*, pp. 3–5). "A dead teacher is much easier to follow than a living specimen" (*ibid.*, p. 5). The cover of Dr. Warren's book describes her interest in writing devotional songs honouring Shirdi Sai and Satya Sai, which may explain why she is so amenable to the subject of miracles.

17. Dabholkar's devotional work was written in Marathi verse, and published in 1929. He assimilated Sai Baba to the Hindu *bhakti* tradition of Maharashtra, and did not understand much about Sufism, it has been concluded. H. S. Dixit added a foreword which merits criticism for having obscured the saint's Muslim background with a divine incarnation theory. Hari Sitaram Dixit was a prominent Hindu devotee who seems to have first visited Shirdi in 1909. He was a lawyer by profession. See Dabholkar, *Shri Sai Satcharita*, trans. I. Kher (Delhi: Sterling Publishers Ltd, 1999). A popular adaptation in English of this work was produced by N. V. Gunaji and published in 1944. See *Shri Sai Satcharita or The Wonderful Life and Teachings of Shri Sai Baba* (tenth edn, Bombay: Sri Sai Baba Sansthan, 1982). Dr. Warren has emphasized that, although many readers have assumed Gunaji's book to be a verbatim translation of Hemadpant, this is far from being accurate. Gunaji both omitted and added, and his additions include frequent Hinduizing interpretations from his own zealous pen. See Warren, *op. cit.*, pp. 3ff. See also note 77 *infra*. Dr. Warren has criticized both Dr. Rigopoulos and myself for not using the Marathi text of Hemadpant (*ibid.*, pp. 15, 18). I am happy to accept that particular criticism. *Gurus Rediscovered* was not a Ph.D. thesis, and I do not read Marathi. Dr. Warren has herself confirmed several aspects of my unconventional monograph. As for Gunaji's misleading adaptation, it made far greater sense to me to rely upon the non-Hinduizing assertions of writers like C. B. Purdom and Dr. Ghani that Sai Baba was a Muslim.

18. Rigopoulos, *op. cit.*, pp. 4–5.

19. C. B. Purdom, *The Perfect Master* (London: Williams and Norgate, 1937), p. 25. The present writer drew attention to Purdom's notice in *Gurus Rediscovered*, p. 5. This notice had formerly been ignored in accounts of the subject.

20. Purdom, *op. cit.*, p. 26. Purdom's information was basically derived from materials supplied by Parsi followers of Meher Baba, who were neutral to the question of Hindu or Muslim origins. It made no difference to them what Sai Baba's religious background was, and this early report is thus particularly relevant.

21. *Ibid.*, p. 26. Cf. B. Kalchuri, *Lord Meher Vol. 1* (North Myrtle Beach, S.C.: Manifestation, 1986), pp. 64–83. This work is a translation from the Hindi original *Meher Prabhu* dating to the early 1970s. Kalchuri's chapter on Sai Baba is to some extent influenced by Hinduization, though it does also contain a strong acknowledgement of the Muslim components, as evidenced in the title "Sai Baba, the Fakir of Allah." The basic conclusion is that "he belonged to no caste or religion or ism" (*ibid.*, p. 66). Kalchuri also states that "some believe that Sai was born into a Brahmin family, that his parents died and he was then raised by a Muslim ascetic. Some believe, however, that he was born in a Mohammedan family and most biographers agree with this belief " (*ibid.*, p. 67). However, most biographers appear to be Hinduizers. It is notable that Kalchuri commences his chapter by quoting the saint's daily invocation at Shirdi: "Allah is the Protector of the poor. There is nothing besides Him. The name of Allah is eternal: Allah is All in all" (*ibid.*, p. 64).

22. Cf. Rigopoulos, *op. cit.*, p. 3, who says that "no historical evidence is available concerning the time and place of his birth, the identity of his parents, or his religious affiliation and training."

23. The Marathi work known as *Bhaktalilamrita*, penned by Das Ganu, was summarized by the Muslim writer Dr. Abdul Ghani Munsiff in his article "Hazrat Sai Baba of Shirdi," *Meher Baba Jnl* (Ahmednagar, 1938–9) Vol. 1. Similar to Charles Purdom, Dr. Ghani identified Sai Baba as a Muslim, though his contribution was neglected prior to *Gurus Rediscovered*, pp. 5ff., where I stated in support: "It seems fairly certain that Sai Baba was actually born of a Muslim family." Rigopoulos has since mentioned Ghani's early article (pp. xxv, 33 n.52), though modifying the Muslim element. Cf. Warren, *op. cit.*, p. 9, who does not do justice to Dr. Ghani's liberal attitude, and who also writes as a partisan of Satya Sai.

24. Ganapat Rao Dattatreya Sahasrabuddhe became known as Das Ganu Maharaj, and gained the repute of being one of Sai Baba's close disciples. His reliability has come under question. He was born at Akolner in 1868, and was a police constable when he first visited Shirdi in 1894. He gave up his role in the police department in 1903, and is believed to have been engaged upon research into the saint's early years, a task supposedly facilitated by his trip to Selu in 1901, where he investigated the memory of Gopalrao Deshmukh. A literate *brahman*, Das Ganu gained the reputation of a pundit among the Shirdi villagers. He was fond of singing hymns in praise of Sai Baba and other saints, and performed regularly at the *urs* fair in Shirdi from 1897. He composed devotional works in Marathi praising Hindu saints and Sai Baba, including *Bhaktalilamrita* and *Shri Sainath Stavanmanjari* (trans. Z. Taraporewala, Bombay: Sai Dhun, 1987). He is documented in Narasimhaswami, *Life of Sai Baba Vol. 2*, pp. 122ff. Cf. M. V. Kamath and V. B. Kher, *Sai Baba of Shirdi: A Unique Saint* (Bombay: Jaico, 1991), pp. 28–9, which strongly questions Das Ganu's reliability with regard to his research on Gopalrao Deshmukh, and which states that Das Ganu rarely saw Sai Baba. "Even when he was in Shirdi, Baba would not allow him to stay long with him; on his own admission Das Ganu got from Baba very few autobiographical details" (*ibid.*, p. 29). Narasimhaswami helped to make Das Ganu famous, and adopted his theory about the Selu guru. Das Ganu is more convincing in stating that Sai Baba was a Muslim despite his (Das Ganu's) own preference for a Hindu identity (Warren, *op. cit.*, p. 105); this controversial but honest reference comes from a verse in his *Stavan-manjari*.

25. Rigopoulos, *op. cit.*, p. 35 n.68, says that there is a discrepancy in my *Gurus Rediscovered* in relation to Narasimhaswami, locating Sai Baba's birthplace at Selu instead of Pathri, and positing Shelwadi as the locale of Venkusha's ashram. In my earlier book, I drew upon Dr. Ghani's article, which identifies the saint's birthplace as Selu, and which says that his father died, and so his mother became a mendicant and took him at the age of five to Gopalrao Deshmukh at Shelwadi. Shelwadi appears to correspond with Shailud, which is an orthographical variant of Sailu, a town which changed name to Selu after Indian Independence in 1947. Selu is very closely adjacent to Pathri, a village now believed by many Hindus to have been Sai Baba's birthplace. There is no proof of where he was born. Rigopoulos does not appear to have read Dr. Ghani, whom he lists as a primary source; he cites some sources in the Meher Baba literature without acknowledgment that it was me who first drew attention to them in the context afforded. The chronological table of primary sources arrayed by Rigopoulos (*ibid.*, pp. xxiv–xxvi) reveals that Dr. Ghani's article ranks as third in order, even though Rigopoulos does not cite any page number from that article in his amplified doctoral thesis. As the primary sources prior to the 1950s extend to only five works, he might have spent more time studying the sole Muslim version listed (and which was first used by me as a source). The only two sources earlier than Ghani were Hemadpant and the memoranda of H. S. Dixit. Furthermore, the sole recognition made by Rigopoulos of my use of the Meher Baba literature was very misleading in a work that is supposedly expert in the sources cited. Rigopoulos states: "Shepherd's portrayal of Sai Baba as a Sufi owes much to the views of Meher Baba and his devotional milieu" (*ibid.*, p. xxvii). My portrayal owes nothing to the devotional milieu of Meher Baba, of which I am very critical. That milieu is in general completely unconcerned with the issue of whether Sai Baba was a Sufi. My portrayal does owe something to the views of Meher Baba, Dr. Ghani, and C. B. Purdom. The last two men were comparatively independent thinkers in Meher Baba's following, possessing a more extensive intellect than most others. Purdom's biography of Meher Baba was remarkably objective in style. Both that and Dr. Ghani's article date well prior to the devotional period of the 1950s and 1960s, when Hindu, Parsi, and Western devotionalism markedly increased in the Meher Baba movement, causing distortions and misapprehensions. Cf. Kalchuri, *Lord Meher Vol.*

1, pp. 67–8, who also presents the report that Sai Baba was born in Sailu (Selu), and who also locates Gopalrao Deshmukh in Shelwadi. The same writer adds that "recent evidence points to his birthplace as being in Pathri village in the Parbhani district" (*ibid.*, p. 67). Kalchuri reports the date of 1838 in relation to the posited birth at Sailu, and accepts the date of 1858 (associated with Hemadpant) in relation to the subject's second arrival in Shirdi (*ibid.*, p. 73).

    26.   Kamath and Kher, *op. cit.*, pp. 24ff., referring to Sai Baba as "a child of a fakir" in Das Ganu's version, and to "the fascination of a saintly brahmin for a Muslim boy" (*ibid.*, p. 26). The authors question Das Ganu's reliability, and urge that Gopalrao died in 1802, which is too early for him to have made a disciple of Sai Baba. While this may indeed be a relevant consideration, the fifth chapter in that book (*ibid.*, pp. 128ff.) is very much concerned with promoting the image of Sai Baba as a miracle saint. Cf. Kalchuri, *op. cit.*, pp. 68ff., for another version of Das Ganu, and which likewise refers to Sai Baba as a Muslim boy.

    27.   Rigopoulos, *op. cit.*, p. 13.

    28.   C. Vaudeville, *Kabir Vol. 1* (Oxford University Press, 1974), p. 32. See also Vaudeville, *A Weaver Named Kabir* (Delhi: Oxford University Press, 1993), pp. 69–70, who says that Kabir was a *julaha* or weaver, an Indian Muslim whose ancestry is traceable to one of the *shudra* castes which converted *en masse* to Islam at some time between the twelfth and fourteenth centuries. The weavers retained their low status even as Muslims. Vaudeville provisionally accepts the first half of the fifteenth century as Kabir's *floruit* (*ibid.*, p. 55).

    29.   Stories of Sai Baba's birth at Pathri are not historically proven. One theory on this matter speculates that he was born into the brahmanical Bhusari family of Pathri. See Kamath and Kher, *op. cit.*, pp. 14ff. However, the same book cites H. S. Dixit, a *brahman* devotee of Sai Baba, who wrote: "It cannot be stated with certainty that he was born in Pathri. It cannot be said also definitely whether Sai Baba was a brahmin or Muslim by birth" (*ibid.*, p. 11). All we can be sure of is that Sai Baba made references in conversations to places like Selu, Pathri, Parbhani, and Aurangabad. Even Narasimhaswami had to admit to an ignorance of Sai Baba's birthplace and parentage. Kamath and Kher cite his statement: "The birth and parentage of Sai Baba are wrapped in mystery. We have not come across a single person who has any direct knowledge of them" (*ibid.*, p. 10). The authors refer to that writer as B. V. Narasimha Swamiji, and state that his *Life of Sai Baba* was "first written in 1955, some 37 years after the passing away of the saint" (*ibid.*). Elsewhere, 1955 has been credited as the year of publication (see note 13 *supra*). The reflections of H. S. Dixit, with one or two exceptions, tend to be in the Hinduizing mould. His foreword to Hemadpant was supplemented by his contributions translated in M. V. Pradhan, *Shri Sai Baba of Shirdi* (1933; repr. Shirdi: Sri Sai Baba Sansthan, 1988).

30. A. Osborne, *The Incredible Sai Baba* (London: Rider, 1958), p. 78. Cf. Rigopoulos, *op. cit.*, p. 13, who expresses agreement with Osborne's interpretation, though apparently not realizing the full implications, instead defending the very Hinduizing version of Narasimhaswami and Satya Sai, who has promoted the theory of a Hindu birth.

31. *Gurus Rediscovered*, p. 76 n.21.

32. Kamath and Kher, *op. cit.*, p. 18.

33. *Ibid.*

34. *Ibid.*, p. 13.

35. Rigopoulos, *op. cit.*, p. 5. In *Gurus Rediscovered* I was too moderate towards the Hindu view on this point, referring to "a nondescript robe that might have been worn by either a Muslim or a Hindu" (p. 69).

36. Shepherd, *Gurus Rediscovered*, pp. 16ff. Cf. Rigopoulos, *op. cit.*, pp. 5–6, who acknowledges my contribution, but who typically tries to modify the implications. "The term *majzub* never occurs in our sources on the *faqir's* life" (*ibid.*, p. 6). I never said it did, and only a pedantic attitude would imagine that Hinduizing sources must include the word *majzub* if any associations are deemed possible. Rigopoulos perhaps means that Satya Sai Baba is not in the habit of using the elusive word found in non-Hindu sources. Rigopoulos does not cover most of the themes I expressed, though he does acknowledge some similarities in teaching and behaviour between *majazib* and Sai Baba. He quotes a contracted perspective by R. M. Eaton, whose otherwise commendable research may be found in Eaton, *Sufis of Bijapur 1300–1700: Social Roles of Sufis in Medieval India* (Princeton University Press, 1978). It is unnecessary to adopt Eaton's generalizing view which equates drug use (or drinking *bhang*) with *majazib* lifestyles. The details of this movement are often piecemeal, and do not extend to detailed individual biographies. A substantial number of *majazib* seem to have been affiliated to the Chishti order; they did not leave any writings, and are reported by opponents and flimsy hagiographies. A flexible interpretation is required to ensure due justice. The Chishti order proscribed drugs and alcohol, and unorthodox affiliates need not be regarded as degenerate. I was not attempting to establish any "certain identification" between Sai Baba and *majazib*, but pointed to a wider circuit of liberal Sufis who included "the heretical Jewish sufi known as Sarmad" who was "a highly literate *majzub*" (*Gurus Rediscovered*, p. 21) of the type evidently unknown to Satya Sai preferences (Rigopoulos failed to include my book *From Oppression to Freedom* in his bibliography). A rather more serious confusion of the *majazib* issue has appeared in Warren, *Unravelling the Enigma*, pp. 111–112, who evidences a sweeping disregard for the context supplied in my

Gurus Rediscovered, and who instead attributes to me a theme which cannot be found in *Gurus*, including the cited page 19. The coincidence of certain phraseology leads one to believe that Dr. Warren was confusing my version with the passage in Rigopoulos (p. 6 top line, "attracted to God," a phrase not used by the present writer). Some adapted Ph.D. dissertations require a more reliable method of citation and analysis. Neither Rigopoulos or Warren shows any cognizance of my themes such as the "popular attempts to imitate the impact of entities like Sai Baba who are imperfectly remembered and interpreted; the principle of imitation often amounts to a sheer distortion" (*Gurus*, p. 15). Instead those scholars have elevated the imitation known as Satya Sai Baba, and observers are at liberty to carp at Ph.D. dissertations of that type. Dr. Warren partially compensates for her misrepresentations by devoting a chapter to the Maharashtrian trend towards syncretism between Sufism and Hinduism. The basic syncretism (or symbiosis) was in process from the Mughal era, varying in expression from some exponents in dervish orders to the Kaivan school (see Shepherd, *From Oppression to Freedom*, Cambridge 1988, Part 2). A poetic Maharashtrian variant contributed by Sufis existed from the sixteenth century, and is covered in Warren, *op. cit.*, pp. 156ff. The Muslim version is little known by comparison with the Hindu *bhakti* tradition of Maharashtra. A recent and significant example of this "Maharashtrian" fusion was provided by the teaching of Meher Baba, whose non-poetic magnum opus (published in 1955) combined the terminologies of Sufism and Vedanta. See Shepherd, *Meher Baba, an Iranian Liberal* (Cambridge, 1988), pp. 66ff. That book of mine was ignored by both Rigopoulos and Warren, though the latter included it in her bibliography with the wrong date of publication (Warren, *op. cit.*, p. 426). Shirdi Sai did not produce any systematic correlations between the terminologies involved, and Satya Sai is noted for his Hindu confines. Shirdi Sai was not in any deep affinity with Shaikh Mahammad (d. 1650), whose "missionary impulse as a Sufi was strong" (*ibid.*, p. 167). Shirdi Sai Baba was definitely no missionary, and nor was he a poet. Shaikh Mahammad is associated with Ahmednagar, as also is Meher Baba, whose version of the syncretism was not sectarian. The latter was born a Zoroastrian, and was neutral to the two major religious traditions he encompassed. On the medieval *bhakti* and Sant traditions, see also Shepherd, *Some Philosophical Critiques and Appraisals* (Dorchester, Dorset: Citizen Initiative, 2004), pp. 144ff.

37.   Rigopoulos, *op. cit.*, p. 8, who here seems in strong support of Muslim elements, despite his noticeable attempt to minimize the "ground-breaking" contribution in *Gurus Rediscovered* on p. xxvii of his prologue. The tendency of the academic thesis to borrow from the contribution of rivals even while attempting to undermine them is perhaps

symptomatic of the snobbery involved in the academic pursuit of career prestige, something diametrically opposite to the vocation of a Shirdi Sai Baba, whose eccentricities were clearly in revolt against establishment thinking and caste complacency. It is very possible that Rigopoulos did not like my "underplaying the miraculous element present in the sources" (*ibid.*), in contrast to the high relief he affords that element in his own work.

38. Rigopoulos, *op. cit.*, p. 8.

39. Kamath and Kher, *op. cit.*, p. 7.

40. *Ibid.*, p. 123.

41. *Ibid.*, p. 8.

42. *Ibid.*, p. 284.

43. Rigopoulos, *op. cit.*, p. 14, and citing A. E. Bharadwaja, *Sai Baba the Master* (Ongole, 1983), p. 12. See also S. S. Anand, *Shri Sai the Superman* (Bombay: Shirdi Sansthan, 1962).

44. Kamath and Kher, *op. cit.*, p. 31.

45. *Ibid.*, p. 30.

46. *Ibid.*

47. *Ibid.*, p. 80, adding that there seems to be no correct information on this matter. Writers like Arthur Osborne were misled by the Venkusha myth, which tended to provide a portrait of a Hindu guru. The present writer made concessions to that myth in *Gurus Rediscovered*, concessions which I now withdraw, in view of the fact that it has become more obvious as to what extent the Hinduizing versions are misleading. On this, see Warren, *op. cit.*, pp. 37ff., who is critical of most sources except Satya Sai Baba. Dr. Warren's attempted identification of "Venkusha" with the legendary Venka Avadhuta celebrated in the Satya Sai lore has aroused scepticism (cf. *ibid.*, pp. 41, 370ff.). That theory stretches scholarly credulity to an extreme.

48. Kamath and Kher, *op. cit.*, p. 81. It was Kamath who wrote *A Unique Saint*, and he is here reporting Kher's communication to him. V. B. Kher supplied the English translation from Marathi and Gujarati sources, and also much of the data. Kher wrote a string of research articles in the monthly journal *Shri Sai Leela* from 1976 onwards, including "Sai Baba and Sufis" (Feb. 1990). Kher believes that Sai Baba left his *brahman* family at Pathri at the age of eight to accompany a Sufi faqir, and seems to credit 1850 as the latest possible date for this event (*A Unique Saint*, p. 6). The date of birth is here placed between 1838 and 1842. The subject did not arrive at Shirdi until 1868 at the earliest (*ibid.*).

49. B. K. Narayan, *Saint Shah Waris Ali and Sai Baba* (1995) p. 36. This book gives a glowing account of Shah Waris Ali, and includes reference to miraculous phenomena. One source cited is S. I. Husain, "A Nineteenth Century Saint," an article originally published in 1922 and reprinted at Lucknow in 1980.

50. Narayan, *op. cit.*, p. 49, which says that "thousands of Hindus are also stated to have received initiation from the master's hands."

51. *Ibid.*, p. 94–5.

52. *Ibid.*, p. 95.

53. *Ibid.*, p. 99.

54. *Ibid.*, p. 100, reporting on *Al Basheer*, April 18th, 1905. I am quoting Narayan, who is detailing the newspaper tribute.

55. *Ibid.*, covering an entry in *Akhbar Vakil*, January 27th, 1909.

56. *Ibid.*, p. 102.

57. *Ibid.*, pp. 104–5.

58. *Ibid.*, p. 105.

59. *Ibid.*, pp. 7–8.

60. *Ibid.*, p. 14.

61. *Ibid.*, pp. 108, 15–16.

62. This was the purport of my comment in *Minds and Sociocultures Vol. 1*, p. 214, that he "may have possessed the predominantly Turkish blood which flowed in the veins of many Indian Muslims." I am inclined to believe that the subject was born a Muslim, but the nature of the sources does not permit categorical statements.

63. Kamath and Kher, *op. cit.*, p. 31. Cf. Rigopoulos, *op. cit.*, p. 7. Cf. R. D. Ranade, *Mysticism in India: The Poet-Saints of Maharashtra* (Albany: State University of New York Press, 1983), p. 214.

64. Kamath and Kher, *op. cit.*, p. 39.

65. When *Gurus Rediscovered* appeared, some parties were unhappy with the description of Sai Baba as a sufi (small s), despite all the evidence and indications that he was a Muslim. So in this volume, I will refer to him by the neutral term of saint.

66. M. Sahukar, *Sai Baba, the Saint of Shirdi* (third edn, Bombay: Somaiya, 1983), p. 22. Cf. Kamath and Kher, *op. cit.*, p. 74, which calls the *Shri Sai Satcharita* a "hallowed text" but which also cautions that "the core of it is in essence a legend rather than historical truth."

67. Sahukar, *op. cit.*, p. 24.

68. Osborne, *The Incredible Sai Baba*, pp. 15–16. In response to such statements, the present author countered with: "It seems fairly certain that Sai Baba was actually born of a Muslim family" (*Gurus Rediscovered*, p. 5). My cues for that conclusion were principally Purdom and also Ghani's version of Das Ganu, though I also had in mind the Muslim minority at Shirdi who claimed the saint as a Muslim. The fact that he was identified as a Muslim saint even by local Hindus is surely not a factor to be overlooked.

69. Osborne, *op. cit.*, p. 16.

70. *Ibid.*, p. 69.

71. *Ibid.*

72. *Ibid.*, p. 73.

73. M. H. Harper, *Gurus, Swamis, and Avataras: Spiritual Masters and their American Disciples* (Philadelphia: Westminster Press, 1972), p. 17.

74. Rigopoulos, *op. cit.*, p. 5.

75. Harper, *op. cit.*, p. 20. Harper visited Shirdi in the 1960s.

76. *Ibid.*, p. 23.

77. See Warren, *Unravelling the Enigma*, pp. 5ff., who duly emphasizes the drawbacks in Gunaji's version of Hemadpant, and who stresses that some writers have inaccurately assumed that Gunaji made a faithful translation of Hemadpant. This has led to the situation in which Gunaji's Hindu exegesis has been mistaken for the actual words of Sai Baba (*ibid.*, p. 6). In fact, Gunaji and Hemadpant must be recognized as quite separate versions of the Shirdi saint, the former much less reliable. Amongst the errors of Gunaji was to ignore the significance of Sai Baba having been in the habit of speaking in Deccani Urdu, a Muslim language (*ibid.*, p. 7).

78. Rigopoulos, *op. cit.*, p. 70.

79. The dating for this event is a vexed issue. I here defer to the calculation of V. B. Kher which states 1868–72, and which amounts to a modification of Narasimhaswami. The saint settled on his second visit to Shirdi; the first visit is placed only two months earlier in Kher's version (*A Unique Saint*, p. 6), though other writers have implied a longer period. In particular, Rigopoulos seems to give some weight to the claim of Satya Sai Baba that Shirdi Sai was born in 1835 and reached Shirdi in 1851, following the conventional estimate of sixteen years of age (*Life and Teachings of Sai Baba*, p. 45). Rigopoulos also comments that this number could be symbolic (*ibid.*, p. 52 n.3). Kher is perhaps more realistic in believing that the subject was at least twenty-five when he arrived in Shirdi (*A Unique Saint*, p. 6). No definite date or age can be given by anyone not claiming omniscience.

80. Rigopoulos, *op. cit.*, p. 60.

81. *Ibid.*, p. 52.

82. *Ibid.*, p. 17, and citing Narasimhaswami, *Charters and Sayings*, p. 207. Cf. Osborne, *op. cit.*, p. 69.

83. Rigopoulos, *op. cit.*, p. 18, who says of the *dhuni* fire that "we find it widely attested to among Sufi orders and *faqirs.*" Cf. Osborne, *op. cit.*, p. 14, who thinks that Sai's habit of maintaining the *dhuni* was "more like a Parsi than a Muslim." Cf. Shepherd, *Gurus Rediscovered*, p. 28, observing that Muslim *faqirs* had adopted the Hindu custom.

84. Shepherd, *Minds and Sociocultures Vol. 1*, p. 461.

85. Osborne, *The Incredible Sai Baba*, pp. 106–7.

86. Rigopoulos, *op. cit.*, p. 47, and even finding yogic significance in Sai Baba's habit of not resting his back against the wall (*ibid.*, p. 84), which seems an extreme deduction. Rigopoulos cites Gunaji's version of the *Sai Satcharita*, a habit which Warren duly regards as a flaw. See Warren, *op. cit.*, p. 18.

87. Rigopoulos, *op. cit.*, p. xxvii.

88. The mosque or *masjid* is described in the sources as a ramshackle structure. Osborne refers to "a dilapidated mud structure with walls only eight feet high by fourteen feet long running round three sides, while the east side stood open to wind and rain" (*The Incredible Sai Baba*, p. 77). The roof was in serious decay, or rather that part of it which was still in existence. Kalchuri refers to the mosque as a "small tin shed" (*Lord Meher Vol. 1*, p. 73), perhaps because tin was used for the roof, or as repairs for the roof. At some uncertain date, the saint allowed devotees to repair the structure, which he refused to vacate, despite attempts at persuasion. He insisted upon details of formal Islamic architecture, complete with minarets and a nimbar facing Mecca (Osborne, *op. cit.*, p. 78). An innovation was the *dhuni* or fireplace.

89. Rigopoulos, *op. cit.*, p. 62, who feasibly explains that the visit to the Khandoba temple is not necessarily to be interpreted as a hagiological embellishment. Cf. Kamath and Kher, *op. cit.*, p. 78, which stresses that accounts vary on a number of particulars relating to the early period at Shirdi. It is here said that there is no confirmation for the story of the saint dancing with *ghungarus* (bells) tied around his ankles. Sai Baba is said to have sang and danced on occasion. With regard to his apparel, Mahalsapati has been quoted as saying that the saint initially wore a *kafni* and cap of ochre colour, which is the colour favoured by Hindu holy men. Yet a tailor is reported to have stitched a green *kafni* and cap for him, the colour green being associated with Muslims. Kamath and Kher insinuate that these might be contrived stories. The conventional report that Mahalsapati identified Sai Baba as a Muslim at their first encounter tends to belie the story of ochre garments. Cf. Rigopoulos, *op. cit.*, pp. 64, 105–6, who relates that Sai Baba would sometimes make nocturnal visits to a hospice for Muslim visitors and there sing hymns in languages that the local people could not understand, apparently Persian or Arabic for the most part, though with some more popular songs of Kabir in Urdu. At the hospice he was in the company of Muslim dancers and musicians (*ibid.*, p. 292). Rigopoulos compares this singing and dancing to the Sufi practice of *sama*, and credits that it ceased about 1890. At some time during his stay at the mosque, the saint began to listen on some evenings to sessions of devotional music performed by Muslim or Hindu artistes. He would sometimes participate by singing or dancing (*ibid.*, p. 85), to judge from a report of 1911–12, though there is some doubt about this.

90. Rigopoulos, *op. cit.*, p. 64, citing Narasimhaswami, *Life Vol. 1*, p. 20.

91. *Ibid.*, p. 64.

92. *Ibid.*

93. Kamath and Kher, *op. cit.*, p. 7.

94. The sources refer to an early group of Hindu followers. It seems that two men in particular became personal attendants of Sai at the mosque, namely the priest Mahalsapati and Tatya Kote. "Many of the villagers would sarcastically refer to them as 'the trio of the Masjid' " (Kalchuri, *op. cit.*, p. 73), a stigma which implies that some time elapsed before local assessment changed in favour of the *faqir*. That change was probably due to his ministrations involving herbs and inexpensive drugs acquired from village shops. He is said to have cured snake-bite and even leprosy, with the consequence that he became known as a *hakim*, a term for doctor in Islamic sectors (Rigopoulos, *op. cit.*, p. 65).

95. Cf. Rigopoulos, *op. cit.*, pp. 68–9; Kamath and Kher, *op. cit.*, p. 7.

96. Kamath and Kher, *op. cit.*, p. 8.

97. Rigopoulos, *op. cit.*, p. 89.

98. Kamath and Kher, *op. cit.*, pp. 86, 90.

99. *Ibid.*, p. 14.

100. Rigopoulos, *op. cit.*, p. 70.

101. *Ibid.*, p. 69.

102. Kamath and Kher, *op. cit.*, pp. 8, 126.

103. Rigopoulos, *op. cit.*, p. 91.

104. Cf. Rigopoulos, pp. 91ff., who refers to the event of apparent expiry as "all-important," and who encourages interest in "the powers (*siddhis*) which can be attained through yogic exercises" (*ibid.*, p. 93), and who urges that "properly executed, *pranayama* has great curative value" (*ibid.*). There is no proof that *pranayama* was involved in the 1886 episode, and Sai Baba himself has been elsewhere quoted as pointing out the dangers in such a practice. "Whoever proceeds by means of *pranayama* will have to come to me ultimately for further progress" (Osborne, *The Incredible Sai Baba*, p. 106). Upasni Maharaj discovered that complexity somewhat to the cost of his health. The misguided enthusiasm which some academics entertain for distractions is perhaps more remarkable than some of the fake miracles popularly feted in India. It is much easier to agree with Rigopoulos that the *Shri Sai Satcharita* was far more unsentimental in reporting the event under discussion than Narasimhaswami, eschewing any miraculous overtones and relating that the attempt involved was to overcome asthma. Yet the same scholar's resort to a footnote discussion of the symbolism of the number three in relation to the 1886 episode may be treated as an unnecessary diversion

(Rigopoulos, p. 96 n.43). The citation of J. Gonda's *Triads in the Veda* is surely an academic exercise in superfluous bibliography for the Sai Baba context. Cf. Warren, *op. cit.*, pp. 45–6, who interprets the episode in terms of "a direct experience of union with God."

105. Kamath and Kher, *op. cit.*, p. 8; Narasimhaswami, *Life Vol. 2.*

106. A report appeared in Narasimhaswami's *Devotees' Experiences of Sai Baba*, and was also furthered by Gunaji. Narasimhaswami was very influential in his conclusion that Sai Baba knew Sanskrit. That interpretation was followed by other writers, and served to strengthen the tendency to portray the saint in a Hinduized manner. See, e.g., Osborne, *op. cit.*, p. 22ff.; Kamath and Kher, *op. cit.*, pp. 18ff.; Rigopoulos, *op. cit.*, pp. 128ff. Cf. Warren *op.cit.*, pp. 356ff., 410ff., who is more convincing on this matter, observing that Sai Baba's interpretation of a *Gita* verse was "totally different" from the version of Shankara and other Hindu commentators. The circumstances of his exposition were such that he did not need to know Sanskrit, as Chandorkar supplied him with the verbal cues necessary.

107. *Gurus Rediscovered*, p. 34. I cited Osborne's account, which merely mentions the name Nana, and did not adequately correlate with other sources.

108. Kamath and Kher, *op. cit.*, p. 270.

109. Osborne, *op. cit.*, p. 21.

110. *Ibid.*

111. Narasimhaswami, *Life Vol. 1*, pp. 26ff.; Kamath and Kher, *op. cit.*, pp. 8, 102–3; Rigopoulos, *op. cit.*, pp. 102–3.

112. Narasimhaswami, *Life Vol. 3*, pp. 171ff. Abdul gains only a few pages in the *Life*, as contrasted with thirty pages on Das Ganu, forty pages on Mahalsapati, and a yet larger number on Nanasaheb Chandorkar in Vol. 2. An improvement has occurred in M. Warren, *Unravelling the Enigma: Shirdi Sai Baba in the Light of Sufism* (1999), pp. 261ff., which includes a translation of Abdul's notebook.

113. This appears to mean *fiqh*, Islamic law.

114. *Tariqat* signifies the Sufi way.

115. A word otherwise rendered as Qadiriyya.

116. A word more usually rendered as Chishtiyya.

117. Kamath and Kher, *op. cit.*, p. 93.

118. Warren, *op. cit.*, pp. 120–1. Cf. Rigopoulos, *op. cit.*, pp. 111–12, citing the report in Gunaji, and believing that *Rama-Navami* "was, for many years, the only Hindu festival that Baba showed interest in celebrating." Cf. Kamath and Kher, *op. cit.*, pp. 125–6. The *Rama-Navami* festival eventually dominated the Muslim partner, which lost profile after the saint's death. The historical irony is that "in defence of Sai Baba's Hindu status, Hindu devotees often cite the fact that Sai Baba celebrated the Hindu festival" (Warren, *op. cit.*, p. 120).

119. Rigopoulos, *op. cit.*, p. 109.

120. *Ibid.*, p. 20.

121. Cf. *ibid.*, p. 105, who makes no comment on the report cited from Narasimhaswami (*Life Vol. 3*, p. 173). The saint is reported to have gone into ecstasy on occasions when he passed the Maruti temple. I would like here to correct a statement made in *Gurus Rediscovered*, p. 70, that during the Great War Sai Baba "would regularly visit the main Hindu temple in the village." I borrowed from a devotional report which was misleading. It seems that the saint never entered any of the Hindu temples, though he regularly passed by the Maruti temple. The building which he did regularly visit was the *chavadi*, an edifice used as a hostel for visitors. From an early date he had been in the habit of sleeping alternate nights at this *chavadi*, perhaps because it was more commodious than the ruined mosque. Whenever he left the mosque for the *chavadi*, he had to pass the Maruti temple, though a distance of about twenty yards intervened between his route and the temple. I have been unable to verify the report that Sai Baba caused a temple to be erected near the mosque in honour of his guru Gopalrao Deshmukh (Kalchuri, *Lord Meher Vol. 1*, p. 79, who also says that *arati* and *puja* would be performed in that temple). It is also said that "when Sai Baba would come from the mosque to the temple of Gopal Rao, his arti would be sung between these two buildings" (*ibid.*, p. 80). Kalchuri associates this practice with the four years of the Great War, i.e., the First World War of 1914–18. A confusion seems to have occurred with the *chavadi*, which was not a temple but a hostel. At the mid-way point between the mosque and *chavadi*, devotees often performed the *arati* ceremony. Dr. Ghani early described this situation in his article "Hazrat Sai Baba of Shirdi" (1938–9), p. 56, emphasizing the years of the Great War and the distinctive "signs in the air" made by the saint (or master) while in a radiant mood. Ghani emphasized the subject's "peculiar lustre and radiance" at such times.

122. At these times of worship, in his more benign moods, Sai Baba would allow devotees to adorn him with flowers, and even to smear sandal paste and vermilion on his forehead in accordance with Hindu customs. This concession gave rise to the theme that "he dressed like a Muslim and bore the caste marks of a Hindu" (Sahukar, *op. cit.*, p. 24). This rather misleading statement is repeated by Kalchuri, *op. cit.*, p. 80, likewise not providing the context for the supposed caste marks.

123. Rigopoulos, *op. cit.*, p. 70.

124. *Ibid.*, p. 141.

125. Narasimhaswami, *Charters and Sayings*, p. 262. Formerly cited in Rigopoulos, p. 189, who does not, however, draw the full implications relevant to the situation. It is perhaps little wonder if Sai called himself a *brahman* in the face of caste snobbery, and one does not really need to attach much symbolic importance to any such reference.

126. Chokhamela lived in Sangli district and was a devotee of the god Vithala at Pandharpur. Because he was an outcaste, he could only pray to his deity outside the temple (Kamath and Kher, *op. cit.*, pp. 52–3).

127. Osborne, *op. cit.*, p. 108, who observes the similarity on this point with Ramana Maharshi.

128. Rigopoulos, *op. cit.*, pp. 114–16, who suggests that the plank might have been in use for a short period only, and who points out discrepancies in the sources. Rigopoulos seems to suggest that this was an act of *siddhis*, i.e., levitation, and classifies it as a miracle in his index (*ibid.*, p. 458 col. 1). Cf. Shepherd, *Gurus Rediscovered*, pp. 38–9.

129. Cf. Rigopoulos, *op. cit.*, pp. 106–7, who narrates the hagiology as if it were fact, though he observes that "the miracle of changing water into oil appears to be a prodigy often attributed to heterodox Sufis." Cf. Osborne, pp. 14–15, who also seems to regard the popular report as fact. Cf. Shepherd, *Gurus Rediscovered*, p. 30, which is critical of Narasimhaswami's version of events.

130. Kamath and Kher, *op. cit.*, p. 9.

131. *Ibid.*, p. 14.

132. See also Shepherd, *Minds and Sociocultures Vol. 1*, p. 200 n.274. See also note 13 *supra*. See also Rigopoulos, *op. cit.*, pp. xxv–xxvii, who lists amongst his primary sources Ramalingaswami, *Ambrosia in Shirdi* (Shirdi 1984), and describing this as presenting "within a hagiographic mould, about two hundred episodes of Sai Baba's miraculous feats." Half of those feats are said to have occurred after the saint's death. The strange license given to some popular ideas in an academic book published by a University Press is sufficient for amateurs to abandon officious lists of primary sources in the endeavour to ascertain history as distinct from hagiology. *Ambrosia in Shirdi* also dwells upon the ritual activities promoted at Shirdi by the Shri Sai Baba Sansthan, a Hinduizing organization or public trust created by H. S. Dixit in the 1920s. In several respects, Rigopoulos is an apologist for this organization, failing to penetrate the devotional glosses and miracle lore.

133. Rigopoulos, *op. cit.*, pp. 139–40, stating that Sai never asked his vegetarian devotees to eat non-vegetarian food.

134. Cf. Kamath and Kher, *op. cit.*, p. 18. See also Kalchuri, *Lord Meher Vol. 1*, p. 77, who says that on rare occasions Sai Baba would himself cook meat and distribute it to those around him. Cf. the more detailed references in Warren, *op. cit.*, pp. 5, 105–6.

135. Rigopoulos, p. 123, and citing Ramalingaswami, *Ambrosia in Shirdi*. Rigopoulos says that "sharing the pipe of a holy man ... is traditionally believed to carry a special blessing or reward due to one's good conduct" (*ibid.*). However, Sai Baba often seems to have been in the mood to test conduct, one would infer from varied episodes. Cf. Kalchuri, *op. cit.*, p. 64, who misleadingly refers to Sai Baba as smoking "a *chilum* pipe of opium," which contrasts with other explicit references of the same writer to Sai Baba's use of tobacco. How that confusion arose is not clear, as Kalchuri does not cite any sources in his chapter on the Shirdi saint. Other accounts refer to tobacco as the commodity, a factor underlined by the large number of devotees who shared in smoking the pipe and who knew the difference between the substances here referred to. We may therefore accept that Sai Baba was a tobacco-smoker on a regular basis. He used the rustic clay pipe known as *chilim*, an item which quickly wore out. On some occasions he employed his pipe for the purpose of offputting urban visitors who did not like foul-smelling tobacco pipes, a typical gesture of the type which it is relevant to understand in any analysis of Shirdi Sai Baba. Tobacco was popular amongst Muslims in that region of India, as attested by the *1884 Gazetteer of the Bombay Presidency*. See also Warren, *op. cit.*, pp. 105–106, who observes that "there is no hint anywhere in the literature that Sai Baba ever smoked or consumed" the hemp or *bhang* that some *faqirs* resorted to. Kalchuri may be considered accurate in stating that "whatever food or tobacco he (Sai) wanted he begged for" (*Lord Meher*, p. 73). The saint's begging round was noted for his continual request for food, tobacco, and lamp oil, and as this activity was the source for anything he consumed, one may conclude that he was typical of the Muslim partiality for tobacco in the Ahmednagar region.

136. E.g., Professor G. G. Narke, who became a devotee in 1913, reports that Sai frequently spoke of his travels in an invisible body over great distances (Osborne, *op. cit.*, p. 86). Narke was a Professor of geology and chemistry at the Poona College of Engineering, and is probably one of the most reliable witnesses described by Narasimhaswami (*Life* Vol. 3, pp. 111ff.). Narke also attested that the saint's language was "highly cryptic – full of symbology, parable, allegory and metaphor" (*The Incredible Sai Baba*, p. 85). He also reported that most of the people who visited Sai Baba "were superficial and sought only material benefits" (*ibid.*, p. 57). Osborne emphasized that the saint often refused to give cures, and that in some cases where he was asked to bless with progeny he would affirm that "there was no child in that person's destiny" (*ibid.*, pp. 57–8). Rigopoulos reiterates that "most people, in fact, went to Shirdi because of poor health or problems of the most various sorts" (*Life and Teachings of Sai Baba*, p. 152), though his account strikes some readers as being uncritical in certain respects.

137. Rigopoulos, *op. cit.*, p. 161, who is citing P. S. Bharucha, *Sai Baba of Shirdi* (Shirdi: Shri Sai Sansthan, 1980), p. 68. Both Rigopoulos and Bharucha supply a version of the "cholera antidote" episode.

Bharucha's devotional book relies heavily upon Gunaji's version of He-madpant, which has been considered very misleading. See Warren, *op. cit.*, p. 6, who says that Bharucha "places much of Gunaji's Hindu inter-pretation as coming directly from the lips of Sai Baba."

138. Rigopoulos, *op. cit.*, p. 160, who overworks the theme of sym-bolic grinding, associating Sai Baba's grinding-mill with stories of Ram-das and Kabir which do not tally with the Shirdi event.

139. Narasimhaswami, *Charters and Sayings*, p. 7.

140. The report of Narasimhaswami refers to the four *sadhanas* and six *shastras*, which have been defined as the four *margas* or yogas (*kar-ma, bhakti, jnana*, and *raja*) and the six *darshanas*. See Rigopoulos, *op. cit.*, p. 211 nn.19–20. On the *darshanas*, see Shepherd, *Minds and Socio-cultures Vol. 1*, pp. 625ff.

141. Rigopoulos, *op. cit.*, pp. 154–5, citing A. E. Bharadwaja, *Sai Baba the Master*, pp. 21–2. It is very probable that Bharadwaja's brief ac-count of Balakrishna and his brother represents a devotional "miracle" report of Upasni Maharaj and his brother Balakrishna, who was a Profes-sor at the Poona Training College.

142. Osborne, *op. cit.*, p. 106.

143. Rigopoulos, *op. cit.*, pp. 104, 144, says that the request for *dak-shina* coincided with the inauguration of congregational *puja*, during the same year of 1908. Cf. Kamath and Kher, *op. cit.*, p. 9, stating that the congregational worship commenced in 1909.

144. Kamath and Kher, *op. cit.*, pp. 246ff.; Rigopoulos, *op. cit.*, pp. 144ff.; Osborne, *op. cit.*, pp. 93ff. Cf. Shepherd, *Gurus Rediscovered*, pp. 48ff.

145. Kamath and Kher, *op. cit.*, p. 118. Cf. Rigopoulos, *op. cit.*, p. 223, citing Bharadwaja, who says that the family of Ramadasis be-longed to the Kabirpanth.

146. Kamath and Kher, *op. cit.*, pp. 112–14. Cf. the condensed ver-sion in Osborne, *op. cit.*, pp. 44–5, who says that Sai Baba requested some ochre dye to colour his robe, but did not in fact dye it or wear ochre, instead continuing to wear his accustomed white *kafni*.

147. According to Sahukar, *op. cit.*, p. 52, "he relaxed this severe dis-cipline and would partake of the *naiveda*, i.e., food given as offering by any of the visiting devotees."

148. Kamath and Kher, *op. cit.*, p. 293.

149. Cf. Shepherd, *Minds and Sociocultures Vol. 1*, p. 833 n.27. Cf. Rigopoulos, *op. cit.*, p. 226. Although some Hindus have denied that Sai Baba was circumcised, it is possible that Sai Sharan Anand and others glossed over a problem in exegesis. Cf. Kamath and Kher, *op. cit.*, p. 18, who affirm: "It has been said that he was not circumcised, again a sure indication that he could not have been born to a Muslim family." This interpretation in effect denies Hemadpant, who states that the saint was circumcised. See Warren, *op. cit.*, p. 352. See also *ibid.*, p. 105, stating "we may infer that Sai Baba was almost certainly circumcised."

150. Rigopoulos relates this story with apparent approval (*op. cit.*, pp. 224–5). That acceptance seems the more facile to the present author in view of the same writer's criticism of my view of Narasimhaswami's hagiographic tendencies (*op. cit.*, p. xxvii). The fact that someone can be stigmatized by an academic "expert" for detecting hagiographic flourishes in the Sai literature is perhaps reason for amateurs to be more sceptical of academic "one-up" tactics, particularly in the ranks of those partisan to Satya Sai Baba. A healthy rationalism is surely long overdue in these subjects. See also note 167 *infra*.

151. Ramalingaswami, *Ambrosia in Shirdi*, pp. 100ff., cited in Rigopoulos, *Life and Teachings of Sai Baba*, pp. 223–4.

152. Rigopoulos, *op. cit.*, pp. 227–8, citing the diary of G. S. Khaparde in *Shri Sai Leela* (February 1986), p. 13. Khaparde was a close colleague of Tilak, and a devotee of Sai Baba. He had gone to Shirdi in 1910 in flight from the repressive political situation affecting the nationalist party. See Narasimhaswami, *Life Vol. 2*, pp. 298ff. Khaparde stayed in Shirdi for a week in December 1910, and for three months in 1911, and also thereafter; his diaries have been published at Shirdi. He was a wealthy man because of his legal practice. See also Kamath and Kher, *op. cit.*, pp. 286ff.

153. Rigopoulos, *op. cit.*, p. 233, citing Ramalingaswami, *Ambrosia in Shirdi*. Some readers have found amusing the suggestion of Rigopoulos that pseudo Satya Sai Babas may be operating across the Indian subcontinent (*ibid.*, p. 252 n.52). While that is by no means impossible, it seems not to occur to him that the major imitator of Shirdi Sai is endorsed by his book. Rigopoulos gives several indications that he is a sympathizer with the Satya Sai cult.

154. Kamath and Kher, pp. 295–6. Narasimhaswami included a version of this in his *Charters and Sayings*, and has Sai say "After the temple is built, we shall reside there" (see Rigopoulos, *op. cit.*, p. 237).

155. See Kamath and Kher, pp. 6, 9. Bade Baba was also known as Faqir Baba and Faqir Pir Muhammad Yasin Mian. Sai is said to have taught him for twelve years in the Aurangabad vicinity prior to the first arrival at Shirdi. Bade Baba himself came to stay in Shirdi in 1909. These details indicate a relationship that was obscured by the later Hindu following, though Bade Baba is mentioned by Narasimhaswami.

156. Kamath and Kher, *op. cit.*, pp. 291–2. Cf. Rigopoulos, p. 254 n.77 referring to the report of Narasimhaswami. Cf. Shepherd, *Gurus Rediscovered*, p. 29, which reports Meher Baba's assessment of Banemiyan as a *majzub* in the very specific sense of a God-merged entity. Meher

Baba referred to this Sufi as Banemiyan Baba. Cf. Osborne, *op. cit.*, p. 121, who refers to the recipient of Sai Baba's message as "another Muslim saint." This Sufi died in 1921. Cf. Warren, *op. cit.*, pp. 116ff. and plate 17.

157. Kalchuri, *op. cit.*, p. 83. Cf. Kamath and Kher, *op. cit.*, p. 293, stating that "the fever subsided after three days but Baba abjured all food and became progressively weak."

158. Kamath and Kher, *op. cit.*, p. 293, and specifying the presence of Nana Nimonkar, Bhagoji the leper, Madhavrao Deshpande, Bayaji(bai) Kote, Lakshmibai Shinde, and others. Kher's version seems unembroidered, and one may believe that he has corrected another misconception. Some writers say that Sai's very last words were "Ah, Deva!" (Oh God), but according to Kher, it was Nimonkar who uttered "Deva," while Sai merely responded with "Ah" in a weak voice (*ibid.*).

159. *Charters and Sayings*, p. 138.

160. Rigopoulos, *op. cit.*, p. 239.

161. *Ibid.*, p. 238.

162. Osborne, *op. cit.*, p. 122, who says that only two *brahmans* remained with the saint at his death. In *Gurus Rediscovered*, p. 71, I followed the version of Osborne, which appears to be defective. There were apparently at least six devotees with the saint at the end. The person whom he leaned against when expiring was Bayajibai Kote, a Hindu woman of high caste who had been one of his earliest devotees in Shirdi.

163. Osborne, *op. cit.*, p. 122.

164. Rigopoulos, *op. cit.*, p. 241, quoting a report by Bappa Baba, an old devotee of Shirdi said to have witnessed the events. The argument over the saint's burial has elsewhere been viewed as the real beginning of the Hinduization process, which does not seem to have been total amongst the Hindu devotees at that early date.

165. *Ibid.*, pp. 241–2.

166. *Ibid.*, p. 243.

167. *Ibid.*, p. xxvii, mentioning "hagiographic and apologetic concerns" in a manner which has conveyed the impression to unversed readers that my "opinion" is erroneous. Rigopoulos failed to convey that my data on these two concerns was directly derived and cited from a diary on Meher Baba dated 1954, a diary which Rigopoulos failed to mention. This detail was surely relevant in a book which assumed an air of expertise on Meher Baba, to judge from the bibliography cited by Rigopoulos (*ibid.*, pp. 427–9). At least equal justice should have been given to the opinion of Meher Baba as was given to the opinion of Satya Sai Baba, especially as Meher Baba was actually in physical contact with Shirdi Sai, Upasni Maharaj, and Narasimhaswami, unlike Rigopoulos or Satya Sai. See further note 388 *infra*. The Kishan Singh diary has also been neglected by Dr. Warren's version of one-upmanship.

168. Rigopoulos, *Life and Teachings of Sai Baba*, p. xxv.

169. Cf. *ibid.*, p. 255 n.104, citing Narasimhaswami, *Life Vol. 2*, pp. 339ff.

170. Osborne, *op. cit.*, p. 125, who uncritically endorsed popular beliefs. Osborne refers to Swami B. V. Narasimhaswami in his Acknowledgment, which clearly follows the President of the All India Sai Samaj.

171. Quoted in Rigopoulos, *op. cit.*, p. 246, who is citing Narasimhaswami, *Life Vol. 2*, p. 348. Rigopoulos also observes here that Narasimhaswami gave "involuntary support" to the claims of Satya Sai by dedicating a chapter of his *Life Vol. 4* to a description of Shirdi Sai's "numerous *lilas* in southern India, and particularly in Andhra" (Rigopoulos, p. 249). The subject of *lila*, literally meaning play, but here meaning posthumous miracles, is not taken seriously by most historians.

172. Rigopoulos, *op. cit.*, p. 249.

173. Despite the attempts of some Satya Sai partisans to depict their figurehead as gaining ground in this direction. For instance, Rigopoulos finds it significant that Mani Sahukar added a favourable chapter on Satya Sai in the third edition of her popular book on Shirdi Sai (*ibid.*, p. 257 n.124). Sahukar's contribution is a devotional work fairly typical of the disposition which does not sufficiently analyse details incorporated. Yet Sahukar did refrain from identifying the two Sais as the same entity (*Sai Baba the Saint of Shirdi*, p. 89). She noted that Satya Sai's "bizarre miracles" of "producing 'uddhi' from empty space and the materialization of all kinds of silver and gold images and rings from his mouth give one a queer feeling of apparent showmanship which is not attractive" (*ibid.*, p. 90). She was one of those impressed by the hospitals and schools which Satya Sai established, though critics take the view that his ashram funds are more than adequate to such ventures, which are very suspect when closely analysed, as in the case of the Super Speciality Hospital. See also note 2 *supra*, and especially Appendix One *infra*.

174. Cf. Rigopoulos, *op. cit.*, p. 372, who in his advocacy of the blanket term, actually tries to present Satya Sai as having improved upon Shirdi Sai in respect of asserting "it is significant that Satya Sai Baba has extended Shirdi Baba's universalism to comprehend the five main religions present on Indian soil" (*ibid.*, p. 372). This refers to Hinduism, Islam, Buddhism, Christianity, and Zoroastrianism. Rigopoulos relies upon the simple emblem of a lotus flower whose five petals contain the symbols of these religions. Some say that Satya Sai merely copied the concept embodied in the "mastery in servitude" emblem promoted by Meher Baba in which symbols of the same five religions appeared in some earlier publications dating back to the 1940s. See note 403 *infra*. That symbolism is not to be derived from Shirdi Sai. Such gestures of universalism do not necessarily amount to anything more than a glib ecumenicism, and are very suspicious when attended by sleight of hand "miracle" phenomena. Rigopoulos makes no mention in his misleading book of these very questionable devices to deceive the gullible, and instead chooses to close his epilogue with an evident tribute to Satya Sai in terms of deeming the latter's worldwide fame to be "an amazing religious phenomenon" (*ibid.*, p. 377). Cf. Shepherd, *Minds and Sociocultures Vol. 1*, pp. 714–16, for a critical view.

175. The popular work is B. V. Narasimhaswami and S. Subbarao, *Sage of Sakuri: Life Story of Shree Upasani Maharaj* (Madras, 1938; fourth edn, Sakori, 1966). This book received a critical assessment from Meher Baba, who knew the subject quite well. See Shepherd, *Gurus Rediscovered*, pp. 3–4, 74 n.7. See also note 388 *infra*. A subsequent version of Upasni appeared as one of the chapters in Narasimhaswami's *Life of Sai Baba Vol. 2*, to which was appended an argument that Sai Baba had no successor because his divine miracles needed no other intermediary after his death. This view of the situation merits strong criticism, especially as it has been such an influential doctrine intended to enhance a tomb cult.

176. Kalchuri, *Lord Meher Vol. 1*, p. 87, from the chapter entitled "Upasni Maharaj, King of the Yogis." Cf. Purdom, *The Perfect Master* (1937), p. 27, who wrote of Upasni's childhood that "nothing gave him so much joy as the offering of prayers, participation in the performance of ceremonies, and the hearing of sermons." It seems that he outgrew the ritual aspect of Hinduism. Purdom's early version of Upasni's biography may be compared with Dr. C. D. Deshmukh's monograph "Shri Upasni Maharaj of Sakori" in the *Meher Baba Journal*, a source which I followed to some extent in *Gurus Rediscovered*, though it has elsewhere been generally ignored, probably because it was relatively inaccessible, despite a 1965 reprint in *The Awakener*, another periodical devoted to Meher Baba. Deshmukh was a Hindu follower of Meher Baba, a Professor of philosophy at Nagpur University, and his article on Upasni is non-hagiological.

177. M. H. Harper, "The Saint who Suffered: Sri Upasni Baba Maharaj" (35–53) in *idem, Gurus, Swamis, and Avataras* (1972), p. 36. Harper erratically deduced that Upasni was "apparently attracted much more to the weird and supernatural side of his grandfather's teachings than to their practical and vocational aspects" (*ibid.*), which might bear out the subject's penchant for contemplation rather than priestly ritual.

178. *Ibid.*

179. Kalchuri, *op. cit.*, pp. 87–8, who refers to "the pain of a burning fire that had been lit in his heart while keeping the old woman's company as he soon discovered that she was no witch, but a lover of God." This strange episode would suggest that his introspection was triggered by emotions associated with *bhakti* rather than Patanjali Yoga.

180. See Purdom, *op. cit.*, pp. 27–8, who says that Upasni first left home when he was scarcely twelve years old, travelling from Dhulia to Nasik. I followed this version in *Gurus Rediscovered*, pp. 84–5. Other versions state that this departure occurred shortly after his marriage.

181. Cf. Narasimhaswami, *Sage of Sakuri*, pp. 9ff. Cf. Harper, *op. cit.*, pp. 36–7. Cf. Kalchuri, *op. cit.*, p. 88.

182. K. K. Klostermaier, *A Survey of Hinduism* (Albany: State University of New York Press, 1989), pp. 389–90.

183. Narasimhaswami, *op. cit.*, p. 12; Harper, *op. cit.*, p. 37.

184. According to Purdom, *op. cit.*, p. 28, the subject was "about twenty," though some other sources, e.g., Kalchuri, *op. cit.*, p. 90, are more explicit in giving the date of 1890. In *Gurus Rediscovered*, p. 85, I set down the date as 1899, which represents an error of transcription, as does the date of July 1900 (*ibid.*, p. 86) for the return to Satana, which should read July 1890. Though Kalchuri's chronological framework for the years 1890–1910 is probably correct, in other respects he follows Deshmukh and likewise omits controversial data relevant to the later phase at Sakori. Kalchuri frequently writes in a poetic style, and there is a trace of hagiology. There are related problems in Narasimhaswami, who created the trend for describing the "samadhi" of Upasni in the Bhorgad cave, e.g., Sahukar, *op. cit.*, p. 79, writes that "as soon as he sat there, a strange peace enveloped him, completely absorbing him in deep *samadhi*, and in this blissful state he remained immersed for a full year without moving."

185. Purdom, *op. cit.*, p. 29. Some writers date this sojourn to 1892–5. I should here correct my reference to "about the end of 1903" (*Gurus Rediscovered*, p. 87). I was uncertain about exact chronology owing to some discrepancies encountered in published sources and amongst informants.

186. This was known as the Rama Ashram. A photograph taken of Upasni when he was an Ayurvedic physician reveals him as wearing the mark of Vishnu on his forehead (see Kalchuri, *op. cit.*, p. 91). That is sufficient to attest Vaishnava affiliations, though in later years he also acquired Shaiva associations.

187. Cf. Purdom, *op. cit.*, p. 29, who does not refer to the Gwalior phase, and says "he gave free treatment to the poor, and was far more bent on restoring health than upon making money." This version influenced the first draft of *Gurus Rediscovered*, and I failed to duly amplify the matter in the second draft.

188. E.g. Sahukar, *op. cit.*, p. 79, who says that Upasni "repaired to a forest where he plunged into deep meditation." See also Shepherd, *Gurus*

Rediscovered, pp. 88–9, in which I felt persuaded that "difficulties of this nature are usually induced by the practice of *pranayama*, the yogic science of breath.... But Upasni had not been undertaking any such exercises." I now take the view that I was misinformed about what he did not undertake. Purdom did not refer to the episode. Kalchuri attributes the problem to "the inner experience of occult power" (*op. cit.*, p. 92), which is perhaps misleading. Cf. the version of Dr. Deshmukh, *art. cit.*

189. Harper, *op. cit.*, p. 39, says "Kashinath decided to revive his old practice of *pranayama*." Harper was here basically following Narasimhaswami, though with a few additional sources. I believe that this version is correct, and that the disruption to breathing was caused by *pranayama* and aggravated by intensive meditation. If even Hindu *tapasvins* like Upasni can reap such troubles through traditional practices, one may wonder at the problems likely to be incurred by Western enthusiasts who are that much less accomplished.

190. Purdom, *op. cit.*, p. 30, says that the yogi "strongly requested him to pay a visit to the Hazrat Sai Baba, but Kashinath declined to do so for the reason that Sai Baba was a Mahommedan." Cf. Harper, *op. cit.*, p. 39, who says: "Assuming that Sai Baba was Muslim, Kashinath, a Brahmin, refused this advice."

191. The term *samadhi* has gained rather varying definitions. Professor Klostermaier opts for "deep concentration" (*A Survey of Hinduism*, p. 529). Swami Vivekananda defined *samadhi* as "superconsciousness" (*Complete Works Vol. 1*, p. 180), though he specified different states of *samadhi* (*ibid.*, p. 159). Harper translated the word to mean "loss of all consciousness" (*op. cit.*, p. 37), which seems an unduly reductionist interpretation.

192. Kalchuri, *op. cit.*, p. 40, who attributes to Narayan a spiritual perfection. The *sadguru* of Kedgaon patronized the best tailors from Bombay, and wore silk and velvet clothes featuring gold embroidery and diamond buttons (*ibid.*, p. 39).

193. Different thrones were employed, all of them lavishly ornamented. The most elaborate was a silver-plated extravagance nearly ten feet high (*ibid.*, p. 42). A photograph of this throne (*ibid.*, p. 43) is offputting to those who feel that the money involved could have been put to better use outside the field of ritual celebrations and devotional etiquette, although Narayan Maharaj is known to have distributed food and money amongst the poor at religious festivals.

194. Kalchuri, *op. cit.*, p. 98.

195. Shepherd, *Gurus Rediscovered*, p. 101. Cf. Kalchuri, *op. cit.*, p. 100, who says that Sai Baba visited the Khandoba temple to utter these words, which seems to be an error.

196. Cf. Narasimhaswami, *Sage of Sakuri*, pp. 38ff. Cf. Shepherd,

Gurus Rediscovered, pp. 94ff. Cf. Kalchuri, *op. cit.*, pp. 96ff. Cf. Rigopoulos, *Life and Teachings of Sai Baba*, pp. 178–9, 185ff., 192ff.

197. Harper's contribution is a convenient index to this interpretation. His chapter on Upasni is entitled "The Saint Who Suffered," and contains such statements as: "In that dark cell (Khandoba's temple) he had been held as a virtual prisoner by the command of his guru, Sai Baba" (*ibid.*, p. 35). Harper might be considered a victim in that he fell prey to the Hinduizing interpretation of Sai Baba and the most influential account of his "suffering" disciple presented in Narasimhaswami's *Sage of Sakuri*. Harper presents the entire phase at Khandoba's temple as a *sadhana*, and states: "For three years Upasni Baba endured the trials of the rigorous spiritual discipline imposed upon him by Sai Baba" (*ibid.*, p. 43). He cites Narasimhaswami's assessment of Pundit Kashinath (alias Upasni): "He was to emerge into a new life as a God-man with myriads of worshippers, with power to grant them salvation and earthly blessings also" (*ibid.*, p. 42, citing *Sage of Sakuri*, p. 39). Critics deem that to be a hagiographic statement.

198. See *Gurus Rediscovered*, part two chapter two.

199. Harper, *op. cit.*, p. 42.

200. Rigopoulos, *Life and Teachings of Sai Baba*, p. 193.

201. Kalchuri, *op. cit.*, p. 101. Kalchuri's version was ignored by Rigopoulos, perhaps because this represents the "Meher Baba interpretation," which differs from Narasimhaswami. It is worth noting that Meher Baba, from 1914 onwards, himself underwent strange introspective states which seemed to outsiders (including his mother) to be madness or suffering, though according to his own description, he was actually experiencing an acute inner bliss, if accompanied by complexities of suffering caused by "returning" to normal consciousness. As these subjects are not amenable to contemporary analysis, one will have to pass on to subjects that are more amenable.

202. See B. Natu, *Glimpses of the God-Man Meher Baba Vol. 6* (Myrtle Beach, S.C.: Sheriar Foundation, 1994), p. 23, who writes: "At that time, Maharaj was refusing to allow anyone near him, hurling abuse and stones at all who approached."

203. Kalchuri, *op. cit.*, p. 101.

204. See Rigopoulos, *op. cit.*, p. 193, who utilizes an English version of a discourse given by Upasni in February 1924, and citing Godamasuta, ed., *The Talks of Sadguru Upasani Baba Maharaja Vol. 1* (repr. Sakori, 1978), p. 111. The talks collected by Godamasuta were first published in 1957 and purport to be accurate representations of Upasni's teaching. Usage of these talks in the Daist sector has been attended by misconceptions and misrepresentations. See note 257 *infra*.

205. Rigopoulos, p. 194, citing Godamasuta, *Talks Vol. 1*, p. 600.

206. *Ibid.*, p. 194, and reproducing the complex statement: "It was the Brahmarandhra that had got opened and that inner eye was seeing the whole Brahmanda." The term Brahmanda means literally "Brahma's egg" and signifies the universe (*ibid.*, p. 215 n.110). On the intangible known as the *brahmarandhra*, see Shepherd, *Minds and Sociocultures Vol. 1*, p. 473.

207. See Kalchuri, *op. cit.*, p. 102, who says that Upasni's fast of one year ended when Sai Baba sent to him a devotee with food and coffee for him. "From then on, Upasni ate and drank regularly in small amounts until he regained full gross consciousness" (*ibid.*). Some other reports sketch a longer period of fasting, though apparently there were breaks in this. Meher Baba is reported to have said of his meeting with Upasni at Khandoba's temple in December 1915: "He (Upasni) had been living on water there under Sai Baba's direct guidance for over three years." See D. E. Stevens, ed., *Listen Humanity* (New York: Dodd, Mead & Co., 1957), p. 249. According to Kalchuri's version: "Between 1912 and 1914 was Upasni's period of regaining creation consciousness" (*Lord Meher Vol. 1*, p. 102).

208. It is not clear whether this occasion marked the end of the year long fast, or a second fast. If it was the end of the first fast, then that would appear to have lasted longer than a year. The intensive period of introspection at the Khandoba temple from mid-1912 to mid-1914 was marked by very severe fasting. The details of the interaction between Upasni and Sai Baba are largely lost. Upasni appears to have reacted against taking any solid food for about two years.

209. It is possible that the episode concerning the oppressive Nanavali coincided with this occasion.

210. Narasimhaswami, *Sage of Sakuri*, p. 84; Rigopoulos, *op. cit.*, p. 195.

211. Rigopoulos, *op. cit.*, p. 195, thinks that Upasni "could not understand Sai Baba's whole attitude towards him."

212. Purdom, *op. cit.*, p. 32. Purdom's early version differs from some others more well known. According to his report, Sai Baba had imparted "God-realization" to Upasni "in a few days" after settling at Shirdi, when he was about 42. The entire period at Khandoba's temple is viewed as an extension of that achievement. Being "possessed only of a little earthly consciousness, he sometimes acted like a madman." After four years at the Khandoba temple he became a *sadguru*, having gained full consciousness of the outer world in addition to his inner realization. "Soon after becoming a *sadguru*, Upasni Maharaj left Shirdi" (*ibid.*) en route to Kharagpur. Thus the impression was given that 1916 was the year of departure. I followed this version in the first draft of *Gurus Rediscovered*, and did not alter it in the final version (p. 108). Kalchuri gives the conventional date of July 25th 1914 (*Lord Meher Vol. 1*, p. 102), and I will follow suit here.

213. Kamath and Kher, *Sai Baba of Shirdi, a Unique Saint* (1991), p. 258. In this work of 300 pages, there are only three very brief references to Upasni, amounting to several lines only. It is not even stated that he returned to Shirdi after leaving for Shinde and other places. Even Narasimhaswami's *Sage of Sakuri* is not listed in the bibliography. Cf. Rigopoulos, *op. cit.*, p. 178, who improves upon the curtailed picture by describing Upasni as Sai's "most highly developed *shishya*," though he thinks that the departure in 1914 means that Upasni was "possibly irritated by Baba's enigmatic behaviour" (*ibid.*, p. 201).

214. B. Natu, *op. cit.*, p. 23; Kalchuri, *op. cit.*, pp. 102–3. Meher Baba called this woman Durgamai. It may be suggested that she was the same female elsewhere referred to as Chandrabai Borkar.

215. W. Doniger, trans., *The Laws of Manu* (Harmondsworth: Penguin, 1991), p. 242.

216. G. Flood, *An Introduction to Hinduism* (Cambridge University Press, 1996), p. 61.

217. See Doniger, *The Laws of Manu*, pp. 236ff.

218. Flood, *op. cit.*, pp. 58ff.

219. Cf. Kalchuri, *op. cit.*, pp. 102ff.; *Gurus Rediscovered*, pp. 108ff.; Narasimhaswami, *op. cit.*, pp. 90ff.; Harper, *op. cit.*, p. 44.

220. Purdom, *op. cit.*, p. 32, says that Upasni gained hundreds of Muslim admirers at Kharagpur, and scores of Christian admirers. Cf. Kalchuri, *op. cit.*, p. 104, who says that Upasni once entered a mosque and sat talking with several Muslims about the prophet Muhammad. He is also said to have visited the homes of Christians and Zoroastrians at Kharagpur.

221. A glowing report of this meeting is given in Kalchuri, *op. cit.*, pp. 81, 217ff., who records that it was Hazrat Babajan who first suggested that Merwan should visit Shirdi. Merwan went there in the company of his friend Khodu Irani, who had heard of Sai Baba's reputation as a miraculous healer, but who was startled by the boisterous greeting of the old *faqir*. Khodu was a strong and muscular young man, and the saint slapped him hard on the back. Kalchuri's account has some hagiological flourishes, but the basic details seem accurate. Cf. Purdom, *The God-Man* (London: George Allen and Unwin, 1964), p. 23, for a brief reference. In Kalchuri's more detailed version, Sai Baba is reported to have uttered the word *Parvardigar* three times and prostrated himself before Merwan, after the young man had fallen at his feet. A footnote in Kalchuri says that the term *Parvardigar* is a Sufi term meaning the Preserver of creation. Cf. Rigopoulos, *Life and Teachings of Sai Baba*, p. 208, whose report actually derives from D. E. Stevens, ed., *Listen Humanity* (1957), pp. 248–9, which represents a record of Meher Baba's own statements. According to Rigopoulos, the term *Parvardigar* "seems to be of Persian origin," and "was apparently a favourite expression" of Sai Baba (*op. cit.*, pp. 28–9 n.11). Narasimhaswami reports Sai as affirming "I am Parvardigar" (*Charters and Sayings*, p. 10), and it is evident that the term had a deep significance in the saint's gnostic vocabulary.

222. Kalchuri, *op. cit.*, p. 108, says that Upasni was sitting naked on the steps of his temple when Merwan Irani arrived. Cf. *ibid.*, p. 221, which describes Upasni on that occasion in terms of "virtually as thin as a skeleton." Cf. Kishan Singh's diary as reported in *The Glow Quarterly Vol. 10 no. 2* (Dehra Dun, May 1975), p. 4 col. 2, which states "Maharaj was very lean."

223. Kalchuri, *op. cit.*, p. 107.

224. At a late date, Narasimhaswami redressed the balance in the Sai Baba literature by writing a chapter on Upasni in his *Life*, though with some controversial accents that justified the idea of "no successor." See note 175 *supra*.

225. Harper, *op. cit.*, p. 53, and citing S. N. Tipnis, *Contribution of Upasani Baba to Indian Culture* (Bombay: New Bharat Printing Press, 1966), which is an "orthodox" work.

226. Harper, *op. cit.*, p. 53, who concludes that "there were many paradoxical elements in the life and teachings of Upasani Baba." A graphic example of the subject's paradoxical approach is afforded in an episode concerning Chhagan Sitaram Dattatrey, a young *brahman* of Bhingar village near Ahmednagar. He was a frequent visitor to Sakori in 1925, but was shocked to hear from some informants that the chief disciple of Upasni was not a *brahman* but an Irani, namely Meher Baba. Chhagan subsequently became reconciled to meeting the non-Hindu, and even joined his ashram at Meherabad. Chhagan's father related the news to Upasni, who expressed annoyance and is said to have complained that the son of a *brahman* had been allowed to go to an Irani who ate with untouchables, thereby spoiling the "religious purity" of Chhagan. The parent then went to Meherabad, but found that his son refused to leave that ashram. The father returned to Sakori. This time Upasni took a very different attitude, dismissing the issue of untouchability as irrelevant. He is reported to have said: "You did not know this, but I will tell you now that I, too, have mingled and lived among the outcastes. Who says religion is affected by their contact?" See Kalchuri, *Lord Meher Vol. 2* (Myrtle Beach, S.C.: Manifestation, 1987), pp. 706–8.

227. M. Piantelli, foreword to Rigopoulos, *op. cit.*, p. xi.

228. Kalchuri, *op. cit.*, pp. 284–5. This report seems to be basically reliable, and fits the irascible disposition of Upasni that emerged in situations of crisis and human stupidity.

229. A report on Gulbai (Gulmai) Irani appeared in the series "Those who met the Master" included in the *Meher Baba Journal* (1938–42). See also Kalchuri, *Lord Meher Vol. 1*, pp. 274ff., 301–2; *id., Vol. 2*, p. 330. Cf. pp. 82ff. of my *The Life of Meher Baba Vol. 1*, written in 1967–8 for my own edification. This unpublished work later became known through hearsay and by title to the Western leaders of the Meher Baba movement, but only Murshida Ivy Duce expressed any interest in it. The outlook of these leaders was one of sectarian insularity. I have no intention of publishing the unwanted biography, and am quite content to regard it as being immature in style and incomplete in many respects. However, Bhau Kalchuri's canonical version is also not complete, for instance missing out details of Gulmai's early life. Critics view certain devotional stylisms in Kalchuri's multi-volume work as a flaw, though it is undeniably a very informative work. Some other criticisms also apply, though these are unwelcome in devotional ranks.

230. Kalchuri, *Lord Meher Vol. 2* (North Myrtle Beach, S.C.: Manifestation, 1987), p. 332.

231. According to Purdom's report, Merwan Irani at first took food only once in two or three days during his sojourn of six months at Sakori. Yet during the last month, he was eating four meals a day. Purdom says that Merwan and Upasni "used to spend a number of hours together at night and every day" (*The Perfect Master*, pp. 36–7). Cf. Natu, *Glimpses of the God-Man Meher Baba Vol. 6*, pp. 16–17, who says that Yeshwantrao made Merwan a coat from a coarse blanket known as *kamli*, in order to keep him warm in November and December (this *kamli* coat has since become a relic). Natu says that the sessions in the jhopri were generally over by 2 a.m. Cf. Kalchuri, *Lord Meher Vol. 1*, p. 320, who says that the sessions lasted until up to 4 a.m., and that Merwan never slept during this period. Although Yeshwantrao prepared him *pan*, it was Durgabai who cooked his meals. Merwan was liable to begin spontaneously singing at any time of the day or night (*ibid.*, p. 321). At the end of the sojourn, Upasni would tell others: "Go to Meher. I have given over my charge and authority to him. Meher now holds my key." (*Ibid.*, p. 322). Cf. Shepherd, *Life of Meher Baba Vol. 1* (unpublished), p. 97, which states the general emphasis as: "Maharaj said that he had given Merwan everything, and added: 'I have given my charge to Merwanji. He is the holder of my key.'" Upasni always referred to his Irani disciple by his original name; he usually spoke in Marathi, and used the respectful suffix -ji when naming Merwan. To Sadashiv Patel, Upasni said: "He (Merwan) now has all that Sai Baba gave me" (Kalchuri, *Lord Meher Vol. 1*, p. 322). Cf. Shepherd, *op. cit.*, p. 97, which reports the words "Merwanji has received from me all that Sai Baba gave me." Sadashiv Patel was a low caste Hindu of Poona who had for several years been an admirer of the

194

"mad Irani," perceiving him to be a rare type of saint. Late in 1921, the Parsi named Gustadji Hansotia was summoned to Sakori, and Upasni told him: "I have made Meher perfect. From now on, hold on to him" (Kalchuri, *op. cit.*, p. 322). Cf. Shepherd, *op. cit.*, p. 98, which reports this communication to Gustadji as: "I have made Merwanji perfect. He is the *sadguru* of this age. Now you have to leave me and keep with him. Hold on to him through thick and thin."

232. "By the beginning of 1921 Meher was three-quarters normal" (Purdom, *The Perfect Master*, p. 36).

233. See, e.g., the account in C. B. Purdom and M. Schloss, "Three Incredible Weeks with Meher Baba," *The Awakener* (1955) 2(3):52, which reports Meher Baba as saying: "Maharaj encouraged them (the *brahmans*) to be jealous of me, and to be bitter, and to hurt me. But Maharaj told Durgamai and Yeshwantrao that Merwan is now 'Malik' of the universe. When the Brahmins heard me called '*Malik*,' they wanted to kill me." The reason why Upasni encouraged *brahman* hostility is not stated. Durgabai (Durgamai) and Yeshwantrao Bhorawke were the two Hindus at Sakori who regarded Merwan as a special disciple. It would seem that in encouraging *brahman* activities and attendance at Sakori, Upasni gave the impression that he had sided with the majority, although in private he made utterances which totally contradicted this. Such paradox was apparently one of his strategies, perhaps similar to the issue of untouchability. There is no possible doubt from the sources that Upasni highly esteemed Merwanji Irani. See Kalchuri, *Lord Meher Vol. 1*, p. 322, who lists statements made by Upasni about Merwan. See also *Lord Meher Vol. 2*, p. 372, for a significant statement made by Upasni at Sakori in May 1922.

234. Kalchuri, *Lord Meher Vol. 1*, p. 320, who also says that the Sakori villagers honoured Merwan as the spiritual heir of Upasni, though a few *brahman* devotees thought of him merely as a penitent (or *sadhaka*). These men became jealous and even plotted to kill him. They were especially irate when Upasni called the young Irani "Mahadev," an epithet of Shiva which means "Great God."

235. Natu, *op. cit.*, p. 18. The new *jhopri* (hut) subsequently became integrated in the expanding ashram, the locale undergoing a pronounced change over the years.

236. This statement comes from the diary of Kishan Singh, dated September 1954 (*The Glow Quarterly*, May 1975, p. 5 col. 1).

237. *Ibid.* According to Meher Baba, "the poison given to Maharaj was so deadly that its dose can kill all of us, yet he withstood it" (*ibid.*). The date is not specified, save in that the dire episode occurred prior to the coming of Godavri Mataji. It is little wonder that Upasni Maharaj later said that he did not want "the *brahman* atmosphere of men" which dominated Sakori.

238. The present writer was in correspondence with Gulmai's son Adi K. Irani during the mid-1960s, not long after her death. Adi had long since become Meher Baba's secretary. He took the view that Meher Baba eclipsed the importance of Upasni, and tended to be sensitive on the subject of his mother, who so notably divided her allegiance between these two figures. Adi's articles detailing his early contact with Upasni and Meher Baba appeared in the Indian journal *Divya Vani* (Hyderabad) at the time of my correspondence with him. The treatment of Gulmai is unsatisfactory in some devotional literature of the Meher Baba movement. Cf. Natu, *Glimpses of the God-Man Meher Baba Vol. 6*, pp. 14–15, who gives a brief history of Gulmai that evidences devotional biases of the post-New Life phase of the Meher Baba movement. The interpretation adopted is that of a divided allegiance between the *sadguru* and the *avatar*. Natu states that Gulmai first visited Upasni in 1921, whereas the date of this event was actually 1919, and there are some other misleading accents in the chronology. An event in 1936 in which Upasni visited her later home at the Khushru Quarters is interpreted in terms of: "Perhaps, in fact, it was at this moment that Gulmai truly accepted Meher Baba as the Avatar of the age" (*ibid.*, p. 15). This gloss represents devotional sentiment interposed from a later period. In reality, Gulmai was not subject to the uncertainties which are often attributed to her by sectarian attitudes. Her home in Ahmednagar known as the Khushru Quarters has since become the Avatar Meher Baba Trust Compound, and past events associated with the environs tend to have the obsession with Avataric identity imposed upon them. Bal Natu, a Hindu devotee of Meher Baba, was not present at the 1936 event, unlike Gulmai's son Adi, and the latter well knew the degree of his mother's "dual" orientation, which was effortless to her. In later years, Adi K. Irani obfuscated this issue, and contributed to the general misconceptions of myopic sectarians.

239. This refers to the secluded meeting at the Dahigaon hut in October 1941. That event was described in the diary of the *Meher Baba Journal* (November 1941). The intermediary between Upasni and Meher Baba on that occasion was Gulmai.

240. The author was Ahmad Abbas, alias Khak Saheb, an Indian Muslim of Poona who had a reputation as a poet in Persian and Urdu. It has been said that he collaborated with Dr. Abdul Ghani Munsiff, another of Meher Baba's Muslim pupils at Manzil-e-Meem. However, it seems that the Muslim known as Asar Saheb was the actual collaborator, Ghani merely helping in the distribution of the book, which was published by Circle & Company in November 1922 (Kalchuri, *Lord Meher Vol. 2*, pp. 443, 455), a venture led by Rustom K. Irani, a son of Gulmai. Some of the men involved in this project were criticized by Muslims for promoting a Hindu guru.

241. This commission seems to have been facilitated by the identity of Sai Baba as a Muslim. Some Indian Muslims were more favourable to Meher Baba than to Hinduism, and were impressed by his affinity with Sufism.

242. The Marathi version was entitled *Sadguru Upasani Maharaj Yancha Charitra*, and was published at Bombay in 1923 by Rustom Irani on behalf of Circle & Company, which dissolved soon after.

243. This work was entitled *Sakori na Sadguru* (*Sadguru of Sakori*), and was published in 1923. The author was Behli J. Irani. See Kalchuri, *op. cit.*, pp. 406–8, which reports the initial resistance of Desai to the project and his subsequent enthusiasm for it.

244. Kalchuri, *op. cit.*, pp. 489–90. Upasni even told Gulmai to stay away from Meher Baba, though to no avail. She tended to acknowledge the priority of Meher Baba, though she remained loyal to Upasni until his death. It was her conclusion, and that of other disciples of Meher Baba, that the two saints drew a line between their respective modes of "work," and deliberately tested reactions amongst a large number of people.

245. *Ibid.*, p. 445. Kalchuri adopts the interpretation that the real reason for Meher Baba's visit to Sakori was to select Mehera J. Irani, a Zoroastrian visitor at the ashram who later became his closest female disciple. Others suspect that this was only one of the reasons involved. Devotional interpretations often seem to narrow down the context, even when the hagiological flourishes are relatively mild.

246. Purdom, *The Perfect Master*, p. 57. Cf. Kalchuri, *op. cit.*, p. 452.

247. Kalchuri, *op. cit.*, pp. 488, 420, reporting that Upasni was prepared to receive half the profits involved in the books written about him. That arrangement was made in October 1922 via Sadashiv Patel. Kalchuri deems all this a "divine joke." It is evident that there was a certain amount of banter occurring between the two saints. Upasni had idiosyncratically given his permission for the biographies to be published, it is legitimate to conclude.

248. Kalchuri, *op. cit.*, p. 492. Cf. Purdom, *op. cit.*, pp. 57–8.

249. Rustom K. Irani had known Upasni for a few years and had a high regard for him, as did his family. One interpretation of the episode is that in making impossible demands, Upasni was deflecting Rustom's deference from himself to Meher Baba, who required a full commitment at this period. Upasni had already told such men that they should adhere to Baba and not to him, and so the interpretation does afford some logical sense. It was Gulmai who was left in a unique category of "divided allegiance" that was seldom understood in later years.

250. This date has been differently reported. Kalchuri, *Lord Meher Vol. 1*, p. 110, gives the date as December 25th 1921, which is also followed by Harper, *op. cit.*, p. 48. Yet in his second volume, p. 461, Kalchuri has a different and more reliable assessment which states that on December 24th 1922, Meher Baba told his men that Upasni had recently imprisoned himself in a bamboo cage. In *Gurus Rediscovered*, p. 126, I reported the date as December 21st 1922, based on Deshmukh and other reports, not Narasimhaswami. Discrepant dates are fairly frequent in the literature on Upasni Maharaj, and require due patience and analysis. I myself was misled by certain reported dates in my youth.

251. Kalchuri, *Lord Meher Vol. 2*, p. 488.

252. *Ibid.*

253. *Ibid.*

254. *Ibid.*, pp. 507–8.

255. This was the impression conveyed to Harper, *op. cit.*, p. 47, who cites Tipnis, *Contribution of Upasni Baba to Indian Culture*, p. 102.

256. See *Upasani Vak Sudha* (Sakori: R. G. Vakil, 1934).

257. See Godamasuta, ed., *The Talks of Sadguru Upasani Baba Maharaja* (4 vols, 1957; repr. Sakori: Upasni Kanya Kumari Sthan, 1978). This version of Upasni's teaching has led to misrepresentations in the sector of Daism, i.e., the followers of Da Free John. A very misleading reference to Upasni appeared in G. Feuerstein, *Holy Madness* (New York: Paragon House, 1991), p. 25, who evidently wants to believe that Upasni was "notorious for speaking quite openly about sexuality and for using coarse language." Though Upasni did use coarse language when angry, the context afforded by Feuerstein amounts to gross misrepresentation. Godamasuta's version was not prepared with the intention of depicting Upasni Maharaj as an Indian version of Da Free John. Feuerstein's use of a single quote from Godamasuta (Vol. 2) appears to borrow from the librarian of the American Trickster Library, a library which belongs to the Free Daist Communion and which deems itself expert on "crazy wisdom," but whose interpretations of religion should be regarded as very dubious and misinformed (cf. Feuerstein, *op. cit.*, p. 262 n.5, who acknowledges this library as the source of many of his bibliographic references). Feuerstein's book strongly reflects the influence of Da Free John (alias Da Avabhasa), despite the author's disillusionment with that American guru. Feuerstein tries to find evidence that various saints were exemplars of "crazy wisdom," a subject associated with Da Free John. In this respect, I will here revise my earlier statement that Upasni "never lent importance to religious tradition of the extroverted type" (*Gurus Rediscovered*, p. 130). Retarded pseudo-mystics such as Da Avabhasa (Adi Da) tend to imagine that an aversion to formal religion means antinomian license. People like Dr. Feuerstein are perhaps unlikely to comprehend the genuine saints, instead confusing them with the delinquent category of mystics like Neem Karoli Baba. Upasni Maharaj upheld the

moral and ascetic dimensions of Hinduism, and permitted orthodox religious observances of both renunciates and householders.

258. Harper, *op. cit.*, pp. 46–7, citing *Upasani Vak Sudha*.

259. In some moments of anger, Upasni was liable to slap or hit an erring man. This is the most problematic of his traits, and does not appeal to some analysts, the present writer included. By far the strongest report I have seen on this matter is "he swung 180 degrees from his heels and really knocked them flat, being a brute of a man over six feet tall and very stockily built." This detail comes from I. O. Duce, *How a Master Works* (Walnut Creek, California: Sufism Reoriented, 1975), p. 641, reporting A. Hassen's version of comments made in 1970 by F. N. Driver (Padri), a Zoroastrian follower of Meher Baba. Padri had little to do with Upasni and may have been exaggerating (Meher Baba's *mandali* did sometimes overstate in their conversations with visitors to Meherabad after Baba's death). If Padri's report is accurate, then it must surely represent an extreme manifestation of displeasure. However, the manifestations of violence evidently varied somewhat, and were perhaps seldom so drastic. Upasni's displeasure was administered as a form of chastisement to men considered obtuse in their attitudes. It was Sai Baba who had inaugurated the "thrashing" administered by Upasni. The old *faqir* sent several conceited men to his Hindu disciple for chastisement, though without telling them of what would transpire (*Gurus Rediscovered*, pp. 116–117). The injury was to self-esteem, not to the body, and this factor needs stressing. Upasni seems to have favoured a form of rebuke in which the erring party were made to look like a naughty child being spanked over the father's knee. He was strong enough to lift a man off the ground. It is possible that a resisting man, or an unusually strong one, could have received tougher treatment, but the context should be understood. Sai Baba had also tended to be demonstrative in this manner, his Muslim disciples having a regard for such chastisement from a saint. Hindus were perhaps somewhat less prepared for the confrontation. Pretentious holy men were amongst the targets. Spectators like Gulmai Irani had many opportunities to observe the limiting attitudes with which Upasni was often faced. The recipients of his wrath often seem to have been *brahmans*, which may have pleased untouchables. The misleading report of Padri does not mention Ardeshir (Kaka) Baria (1891–1969), one of Meher Baba's *mandali* who was originally a follower of Upasni for over a year. This Parsi would stay at Sakori for two or three days at a time before he encountered Meher Baba in 1928. His confrontation with Upasni was of an unusual kind. When Kaka was feeling inclined to visit Meher Baba, the Sakori saint made things easier for him by leading Kaka to one of the Hindu temples and repeating many times: "This God is false!" Brahmanism was being snubbed, as when Upasni

199

subsequently told Kaka: "I am false" (Shepherd, *Life of Meher Baba Vol. 1*, pp. 279–80, unpublished). Shortly after, Kaka Baria visited Meher Baba's temporary ashram at Toka, though he was not allowed to join the *mandali* until 1930. His energy was later put to use in the *mast* work. Cf. Kalchuri, *Lord Meher Vol. 3* (1988), p. 1067. See also note 460 *infra*.

260. According to Kalchuri, *Lord Meher Vol. 4* (North Myrtle Beach, S.C.: Manifestation, 1989), p. 1388, the encounter occurred in (or soon after) 1924. Kalchuri's version of the event is brief. Cf. Purdom, *The God-Man*, p. 95. Cf. Shepherd, *Gurus Rediscovered*, pp. 130–1. The date of 1927 has also been given for the encounter.

261. See Kalchuri, *op. cit.*, pp. 1382ff., 1388ff., 1445ff., 1513ff.; *Vol. 5* (1990), pp. 1714ff., 1726ff., 1772.

262. E.g., in September 1931, Meher Baba privately accused Gandhi of being inconsistent in his policies. Meher Baba was sympathetic to both the Muslim and the Untouchable parties who were in friction with Congress, though he was not dogmatic over the issues involved, respecting Gandhi's struggle for national independence. He was prepared to take Gandhi at his word in advocating the abolition of untouchability, though he pointed to the discrepancies in the policy of the Congress party (see Kalchuri, Vol. 4, pp. 1385–7). He also said: "To raise one to the seventh heaven and to cry out 'Mahatma Ki Jai' has made a man like Gandhi vain and brought him down" (*ibid.*, p. 1386). See also the disclosure made in July 1940: "Gandhi is impractical, but a very good man." This appears in Kalchuri, *Lord Meher Vol. 7* (Myrtle Beach, S.C.: Manifestation, 1994), p. 2580. Meher Baba was here criticizing Gandhi's policy of non-violence in the face of Hitler's aggression. He described Hitler as a beast, and said that both Gandhi and Hitler were mad in their adoption of extremes. His views tend to converge here with those of Dr. Ambedkar, who said that Gandhi's policy of non-violence during wartime was madness, and who urged the untouchables to join the British army in order to defend India against Hitler and the Japanese. While Gandhi was anti-British, Ambedkar was ironically pro-British.

263. Nevertheless, Purdom wrote that "the temple is open not only to the Hindus of low as well as high caste, but also to non-Hindus" (*The Perfect Master*, p. 33).

264. L. Fischer, *The Life of Mahatma Gandhi* (London: Jonathan Cape, 1951), p. 419, citing *Young India*, October 6th 1921.

265. *Ibid.*, pp. 419–20.

266. Cf. *ibid.*, pp. 383ff., who writes of Ambedkar that "age-long Hindu cruelty to his unhappy brethren filled him with anger, spite and vindictiveness" (*ibid.*, p. 391).

267. *Ibid.*, pp. 182ff.

268. Klostermaier, *A Survey of Hinduism*, p. 327, and citing B. R.

Ambedkar, *What Congress and Gandhi Have Done to the Untouchables* (Bombay 1945, second edn 1946).

269. See V. Jha, "Stages in the History of Untouchables," *Indian Historical Review* (1975) 2: 21ff., and citing Ambedkar, *The Untouchables* (Delhi, 1948).

270. Klostermaier, *op. cit.*, p. 485 n.34, citing R. P. Mukane, "Harijan's Plight," *Times of India* (Bombay), 20th March, 1968. The atrocities included a Harijan youth being roasted alive in Andhra on a charge of theft. Far less guilty of any crime were three Harijans who were shot dead by caste Hindus for growing their moustaches upward instead of downward.

271. Cf. Harper, *op. cit.*, p. 52, who says that "he held traditional ideas of the home, yet he advocated 'family planning' long before it became a real issue in India."

272. I am here following the data given by Sahukar and other writers. However, Kalchuri, Vol. 1, p. 111, says that Godavri was nine and visited in 1923.

273. Feuerstein, *Holy Madness*, p. 25, has conveyed a misleading impression to some readers by his statement that Upasni caused "a public outcry when he revived the ancient Vedic custom of 'spiritual marriage' (*brahma-vivaha*), marrying no fewer than twenty-five virgins." The general context of this exaggerated statement is Daist, and also convergent with Tantra, especially in view of the fact that the preceding paragraph refers to Neem Karoli Baba's belief in sexual energy as a vehicle for the transmutation of consciousness. See also note 257 *supra*. Upasni was not a Tantric. See further Shepherd, *Some Philosophical Critiques and Appraisals*, p. 273 n. 232. The number of *kanyas* at Sakori during the lifetime of Upasni was small, six women appearing on photographs. That number did not swell to twenty until some years after his death.

274. Sahukar, *Sai Baba the Saint of Shirdi* (third edn), p. 77.

275. *Ibid.*, p. 78.

276. On Gargi, see Shepherd, *Minds and Sociocultures Vol. 1*, pp. 557, 619.

277. Sahukar, *op. cit.*, p. 81.

278. *Ibid.*

279. See Natu, *Glimpses of the God-Man Meher Baba Vol. 6*, pp. 23–6. Cf. Kalchuri, *Lord Meher Vol. 12* (1997), pp. 4384–5 and note; the narration is rather fantastic, and includes some uncertain details.

280. Natu, *op. cit.*, p. 25. In his youth, Natu was influenced by the hostile articles of these scholars, but later learnt how false they were.

281. A brief account came from Adi K. Irani, brother of Rustom K. Irani and son of Gulmai; he knew in detail of Upasni's activities from 1920 onwards. This account comprised the record of a talk he gave, and was not written by him. I relied upon this version in *Gurus Rediscovered*, pp. 136ff. It is reported that Upasni thwarted the wishes of *kanya* relatives who wished to take away the young nuns due to the gossip of detractors. He would not allow those nuns to be taken away against their wishes, and insisted that their "spiritual marriage" with him was a relevant commitment in accordance with Hindu codes. He appeared at a law court in an ongoing situation that is missing in most accounts of him. See my text relevant to note 360 *infra*. The report transcribed from Adi. K. Irani in *The Glow Quarterly* (1977) indicated that Upasni was aged sixty-eight at the time of his "marriages," but it is necessary to revise this in terms of his early sixties. However, the legal extensions of this issue took some time to resolve, and Durgabai's apology was not made until about 1938. The number of "marriages" specified is six. In *Gurus*, p. 137, I referred to "six wives," though events did not signify a marriage of the kind that is usually envisaged. Adi K. Irani's account was not comprehensive, though unusual at that time for the information given.

282. Natu, *op. cit.*, p. 25.

283. "His food is as simple as his clothing" (Purdom, *The Perfect Master*, p. 33).

284. Sahukar, *op. cit.*, p. 82.

285. One report states: "For his last fourteen months and twelve days, he lived in a bamboo cage and took nothing but coffee once a day. The cage was about 3 feet by 3½ feet so that he could not lie down" (Purdom and Schloss, *Three Incredible Weeks with Meher Baba*, p. 48). The writers involved here both visited Sakori in September 1954 in the company of Meher Baba. It is difficult to ignore this version (cf. Deshmukh, *art. cit.*), although some qualification seems relevant. (Details in various reports often suffered compression, e.g., Purdom and Schloss say that Godavri Mataji first met Upasni when she was two and a half years old). Upasni does not look emaciated in photographs taken of him at this period, and one may question that the fast was so severe. The bamboo cage had undergone some adaptation, Upasni being annoyed with the silver bars and insisting that this innovation be altered, though he seems to have compromised. Yet the dimensions remained the same, admitting a greater length than three and a half feet; he had been able to lie down in the cage during his 1920s interment. He definitely did not live continually in the cage at the end of his life, instead undertaking visits to various places and dying in his hut. (Purdom and Schloss were aware that he died in a separate structure to the cage, as they report that he died in a room shown to them). I included the Purdom-Schloss version in *Gurus Rediscovered*, p. 139, not altering the first draft (dated 1967) on this point. Yet I now believe that the dimensions given in the Purdom-Schloss report were misleading, and that the cage referred to was the same *pin-*

jra earlier used, being rather narrow but approximately five feet high and about six feet long. The length of time specified is suspect, and may amount to a confusion with the 1922–4 confinement which lasted nearly fourteen months. Yet the duration given is puzzling. In *The God-Man*, p. 252, Charles Purdom wrote of Upasni that "at one time for fourteen months and twelve days he lived in a bamboo cage and took nothing but coffee once a day." Purdom may have meant that as a revision of his earlier report, though the same dimensions for the cage are reiterated. A problem is that other accounts of the early 1920s confinement do not mention a severe fast on coffee. Perhaps this fast occurred at a later date, in combination with visits to the cage, before or after it gained silver bars. Of the *pinjra*, it has been said that "from then on (after January 1924) he would go in and out of it at his will and pleasure" (Natu, *op. cit.*, p. 19). Thus, some event of acute privation may have occurred during later years when much became obscure owing to disturbances within and without the ashram.

286. See Kalchuri, *Lord Meher Vol. 8* (Myrtle Beach, S.C.: Manifestation, 1995), pp. 2723ff., which includes several photographs of the event that earlier appeared in the *Meher Baba Journal* of 1941. The meeting occurred on October 17th, 1941.

287. Harper, *op. cit.*, pp. 50–1, writes: "As far as I could learn, the *kanyas* of the Kanya Kumari Sthan are the only women who are so trained." Harper also says that he was impressed with "the precision and ease with which they performed this extremely difficult task" of reciting the Vedas (*ibid.*, p. 50).

288. See M. Sahukar, *Sweetness and Light: An Exposition of Sati Godavari Mataji's Philosophy and Way of Life* (Bombay 1966). See also S. N. Tipnis, *Life of Shri Godavari Mataji* (Jabalpur: Aryan Press, 1983).

289. Harper, *op. cit.*, p. 192.

290. Sahukar, *Sai Baba the Saint of Shirdi* (third edn), p. 86, from chapter XIV on Godavri.

291. *Ibid.*

292. *Ibid.*

293. *Moha* means delusion, in the context here of external distractions.

294. Sahukar, *op. cit.*, p. 86.

295. Harper, *op. cit.*, p. 193.

296. Sahukar, *op. cit.*, p. 87.

297. See S. Radhakrishnan, *The Bhagavadgita* (second edn, London: George Allen and Unwin, 1949), See also Klostermaier, *Survey of Hinduism*, chapter 6. Cf. G. Flood, *An Introduction to Hinduism*, pp. 124ff., who says that the great popularity of the *Gita* only dates from nineteenth century Hindu revival movements, though it had an earlier theological importance.

298. Harper, *op. cit.*, p. 193.

299. *Ibid.*, pp. 192–3, who states that he was told by Dr. Tipnis that harassed businessmen finding a quiet retreat at Sakori in the presence of Godavri "are prepared to make a significant spiritual contribution to the life of the nation" (*ibid.*, p. 193).

300. An incomplete account of this activity appeared in Purdom, *The Perfect Master*, pp. 87ff. Less satisfactory is the version in J. Adriel, *Avatar: The Life Story of the Perfect Master Meher Baba* (Santa Barbara, Calif.: J. F. Rowny Press, 1947), pp. 84ff., who makes too much of Baba as an advocate of vegetarianism, not comprehending the full situation.

301. Shepherd, *Life of Meher Baba Vol. 1* (unpublished manuscript), pp. 236–7. Cf. Kalchuri, *Lord Meher Vol. 2* (1987), pp. 699–700. My version of events derived from reports traceable to such men as Vishnu Narayan Deorukhkar, who was the teacher of the untouchable boys at the Hazrat Babajan School. Deorukhkar was a caste Hindu disciple of Meher Baba, and one who set very high standards of humanitarian attitude. Prior to joining the *mandali*, he had given voluntary service as teacher to a night school for untouchables.

302. Kalchuri, *op. cit.*, p. 700.

303. This episode was first reported in *The Meher Message Vol. 1 no. 12* (Meherabad 1929), pp. 60–1. Variants of this episode have also appeared in print, sometimes with an abbreviated wording.

304. All his followers were free to maintain their native religious traditions and customs, though he never incited to ritual observances. If Muslims wished to go to a mosque, they were free to do so. His Muslim followers were not fundamentalists, and his Hindu followers did not wish to be associated with the strictures of caste Hinduism. The Zoroastrian contingent was disillusioned with orthodox Mazdaism and regarded him as their sole leader.

305. See B. Kalchuri, *Let's Go to Meherabad* (Berkeley, California: Beguine Library, 1985), p. 118, who says that the four symbols placed on the upper four corners of the tomb were "a mosque representing Islam, a temple for Hinduism and Buddhism, a cross and fire container for Christianity and Zoroastrianism." Kalchuri's account is devotional in tone and extols the unique importance of the tomb and Meherabad. He resorts to a dialogue form to narrate details, which is rather offputting to some readers.

306. There are, however, two atypical reports involving *udi* which date to 1929. The Parsi devotee K. J. Dastur claimed that a diseased Irani woman had been cured by Meher Baba as a consequence of swallowing a few particles of ash from Baba's *dhuni*. Dastur says that Meher Baba gave a similar instruction to this woman's daughter; however, Baba also specified an injection in this case. The daughter slowly recovered from her malady, and there is no need to regard the cure as a miracle. Cf. the editorial diary in Dastur's periodical *The Meher Message Vol. 1 no. 8* (Meherabad 1929), pp. 28ff. Such an instruction to swallow ash was a novelty for Meher Baba, who was inclined to prescribe conventional medicines for illness. The recourse to *udi* is at odds with other features of his life, despite the very late oral report of Mansari Desai, who said that in the 1920s she was given a bottle of *dhuni* ash and told to take a pinch of ash every morning and repeat his (Baba's) name in order to eliminate her skin disease (*Meher Baba Association Newsletter*, London, January 1997, p. 3). Such a recourse seems to have been rare on the part of Meher Baba. Ivy Duce relates how during the 1950s a young man who had visited Meherabad ashram brought back to America a jar of *udi* and sent packages of this to various Americans, telling them to place the ash on their forehead or under the tongue. How he got this notion is not clear, but when Meher Baba was informed of the innovation, he told his sister Mani to write to the young man and have the packages recalled. See Duce, *How a Master Works* (Walnut Creek, California: Sufism Reoriented, 1975), p. 559. What seems to have happened here is that the *dhuni* ashes had gained a popular repute for healing qualities. It is said that people would write and ask for a pinch of ash (*ibid.*, p. 79). Yet Meher Baba himself said that the "real *udi*" was the "ash (produced) from the burning up of our desires and cravings" (*ibid.*). According to Mani Irani's version of his emphasis in 1960, the ash given by a spiritual master was merely a symbol "signifying that you have to burn your desires and cravings to ashes" (*ibid.*).

307. Meher Baba did not publicly declare himself to be the *avatar* until 1954. By 1960 this term had become a common description employed by his devotees, facilitated particularly by the secretarial flourishes of Adi K. Irani, who became increasingly dogmatic from about 1956. See Shepherd, *Meher Baba, an Iranian Liberal* (Cambridge 1988), p. 265. The title of Shri Meher Baba was still the official mailing identity employed in letters to the subject from his followers in December 1956. See *The Friends of Meher Baba Newsletter* (London, December 5th, 1956), which bears the name of the Hon. Secretary Dorothy Hopkinson. The message was conveyed in this document that Meher Baba wished each of his followers to write a short letter to him. That was a rare gesture. The postal address specified was Shri Meher Baba, Grafton Camp, Satara, Bombay State. Hopkinson ended the news with the simple greeting "In the Name of Baba." Nothing Avataric. I possess an original copy of this newsletter given to me by Ann Powell, a British devotee who died in 1965.

308. See Part 3 of *Iranian Liberal*.

309. See Purdom, *The God-Man* (1964), p. 303. Meher Baba awarded Mahavira a high spiritual status as a *sadguru*, a term he rendered in English as "perfect master." That category of exalted description often excites scepticism. Though the theme of five elite masters is generally associated with the Sufi concept of a spiritual hierarchy, there are also correspondences with a Hindu theme. On this, see Rigopoulos, *Life and Teachings of Sai Baba*, p. 218 n.171, referring to "the popular theory of the *Nath-pancayatan*, that is, the existence of five perfect masters."

310. Meher Baba visited Assisi during his travels to Europe in the early 1930s. During his visit to Avila in 1933, he also expressed an affinity with John of the Cross and St. Teresa, though he did not award them the same status he assigned to Francis.

311. Sant Tukaram (1598–1649) was an important mystical poet of Maharashtra. See R. D. Ranade, *Mysticism in India: The Poet-Saints of Maharashtra*, Part IV.

312. Guru Nanak is the figurehead of the Sikhs, with whom Meher Baba was on good terms. See *Iranian Liberal*, p. 46.

313. Bab (meaning "Gate") was the special title claimed by Mirza Ali Muhammad (1819–1850), the Iranian radical Shi'ite Muslim from Shiraz who was executed at Tabriz. The young Merwan Irani probably heard much about the Bab from his father Sheriar Mundegar Irani, who had become a *dervish* in Iran. The Babi sect developed pacifist extensions after 1860, and were then sympathetic to Zoroastrians. See Shepherd, *From Oppression to Freedom* (Cambridge, 1988), pp. 20ff.

314. Books on the subject such as those of Charles Purdom are completely free of extravagant attributions. Works of a more devotional category sometimes exhibit peculiarities, and also the account by Ivy O. Duce. The lavish multi-volume work of Bhau Kalchuri, cited in these notes, occasionally attributes to Meher Baba extensive abilities in national and international events, though this tendency does not revolve around the fascination with *siddhis*. Meher Baba was definitely not a saint who promised offspring or who performed sleight of hand to entertain caste Hinduism with deceptions of bounty denied to those of lowly status from birth.

315. Purdom and Schloss, *Three Incredible Weeks with Meher Baba* (1955), p. 50.

316. *Ibid*. In this 1954 communication to a party of Westerners, who included the literate diarists Charles B. Purdom and Malcolm Schloss, Meher Baba added a warning about the miracle atmosphere at Shirdi. He also reflected that Sai Baba was being commercialized, his picture even being found on match boxes. "The state of affairs at Shirdi I do not like," said this supposed representative of the "Sai Baba movement" which has been invented by academic theorists influenced by Satya Sai.

317. The Universal Prayer is now often known as the Parvardigar Prayer, due to a reference in the first line. It was originally known as the Master's Prayer, under which title it was reproduced in an early issue of *The Awakener* (1953) 1(2): 18–19. See also *Life Circular No. 15*. It was dictated in August 1953 at Dehra Dun. Whereas the Prayer of Repentance dates from 1952. There were no special rules for the recitation of these prayers amongst Meher Baba's following, a matter which was left entirely to individual inclination. The Prayer of Repentance had a prelude which is not included in all printed versions (though given in full by Purdom in *The God-Man*, p. 238). An abbreviation for this prelude which appears in some versions is: "*Om Parabrahma-Paramatma, Ya-Yazdan, La ilaha illallah*, O God, Father in Heaven!"

318. Purdom, *The God-Man*, pp. 236ff., reporting an event in 1954. A fuller report was made in *Three Incredible Weeks*, pp. 22ff. On other occasions Baba also included a Sikh prayer. In addition to the traditional "orthodox" prayers that were recited, there were many other prayers which Meher Baba himself dictated and which did not become generally known, even though he repeatedly had these recited in his presence. He personally participated in the solemn prayer sessions. According to Eruch Jessawala, who kept an unpublished "prayer book," the process of dictation was complex. "Some words were in Gujarati, Urdu, some in Hindi or Persian, most in English." The spontaneous dictation was afterwards subject to a "dressing-up in English" which was read out to Baba for approval. He also asked the men *mandali* to recite the "101 Names of God" according to the Zoroastrian prayer book, and they would comply without knowing the meaning of the terminology. Meher Baba translated each one of the 101 names, e.g., he rendered Ezad as "the one worthy of worship." For the translation, see "The 101 Names of God," *The Awakener Vol. IX no. 3*, pp. 37–9. According to Eruch, the Names are in "a dead language of ten thousand years ago." See "Eruch on the Master at Prayer," *Meher Baba Association Newsletter* (London), November 1991, pp. 2–3, reproducing extracts from *The Awakener Vol. XIX no. 2*. The chronology is apparently derived from Meher Baba, who is also reported to have given an early dating for Zarathushtra which is puzzling to scholars of that subject, though reminiscent of some ancient Greek estimates. Baba said that the Iranian prophet lived some six thousand years ago, and that his master was a Hebrew; Meher Baba is also reported to have said that Zarathushtra was "the greatest Sufi" (Kalchuri, *Lord Meher Vol. 4*, p. 1196). On another occasion he said that Zoroastrianism was almost 6,000 years old, and that the original teachings of Zarathushtra had not survived (*ibid.*, p. 1352). It is not clear whether he regarded the Gathas as a later priestly attribution, though some of his communications might indicate that.

319. His statements against drug use have appeared in various publications, especially *God in a Pill? Meher Baba on LSD* (San Francisco: Sufism Reoriented, 1966). See also note 450 *infra*.

320. On Rajneesh in Poona, See H. Milne, *Bhagwan: The God that Failed* (London: Caliban Books, 1986), pp. 106ff. On Rajneesh in Oregon, see L. F. Carter, *Charisma and Control in Rajneeshpuram* (Cambridge University Press, 1990). Professor Carter, though a sociologist, failed to observe basic differences of emphasis in stating that "the Meyer (*sic*) Baba movement of the late 1960s was perhaps most similar to the Rajneesh movement in origin (Poona, India), teachings, relationship between master and disciples, and pattern of organizational development" (*ibid.*, p. 273 n.1). American sociology still has to correct misconceptions engendered about similarities, and ought at least to render the name of the obscured Irani correctly. Professor Carter, of Washington State University, has written a very useful book on Rajneesh, but appears to rely for his information about Meher Baba solely upon J. Needleman, *The New Religions* (New York: Simon and Schuster, 1972), pp. 74ff. Needleman affords an inadequate and partly misinformed view which does not compare Meher Baba with Rajneesh. Insofar as geographical origins are concerned, the Meher Baba "movement" that later developed can be ascribed to Meherabad ashram, near Ahmednagar, rather than Poona, if the sources are more closely examined, though the late 1960s permutation was at least in part American in componency and should be carefully distinguished from some earlier manifestations not widely studied. The teachings of Meher Baba were so far removed from many emphases of Rajneesh that it might yet take American sociology some centuries to cognize the differences when only one secondary source is cited. For instance, in the early days at Meherabad, Meher Baba's stress upon the value of restraint and the karmic dangers of promiscuity was so pronounced that many Americans would be incapable of meeting his requirements and ideals (e.g., the discourse of October 11th, 1928, reproduced under the title "Sex and Sanskaras" in *The Glow Quarterly*, ed. N. Anzar, August 1973, pp. 2–3). By contrast, Rajneesh was morally retarded to an acute degree, and is more compatible with some of the norms in contemporary American socioculture. Rajneesh incited his followers to constant promiscuous relationships, making them believe that this lifestyle was beneficial for them. In contrast, Meher Baba taught that even a fleeting promiscuous encounter will contract binding impressions (*sanskaras*) of lust transferred from the partner that are enough to complicate further evolution towards spiritual emancipation. Thus, according to this perspective, the American Rajneeshis who so gleefully pursued the ideals of Rajneesh in the contemporary American spirit of hedonistic liberation were creating for themselves a much stronger ball and chain that will weight them down over diverse reincarnations until they psychologically scream to free themselves from tunnel vision. The differences in perspective ought really to be vaguely mentioned even in universities where primary and supplementary sources are overlooked in the spirit of sociology inherited from Comte, Weber, and Parsons. Meher Baba's discourse "The Sanctification of Married Life" clearly deters against promiscuous relationships. See his *Discourses Vol. 1* (sixth edn 1967), pp. 148ff. When the radical difference in teaching between Rajneesh and Meher Baba is understood, then it also becomes very obvious from the data that the relationship between "master and disciples" was very different in their respective cases. Insofar as organizational developments are concerned, Meher Baba stressed that he did not want to establish any religion and did the exact opposite of creating an order of permissive neo-*sannyasins*, which was one of the extremely dubious tactics of Rajneesh. Why such differences cannot be comprehended by academics is surely a matter for due analysis when sociology cares to investigate the sources more closely.

321. Beryl Williams of New York drew my attention to this detail in 1966, when she informed me that Meher Baba's hair was originally auburn or reddish-brown and darkened in colour over the years. She sent me a clip of his hair dating to the 1930s, which confirmed the matter. Williams, a black American, had met resident Zoroastrian women at the two ashrams near Ahmednagar, and they had informed her of such details and given her a quantity of his hair which they regarded in the manner of a sacred relic. Beryl Williams had first met Baba in 1952 and was treated virtually as an untouchable by some white American devotees. She was more literate than many of the whites and wrote long letters in a very neat hand which expressed good and clear English.

322. The title of my book *Meher Baba, an Iranian Liberal* (1988) created some puzzlement amongst those readers unaware of ethnic complexities. It has been assumed by some writers that Meher Baba was an Indian Parsi. Yet it is technically incorrect to call him a Parsi. He was an Irani, with very strong ancestral roots in the villages of the Yazd locale of Central Iran. The term Irani designates a Zoroastrian of the mother country, i.e., Iran. The Iranis distinguished themselves from the Parsis, though no hostilities were involved. The distinction between these two Zoroastrian contingents is marked in early twentieth century literature, and is also found in the circulars despatched to the followers of Meher Baba at his instruction. Thus, although Meher Baba was born in the India of the British Empire, the full flavour of his ethnicity is lost unless his Iranian links are established. Both of his parents were involved in the ethnic drift from Iran to Western India.

323. One of the most proficient teachers at the Meher Ashram was

Kaikhushru Asfandiar Afseri, an Irani Zoroastrian from Teheran, who held the academic credentials of a B.A. He was a disciple of Meher Baba and was respected by Shi'ite Muslims; he had considerable gifts of tact and diplomacy. He was the author of *Kashf al-Haqaiq* (Ahmednagar 1929), on which see *Iranian Liberal*, p. 254.

324. The checklist is accessible in *Ramjoo's Diaries 1922–1929*, ed. I. G. Deitrick (Walnut Creek, California: Sufism Reoriented, 1979), p. 502. The relevant account is an edited version of an earlier book by Abdul Karim Abdulla, nicknamed Ramju, an Indian Muslim pupil of Meher Baba. Cf. *Iranian Liberal*, p. 255.

325. This honorific was employed as a sign of great honour. The term *qibla* refers to the direction of prayer, being synonymous with the niche or *mihrab* in the walls of mosques; the term is not lightly bestowed on anyone by Muslims. The title reflects the considerable esteem in which Meher Baba was held by some Indian Sunni Muslims and by some Iranian Shia Muslims. The sub-title of Ramju Abdulla's *Sobs and Throbs* (1929) was *A Real Romance about the Meher Ashram Institute, and the living miracles of Hazrat Qibla Meher Baba*. Ramju was not referring to hagiological miracles, which Meher Baba disdained, but to the interactions between Baba and the inmates of the Meher Ashram. The account is factual, if very colloquial in tone. The American version (see note 324 *supra*) was heavily edited in places, and omitted the introduction of Maulana Mazhar al-Haque, which more or less proclaimed the original as a "Muslim" book. Furthermore, the editing in *Ramjoo's Diaries* does not elucidate various ethnographic and sociological data that are helpful in reading such accounts of bygone times. An inchoate attempt of mine to do so was incorporated in *The Life of Meher Baba Vol. 1*, pp. 287–402, an unseen manuscript discounted by the Meher Baba movement, though Ivy Duce did acknowledge the existence of that non-canonical work. When a copy of *Iranian Liberal* and an accompanying goodwill document was sent in 1988 to Sufism Reoriented in California, there was no reply. The policy of that organization mirrors the general attitude of the devotional movement. Devotees currently appear to think that the last word on the subject of Meher Baba has been said in Bhau Kalchuri's biographical volumes, and that contributions from independent researchers like myself are superfluous. Flaws are discernible in Kalchuri's work, and improvements are quite conceivable. However, even slight criticism risks sectarian displeasure. My own version of the biography never having been written for commercial purposes, and myself having long recognized the immaturity of my manuscripts, I am disposed to think now that there is no discriminating demand for a newly written *Life* from me. I do not feel that it is possible in the current climate of the erroneous "Sai Baba movement" to produce worthwhile interest in an entity who has become regarded by many as a rather ridiculous cult figure owing to the presentations of devotees – especially in view of the fact that even professional sociologists have not bothered to ascertain the differences between Meher Baba and Bhagwan Shree Rajneesh. All I can do is supply some data here that may be of interest to future researchers who might penetrate some of the mists created by sects and "new religions." See also notes 341 and 396 *infra*.

326. See *Iranian Liberal*, p. 255.

327. Cf. *Ramjoo's Diaries*, p. 529, which does not express the full complexion of the situation. My version has the addition: "Within a short while he was rescued from his unpleasant predicament by news from Meherabad" (*Life of Meher Baba Vol. 1*, p. 395).

328. Shepherd, *Life of Meher Baba Vol. 1*, p. 395. Cf. *Ramjoo's Diaries*, p. 530. For Kalchuri's version of the Meher and Prem Ashrams which has additional details to those supplied by Ramju, see *Lord Meher Vol. 3* (North Myrtle Beach, S.C.: Manifestation, 1988), pp. 893ff. The page numbers in Kalchuri are consecutively spread throughout the volumes, and do not represent the number of pages in each volume.

329. Her father was Dorabji Khooramshari. See *From Oppression to Freedom*, p. 56, where I followed Purdom's rendition of this village name as Khooramshah. Another spelling that I have encountered is Khooramsharh.

330. Shepherd, *Life of Meher Baba Vol. 1*, p. 421.

331. The Babis were followers of the Bab, a radical religious leader executed in 1850. The Bahais were followers of Bahaullah, who in 1866 had declared himself to be a prophet, and who taught a pacifist outlook which was accepted by many Babis, who thus came to be known as Bahais. Bahaullah declared his new dispensation in terms of a universal religion; his priority was humanitarianism and not patriotism. He sought to conciliate with the Qajar government and to gain their support against the Muslim *ulama* (theologians), though at the same time he warned his followers against political involvement. He urged religious tolerance, himself suffering exile in Turkey and Palestine. See, e.g., M. Bayat, *Mysticism and Dissent: Socioreligious Thought in Qajar Iran* (New York: Syracuse University Press, 1982), pp. 126ff. Although in some general features, Meher Baba's teaching might be compared with that of Bahaullah (e.g., pacifism, universalism, non-political involvement, non-patriotic ideology), in many other respects the emphases were very different.

332. Kalchuri, *Lord Meher Vol. 4*, p. 1238.

333. Shepherd, *Life of Meher Baba Vol. 1*, p. 424. The source here is the account appearing in *The Meher Message* (1929), a journal edited by the capricious devotee K. J. Dastur. Cf. Purdom, *The Perfect Master*, p. 140. Cf. Kalchuri, *op. cit.*, pp. 1220ff., which is also incomplete.

334. An *anjoman* is a local Zoroastrian assembly, a continuation of the traditional council of elders, and a body distinct from the priestly assembly known by the same term. Such bodies collected funds for charitable enterprises, including educational and medical care.

335. Kalchuri, *op. cit.*, p. 1370.

336. Purdom, *op. cit.*, p. 157.

337. *Ibid.*, p. 162.

338. *Ibid.*, p. 164.

339. One of these women was Kitty Davy, who later penned her memoirs. Of their trip to India in 1933, she wrote: "On that initial trip, we were more like children on a holiday.... For instance, one or two of us had taken special dresses along for this occasion among our rather extravagant and unnecessary wardrobes. I mention this *en passant*, because it shows how little some of us understood, in those early days, what life with a spiritual master meant, or the real significance of Baba's breaking his silence." See Davy, "Twenty Years with Meher Baba Pt. 2 – Our Life with Baba in India: The First Trip 1933," *The Awakener* (1955) 3(1): 6. This passage is missing from Davy's edited version of the memoirs in *Love Alone Prevails: A story of life with Meher Baba* (North Myrtle Beach, S.C.: Sheriar Press, 1981), p. 91. The missing passage is rather allusive. It seems that the special dresses mentioned were "God-realization dresses," novelties which appear in other reports pertaining to the years 1932–3. In 1933 Baba was still indicating or joking that he would break his silence in the Hollywood Bowl. Perhaps he deemed this quip to be in keeping with the aptitude of the Western visitors who regarded their visit to India as a "pleasure trip," to quote Davy's phrase. Cf. Duce, *How a Master Works* (1975), p. 163, who refers to the visit to Hollywood in 1932. Cf. Shepherd, *Iranian Liberal*, pp. 27, 200–1, 245 n.267. Cf. D. De Leon, *The Ocean of Love: My Life with Meher Baba* (Myrtle Beach, S.C.: Sheriar Press, 1991), p. 56, who says that Baba "had told us we would all get God-Realization when he spoke, and Norina and Minta had bought special dresses for the occasion." Cf. Kalchuri, *Lord Meher Vol. 5*, pp. 1661–4, who reports that it was the English devotee Quentin Tod who persuaded certain women to obtain "fancy God-realization dresses made for the occasion, assuring them Baba would give them God-realization at the time, though Baba himself never indicated anything like this." Baba's younger brother Adi S. Irani was horrified at some of the enthusiasms in evidence and complained to Baba; Adi never lost his suspicion of the Western women like Princess Norina Matchabelli, one of those who obtained a fanciful dress. The careful reader will note that the late Delia De Leon was still party in her last years to the belief that Baba had specified God-realization for her group. The various misapprehensions that occurred over the years are a relevant investigation in sorting out who did not understand what in the creation of the Meher Baba movement, as some analysts term the phenomenon.

340. The "Kimco" group of British women later tended to preen themselves upon their contact with him, though they did not consider themselves to be mystical experts but leading devotees. Kitty Davy participated in the founding of the Myrtle Beach Centre in South Carolina, a place which Meher Baba visited in the 1950s. Davy died a centenarian. Delia De Leon also lived to a ripe old age, being over ninety when she died in 1993. Some confusion has recently arisen concerning her autobiographical memoirs in a book bearing the lavish title of *The Ocean of Love* (1991). Letters reproduced in that work bear rather effusive greetings like "My darling Leyla," apparently addressed to her by Meher Baba. Yet the book in question does not explain the process of transcription operative in correspondence (cf. *Iranian Liberal*, p. 287). The Parsi devotee F. H. Dadachanji, generally known as Chanji, was Baba's amanuensis during the 1930s, and he often adopted a sentimental "dear darling" style in wording letters to the Western female devotees. De Leon remained under the impression that most of the wording in her letters was that of Baba. It is true to say that he sanctioned the wording of such letters, but equally relevant to point out that there was rarely any close dictation involved; the secretary was free to round out the brief communications relayed on the alphabet board which Baba used. Meher Baba himself never wrote anything except his signature after January 2nd 1927. De Leon's memory for factual details was not infallible; her interpretations were frequently questionable, and she tended to place too much reliance upon the words of other prestigious devotees. Many relevant details are missing from her book, perhaps due to her age at the time of compilation; she was then ninety. Various letters from Meher Baba worded by Chanji, Dr. Donkin, Mani Irani, and Adi K. Irani confirm that the covering idiom of communication varied markedly with the editor. This is also apparent in many of the messages and discourses transmitted by Meher Baba. In letters bearing his signature he generally communicated a core message which was grammatically expanded by the amanuensis. From January 1927 onwards he never wrote anything, but merely applied his signature of M. S. Irani. The most direct rendition of his words occurred in cablegrams.

341. See K. Davy, *Love Alone Prevails*, pp. 16ff. Some more extensive information about Meredith Starr appears in Kalchuri (Vols 3, 4, and 5). Further details about Starr, supplied by Ann Powell, were incorporated in my unpublished *Life of Meher Baba Vol. 2*. That *Life* was listed in the bibliography of *Iranian Liberal* (pp. 271–2), which was suppressed at the Myrtle Beach Baba Centre as heretical. The related *Life* is apparently considered a diabolical rival work that should not even be heard of. Love alone prevails to the extent of suppression and rabid intolerance, one might well conclude. See also note 325 *supra*. I believe it would be rather futile to engage further in writing or preparing books about cult figure-heads who are credited with posthumously directing the whims and biases of the cult devotees. Conversely, there may be a need for books which do not accept cult interpretations.

342. See *Iranian Liberal*, pp. 146ff. Cf. P. Brunton, *A Search in Secret India* (London: Rider, 1934), chapters 4 and 14, which comprise a very misleading report, though frequently cited as an authority on the subject by those ignorant of background details. Brunton was far more interested in Meher Baba's abilities than he chose to disclose. He does accurately report that he was given diaries to read. I formerly stated that the diaries were those of Ramju Abdulla and Behli J. Irani, which I can here revise. Kalchuri's version is disappointingly facile, though I accept that the diaries were those of Ramju and Chanji (cf. *Lord Meher Vol. 4*, pp. 1346ff., 1358–9). Purdom saliently mentioned "the diaries of Behli J. Irani" in the Preface to *The Perfect Master*, which led some to believe that they were a major source. Chanji's diaries were a source for Ramju in his book on the Prem Ashram. Kalchuri's volumes are not annotated in respect of the sources utilized, a fact which makes checking more difficult. It is known that Kalchuri had ready access to all the diaries and other materials that were available to him after Baba's death. A question exists as to whether all the reported statements of Meher Baba are correctly transliterated in *Lord Meher*. Cf. *Minds and Sociocultures Vol. 1*, p. 854 n.152. Kalchuri's account of Brunton's visit to Meherabad is totally uncritical of the conversation; he also inserts the word *avatar* several times, a word which does not appear once in Brunton's version. This detail might serve to cast doubt upon Kalchuri's frequent use of the term *avatar* in his early volumes. Professional researchers might care to investigate such matters in the future.

343. See J. Masson, *My Father's Guru* (London: Harper Collins, 1993), pp. 160ff. See also *Minds and Sociocultures Vol. 1*, pp. 200–1 n.275.

344. Furthermore, on January 3rd 1932, Baba is reported to have told Gandhi, during their meeting in Bombay, that "I have already advised these Untouchables and their leaders who came to me.... In Nasik, the leaders of both the Brahmins and the Untouchables come to me for help" (Kalchuri, *Lord Meher Vol. 4*, p. 1518).

345. Kalchuri, *Lord Meher Vol. 5*, p. 1713.

346. *Ibid.*, p. 1714.

347. *Ibid.*, pp. 1714–17.

348. *Lord Meher Vol. 4*, p. 1518. Cf. the report of Adi K. Irani included in Duce, *How a Master Works*, pp. 572–3, which has some different accents to Kalchuri's version. Adi K. Irani tended to take a sectarian view of past events by 1970, the date of his report, which was given in San Francisco. Kalchuri's version is far more amenable to Gandhi, and states: "At the end, Baba urged Gandhi to come to him, warning him that his life was in danger" (*op. cit.*, p. 1518). That detail is in query. When Meher Baba was informed of Gandhi's death in January 1948, he paid tribute to the memory of the Hindu leader by conveying: "Gandhi's whole political life of sacrifice and selfless service was for his love of God, whom he longed to see until the very end." That quotation comes from Kalchuri, *Lord Meher Vol. 9* (Myrtle Beach, S.C.: Manifestation, 1996), p. 3236. Kalchuri does not here mention any request of Baba that Gandhi should go to him, and merely says that Chanji and Dr. Deshmukh "had met him a number of times" (*ibid.*) since Baba had last encountered him, though Gandhi "had even promised Baba to join him after India was freed" (*ibid.*). Some of the *mandali* (primarily Adi K. Irani) made too much of this theme in later years. After Gandhi's death, the Indian leader gained many public tributes, including one from Shri Aurobindo Ghose. Meher Baba described Aurobindo as "a real advanced saint and a good soul, but not having realized God, he still thinks of politics" (*ibid.*, p. 3237). Some of the *mandali* seem to have been annoyed that Gandhi was acclaimed by some parties as an *avatar*, and in response to circumstances, Baba asked all the *mandali* to write down their views on the matter of his (Baba's) precise status. A number of the responses have been published (*ibid.*, pp. 3237–9), with some differences to Kitty Davy's brief version (see note 398 *infra*), which was written closer in time to the event described, originally appearing in *The Awakener* journal. Pendu (A. R. Irani) was one of the men who were unconcerned with the definition of status tags. He wrote: "As you know well, I have nothing to do with this Avatar or God business. I know only one thing, that I have to serve you" (*ibid.*, p. 3239). It is evident that Meher Baba was not concerned at this period (the late 1940s) with promoting any image of himself as the *avatar*, and that a number of the *mandali* were not certain how to classify him.

349. Shepherd, *Life of Meher Baba Vol. 1*, pp. 252–3. Cf. the *Message to India* dated 1932–3 in which Meher Baba does not mention the untouchable issue. See *Messages of Meher Baba delivered in the East and West* (Ahmednagar: Adi K. Irani, n.d.), p. 5. However, the subject is known to have made various informal statements about his opposition to caste. Even Paul Brunton, who was bent upon caricaturing the "Parsee messiah," credits him with the statement: "In India I shall not rest till the pernicious caste system is uprooted and destroyed.... When the outcastes and lower castes are elevated, India will find herself to be one of the influential countries of the world" (*A Search in Secret India*, p. 51). That cannot be regarded as a verbatim report, though it does match the context found in some other sources. Brunton's narrative is basically untrustworthy, his profile of Meher Baba resulting from a mood of pique. His description of Baba's physiognomy is blatantly inaccurate, and even partisans of Brunton have winced at that description found in a work that was clearly written for commercial ends.

350. This quotation is from "The Need for Creative Leadership in India" in *Messages of Meher Baba delivered in the East and West*, p. 40. That message was issued for the benefit of political leaders in March 1942, at the time of the proposal made by Sir Stafford Cripps at New Delhi. See also Kalchuri, *Lord Meher Vol. 8* (1995), pp. 2772ff. The Cripps Mission failed, and official British sources blamed this upon Gandhi's pacifism. See L. Fischer, *The Life of Mahatma Gandhi* (London: Cape, 1951), pp. 447ff. Meher Baba is not mentioned in the standard biographies of Gandhi, and the British probably did not give much attention to the message of a non-politician. Yet his contribution perhaps had significance. He was not pro-British, but at the same time, he was not anti-British, remaining distinctively neutral in the Churchill versus Gandhi conflict. "Gandhi is impractical, but a very good man," he said in July 1940 (Kalchuri, *Lord Meher Vol. 7*, p. 2580).

351. In early April 1942, Chanji (F. H. Dadachanji) was despatched once more to Delhi to call on Gandhi. (Chanji was a very likeable Parsi, an earnest devotee of Meher Baba who was conciliatory towards other parties, and who made an appropriate emissary). Afterwards several letters passed between Chanji and Gandhi on the subject of Baba's advocacy of "non-violent violence." Dr. Deshmukh, of Nagpur University, was also asked by Baba to see Gandhi for the purpose of making a clear explanation of the controversial issue. (Deshmukh was a Hindu devotee, and one of the more intellectually accomplished men in Baba's contact). On April 15th, Deshmukh visited Gandhi at his ashram in Wardha, but the Mahatma was adamant in denying the validity of Baba's viewpoint. See Kalchuri, *Lord Meher Vol. 8*, pp. 2787, 2789.

352. Kalchuri, *Lord Meher Vol. 5*, p. 1847.

353. This was M. R. Dhake Phalkar, who had a degree in law.

354. Upasni always referred to Meher Baba by his original name, clearly intended as a term of familiarity and endearment harking back to their early acquaintance. Upasni consistently used the respectful form of Merwanji, the suffix *ji* being used amongst both Hindus and Zoroastrians in India.

355. Kalchuri, *Lord Meher Vol. 6*, p. 1915.

356. *Ibid.*, p. 1916, who says "there was a continuous exchange of such strange messages between Meher Baba and Upasni Maharaj."

357. The women's ashram at Meherabad was not inferior to the Sakori women's ashram of *kanyas*. Meher Baba's counterpart had a date of origin in the early 1920s, and thus antedated the elevation of Godavri

Mataji at Sakori. During the 1930s, the Meherabad women's ashram was larger than the *kanya* grouping. The core of the Meherabad women's ashram was Zoroastrian, early members including Gulmai Irani and Mehera J. Irani. Mani S. Irani, Baba's sister, did not join until 1932, but during the 1950s her salience as a writer of newsletters eclipsed the memory of Gulmai amongst Western devotees, who assumed that Mani and Mehera were the two most important women in Baba's contact. This belief may be doubted. Even the diligent Charles Purdom was under the erroneous impression that Gulmai died in 1942 (*The God-Man*, p. 29). This may have been a misprint, yet a number of readers were led to believe that she was a deceased figure whose importance had long faded. In reality, she died in 1962, only seven years before Meher Baba. See Mani Irani, *Family Letter no. 48* (Meherazad, August 16th, 1962), pp. 2–3, which reports the death of Gulmai on August 10th 1962, and which describes her as "one of the oldest and closest of Baba's disciples," and adding that it was due to her efforts that Meherabad ashram was acquired forty years earlier. Baba made a special visit to Gulmai's home in Ahmednagar the day before her death. As for Mani, she was respectfully known as Manija after Baba's death, and was then very much in the limelight with the many visitors to Meherabad and Meherazad. She was regarded as a major representative of her brother until her death in 1996. Whereas Gulmai, like Mehera, was far more retiring in disposition, and did not write memoranda. Gulmai's relationship with Upasni Maharaj was viewed as a contradiction of loyalties by some zealous devotees of the Avatar Meher Baba movement after the nominal founder's death. It is often necessary to query devotional interpretations in the interests of accuracy. Mani was literate in English, witty, and very conversational; she was very popular with Western visitors to the ashram after Baba's death. It does not necessarily follow that she was superior in spiritual characteristics to Gulmai.

358. A. K. Irani, "Shri Upasani Maharaj's Visit to 'Khushru Quarters,'" *Meher Baba Journal* (Nov. 1938) 1(1): 33.

359. *Ibid.*, p. 34. Elsewhere, Adi K. Irani says that after the *arati* performance, Upasni told Gulmai and himself that Meher Baba was the *avatar*. This second report dates from after Baba's death. No reference to the term *avatar* appears in the *Meher Baba Journal* article. A third report appeared in Purdom, *The Perfect Master*, p. 226, which is clearly abbreviated and includes the phrase "Meher is my loving child." Cf. Kalchuri, *Lord Meher Vol. 1*, p. 114, who has it that Upasni said on this occasion: "Do you really know who he is? He is the Avatar." This detail might be true, although less certain than the earlier reports. Cf. Kalchuri, *Lord Meher Vol. 6*, pp. 1985–7, who gives a reasonably accurate version of Adi K. Irani's abovementioned report (without citing that item), though his assertion that Khushru Quarters was the same building at which Upasni had stayed in 1921 is in contradiction to Adi's explicit statement to the contrary (*art. cit.*, p. 32 col. 2). Kalchuri ends his account of the 1936 episode with a devotional verse in praise of Upasni and Meher Baba, deemed superfluous to the narrative by some readers.

360. Kalchuri, *Lord Meher Vol. 7*, p. 2559.

361. *Ibid.* Kalchuri's account is not totally clarifying, and he resorts to surmisals on p. 2560. "It was their divine humour to engage in such play," he says of the two saints. Some analysts find such aspects of Kalchuri's work irritating and misleading. It was not play when Meher Baba foiled the plans of Upasni's detractors in the law courts, and he was in real earnest about the elimination of caste Hindu stigmas and ritual dominance at Sakori. The priestly setbacks obscured the factor of Upasni's sympathy with untouchables. If that sympathy amounted to play, then Upasni had bad tastes in humour. Meher Baba definitely had good tastes, and was strongly opposed to bad tastes in this respect. Meher Baba was averse to those who supported caste suppression of untouchables, and he was perhaps very annoyed with Upasni's ambiguous standpoint in relation to that matter; he would doubtless have raised the high sum required to buy the Sakori ashram if events had proved more congenial to progress in that camp. Kalchuri's work does not mention the issue of untouchability in relation to Sakori, one of the many flaws in his devotional text. On the credit side, he gives much information difficult to find elsewhere, providing the most detailed of the biographical works on Meher Baba.

362. Kalchuri, *Lord Meher Vol. 8*, p. 2729. Cf. Purdom and Schloss, *Three Incredible Weeks with Meher Baba*, p. 52, which records Meher Baba's words in September 1954 and which reports Upasni as saying "You are *Adishakti*" and "Keep your eye on Sakori." Cf. Natu, *Glimpses of the God-Man Meher Baba Vol. 6*, p. 27, who reports Baba's reminiscences in March 1954, which include the information that Upasni three times asked him to break his silence, though the reply (via gestures) was that the time had not yet come. The earliest version of the Dahigaon meeting was in the *Meher Baba Journal*, only one month after the event. Different wordings in the reports are due to the different occasions of reporting and the different editorial hands involved, a common feature of the Meher Baba literature and one requiring due flexibility in coverage. Photographs of the two mystics were taken by Padri, a Parsi member of the *mandali* who had to beg Meher Baba to allow his inclusion in the small travelling party. The event is otherwise notable for the privacy and non-publicity involved. It is on record how Padri feared that Upasni would destroy his camera, the Hindu sage apparently being averse to gadgets.

363. Kalchuri, *op. cit.*, p. 2757.

364. *Ibid.*, p. 2746. In a conversation with Minoo Bharucha shortly after Upasni's death, Meher Baba said that "a man living near Tibet" had taken the place of the deceased *sadguru*. There does not appear to have been any further clarification. Minoo Bharucha was a Parsi of Nasik who had been very devoted to Upasni Maharaj. His wife was named Aimai, "who once was a nun at Sakori." Meher Baba called them both to Meherabad and told Minoo that there was no difference between Upasni and himself. The careful investigator will note that Baba did not say that Godavri Mataji had replaced Upasni.

365. Purdom and Schloss, *Three Incredible Weeks*, p. 52. This disclosure was made at Meherabad.

366. This statement comes from the diary of Kishan Singh, relevant to September 1954 when the diarist accompanied Baba and the group of Western men on a visit to Sakori. See "At Sakori with Baba" in *The Glow Quarterly* (May 1975) 10(2): 5 col. 2.

367. *Ibid.*

368. Purdom and Schloss, *op. cit.*, p. 52. "Her loving influence overcame the Brahmin atmosphere; she at last saw me at Nagar (Ahmednagar) and asked me to come once to Sakori."

369. See R. Abdulla, "Meher Baba's Fiery Life and External Activities," *The Awakener* (July 1953) 1(1): 26–7. Cf. Natu, *Glimpses of the God-Man Meher Baba Vol. 3*, p. 196. Godavri Mataji is not mentioned in these accounts, though it is clear that Baba was welcomed with respect and warmth. According to Ramju Abdulla, it was past sunset when the visitors arrived. Meher Baba's intention seems to have been limited to visiting the tomb of Upasni and honouring that structure by placing his forehead to it. When he got up he conveyed to his companions: "Maharaj is here and not there." This was a daring statement meaning that Maharaj was in him and not in the tomb. He was briefly shown around the ashram and his party were offered refreshment. They afterwards moved on to briefly visit Shirdi that same night, where Meher Baba offered his respects at the shrine of Sai Baba, subsequently visiting the mosque and the Khandoba temple. Ramju's account makes it evident that Meher Baba went to Shirdi as an outsider. The visit was incognito, with no fanfare or *darshan*. Ramju comments that "those who had lived with Sai Baba found it hard to recognize the original sites and scenes" at Shirdi because of "the erection of huge modern structures" (*art. cit.*, p. 26). Baba had hitherto avoided Shirdi on his travels. One of the party, Gustadji Hansotia, had once lived at Shirdi for six months as a disciple of Sai Baba. Ramju refers to Sai Baba's shrine as "the temple-like *dargah*," indication of his Muslim perspective. They moved on to the *dargah* of Hazrat Babajan at Poona, arriving there by 2 a.m. in the morning of November 15th, 1952. Baba's express purpose in this trip was "for the first and last time to pay homage to the three masters with whom I have been connected, viz., Sai Baba, Upasni Maharaj, and Babajan" (*ibid.*, p. 25).

370. Natu, *Glimpses of the God-Man Meher Baba Vol. 6*, p. 20. Bal Natu, a Hindu devotee of Meher Baba, was given permission to accompany the party to Sakori. It is significant that, during his teens, he had been influenced by slanderous articles against Upasni Maharaj which appeared in a Marathi monthly, written by detractors. "In my ignorance of true spirituality and in my youthful patriotic fervour, I regarded Maharaj as a parasite on society" (*ibid.*, p. 12). He had since altered his perspective quite radically, and had felt guilty for sarcastic remarks he had once made about the Sakori saint.

371. The diary of Kishan Singh reports Baba as saying in September 1954: "She (Godavri) welcomed me, bowed down to me, performed my *arati*, made me sit on the *jhula*, and that group of Wagh fell numb." See *The Glow Quarterly*, 1975, 10(2): 20. It is evident that much tension existed amongst the males in the reception party. Baba afterwards embraced Wagh, who is said to have felt relief. Baba then embraced all the other men of Sakori ashram, and they are said to have softened (*ibid.*). Bal Natu omits these details, possibly as part of a public relations policy between ashrams. His account (*op. cit.*) dwells very much on harmony, but this is not totally realistic.

372. Natu, *Glimpses of the God-Man Vol. 6*, pp. 21ff., 26. The author makes clear that his report of Meher Baba's statements is not verbatim. "I had to read between the lines and reconstruct the flow of ideas as best I could" (*ibid.*, p. 21). That is a very honest reflection. So many other reports give the impression that a verbatim specimen is being presented. Even when Meher Baba was verbalizing in only one language, a verbatim report was not always easy. Translation and editing are further complications. A large number of the renditions of his communications in the volumes of Kalchuri's *Lord Meher* can only be considered approximate. For instance, the inclusion of avataric phraseology from a later period is always suspect unless close evidence is available for early years of the "Old Life." It is evident from such reports as that of K. J. Dastur that Meher Baba was making non-public references to *avatar* status as early as the late 1920s – long before the spate of Hindu avatars who used the key term in varying senses. According to Bal Natu's approximate report, Baba conveyed at Sakori in March 1954: "He (Upasni) only made me *know* my Ancient One status as the Avatar" (*ibid.*, p. 25). Upasni had also been known to use the phrase "Ancient One" according to some translations, but not in the sense of *avatar*.

373. *Ibid.*, pp. 28–9.

374. *Ibid.*, p. 33.

375. *Ibid.*

376. Purdom and Schloss, *Three Incredible Weeks*, p. 48; Purdom, *The God-Man*, p. 253. See also Natu, *op. cit.*, pp. 123–4. See also the report of the Western followers in "Facets of the Diamond," *The Awakener* (1955) 2(4). See also the report of Kishan Singh, which is the most detailed one for the visit to Sakori (*The Glow Quarterly*, 1975, 10 no. 2, pp. 1–4).

377. This report appeared in "Facets of the Diamond" and was reproduced in Duce, *How a Master Works*, p. 191.

378. *Ibid.*

379. Purdom, *The God-Man*, p. 253. The fullest account exists in the diary of Kishan Singh, cited above.

380. K. Singh, "At Sakori with Baba," *The Glow Quarterly* (1975) 10(2): 4 col. 1.

381. *Ibid.*

382. *Ibid.*

383. *Ibid.*

384. *Ibid.* Narasimhaswami was influenced by the hostile brahmanical slanders of the 1930s, a factor which caused him to relegate the importance of Upasni after writing the biography.

385. *Ibid.*, p. 4 cols 1 and 2. This detail apparently refers to the year 1936.

386. *Ibid.*, p. 4 col. 2.

387. *Ibid.*, p. 20 col. 1. The diary is presented in a rather disjointed manner, but is unedited in content. The style is simple and clear.

388. I have here given details of Meher Baba's reported words to confirm for the benefit of unbiased readers that I was following his version of events in *Gurus Rediscovered*, pp. 2–4, 134–6, and not inventing an interpretation of my own. I entered the Kishan Singh diary in note 7 on p. 74 of *Gurus*, though that observance of annotation protocol was not sufficient to stop Antonio Rigopoulos from adversely pronouncing upon my "opinion" that the works of Narasimhaswami were marked by "hagiographic and apologetic concerns" (Rigopoulos, *Life and Teachings of Sai Baba of Shirdi*, p. xxvii). Dr. Rigopoulos should instead address himself to the opinion of Meher Baba, which is surely more pressing than mine, and very relevant in a work of the kind he wrote. Rigopoulos shows no acquaintance with the Kishan Singh diary and related sources, though he insinuates that my version of Sai Baba was deficient; he also omitted my book *Iranian Liberal* and Bhau Kalchuri's multi-volume work on Meher Baba from his supposedly authoritative bibliography on the "Sai Baba movement" that is assumed by him. Readers should decide for themselves whether Rigopoulos was justified in his Satya Sai-oriented defence of Narasimhaswami, or whether what Meher Baba said has some relevance to the situation of "Sai Baba movement." Cf. M. Warren, *Unravel-*

ling the Enigma, pp. 15, 24 n. 38, 354, for some distortions and another failure to consult the Kishan Singh diary, despite many references to Meher Baba, whose own emphases are ignored and replaced by a vindication of Narasimhaswami's integrity. In future, academics who write theses on the "Sai Baba movement" should check all the literature in which they presume to be non-opinionated experts (as an amateur, I am no expert, and disclaim any such honours). That would surely be a better procedure than assuming that cult literature of the Narasimhaswami category amounts to a faithful picture of events so convenient to Satya Sai Baba. See also note 167 *supra*.

389. Although Narasimhaswami's second multi-volume work is of some documentary relevance, many interpretations embodied in it are very questionable, and that work did not in any way serve to annul the miracle instinct he had created amongst many readers. Thus, Narasimhaswami's *Life of Sai Baba* was party to the popular scenario he had earlier created, and has to be used with considerable caution. Rigopoulos, *Life and Teachings of Sai Baba*, relies heavily upon that work, and eschews other material such as is contained in the Kishan Singh diary.

390. Purdom and Schloss, *Three Incredible Weeks*, pp. 9–10. The total number of "women disciples" living at Sakori is here given as thirty, that figure applying to 1954.

391. Purdom, *The God-Man*, p. 270. This kind of acknowledgement was generally reserved for Mehera J. Irani, his own disciple, from about that time on. The similarity to statements made about Mehera in the 1950s and 1960s is quite striking. Devotees of Meher Baba did not generally credit any equivalent to Mehera, though one is left wondering.

392. *Ibid*. The diary of Kishan Singh has Baba's gracious reference to Wagh as the man "who has for years most faithfully and honestly carried [out] the office work and also the arrangements at Sakori ashram." See "The Great Gathering, 1954," *The Glow Quarterly* (1975) 10(2): 15 col. 1.

393. Godavri requested Meher Baba to visit Sakori once more in January 1956, an event celebrated on a more lavish scale than formerly. Baba was asked to visit Shirdi at that time, but declined to do so, being averse to the miracle sentiments there. In April 1957 he again responded to Godavri's request for him to visit Sakori. She in turn attended his birthday celebration at the Meherabad *sahavas* programme in 1958. These events were included in my unpublished *Life of Meher Baba Vol. 4.*

394. The only permanent Western inmate in this ashram was Rano Gayley, an American. A British woman who lived for many years on Meherabad Hill was Kitty Davy, who eventually moved to America at Baba's instigation in 1952. She reports that in 1937 there were over ten Eastern women living at Meherabad, including Gulmai Irani (*Love Alone Pre-*

vails: A story of life with Meher Baba, p. 169). Nearly all of these women were Zoroastrians.

395. See J. Judson, ed., *Mehera* (New Jersey: Beloved Books, 1989). The foreword by Mani S. Irani reports that, although all members of the women's ashram were kept in strict segregation from the men, in Mehera's case there were very special arrangements insisted upon by Meher Baba. "For many years she could not even hear the name of any man, even for example when the newspaper was read out" (*ibid.*, p. IX). Prior to January 31ˢᵗ, 1968, "not once had Mehera ever met or greeted or even seen at close range any of the men *mandali* who lived with Baba" (*ibid.*). On the very late date specified, the men *mandali* met her for the first time at Baba's instruction. He stood by her as she said the words "Jai Baba" in greeting. This very simple greeting was all that most men at first heard from her, and her attentions were mainly directed to female devotees of Baba after the latter's death. Her very cloistered existence for over forty years is reflected in her statement: "At first I was very shy of talking in front of people, especially men, as my life with Baba has been very secluded" (*ibid.*, p. 241). Mehera refers to Meher Baba "undergoing all the austerities and ruining his health with fasts and accidents" (*ibid.*). Her verbal mode of expression fitted the general devotional ambience at Meherazad, though she remained the most distinctive and the most retiring of the women who gained prominence at the ashram. She died the same year her memoirs were published. The volume consists of a compilation from tape recordings, not writings. Mehera reminisced in Gujarati, which was translated into English. A further version of her reminiscences can be found in D. Fenster, *Mehera-Meher: A Divine Romance*, a 3 volume work based on Mehera's personal narrative recorded between 1974 and 1982.

396. This is an angle I attempted to express in my introductory work *Meher Baba, an Iranian Liberal* (Cambridge 1988), which was intended in a rational spirit of analysis. That angle has been repudiated by major Centres of the devotional movement passing under Meher Baba's name, Centres who claim to represent him and who act as if they have a monopoly in the materials concerning him. My book was accused of being hostile to some of his close disciples by daring to criticize aspects of their writings and/or policies, while one party accused me of not clearly stating that Meher Baba defined himself as *the* avatar. The Centre at Myrtle Beach in South Carolina, which ranks as the major Baba Centre in the West, described my book as "purported research" and suppressed *Iranian Liberal* within the environs, afterwards warning some readers that the book was unfit for consumption by Baba lovers (as they call themselves). The fact that I had formerly written a four volume work on the subject, unpublished and unseen by them, was dismissed without further reference. See also notes 229, 325, and 341 *supra*, and notes 445 and 464 *infra*. My "purported research" was based upon many tangible documents such as the first published article on the Meher Baba Centre at Myrtle Beach. Ann Powell had passed to me in 1965 a reprinted item from the *Myrtle Beach News* dated March 21st 1946, and which evidently originated from Elizabeth Patterson and her colleagues. Some extracts may be of interest here to serious researchers. "Myrtle Beach may become one of the leading spiritual centers of the United States, is the prediction of interested friends, who foresee it as the future spiritual Mecca of America" (*Meher Baba Spiritual Center* reprint, p. 1). Does the first half of this sentence mean that the tone was more moderate at that time? Certainly, Meher Baba is only described as a "perfect master" in the article under discussion. The tone was clearly influenced by Baba's humanitarian endeavours at that period, and stated that the Center "will be developed along humanitarian lines" (*ibid.*). Road-building, the introduction of electricity, and a mosquito control project were underway (it was only two or three years since Patterson had located the property after a search instigated by Baba). The property amidst the lakes was not merely conceived as "a sanctuary for wild life" (*ibid.*). "Meher Baba, when he comes here, will guide the actual development of the various activities. This will include several humanitarian institutions, such as a hospital, nursery, rest home for psychological cases, which includes victims of the recent war. Special protection will be given to many of the homeless children who have suffered from the present catastrophes." (*Ibid.*). Meher Baba had described the envisaged Center in terms of "The Abode for One and All" (*ibid.*). I was interested in these diverse plans when I was a boy and wrote to Kitty Davy, a senior British devotee who had lived at the Myrtle Beach Center since 1952 and who was a celebrity there. She was unable to answer all my questions, and I gathered that difficulties had been encountered with some plans. That correspondence occurred in 1965–66. Several years later Ivy Duce recorded that when Baba visited the Myrtle Beach Center three times in the 1950s, he expressed his "wish that it be a great place of pilgrimage" (*How a Master Works*, p. 751). A question might be how this emphasis avoids establishing a religion which suppresses books about the figurehead. To return to the 1946 article. "He (Baba) does not intend to found any new religion or school of philosophy; his influence makes people live up to the truth which underlies all religion, and he trains men to what he calls 'mastery in servitude.'" (*Ibid.*, p. 2). Here we find one of the frequent assertions in the literature about no new religion, although the clause about servitude is more rarely found. As a teenager, I was very interested to find out the precise meaning of the clause. I corresponded with various devotees in America, though the most impressive instance of servitude was a black American named Beryl Williams, who lived in New York. She gave her time and information without stint, and sometimes even sent me free literature without my asking for it. She aided my early research more than any other American. She never made any claim about herself, and I began to see that devotees varied a great deal in their talents, disposition, and understanding. Yet it was Beryl Williams who had to struggle for recognition against some white American devotees who retained nineteenth century attitudes. To return to the 1946 article. "Meher Baba has been devoting energy and resources to the alleviation of starvation in India. He makes it his practice to visit every famine district. He attends to the dying and eases their transition. He has established free dispensaries for the poverty-stricken masses. He has cleansed the lepers personally, as Jesus did centuries ago. Meher Baba also takes personal interest in the upliftment of the depressed classes, and in all his institutions, no distinction is made between Brahmin or Untouchable." (*Ibid.*). As far as my "purported" research has been able to confirm, most of these details are in fact true of the first three decades of Meher Baba's career, though "every famine district" would seem an exaggeration. Some famine districts, yes, and in a manner that achieved for him no obvious gain and almost no publicity. However, I have not been able to confirm the detail about attendance of the dying. Patterson had evidently been inspired by the mastery in servitude theme in formulating her own humanitarian plans, whatever the outcome was. See also note 417 *infra*. See also notes 398 and 437 *infra*. The reprint of the 1946 article appears by courtesy of William A. Backett (d. 1963), and bears his address of Old Oak Cottage, Halstead, Sevenoaks, England. For thirty years Backett and his wife Mary (d. 1962) were the underprofiled backbone of the British devotees, being the main focus for communications from Baba's ashrams that they relayed on a more general basis. I did not meet Backett, who was deceased by the time I heard about him from Ann Powell (d. 1965), who had known him for thirty years. He and his wife had a reputation for sincerity and humility. Will Backett had based his publishing and related activities at an office in Charing Cross. He seems never to have asserted his importance, which other devotees tended to do. He and his wife were originally pupils of Inayat Khan (d. 1927) and later said they had found a greater truth in Meher Baba. Backett was a retired insurance broker and had the demeanour of a lower middle class man. Unlike Delia De Leon (upper middle class), he was not related to a family estate in Panama, and he and his wife gave everything to what they believed in. Meher Baba had made a special visit to their cottage in 1933, which also attracted a small number of British devotees like Ann Powell (Welsh working class). The Backetts imparted to their environment a distinctive rustic flavour, with Mary often sitting at an old spinning wheel. Their simple cottage contrasted with Elizabeth Patterson's luxury home known as Youpon Dunes, near the Center at Myrtle Beach. The Backetts only vacated their cottage when they were seventy years old as a consequence of Baba's wish for them to move to London. They sold the cottage and soon acquired a small bungalow in Acton in 1950. Kitty Davy (upper middle class) lived in Patterson's home during the 1950s, though she had roughed it at Meherabad, a feature of her varied lifestyle which can here be applauded. In the late 1950s Baba is reported to have told Davy that the Myrtle Beach Center "will one day become my Universal Center" (Duce, *How a Master Works*, p. 747). The delay is striking. At what point does that Center become universal? It would seem definite that Princess Norina Matchabelli, one of the founders, died in 1957 in the pre-universal phase. Meanwhile, the Backetts attracted a cosmopolitan audience in their humble London home and related hired rooms, visitors from India finding their venues more accessible in the global chart of official and unofficial centres. Their home was never actually billed as a Meher Baba Centre, but that was the unofficial assessment of their contribution. (However, the Backett abode at Westfields Road, Acton, was listed in the "Centers of Information about Meher Baba" that regularly appeared on the back cover of *The Awakener* journal in the 1950s). Ann Powell was one such assessor. She was an unassuming person, and Fred Marks (lower middle class ex-schoolteacher) conveyed to me in 1965 that she was very similar in disposition to the Backetts, whom he had known very well since the 1940s, being a weekly visitor to Old Oak Cottage. Marks clearly lamented the disappearance of that dedicated couple from the scene owing to decease. I noticed that both Powell and Marks did not use certain terminology employed by the *mandali* and some American devotees. They rarely mentioned the word *avatar* and nor did they resort to the term "Baba lovers" that had become popular in America (though at a later date, Marks did follow suit with the new trend). They had both retained the verbal influence of Will Backett's vocabulary. Backett had achieved the feat of maintaining 1930s and 1940s "Meher Baba movement" vocabulary until the time of his death, assisted by similar idioms of Charles Purdom (middle class intellectual). I was fascinated to compare the differing registers in existence by 1965. Backett produced and influenced many "Friends of Meher Baba" newsletters which are lacking in usage of terms now generally associated with the movement. Even Baba's brother Adi S. Irani did not deviate from the "British" pattern when he became the Hon. Secretary, and in the December 1958 *Friends of Meher Baba Newsletter*, Adi merely stated: "Issued on behalf of the Committee in Baba's Love and Service." The only references to "Beloved" and "Avataric" in that newsletter occurred in the reproduction of a Family letter from Adi's sister Mani. Will Backett did not take up the term avatar, deeming the name Meher Baba sufficient, and he technically remained a "friend" of Baba, not a lover. Yet he was partial to the phrase "Highest of the High" that was found in certain messages, and one of his idiosyncrasies was to inscribe that phrase upon some of his photographs of the ideal. That trait apart, he and Purdom remain memorable as restrained admirers. Only after Purdom's death in 1965 were the ramparts removed against exaggerated stylisms within the London group. Purdom looked askance at the trend promoted by Baba's brother Jal which sold Baba badges and other devotional souvenirs. Purdom would have been nauseated by the tritely emblazoned card which displayed "sayings" like "Don't worry be happy," a novelty which appeared in 1966 in America. Cf. K. Davy, "Thirty Years in the Service of Meher Baba 1932–1962," *The Awakener* (1963) 9(3): 1–18, which is a version of the Backetts penned at Meher Baba's own request, a very unusual gesture for him to make. The couple had first met Baba at the London home of Kitty Davy in 1932, but a drawback is that Davy had not been part of their milieu after the 1937 sojourn at Nasik, and only some basic details are covered in her article. Individuals like Ann Powell are missing from the narrative, which was written at the Myrtle Beach Center. However, Davy does appropriately state that the small house in Acton, though not big enough for large gatherings (which were held elsewhere), "nevertheless has been 'The Meeting House' for East and West up to December 1962" (*ibid.*, p. 13). That tallies with the impression conveyed by Powell, Marks, and others. Thus, a small London bungalow attained celebrity alongside the 500 acre property at Myrtle Beach that was pre-universal. There were other complexities also. I had the opportunity to observe Ann Powell alongside three far more prestigious devotees, namely Delia De Leon, Charles Purdom, and Adi S. Irani (Baba's brother domiciled in London since 1956). The occasion was a group discussion that took place in London in 1965. The three prestige persons dominated the discussion, but there was much argument amongst them. Powell remained silent, no contribution being requested from her by the vocal persons. Purdom was actually quite impressive; he had the strongest intellect in the company, and spoke in comparatively incisive terms, keeping to the point. Adi had by far the greatest personal magnetism; he also had a habit of asserting himself now and again, sometimes invoking his long years of association with his famous relative. De Leon was the most forward of the talkers, and gave the impression that she was one of the "nearest" to Baba and therefore had an important say in matters. (De Leon was known at times to assert, "I am one of Baba's nearest and dearest," a theme which did not convince everyone). De Leon gave the impression that Baba had favoured her by becoming the President of the London group (the Friends), though she had been unable to find a suitable place as a Centre, which he had asked her to do in 1948. There were distinct gaps in her version of events. I found private talks with Ann Powell far more enlightening. Her words and attitudes conveyed much more insight than the prestige entities above-mentioned. Powell had known Baba for as long as De Leon (since 1931), and yet she was almost unknown in the movement. Beryl Williams had not heard of her, as I discovered, and by which time I was aware that very close investigation of various matters was required in order to ascertain what had been happening. For instance, Powell's assessment of De Leon was less flattering than the latter would have wished. According to Powell, it was not De Leon whom Baba had honoured but the Backetts. In 1948 Baba had asked De Leon to create a Centre in London, but the Backetts were the ones he wanted to live in that Centre and run it. The latter couple were so unassuming that they complained of being unfit for any such role, although they agreed to the proposal. Baba became the official President of this new organizational activity, but De Leon failed to find a central building in London, complaining that costs were against her. Yet the redoubtable Backetts sold their cottage, eventually purchased their humble abode in Acton, and unintentionally convinced many devotees that they were the "nearest and dearest" in England rather than the Kimco group (which had included Delia De Leon). The number of Indian visitors to Acton seems to have been noteworthy, and one might infer that the Backetts were more universal than Kitty Davy's operation at Myrtle Beach. A basic factor appears to be that the Backetts were always available to participate in "Baba's work" (if that is the correct description), whereas De Leon (like Adi. S. Irani) was only available at certain times such as monthly group meetings, or the occasional Sunday afternoon. See also notes 467 and 468 *infra*. The intrinsic history of some sects has been obscured by those in assertive roles; that is an anthropographic deduction.

397. The American devotee Jean Adriel (Jean Schloss) entitled her version of Meher Baba as *Avatar*, though being rather careful to insert the sub-title *The Life Story of the Perfect Master Meher Baba* (Santa Barbara, California, 1947). From various references in that work, it is clear that the boundary had not been definitively passed from one status role to another in the mentation of Meher Baba's following. Adriel's basic view seems to be expressed on page 50, which refers to "Avataric cycles," and thus the conception of Meher Baba as a very elevated master is attested. The factor of discrepant ranking is also evidenced by such publications as *Message by Meher Baba the Perfect Master: The Religion of Life* (New York: Circle Production Inc., 1949). This was a booklet issued in close affinity with the formative Meher Center on the Lakes near Myrtle Beach, S.C., and being associated with Princess Norina Matchabelli, a figurehead of that Centre, which was instigated by Meher Baba with some rather complex clauses attached. See note 417 *infra*.

398. See K. Davy, *Love Alone Prevails*, pp. 325–6, who records that Baba sent round a questionnaire on the subject of "What do you take Baba to be?" The men *mandali* gave answers like "Perfect Master," "The Master of the Age," "Sadguru," and "Avatar." Kitty Davy wrote with honesty that she had no real knowing, and also inscribed her entry with a quotation from St. Paul: "Faith is the substance of things hoped for, the evidence of things not seen." I have always admired that sort of honesty, which is far better to my mind than the lavish eulogies sometimes found in devotional literature. At the same time, it is reasonably obvious from the sources that Kitty Davy was not a mystic like Kaikobad Dastur or Chhota Baba, and hence my cautionary reflections in *Iranian Liberal*, pp. 276ff., to the effect that it is unwise to elevate devotees to a status higher than they actually possess, in order that events may be seen in due perspective. That view does not entail any belief that Kitty Davy was not a worthy person (which I believe she was) possessing certain practical talents (with which I do credit her) and honesty (fully conceded here). That view merely means that it is prudent not to confuse her (and others like her penfriend Mani S. Irani) with mystical categories subject to different experiences. The same considerations apply to Elizabeth Patterson, a practical American devotee with considerable business expertise who was closely involved in establishing the Meher Center on the Lakes at Myrtle Beach. Such people, whatever their good qualities, are surely not beyond criticism; once they become regarded as being beyond criticism, as being infallible instruments of a divine cause, then cult attitudes will arise as may be found in the Meher Baba movement.

399. In his book *The God-Man* (London 1964), the British author Charles Purdom annoyed some devotees with his interpretation of the subject's spiritual status (*ibid.*, pp. 390ff.). Purdom was berated by some dogmatic American Baba lovers for some statements in Part 2 section 3 of his longest biography, especially: "To suppose that Baba is the Palestinian Jesus come again, is a fundamental error" (*ibid.*, p. 401). Purdom was indeed concerned about some implications of the *avatar* theme, and he reports that when he was with Meher Baba in India in 1954, the latter said to him: "You are bothered about the idea of *Avatar*. There is no need to be, for we are all *Avatars*" (*ibid.*, p. 391). That is an example of Meher Baba's disarming attitude to problematic issues. Such theological issues do greatly bother some people, and I will leave such matters to theologians and religious scholars who are in the habit of pronouncing upon them. Such matters are not my field. I am prepared to respect Purdom's liberal version of Meher Baba, though even he was perhaps being dogmatic in affirming: "I believe Christianity to be unique, final in its uniqueness" (*ibid.*, p. 402). My own investigation of gurus, saints, and avatars is philosophical and anthropographic rather than theological. See also *Minds and Sociocultures Vol. 1*, pp. 199–200 n.273 for a reference to Purdom.

400. See W. Donkin, *The Wayfarers: An Account of the Work of Meher Baba with the God-intoxicated, and also with Advanced Souls, Sadhus, and the Poor* (Ahmednagar: Adi K. Irani, 1948). The publisher excelled himself in this project, providing a good quality book with diacritical marks, maps, and photographs. A large fold-out map of India was provided, and two supplements followed. A reprint appeared in America (San Francisco: Sufism Reoriented, 1969). See also the remarks in *Iranian Liberal*, pp. 257–8, based upon my own unpublished version of the *mast* work in *The Life of Meher Baba Vol. 3*, an early manuscript written in 1971–3. A version of the mast work can be found in Kalchuri, *Lord Meher Vols 7–9*. Cf. B. Natu, *Glimpses of the God-Man Meher Baba Vol. 1 (1943–1948)* (Walnut Creek, Calif.: Sufism Reoriented, 1977).

401. See G. Feuerstein, *Holy Madness* (1991), pp. 28–30, who discusses Meher Baba as an Indian *avadhuta* in the context of "crazy wisdom," a very inappropriate system of reference. Feuerstein also writes that "the *masts* are not merely insane" (*ibid.*, p. 30), which is an understatement, and neglects to correlate his reference to "God-intoxicated individuals" (*ibid.*, p. 28). The *masts* are not "countercultural heroes," as Feuerstein's chapter title would have readers believe, though they have been made so in the Daist idiom of misinterpretation. Feuerstein insensitively sandwiches the activity of Meher Baba in between the hedonistic exploits of Neem Karoli Baba and sexually active Tantric *bauls*. The *masts* are a Muslim and Hindu subject, and will probably not be understood for centuries in the West, it would seem, despite Dr. Donkin's pioneering book. The Daists, and those influenced by them, distort and misplace many subjects with which they presume to be intimately conversant as experts in mysticism. The publishing blurb of Paragon House states on the dust jacket of *Holy Madness* that Feuerstein "has first-hand experience of crazy wisdom." That confusing theme entails Feuerstein's negative reaction to Meher Baba, who is notably snubbed as representing "desirelessness," in contrast to the "desires" favoured by left hand Tantra (*ibid.*, pp. 250–2). See also note 463 *infra*.

402. E.g., Rigopoulos, *Life and Teachings of Sai Baba of Shirdi*, p. 398, states that "Meher Baba used this word to indicate someone who was 'God-intoxicated,' a mad ascetic." The last two words are very misleading; the description of "mad ascetic" is not that of Meher Baba, but of Rigopoulos or his colleagues. Meher Baba was at pains to point out that this category are not mad. Furthermore, nor is the term "crazy wisdom" any more suitable, contrary to the imposition of that confusing term by Georg Feuerstein.

403. Cf. Rigopoulos, *op. cit.*, p. 372, who refers to the *Sarvadharma* emblem of Satya Sai Baba, without any reference to the "mastery in servitude" emblem associated with Meher Baba. "It is significant that Satya Sai Baba has extended Shirdi Baba's universalism to comprehend the five main religions present on Indian soil" (*ibid.*). This excised version of the extension is very misleading, and perhaps one item of proof that "Sai Baba movement" is a cliche for neglecting unwanted details. A relevant detail is that Meher Baba's emblem gained the addition of a Jewish symbol by the 1960s, proof perhaps that he was not concerned merely with Indian soil (see the front cover and title page of his *Discourses*, sixth edn 1967, which feature the Star of David). This symbol was also copied by the emblem of Satya Sai, the official explanation being that American devotees had requested this addition.

404. The dates and descriptions appended to photographs have sometimes varied. The present writer obtained a large number of photographs from Meherazad ashram during the mid-1960s; these were inscribed on the reverse in a neat hand by Rano Gayley. Her descriptions sometimes differ from those found in the volumes by Kalchuri, which feature many photographs prepared by L. Reiter. For instance, what Gayley inscribed as the first photo of the subject as Meher Baba was dated by her to 1920. Reiter employs the description of "early 1920s," which can give the impression of 1922–4, in which case the description is misleading (cf. *Lord Meher Vol. 1*, p. 222). See also note 480 *infra*.

405. There are various videos in circulation that require comment. The original 8mm. (and 35mm.) films have been edited by devotees, and have undergone some adventures, including over-prolonged stills. These films vary considerably in quality, and include both formal and informal occasions. The earliest films are black and white samples from the 1930s, but many are in colour and date from 1954 onwards. The originals very rarely had a soundtrack, but the popular videos have gained a variety of accompaniments which vary from Pete Townshend's sensitive version of the Parvardigar Prayer to dogmatic doctrinal presentations that sound uninspired.

406. Various versions of the New Life have been published, of which the latest is Kalchuri, *Lord Meher Vol. 10* (Myrtle Beach, 1996). Cf. Natu, *Glimpses of the God-Man Meher Baba Vol. 2* (Bombay: Meher House, 1979).

407. M. Baba, *The Everything and the Nothing* (Sydney, Australia: Meher House, 1963), p. 26, from the discourse entitled "The Four Journeys."

408. N. Anzar, *The Beloved: The Life and Work of Meher Baba* (Myrtle Beach, S.C.: Sheriar Press, 1974), p. 68 n.41, reproducing an extract from the diary of Kishan Singh.

231

409. *Meher Baba's Call given on occasion of Mass Darshan Programme at Ahmednagar on 12th September 1954* (Ahmednagar: Adi K. Irani, n.d.), p. 1.

410. Purdom, *The God-Man*, p. 217.

411. *Ibid.*

412. *Ibid.*

413. *Ibid.*

414. Edited by Adi K. Irani and originally appearing in *The Awakener*, a journal devoted to Meher Baba. This message has since appeared in other publications, e.g., Anzar, *op. cit.*, pp. 116ff. See also *Iranian Liberal*, pp. 51ff., for a critical coverage. Baba's statements in the abridgment did include disapproving references to devotees raising funds in his name. "Even one penny extracted in my name without true foundation is dishonesty."

415. Natu, *Glimpses of the God-Man Meher Baba Vol. 5* (Myrtle Beach: Sheriar Press, 1987), p. 243. Part XI of Natu's book is a devotional account of the Rajahmundry episode but is much more detailed than the earlier brief version edited by Adi K. Irani. Meher Baba said on this occasion: "No one of my *mandali* is Baba; everyone has got weaknesses and defects. Advice you can have from Adi [K. Irani], but not as from Baba through Adi" (*ibid.*, p. 254). Such warnings were generally forgotten in subsequent years.

416. *Ibid.*, p. 243.

417. On the history of the Meher Center-on-the-Lakes, see Davy, *Love Alone Prevails*, pp. 361ff. From India in 1941, Meher Baba despatched two devotees, Elizabeth Patterson and Norina Matchabelli, to find a suitable property in America to be used as a Centre. Two years elapsed before Patterson remembered a tract of land in South Carolina that belonged to her father, and which was subsequently prepared as the new Meher Center, to use the American spelling. This comprised about 500 acres of land, some ten miles north of Myrtle Beach. Baba said that his devotees should make this site "the spiritual abode for one and all" (*ibid.*, p. 372), though the prestigious devotees at that Centre have since decided to suppress books which remind them of the gap between theory and practice. Being intolerant of any constructive criticism, they choose to prohibit any suggestion that they have not achieved the ideal. See Shepherd, *Minds and Sociocultures Vol. 1*, pp. 201–2 n.276, and also pp. 114, 162 for references to "brainwashing" in a context that differs from the standard accusation made against cults. A proscribed book dared to point out that Patterson and others had not furthered the list of projects which Meher Baba had suggested for this site (*Iranian Liberal*, p. 43 and n.16), though I also pointed out that the ideals set were very high and difficult to achieve. Those ideals were listed by Kitty Davy in

Love Alone Prevails, p. 695, though without some of the context afforded. I might be allowed outside the target area to briefly mention here what those ideals were:

1) the spiritual academy that would use "intellectual understanding"; there was no mention of simplified devotional emphases of the type that abound at Myrtle Beach and other Baba Centres.

2) the house of advanced souls, intended to "prepare real mystics of the practical type"; real mystics are not necessarily devotees if intellectual understanding is brought to bear on these matters.

3) the abode of the saints, to consist of "saints who will bestow true knowledge on souls who are ignorant"; anyone who claims to be such a saint at the Meher Center-on-the-Lakes might require to furnish proof of gnosis, which is customarily discounted as a distraction for devotees who wish only to follow the Avatar.

4) the *mast* institute, an ideal surely very difficult to implement outside the East, as Meher Baba himself emphasized that *masts* are not found in the West. This ideal was somehow perpetuated from plans for an earlier Centre at Byramangala, in India.

5) the solitary quarters for meditation, an ideal that appears to be rather at loggerheads with the standard belief of Baba lovers that such ideals are not applicable to them.

6) the resting place for the afflicted, evidently an humanitarian endeavour, though not in any obvious evidence at Baba Centres in the West. However, such a plan was strongly envisaged during the 1940s. See note 396 *supra*.

Purdom's report says that Baba told Patterson that the new Centre was to be devoted to the ideals listed above (*The God-Man*, p. 202). This is a reasonable assessment, though Kalchuri's more recent version has Baba stipulating that the Centre was "to be used for any" of those ideals (*Lord Meher Vol. 11*, p. 3830). Yet Kalchuri lamely adds: "Elizabeth decided that it be a retreat for those who loved Baba and knew of him" (*ibid.*). A degree of evasion may be detected here, especially in view of the accompanying assertion that "the soil of the Center is saturated with tears.... they who visit the Myrtle Beach Center will not leave disappointed" (*ibid.*). Criticism of the hierarchy is deemed "purported research" at the glorified Centre, and critics will court acute disappointment at the absence of an academy employing due "intellectual understanding." Intellectual is a big word, though unfashionable in the devotional sphere and the New Age.

As foreign reminders on these matters are proscribed at Meher Baba's "Home in the West," perhaps some party in America will study the materials to ascertain any possible deficiencies. The situation has nothing further to do with me, as I have no wish to contact Baba Centres, and for many years have not been near one.

418. W. Parks, "The Early History of the Ahmednagar Centre" (8–12) in *Meher Baba Association Newsletter* (London) Nov./Dec. 1995, p. 9, from the message dictated for the inauguration of the Ahmednagar venue, a message read out by Adi K. Irani.

419. *Ibid.*, p. 11 col. 3. Devotional activities still took precedence at the Ahmednagar Centre, and Baba permitted the devotees there to undertake public processions on the occasion of his birthday in 1967–8 (*ibid.*, p. 11 col. 2).

420. *Messages from Meher Baba* (repr., Acton, London: W. A. Backett, 1952, limited edn of 150 copies), p. 10. This is from the message entitled "Meher Baba on Religion and Politics."

421. *Ibid.*

422. *Ibid.*, pp. 10–11.

423. The editorial recensions abundantly reveal that efforts were made to improve upon the loose dictation in English from the alphabet board. The original five volume edition of *The Discourses* was edited by Dr. C. D. Deshmukh. Charles Purdom subsequently produced a different version of this collection in his *God to Man and Man to God* (London 1955), editing and condensing the material after gaining Baba's permission, the aim being to provide a convenient one volume edition. Sufism Reoriented later produced a revised three volume version of Deshmukh's edition. See entry numbers 2–4 in the bibliography of *Iranian Liberal*. Cf. the seventh edition of that collection (Myrtle Beach, S.C.: Sheriar Press, 1987), in which the new editors are named as Eruch B. Jessawala, Bal Natu, and J. Flagg Kris. There are obviously advantages in a one volume edition with a technical glossary, and some think that the new one compares well with Purdom's version. However, there are flaws of sectarian propaganda in the introduction by D. E. Stevens. See note 479 *infra*.

424. See M. Baba, *God Speaks: The Theme of Creation and Its Purpose* (New York: Dodd, Mead & Co., 1955). See also *Iranian Liberal*, pp. 248–9, which makes an objection to some editorial content in the second edition published after Baba's death. The Tibetologist Dr. W. Y. Evans-Wentz wrote an approving review of the first edition which stated that "no other teacher in our own time or in any known past time has so minutely analysed consciousness as Meher Baba has in *God Speaks*." That assessment does not appear to have been cited very much outside the Meher Baba literature, which so rarely supplies the source or even the quotation. See also *Iranian Liberal*, Part 2, for an attempt at overview. Unlike Shri Aurobindo's texts, the works of Meher Baba did not gain popularity in the New Age, a fact which could indicate that these works have profundity and an unfamiliar terminology.

425. Even Baba's brother Adi S. Irani did not read the key text, though he was naively considered an expert on Meher Baba's teaching by other devotees. Adi was by no means illiterate, having attended the Deccan College in Poona (many years after his famous brother Merwan). Yet he did find *God Speaks* very difficult to comprehend. During Adi's stay at Meherazad ashram in December 1968, Baba expressed annoyance with him for having failed to read *God Speaks* after so many years, and made him commence reading the book there and then. Still Adi could not comprehend the meaning, and his pride was humbled as a consequence. The profile of the failed reader was not the common devotee view of Adi, especially as he had tended to assume an air of knowledge. He himself later related the problem to a few people in England. See also note 462 *infra*.

426. Recorded in F. Brabazon, *Journey with God* (Beacon Hill, N.S.W., Australia: Beacon Hill Publishing Co., 1954), p. 29, from a message dictated at Rajahmundry on 27th February 1954.

427. *Ibid.*, p. 33. The date and place is missing in Brabazon's text, but the message from which this statement comes was delivered at Rajahmundry on 1/3/54. See *Meher Baba's Call* (booklet cited above), pp. 5ff. The relevant message was entitled "Existence is Substance and Life is Shadow." The word *talib* is a variant of *dervish*, and is used in different contexts in Sufi literature, sometimes denoting an initiated disciple.

428. Brabazon, *op. cit.*, p. 33.

429. *Ibid.* A *chilla* is a period of intense discipline or penance, and the word is used in Sufi tradition. The practice of *chilla* was sometimes adopted in extreme forms by the members of *dervish* orders, especially in India. Extremist *dervishes* might even hang themselves upside down like some Hindu *tapasvins*, or indulge in contorted breathing exercises (perhaps of Yogic origin) accompanying elaborate vocal *zikr* (repetition). A forty day period was sometimes favoured. Meher Baba's own father had undertaken a contemplative version of such discipline. See Shepherd, *From Oppression to Freedom* (1988), pp. 52–4. Such practices are extremely dangerous. Some Sufi teachers frowned upon such exercises as an extravagance; the basic form was contemplation and fasting, with which extremists could not rest content.

430. Brabazon, *op. cit.*, p. 32.

431. *Ibid.*, p. 34.

432. *Ibid.*, p. 9. Francis Brabazon compiled the messages quoted as a result of his participation in the Andhra tour. He was an Australian who first met Meher Baba at Myrtle Beach in 1952. He was noted for his acquaintance with Sufism in the form associated with Rabia Martin and Baron Von Frankenburg. He frequently stayed at Baba's ashram and became regarded as one of the *mandali*. He wanted to become as "dust" and considered this ideal to be exemplified by the *mandali*, though in practice he became praised by Baba for his poem *Stay With God* (Woombye, Queensland, 1959) and was feted in *The Awakener* journal by devotees. The Sufi dimension to this situation might leave open the question as to how far celebratory exposure can affect the status of abnegation. Baba's strategy was perhaps a test, some would think, though devotees were honouring celebrity (which was reaped by prominent members of the *mandali*). Brabazon may be admired for having renounced his earlier potential role as a *shaikh* in the Inayat Khan movement, though he certainly became lionized in the Meher Baba movement as a major spokesman after Baba's death, when various interpretations passed unchallenged and unquestioned by devotees. See also Brabazon, *The Silent Word: Being Some Chapters of the Life and Time of Avatar Meher Baba* (Bombay, 1978). Brabazon seems to have held a high opinion of his adaptation of the *ghazal* format in Persian poetry. Baba sometimes asked him to write *ghazals* in English, requests to which Brabazon came to attach much significance. At the event known as the "Great Darshan" in 1969, his comments were much in demand amongst visiting Western devotees, who regarded him as an authority figure. Brabazon was apparently happy to accept that role (and such a situation should always be duly questioned). He is reported to have said at that time: "Baba now taught me a poetical form capable of expressing all shades of the impossible relationship of the (mystical) lover and the Beloved. Such a form has not existed in English till now, because the lover-Beloved dilemma was not part of the British-American consciousness. And, of course, beloved Baba being the author of this new form was (or seemed to be) delighted with my exercises in it." These words are recorded in the *Meher Baba Association Newsletter* (London) Jan. 1997, p. 9. It is perhaps prudent to suggest that Meher Baba was not quite so delighted as Brabazon was with the versifications of the real author (i.e., Brabazon). Some analysts think that Brabazon's poetry was at its most fluent in his *Stay with God*, and was thereafter frequently mediocre by comparison.

433. Purdom, *The God-Man*, p. 284, reporting on the *sahavas* programmes held in November 1955 at Meherabad. On those events see also D. E. Stevens, ed., *Listen Humanity* (New York: Dodd, Mead & Co., 1957).

434. Purdom, *op. cit.*, p. 284.

435. This trend was not marked in Britain until the late 1960s, when American influences strongly contributed. Some of the idiom found in Bhau Kalchuri's volumes gives the very misleading impression that the term "lovers" was a norm in the pre-New Life phase. In reality, that term was a late innovation.

436. A prestigious Australian devotee has related his frustration at the absence of news about Baba in some of Mani's newsletters. "Occasionally for something to say, she would tell us about some little incident that was happening in the garden.... But I would get impatient with her because I didn't care what was happening in the garden, I would just want to hear about Baba." See J. A. Grant, *Practical Spirituality with Meher Baba* (Sydney: Merwan Publications, 1987), p. 126. According to John Grant, Mani was not always allowed to give (current) information about Baba, and he tends to justify the style of reporting which caused him frustration. Others think that Mani could have chosen more appropriate materials than her observations about birds and dogs and other matters; there were many records of her brother's past years that were neglected completely, and she had access to them. Cf. Mani S. Irani, *82 Family Letters* (Myrtle Beach, S.C.: Sheriar Press, 1976). Cf. the review of the Family Letters in *Iranian Liberal*, pp. 266–8. It remains to add here that the National Library of Australia filed John Grant's book under Hinduism in their Cataloguing-in-Publication data. It is apparently the devotional complexion of many books on Meher Baba that causes this kind of simplification. Yet due study of all the materials will dispel the impression that he was a Hindu guru. No library can really be blamed for associating the word Avatar with Hinduism, but as this word was in popular vogue amongst Meher Baba's following only from 1954 onwards, and as that following then comprised a Hindu majority, scholarly approaches could usefully set the biography in perspective, as I have been trying to do against overwhelming odds.

437. See Natu, *Glimpses of the God-Man Meher Baba Vol. 3* (Myrtle Beach, S.C.: Sheriar Press, 1982), pp. 22ff., and reporting that on subsequent visits, Baba referred to this Centre as his "home in the West" (*ibid.*, p. 49). That is explicable enough, as it was his home for one month in 1952 and for two weeks in 1958 (with a shorter stay in 1956). Yet Natu also uses some rather exaggerated expressions such as "every structure built on the property, small or big, was endowed with its own outstanding feature and eternal inner importance" (*ibid.*). The reader is also told that "Baba's love and presence experienced by his dear ones and the visitors during the earlier interviews and *darshan* on the Open Day, still permeate the entire property with a penetrating sublimity" (*ibid.*). The sublimity of suppressing a book like *Meher Baba, an Iranian Liberal* is lost upon the present writer. It would seem that the sense of eternal inner importance which has been conferred upon the Meher Center-on-the-Lakes cannot tolerate mild criticism from insignificant parties living elsewhere.

438. Natu, *op. cit.*, pp. 47–8; Duce, *op. cit.*, pp. 91–2.

439. Purdom, *The God-Man*, p. 288. See also F. Frederick, "Journey of the Heart," an account which was serialized in *The Awakener* (New York) soon after the events described. Cf. Duce, *op. cit.*, pp. 243ff.

440. B. Le Page, *The Turning of the Key: Meher Baba in Australia* (Myrtle Beach, S.C.: Sheriar Press, 1993), p. 69.

441. See C. B. Purdom, "The American Sahavas with Meher Baba," *The Awakener* (1958) Vol. 5 no. 3, p. 2, which states that the account was "based on his (Purdom's) own notes and those of Phyllis Frederick and others." Frederick was an American devotee and editor of *The Awakener*. See also Purdom, *The God-Man*, pp. 296ff. Purdom says that 225 people attended the *sahavas*, and that there was no publicity permitted. Some analysts might have difficulty in describing this event, as it was not a devotional programme and nor anything resembling a Yoga class.

442. See J. Spencer Trimingham, *The Sufi Orders in Islam* (Oxford University Press, 1971), p. 185, quoting the *Awarif al-Maarif* on the process in which "the genuine candidate who enters into discipleship (*suhba*) with the shaikh, surrendering himself and becoming like a small child with his father, is reared up by the shaikh in his God-given wisdom." Superficial or uninformed academics who have imagined that the "surrender" taught by Bhagwan Shree Rajneesh was the same as that emphasized by Meher Baba might consider well that such a conflation would be disrupted if the latter figure was more in affinity with Sufi ideals than the licentious neo-Tantric who encouraged four letter word therapy at Poona and in Oregon.

443. Le Page, *The Turning of the Key*, p. 114.

444. *Ibid.*, p. 123.

445. Namely Bill Le Page, who was the senior devotee mentioned in Shepherd, *Minds and Sociocultures Vol. 1*, p. 201 n.276. In 1993 he refused a free copy of my book *Meher Baba, an Iranian Liberal* that was gifted to the library at his centre on Kiel Mountain known as "Avatar's Abode," located near Woombye in Queensland. In defence of the rejected and proscribed work, I might here be allowed to draw the attention of more impartial readers to certain features of presentation. *Iranian Liberal* lists over fifty sources in an annotated bibliography (pp. 248–297). Le Page very briefly lists ten "Major Books by and about Avatar Meher Baba" (*The Turning of the Key*, pp. 412–13), using the status title which perhaps tends to make devotees feel superior. An accompanying page states that "books by and about Meher Baba are available" from four centres, two of which are Avatar's Abode and Sheriar Press of Myrtle Beach. None of these agencies stocks the proscribed book *Meher Baba, an Iranian Liberal*, and Sheriar Press was prominent in suppressing that book in 1988–9. The literary apartheid created by cult personnel like Bill Le Page and others signifies the prestige assumed and exercised by senior devotees who seek to screen out any alternative version of their figurehead that they do not happen to like. The matter boils down to the fact that criticisms (however mild) of senior devotees are unwelcome and regarded as cardinal crimes, and are thus effaced from the cult records. The supposed egalitarian nature of the Avatar Meher Baba cult is a myth, though Meher Baba himself definitely did promote egalitarian ideals.

446. Le Page, *The Turning of the Key*, p. 123.

447. In his book *The Turning of the Key*, Bill Le Page makes a great deal of his centre, known as "Avatar's Abode," as a place of world pilgrimage. Yet Meher Baba appears to have made no statements about the Kiel Mountain property being a prospective pilgrimage spot until 1967, when Le Page visited India. According to the latter's report, at Meherazad in 1967, Baba said that the Kiel Mountain property would become a place of pilgrimage and that Le Page should live there and have the property transferred to him (Le Page), to form a Trust (*ibid.*, p. 198). A problem is that Meher Baba "left unsaid what he meant by development of Avatar's Abode" (*ibid.*, p. 284), though Le Page has given his own interpretation. It was not until 1979 that Le Page moved permanently to Kiel Mountain and started to carry out his plans. He acquired an additional 185 acres adjoining the property, but had to sell this extension in 1992 (*ibid.*, pp. 281–2). It is not easy to follow the reasoning which Le Page applies in his assessment of the situation. He attributes the purchase of the extra land to Meher Baba's blessing, and the forced sale of that same land likewise to Baba's blessing (*ibid.*, p. 282).

448. It is reported that Baba asked one man present whether he would obey if asked to cut his wife's throat; the man answered yes (Le Page, *op. cit.*, p. 116). Meher Baba never gave that sort of instruction, and some think that a true answer would have been to refuse on grounds of conscience rather than to agree on the basis of a fear of being left out of the proceedings. The issue of obedience is awkwardly described in many devotee reports. Cf. Grant, *Practical Spirituality with Meher Baba*, p. 102, who has more details of the event under discussion, stating that the man "slowly and reluctantly" replied in the affirmative, and how Baba emphasized afterwards that he would not ask people to do such things. The incident is an extreme one in the literature.

449. Purdom, *The God-Man*, p. 359. See also F. Frederick, "Notes on the East-West Gathering," an article which comprised a special issue of *The Awakener* in 1963.

450. Kalchuri, *Lord Meher Vol. 19*, p. 6414. Meher Baba was charitable enough to describe Alpert as a sincere seeker, though his injunction to limit intake of LSD to three more trips was ignored by insincerity. "You can, if you want to, take LSD three more times and then you should stop taking it completely" (*ibid.*, p. 6413). See also Shepherd, *Pointed Observations* (Dorchester, Dorset: Citizen Initiative, 2005), pp. 103–4. The reply to Alpert, and other statements, were included in a pamphlet entitled *God in a Pill?* This was circulated to American college students.

See note 319 *supra*. See also "No Drugs – Meher Baba on the LSD Drug," *The Glow* (November 1966), p. 5, which describes the indulgence in drug use as "a state of perverted consciousness." In a message included in *God in a Pill?* Baba further stated: "The experience of a semblance of freedom that these drugs (such as LSD, mescaline, and psilocybin) may temporarily give to one is in actuality a millstone round the aspirant's neck." He also emphasized: "If the student world continues to indulge in the use of LSD, fifty per cent of its intellectual potential will be lost to the nation." The nation here meant was America, to which the message primarily applied. See also A. Cohen, "LSD or Love? – The Master in Action," *The Awakener* (1967) 11(4): 4–13, who states that Meher Baba's anti-drug campaign began in earnest in April 1966 when a letter from the ashram was sent to Dr. Allan Y. Cohen in America, the author of the article. Dr. Cohen observed that "Baba's message on drugs is clear, forthright, and serves to challenge the heart of the pro-psychedelic propaganda" (*ibid.*, p. 9). The campaigning devotees in America resorted to articles and letters published in regional and national publications, many talks and lectures, a distribution of anti-LSD literature, and also several radio and television appearances. "It is no exaggeration to estimate that hundreds of thousands of people have already read or heard of Baba's views on drugs" (*ibid.*, p. 10). A poster appeared in a Berkeley campus bookshop posing the question "Who will win – Meher Baba or LSD?" (*ibid.*). See also A. Y. Cohen, ed., *The Mastery of Consciousness* (Middlesex: Eel Pie Publishing, 1977).

451. Le Page, *op. cit.*, p. 189.

452. *Ibid.*, p. 190.

453. *Ibid.*, stating a total of fourteen *mandali*, though one of these appears to have been a visitor, not a regular member of the *mandali*. The men were Baidul (R. B. Irani), Kaka Baria, Pendu (A. R. Irani), Aloba (Ali Akbar Yazdi), Bhau Kalchuri, Eruch B. Jessawala, and the Australian Francis Brabazon (who joined at a relatively late date in the 1950s). Kalchuri was also a relative latecomer, a Hindu who became one of the *mandali* in 1953, and filling the role known as "nightwatchman" from 1955. See Bhau Kalchuri, *While the World Slept* (Myrtle Beach, S.C.: Manifestation, 1984). Meher Baba said that he wanted his biography written in Hindi for the people of India. In 1971 Kalchuri commenced to write *Meher Prabhu*, his lengthy biography in Hindi which was completed in 1973 at Meherazad, and which he afterwards co-translated into English. This is a prose work, though Baba had actually asked him to write a verse biography. He followed up with *Meher Darshan*, a verse biography in Hindi which was not published until 1985. Meanwhile, *Meher Prabhu* (*Lord Meher*) passed through different editorial hands and began to be published in 1986 in America. Kalchuri also produced a book called *The*

Nothing and the Everything, described as being based on points Baba had given at the end of his life; the extent to which one may regard this as Baba's dictation is uncertain, as the points were evidently amplified by the transcriber. See Kalchuri, *The Nothing and the Everything: Points representing ten per cent of Baba's missing book* (Myrtle Beach, S.C.: Manifestation, 1981). The reference to a "missing book" concerns the document written by Meher Baba at Meherabad in the mid-1920s. No explanation is given for the elusive nature of that early document.

454. According to Eruch Jessawala: "There was nothing much left of his legs, as the muscles of the thighs had lost elasticity and had become solid lumps – having no weight-bearing capacity" (*Meher Baba Association Newsletter*, London, Nov. 1991, p. 5). This deficiency was ultimately derived from his second motor accident in 1956. Meher Baba had great difficulty standing up in 1968 during the recitation of the Universal Prayer in the *mandali* hall at Meherazad, even though he was supported by one or two men, and even though the prayer was read out very fast. It was his habit to stand while that prayer was being recited.

455. H. P. Bharucha, *Meher Baba's Last Sahavas* (Navsari: H. P. Bharucha, 1969), pp. 11–13. The title of this account by a Parsi devotee refers to the first week in February 1969, when Baba's corpse was still visible at his tomb to the large number of visiting devotees who arrived after receiving news of his death. The description of Baba's last days is graphic, though the tone of description in relation to the "last *sahavas*" is at times highly coloured, e.g., Adi K. Irani is described in terms of: "Not only this life but millions of lives he would sacrifice at the feet of Baba" (*ibid.*, p. 39). A very small number of Western devotees made the journey to Meherabad in the short time available, including Delia De Leon from England. Prominent devotees were the first to be informed of the decease. Bharucha names eight Westerners and also Adi S. Irani, who likewise came by aeroplane.

456. This quotation comes from a letter of Will Backett to Ann Powell dated 23rd October 1946, written from Old Oak Cottage near Sevenoaks. This letter, which is in my possession, contains evidence of some distinctive 1940s attitudes to Baba's "speaking." Backett writes: "Baba said years ago when in seclusion – 'Things which are real are always given and received in silence.' We learn this every day, more and more, as we listen to his Inner Voice. Enid Corfe, who is in a displaced Jewish person's camp in Germany, wrote that she sometimes hears him utter one word in her sleep and dreams, and how sweet and wonderful his Voice is." Enid Corfe later moved to America and was a friend of Beryl Williams; she had first met Baba in Paris in 1931, and Backett was in contact with her at the end of the war. Such experiences as Corfe had seem to have been very rare amongst the post-New Life *mandali*. Even the comparatively intellectual Charles Purdom had a mystical attitude to Baba's "speaking," and wrote several years later: "Meher Baba's silence does not mean that he does not speak, for he declares that he speaks to himself; but he speaks to no one else." This comment comes from the introduction to *God to Man and Man to God: The Discourses of Meher Baba* (first edn 1955; second edn, Myrtle Beach, S.C.: Sheriar Press, 1975), p. vi. Cf. Purdom, *The God-Man*, pp. 407ff., reporting Baba's statements "Do you not know I am always speaking?" and "the voice of intuition is my voice" (*ibid.*, p. 413). However, on the same page in his biography, Purdom appears to credit that Meher Baba would eventually speak "the Word," and yet Purdom's version of this event was also mystical. He reflected: "the Word will be an inner word, heard by the inner ear only by those able to hear it" (*ibid.*, p. 414). Some other interpretations were rather less sophisticated. If Purdom was even partially correct, then it would appear that many devotees were stone deaf in terms of mystical audibilities.

457. De Leon, *The Ocean of Love* (1991), p. 207. On the attributed presence, see especially Le Page, *The Turning of the Key*, p. 234, who states: "That Baba did give his *darshan*, I can testify: as I knelt before his chair in Guruprasad, I felt his arms around me as though he were physically there." Another eulogy of the Great Darshan came from Murshida Ivy Duce, who stated that "Baba's silent presence was just as effective at this darshan as when we could see him" (*How a Master Works*, p. 422). Duce asserted that the Great Darshan "differed in no way from every other *sahavas* in which I participated" (*ibid.*), which is perhaps not much of a recommendation for her master-disciple relationship. Cf. Davy, *Love Alone Prevails*, pp. 673ff., whose version of events tends to endorse the rather extreme statements found in various accounts. Kitty Davy says that almost 700 visitors arrived at Guruprasad, Poona, and that the "Great Darshan" was "indeed unparalleled in the tremendous outpouring of Baba's infinite love which, with few exceptions, was felt by all present" (*ibid.*, p. 676). Apparently the devotees managed to exceed the scope of the *darshans* at which Meher Baba was physically present. Davy's glowing account also quotes an American devotee on the Great Darshan: "The hall was filled with Beloved Baba's welcome as he spoke in every heart, 'You see, I *am* here and I love you.' One by one we went up to Baba's chair to receive a personal 'embrace' – a timeless embracing of hearts" (*ibid.*, pp. 677–8). Such interpretations are not supposed to be criticized by those who point out that timeless considerations have an ambiguous relation to empty chairs in ever-loving halls that are soon afterwards demolished in the interests of economic considerations decided upon by the *mandali*. Davy does not refer to the demolition of Guruprasad to make way for high-rise flats. Instead she reiterates the devotional mood of "he has truly come to live within the hearts of his lovers" (*ibid.*, p. 679). Even those who ban books about him, it would seem, in their excess of eternal love. That gushing mood appears to have been triggered by Adi K. Irani's cablegram which informed devotees of Baba's death and which proclaimed that he would "live eternally in the hearts of all his lovers" (*ibid.*, p. 674). If one cuts out the word "eternally," the mood might be considered reasonable, but by the summer, the exaggerations had multiplied. After the Great Darshan, Mani's reflections at Meherazad rounded out the emerging sentiments: "Beloved Baba's presence fills each part and particle of Meherazad" (*ibid.*, p. 679). Guruprasad particles were superfluous, and Mani was one of those influential in the decision to demolish the bungalow in Poona where Meher Baba had annually resided. In August 1969 Kitty Davy continued the correspondence with Mani that is deemed to be so significant by American devotees, and stated: "Baba has broken his silence in the sense that love is pouring out in humanity in more abundance than ever before; groups and centers are popping up everywhere.... Baba is wasting no time in getting his message spread" (*ibid.*, pp. 680–1). Readers might almost be led to believe that devotees who were spreading the "message" were the proof of Baba breaking his silence. Anything can happen in imagination when no concrete knowledge of an event exists amongst sectarian promoters.

458. In *Iranian Liberal*, p. 65, the present author wrote that the Hindu minority in the ranks of *mandali* did not gain eminence after Baba's death. That was true at first, though eventually Bhau Kalchuri gained a high profile. The publication in America of *Lord Meher*, his multi-volume biography, has conferred upon him a role as a leading exegete. His book is regarded as a kind of gospel by devotees. Kalchuri has made visits to the West, and thus succeeded Adi K. Irani as an ashram representative in distant lands. One of his statements regarded as authoritative by devotees is: "After dropping his body he (Meher Baba) is infinitely active in this cleaning work because he has to Manifest, and unless he takes the garbage out of everyone he cannot Manifest. He has been doing this work since he dropped his body, and it will last for one hundred years when he will Manifest universally" (*Meher Baba Association Newsletter*, London, March 1997, p. 3). Critics regard such statements as being improvisations of belief. Also, it is relevant to point out that some loose renditions of Meher Baba's communications have recently appeared, and that the criterion for accuracy are publications which appeared during his lifetime or extant diaries from that period.

459. The standard interpretation which emerged in the movement was definitely sectarian and elevated devotion and personality worship. Because of this, many outsiders have been averse to reading Meher Baba's teachings contained in *God Speaks*, the *Discourses*, and related mes-

sages. Those teachings are in a different category to personality veneration. So also were partisan writers like Charles Purdom, and the differences should be credited.

460. The status of the *mandali* was defined by their proximity to
Baba, which devotees assumed entailed a deep wisdom. It does not necessarily follow that they were expert mentors. Their role during Baba's
lifetime was not that of expositors, but usually of accomplishing manual
or administrative tasks. Their opinions were sometimes to be treated
with caution, e.g., soon after Baba's death, Ali Akbar Yazdi (Aloba) conceived the notion that the deceased master would emerge triumphantly
from his tomb, a belief which surprised even some of the gullible visiting
devotees. Aloba had known Baba since the Prem Ashram days, and was
one of the many men who had gained little profile over the years. There
had earlier been a much larger number of *mandali* in the "Old Life" (i.e.,
prior to the New Life of 1949–52), some not being permanent residents
of the ashram. Certain of them are rarely mentioned in the devotional literature, obscured by later events. Of those long deceased, Dr. Abdul
Ghani Munsiff was unusual for his intellect and his affinity with Sufi literature. The British medic Dr. William Donkin had been a comparatively
isolated figure at the ashram long before Francis Brabazon arrived upon
the scene, and was a very different type to the Australian poet; Donkin
did not express himself in a devotional manner, and nor did Ghani. At
Baba's death, the *mandali* had been in existence for nearly fifty years;
they were an exceptional body in that they did not exhibit the typical ad-
juncts of Indian ashrams, e.g., *tapas*, renunciate garb, *mantras*, Yoga,
caste taboos. They wore ordinary clothes. A few had been married men,
though many of them lived a celibate life of hard work governed by obedience to the directions of their mentor. One of the Hindus, namely Vishnu Deorukhkar (see note 301 *supra*) was depicted by Paul Brunton as a
primitive native of limited horizons in the commercial descriptions provided by *A Search in Secret India* (1934), giving no idea of that man's
humanitarian activities with untouchable children (cf. *ibid.*, p. 51, also
misdescribing Deorukhkar as the secretary, which was the role of Chanji; Deorukhkar is referred to by Brunton as "a short dusky-faced man
who wears the round black cap of the Mahratta people"). Brunton's attitude is that of the Great Western Investigator who sees the natives for
what they are, which was popular fare in the British Empire. The truth is
that Brunton found Meher Baba's ashram too practical and down to
earth. By comparison, Brunton was a superstitious tourist obsessed with
weird-looking holy men, meditation, and occult powers. Deorukhkar died
some years before Baba, but amongst those surviving at the end were
Baidul and Kaka Baria (d. 1969). Neither of these men achieved much celebrity amongst Westerners. Both had taken a major part in the search

for *masts* during the 1930s and 1940s. Baidul was a man of robust strength who excelled in that task; he was an Irani from the village of Jafrabad near Yazd in Central Iran, and was originally an agricultural worker. Ardeshir Shapurji Baria, alias Kaka, had originally been a devotee of Upasni Maharaj, and during the early 1930s was often puzzled and irate at the behaviour of the Western women who mistakenly treated their time with Baba as a holiday. Baba acknowledged Kaka's devotional loyalty and compared him to Hanuman. As a consequence of such associations, Kaka was incorrectly described as a Hindu in *Iranian Liberal*, p. 34, another reason being that the name Kaka has been applied to Hindus. A. S. Baria was actually a Parsi. It is worth observing here that the *mandali* generally made nothing of their religious background, a factor very often reflected in the literature. See also note 259 *supra*. The only member of the *mandali* whom Baba described as being spiritually advanced was Kaikobad Dastur (not to be confused with K. J. Dastur), a Parsi who was subject to strong mystical experiences and with whom Baba would sit in solitary sessions resembling the *mast* work, effectively a mystery to the other *mandali*.

461. Le Page, *The Turning of the Key*, pp. 234–5. Cf. the statement of Mehera J. Irani that at the Great Darshan in 1969 "we greeted them (the devotees) with love, as Baba would wish, but we felt very sad without him" (Judson, ed., *Mehera*, p. 238). It is evident that Mehera knew that Baba was no longer present. Indeed, it is an insult to her prevalent grief at this period to imagine that he was. Her acute grief over Meher Baba's death became well known in the literature, though the implications were not assimilated. It was not until July 1969 that she contributed to the emerging belief that "he is always with us," although in a manner not typical of her companions. She reported seeing Baba's face in the bark of a tree near her window at Meherazad, after "feeling very sad and lonely" in his absence (*ibid.*, p. 238). In her sensitive psychological state, it is not really surprising that this kind of vision occurred. The episode became somewhat exaggerated when all the *mandali* and all the local villagers came to investigate the tree and Mani even took photographs of it which she sent to Western devotees (*ibid.*, p. 240). The *umar* tree became a conversation piece. The present writer can remember Western critics carping at this episode during the early 1970s, though they failed to distinguish between the anguished experience of an Irani nun and the follow-on enthusiasms of persons who were far less devoted to contemplation of the mystical beloved.

462. This orthodox emphasis is contradicted by another reference. In 1962 at the East-West Gathering in Poona, Meher Baba told Charles Purdom (d. 1965) that there would be a successor, though he would not divulge the identity. See *Iranian Liberal*, p. 270. This detail has been overlooked and ignored by the movement. Purdom was not a dogmatic devotee, and was more intelligent and liberal than many others. He did not exaggerate, and was sceptical of the devotional tendency to distort facts. It was he who led the English "Baba group" in London during the early 1960s. In May 1965 I attended his lecture on Ramakrishna (read out by another devotee because of his illness); that lecture was a studious contribution which would have been considered a shocking distraction in subsequent years when the mood changed to insular devotion under the auspices of such speakers as Don. E. Stevens, an American who considered himself an expert on Baba's *Discourses* and who gave "Avatar only" lectures. (Purdom did not believe that Ramakrishna was an *avatar*, but his study was not disparaging, and he was clearly interested in comparisons, not in promoting an insular sectarianism). Purdom was not sure what to make of Baba's disclosure about a successor, and nor was Delia De Leon, who had discussed the matter with him. She told me in 1973 that she and other women had formerly speculated over many years as to who would be Baba's successor. It was not Mehera but a male whom they envisaged. They had been tempted to think that the answer might be Dr. William Donkin, though she admitted that the English women were much swayed by the consideration that he was a tall and handsome Englishman with considerable brain and cultural style. Donkin died in 1970, and so could not be considered a successor. De Leon was unable to give any explanation of what Baba had meant in the communication to Purdom, and seemed confused by the fact that the *mandali* in India were saying that there was no successor. She had been reluctant to discuss the matter in the 1960s. In 1973 Fred Marks of London dismissed the matter, saying that "only Baba counts," reflecting the typical devotee attitude of exclusion. Adi S. Irani, Baba's younger brother who lived in London, was also aware of the issue, and was tempted to think that he was the successor. He lost this assumption at the time of Baba's death, after a visit to Meherazad in which he was rebuked by Baba for not reading *God Speaks* in the fourteen years since publication (see note 425 *supra*). Assumptions about being a "successor" are attractive to fantasy; some claims of this nature have been made in India, and should be met with due caution. It is rather unlikely that any genuine mystic would claim such honours. Upasni Maharaj seems to have been indifferent about being considered the successor of Sai Baba, even though he may have had cause to be viewed in that light. Meher Baba himself had not claimed to be the successor of Upasni (see note 364 *supra*).

463. D. Anthony and T. Robbins, eds., *In Gods We Trust – New Patterns of Religious Pluralism in America* (second edn, New Brunswick: Transaction Publishers, 1990), p. 495, from the editorial conclusion. Dick Anthony is an academic who became a devotee of Meher Baba in the late

1960s. His idea of a monistic "logic" of Meher Baba as the universal self of all persons has been contradicted by the present writer in *Minds and Sociocultures Vol. 1*, p. 162. Dick Anthony was also co-editor of the book *Spiritual Choices: The Problem of Recognizing Authentic Paths to Inner Transformation* (New York: Paragon House, 1987). This volume was considered by some American academics to be a major contribution to evaluation in the field covered. The introduction made some valid points, though some other articles included are far less cogent. Yet what is described as the Anthony Typology (*ibid.*, pp. 35ff.) does emphasize some very relevant considerations such as the misguided confusion of antinomianism with transcendence, and also the mistake involved in choosing "to define as 'mystical' those elements of normal consciousness such as rage, eroticism, grief, and other emotions" (*ibid.*, p. 49). In the interview with Dick Anthony entitled "Meher Baba" (153–192), he describes how he took LSD during an existential phase of academic life and made a visit in the late 1960s to the Meher Baba Centre at Myrtle Beach. He attributes significance to an experience he had there, which he afterwards discussed with his therapist, the issue being whether or not the experience was crazy. The outcome was that the therapist believed Anthony was no longer in need of therapy. He subsequently wrote to Meher Baba and received a reply. Meher Baba died soon after, and Anthony was one of those who attended the "Great Darshan" in Poona. He says that he had an experience at Baba's tomb which strongly affected him, producing "an exalted sort of transcendent state for several years" (*ibid.*, p. 161). He rejected psychotherapy and related interests. "I was celibate, and became ascetic and lived very simply" (*ibid.*, p. 162). After five years he chose to participate in "a Gestalt therapy weekend" and was persuaded that he had suppressed sexuality, anger, and other problems and that he "needed to reconnect with these feelings in order to be a real person" (*ibid.*, p. 162). He afterwards married, and also "did various kinds of therapy" and went "into private practice doing a type of body-oriented therapy, a type that I think of as transpersonal" (*ibid.*). Anthony tends to insinuate that his "ascetic" phase was inferior, and that his subsequent phase as a married therapist was superior. It must have been more lucrative, one would think; a large number of transpersonal enthusiasts became therapists in post-hippy America, and their doctrines have served to obscure the complexities in traditional mysticism. The reader could well wonder why Meher Baba and many of his *mandali* (male and female) lived a permanently celibate and "ascetic" life which lacked any trace of therapy or commercial practice of the same pursuit. An alternative view might even be that Dick Anthony failed to become a mystic for very long and relapsed into contemporary American patterns of life and assumption that are not in fact mystical. Yet he does clearly state the disadvantages of the "guru-

247

therapist syndrome" in terms of a "unilevel monism" (*ibid.*, pp. 64ff.). Anthony's monistic "logic" of Meher Baba is open to strong disagreements, however. One objection I have is that nothing like it was promoted during Meher Baba's lifetime amongst his following, and that the logic involved amounts to sectarian hindsight. Cf. G. Feuerstein, *Holy Madness*, pp. 250–2, whose objection to the Anthony Typology is from a Tantric perspective unable to accept disciplined standards associated with celibacy, and whose desire for an enlightenment filled with desires is very dubious for the future of American yoga; for such left hand Tantrics, desirelessness is puritanical. That could be a symptom of ignorance if enlightenment is worth having. The desire to be a Ph.D. does not automatically confer wisdom. In contrast, Dick Anthony does remember and honour some difficult ideals, but also props up the deficient doctrine of the Meher Baba sect, though his writing is not typical of devotional idioms. He has also tended to support the "non-brainwashed community" image of the Myrtle Beach Centre, which might have made that community feel more justified in their exercise of monistic intolerance in public relations. I might be allowed to remark in passing that Britain has a reputation for conservative attitudes, while America is supposedly liberal and democratic. Britain is indeed insular in the academic world, and from the citizen point of view, almost hopelessly so. Unfortunately, the American situation, even at supposedly liberal levels of "transpersonal" universalism, tends to screen out contributions from European countries. If I might dare to use a cultic illustration for a more general and complacent trend, the Californian Baba Centre (not Sufism Reoriented) wrote to me in 1989 enquiring about *Iranian Liberal* (they were the only Baba Centre to make such an enquiry). The reason for this unique gesture was that Dick Anthony had told one of the people there that he thought *Gurus Rediscovered* was an OK book to read. When I told the enquirer of the suppression tactics awarded to *Iranian Liberal* at the Myrtle Beach Centre, there was no further response. The Californians had evidently sided with the mother Centre against foreigners. The book was not distributed in America at that time, and these people were perhaps persuaded that Meher Baba guides their lives to such an extent that books about him should not be read or tolerated. Liberal California indeed.

464. The present author attempted to give warning about this and other matters in *Meher Baba, an Iranian Liberal* (1988), e.g., pp. 64–5, even supporting the Sufi dimension associated with Meher Baba (a dimension which is somewhat larger than Sufism Reoriented) by referring to the division between *zahiri* and *batini* characteristics – though using the word *batini* in an updated sense of an allusive statement. It was (and is) my view that devotees have presented a very unbalanced portrait of Meher Baba. That view has been confirmed by the response to *Iranian*

Liberal, e.g., see notes 325, 341, 396, 445 *supra*. That book has been variously ignored, suppressed, and proscribed by the Centres of the Avatar Meher Baba movement or cult, despite or because of my attempt to present the subject in a rational manner with critical apparatus. It was considered blasphemous to make any criticisms (however mild) of his "close disciples," who are considered beyond criticism. To many devotees, words like *batini* are merely strange Iranian or Arabic words having no reference to current American or English cliches in the "just love him" idiom. Perhaps Meher Baba was really an American incarnation of the avatar who happened by mistake to get trapped in an Irani entity. It would not surprise me if some Western devotees have already concocted equivalent beliefs under the influence of therapy or other New Age trends.

465. P. Townshend, introduction to De Leon, *The Ocean of Love* (1991), p. xiv, though without any reference to the way in which this harmless caution became a popular slogan.

466. In 1976 Pete Townshend established Meher Baba Oceanic in London, a venture in which his mentor was Adi K. Irani, who visited the new Centre and gave talks. Not long after, Townshend relapsed into a phase of alcoholism and drug-taking which caused a shudder of horror in the movement. His Centre dissolved. See G. Giuliano, *Behind Blue Eyes: A Life of Pete Townshend* (London: Hodder & Stoughton, 1996), chapters 5, 6, and 7. Assessments of the episode have differed. Some critics felt that Meher Baba was inadequate as a guide. The events in question surely cannot be blamed on Baba, as he died ten years earlier. Some thought that devotee leaders like Delia De Leon and Ivy Duce (of Sufism Reoriented) had failed to inspire Townshend sufficiently; however, it is also difficult to blame them, as they opted for a very different lifestyle. Individual decision-making and personal responsibility is crucial, something which devotees can acutely mystify with talk of a deceased mentor who is monistically present in everyone doling out perpetual guidance. To repeat, Meher Baba died in January 1969. It is on record that Pete Townshend had a conflict as to whether he should give up his link with The Who. That seems to be the crucial factor, quite independent of the fantasized monistic avatar.

467. This statement comes from a circular of the Meher Baba Association in London, dated July 1993. It is there affirmed that the Association "was set up on Baba's instruction and he was the President – he remained President at the time of his death, the only Baba group worldwide in which he retained an official position." It is also stated that Delia De Leon felt that this was very important. The circular also informs that the money being requested was for the purpose of paying the travel expenses of one of the *mandali* on a visit to England. The circular neglects to dwell upon the circumstances under which the "Association" came into being, and has no reference to the changes which occurred at the end of Baba's life. The present writer attended at a meeting held in 1965 in London when Charles Purdom, Delia De Leon, and Adi S. Irani (Baba's brother) discussed the matter of their small organization. They did not agree in all particulars, and the impression conveyed was that Meher Baba had been requested to become the President, and had consented subject to certain stipulations with regard to personnel. He would only become President if Charles Purdom and Will (and Mary) Backett were integrated in the project; upon their inclusion the venture depended. Adi S. Irani strongly insinuated that he was also an important component of the London group. Nobody challenged that suggestion, doubtless because of his celebrity as Baba's brother; yet Adi had not been involved in the arrangement made in 1948-9, as he was then still living in India and had not appeared upon the British scene until 1956. De Leon was the only other person who had been allocated a prominent role, though her contribution requires a critical assessment in the light of various facts. See also note 396 *supra* and note 468 *infra*. In 1965 there was still no separate building for the London group, which had not in fact become a Centre. They hired a room in London once every month for a meeting. The London group was not then known as the Meher Baba Association (a later identity) but as the Friends of Meher Baba, and did not resemble sequels of c. 1970, though it did deteriorate after Purdom's death in 1965. One noticeable feature of meetings I attended in 1966 was that Adi S. Irani and Delia De Leon were not in harmony. The former tended to view his own home in Barnes as a Baba Centre. A problem in this respect was that Adi rarely allowed any devotee to visit his home at that period, and De Leon had never received an invitation to do so. The friction between the two seemed more on his part than hers, and seemed to date back to his dislike of the Kimco group of British women in the 1930s. He had considered them to be superficial women of a colonial background who were very slow to learn elementary points about discipleship. A recent video prepared at Myrtle Beach bears the title *Memoirs of the Frivolous Three: An Evening with Margaret Craske, Kitty Davy, and Delia De Leon*. The frivolity may be the reason why some of the *mandali* reacted to them (and their associates) in the early 1930s. Adi was still reacting in the early 1970s. After Baba's death, Adi stopped attending the London meetings, and told me in 1973 that he disagreed with the policies and attitudes of those involved. He was able to point out that the London group had never become a Baba Centre in the conventional sense while his brother was alive, and that the continuing problem with regard to improvised venues was a flaw in De Leon's leadership. (Her protege Pete Townshend later established a distinct Baba Centre in London, but that was nothing to do with the former situation of Meher Baba as President). Adi said that his own home was as much a Centre as anything Delia had created, and I could see the point he was making, despite certain reservations I had about his own policies. He dismissed Delia's theme of Baba as the President of the Association until his death – that was in name only, Adi implied, and even if such auspices could be construed as an encouragement, they could have no possible application after Baba's death. I found that Delia was trying to imply otherwise in 1973, as I gained a lengthy talk with her that same year. I believe that she was confused and had contributed to a limited sectarian outlook. She was unable to correlate various details and left seriously deficient gaps in her exposition of events. She was not sure what to say about Adi; he had retreated without giving any explanation. (He was often called Adi Jnr to distinguish him from Adi K. Irani, Baba's secretary, who was his senior in years, though Baba's brother had an equivalent status amongst devotees). Adi Jnr tended to be very assertive at times, and perhaps tended to overestimate his importance as much as De Leon did hers. Yet he was logical enough in his attitude that "Kimco talk" had obscured what had been happening (and not happening) in the London group. He had been in friction with Kimco for over forty years, and the implication was that these women, especially De Leon, had created a myth about their importance to Baba, who had initially pandered to their tastes in a way that broke down some of their superficial behaviour such as the tendency to act charades at any opportunity. At that period also (early 1970s) I made three visits to the Association meetings in London, and found evidence of a deteriorated content to that operative amongst the Friends of Meher Baba in 1965. Although a number of the new Association recruits were vocally very keen about Meher Baba, they were not interested in any method of inquiry as to the nature of events. A number of the persons I encountered had never seen Adi S. Irani, and had no idea of the ideological gap existing between him and De Leon, together with all that this implied. They had not heard of Ann Powell save in fleeting references, and some of the Indian affiliates of the Friends had reaped total obscurity. There were some very vague notions about the activity of the Backetts, whose early years of disciplined life were a blank in the Association record. Yet far worse, the new recruits did not consider historical details to be important. It was "love and obedience" that were celebrated, even though Meher Baba was dead and no longer gave instructions. Fantasy was the substitute. The new wave had been taught by De Leon that Baba had given her a special place as a kind of apostolic heroine, which is how the new recruits regarded her. The Meher Baba Association established by De Leon (and not by Meher Baba) had gained the status of a divine vehicle of the Avataric will. It was all a matter of "Baba is with us." Yet more realistically perhaps, it was a case of "Delia is with us," along with Pete Townshend, who was idolized in the general confusion of celebrity identities. The subscribers to the beliefs at issue here were notably uninterested in the *mast* work, this being deemed inapplicable to Western devotees who were only interested in Meher Baba. The logic was peculiar, and may have reflected De Leon's sense of unfamiliarity with the thirteen years and more of *"mast* work." Despite her admiration for Dr. Donkin, I am not certain she had ever read the lengthy supplement in *The Wayfarers*, a book which did not fit her ideas about monthly meetings in the British middle class style where visitors had a nice cup of tea, socializing gossip, readings from the *Discourses*, and some poetry. Many of her new followers seemed to be poetry reciters or else guitar enthusiasts. Some of them preferred to read out their own poetry. There were strange beliefs that Baba was invisibly guiding the Association, using even trivial upsets to stir the psyche. Adi Jnr was more sober. He knew that different priorities had been involved at the ashrams where he had been a member of the pre-New Life *mandali*. Circumstances for the male *mandali* were very different before Baba became disabled by his second motor accident. Adi was able to describe how difficult many third class rail journeys with his brother had been; the *mast* work had required men of bull strength like Baidul Irani to keep up with his brother, who could exhibit a galvanic energy when everyone else was exhausted. Adi had in fact been rather grateful to retire from ashram life when he got married, eventually moving to London to gain increased prosperity in the old Empire remains. He was able to lapse from strict ashram discipline and get up late if he wanted to. He also felt that it was difficult to obey someone who had expired; contrary to the ashram rule, Adi drank strong liquor, though he had displayed that partiality prior to Baba's death. Whether Adi was obeying himself or his brother was perhaps a valid question at times, yet in his cynical way, he had penetratingly diagnosed the situation at the Association, where the devotees obeyed Delia De Leon in her version of the Godman. One has to search hard for Meher Baba rather too often when history is desired. The Meher Baba Association have recently joined the advertisements section in a well known New Age magazine that specializes in publicizing many quacks and exploiters in the world of occultism and alternative therapy. See *Kindred Spirit* (1997) 39: 45, 75, which promotes a talk by Bhau Kalchuri at Kensington Town Hall. That talk is apparently on the familiar theme of Avataric uniqueness, and the promotion might demonstrate that post-New Life *mandali* exegesis has become a part of the worst fad in the Western world. It would seem that Delia De Leon (d. 1993) paved the way for New Age messianism, though Meher Baba himself might be writhing in his tomb at the prospect of even more misrepresentation. The New Age ad includes the glib quotation "Don't worry, be happy, I will help you" (*ibid.*, p. 45). Again the lack of context lifted into a sectarian message struggling to find recruits for a new religion which Meher Baba in reality said that he did not want.

468. The Meher Baba Association in London is a derivative of earlier groupings. In November 1948 Delia De Leon sent out a circular letter to British devotees saying that she had recently spent three months in India with Shri Meher Baba, and had been directed by him to establish a non-profit venture in Britain as a branch of "The Universal Spiritual League" (a concept that was intended for America, and which Elizabeth Patterson was then arranging). Baba wished her to raise funds to acquire a suitable property in London. She refers to Baba as "the Avatar of our age" (the original circular is in my possession, given to me by Ann Powell, and which gives the address of William A. Backett of Sevenoaks as the Hon. Treasurer for subscriptions). The proposed Centre never materialized (fuller details are in my *Life of Meher Baba Vol. 3*, pp. 391–2, unpublished; see also note 396 *supra*). This matter was later a sore point with some Indian followers of Meher Baba who resided in England and who attended the London group meetings held at various venues. According to one of the Indians, an intelligent Hindu with a university degree, De Leon had ample assets at her disposal to have established a Centre herself. The Indian contingent appeared on the scene during the 1950s and early 1960s, and comprised Parsis, Hindus, and one Muslim (all of whom I met during 1965–6). Some of these men resented the officiousness of certain British devotees, and were critical of De Leon's estimation of her "very close" link with Meher Baba. One of these critics was Adi S. Irani, Baba's brother who came to live in London during 1956. The tensions between leading spokespersons of the London group were considerable. Charles Purdom had remained aloof (with a few exceptions) from the other British devotees until 1948, when Meher Baba wished him to become the Chairman of the branch League in Britain. Purdom agreed to this, and his isolationism thereafter ceased. (See *Iranian Liberal*, pp. 188ff.). Baba also wanted Will Backett to be the Secretary and Treasurer, and this was likewise agreed. De Leon was given the role of Vice-Chairman, and Baba himself agreed to be the President. The formally elected Committee created a situation that De Leon did not describe in her memoirs. Cf. De Leon, *The Ocean of Love: My Life with Meher Baba* (Myrtle Beach, S.C.: Sheriar Press, 1991), p. 166. It is clear that Baba wanted Purdom and Backett to act in concert; he perhaps considered that their different temperaments could be enhanced if reconciled. The new Committee was certainly a means of drawing Purdom out of his isolationism, and changed Backett's information despatches into more streamlined newsletters. Yet there were problems involved because of personality frictions. De Leon later gave the impression that she was the most privileged member of this Committee, but in reality it would seem that she was the go-between in the attempted fusion of talents possessed by Purdom and Backett. She had neither the intensity of Backett and his wife Mary, and nor the analytical faculties of Purdom. She admired Purdom's intellect, and tended to side with him strongly in disagreements that arose. "Backett could not see eye to eye with Purdom and De Leon, whom he came to regard virtually as the devil and his accomplice" (Shepherd, *Life of Meher Baba Vol. 3*, p. 392). I will attempt to briefly explain this fraught situation. Will Backett was not a typical devotee, and like Purdom, he was not mawkish. However, he lacked Purdom's analytical streak, and seemed too uncritical to Purdom. Backett became much more critical when he moved to Acton from Sevenoaks and was drawn into organizational arguments with his colleagues of the Spiritual League. He was a very placid man, and managed to keep most of his grievances a private matter for some years. A relatively minor issue was that he took exception to Purdom's project of an edited and condensed version of Baba's *Discourses*, himself believing that Deshmukh's text should be left unaltered. That stance was uncritical in some respects, though valid in other ways; the matter had been debated at the ashram, though Baba had finally agreed to Purdom's request to edit. Backett was also disconcerted by Purdom's comparatively professorial bearing; the latter was inclined to lecture, and it was discovered that he could give imposing talks that silenced De Leon's amiable chatter. Purdom was usually in control, but occasionally he seems to have been overbearing. In comparison to his rivals, Backett was more like a reverent Sufi who only wanted the "heart." Yet Purdom had the head, and he could not be ignored. Ann Powell (d. 1965) was one of those who witnessed many public and private tensions. She told me in 1965 that Backett had referred in private to Purdom as "the devil," by which he meant something virtually tyrannical. There were other aggravations in the person of De Leon. In Backett's eyes, Delia was superficial in many ways, and a person who was not sufficiently one-pointed. Formerly a pupil of Inayat Khan, Backett's Sufi training had left him far more contemplative and dedicated to unworldly ideals long before De Leon commenced her frivolous career as one of the Kimco group of admiring women. The differences stood out a mile, it seems. Backett's ex-Sufi approach opted for a "reverent and church-like" atmosphere, as De Leon complained to me in 1966. She said that he was too serious, and not jolly enough. I am not certain that she ever understood what Sufism was, and her acquaintance with the vocabulary of *God Speaks* was very slight. Her idea of group meetings clashed with those of Backett (and often with those of Purdom also, who had a rather more disciplined approach than her). She preferred a musical repertoire of sing-song around a piano, though poetry was also welcome. I came to the conclusion that Backett must have psychologically groaned at the sight of De Leon on many occasions. Unlike both Purdom and De Leon, Backett made his own home available to the devotees in relatively small and private meetings; his sincerity was such that many regarded him and his wife Mary as the pivotal figures in the London group. Purdom did not achieve that level of popularity, and there are indications that De Leon was frustrated with the general verdict. Under Backett's influence, the London group gained identity during the early 1950s as the Friends of Meher Baba. Yet he found that official meetings in the hired rooms were a trial by comparison with the unofficial meetings conducted in his home at Acton. The Chairman and Vice-Chairman wanted their own way of doing things. Backett had little interference with his newsletters, as Purdom wrote books and De Leon merely talked. The latter often talked about her letters from Baba in the 1930s. See note 340 *supra*. There is reason to think that both Purdom and Backett got tired of hearing about the celebrations of "Dearest Darling Leyla," to use Chanji's exaggerated secretarial stylism. Leyla was the nickname Baba had given Delia. Backett perhaps grasped that Purdom was right to be critical of the effusive secretarial flourishes which had been employed by Chanji. Yet the extravagances ceased in 1940, and "after 1940 Baba did not send dictated and signed letters" (*The Ocean of Love*, p. 140). Backett himself gained many more communications from the ashram than De Leon did after 1940. Purdom doubtless exercised his analytical acumen over the question of where Baba's signature had gone. For some reason Baba preferred to withdraw it on a notable scale. Backett received many letters from Dr. Donkin and others with messages from Baba during the 1940s, which De Leon did not. She was relegated to collective cablegrams. Frivolity had lost the ascendancy, as Backett must have perceived. Yet De Leon had been invited to India for three months in 1948, which afforded her a theme of renewed intimacy. Purdom and Backett got their chance with the "three incredible weeks" at Meherabad in 1954, in an event which excluded Western women. In her memoirs, De Leon does fleetingly mention the friction which had commenced in 1940 when she was first asked by Baba to collaborate with Backett. "It was never easy for us to work together as we were poles apart; I, with my theatrical background, was very happy-go-lucky and Will, a Methodist, was rather prim and proper" (*ibid.*, p. 139). The description of Backett as a Methodist is misleading; that was how De Leon conceived of an ex-Sufi who was more than superficially acquainted with Meher Baba. She used the same description in a conversation with me in 1966, and it was difficult to correct her, as she was supposed to know all about the subject. Reference to the biography of Will Backett discloses that he had been so eager to escape his Protestant upbringing that he had lived at a Tolstoy colony, studied Vedanta, and even joined the Theosophical Society. All that occurred before he became a pupil of Inayat Khan (*Iranian Liberal*, p. 189). There is another subtlety involved in this matter. De Leon was no longer receiving privileged letters from the ashram in the 1940s, and yet Backett did receive such communications. Also, a humble social entity like Ann Powell was receiving letters from Margaret Craske in India with messages from Baba. Leyla was becoming outflanked. According to Ann Powell, she gave up trying to talk with De Leon, as the latter tended to assume superior airs in conversation with her. "She would not have fitted in with us," De Leon told me in 1966, this being a reference to Powell's non-eligibility for the "holiday" venues on the Continent in the early 1930s. Probably not, as Powell was not the frivolous type; she certainly did not have the money to buy a God-realization dress such as Delia's sister Minta invested in, along with the well-heeled Princess Matchabelli. See note 339 *supra*. One might take it that Powell was too sensible to join in the charades that annoyed Kaka Baria and other *mandali*. Powell was Welsh working class, not affluent British careers or international nobility. She had the satisfaction of knowing that she was the closest female confidante of Mary Backett, reputed to be more intuitive than her husband, and who was similarly wary of De Leon's airs and graces. Mary Backett did not fit in with Italian holidays either, but that did not stop her from being invited to Nasik in 1937 along with Kimco and others for a lengthy sojourn. De Leon liked Mary Backett, grasping that she was somehow considered important at Nasik, though Delia's memoirs contract the issue to Mary possessing "a great sense of fun" (*Ocean of Love*, p. 140). The fun and games of the Kimco group (who included Delia) are not the best guide to priorities in other case histories. The Backetts were able to observe that although De Leon entertained the belief that Baba would again invite her to India on a privileged basis, this never actually happened. What did happen was that in 1956, Will Backett lost his accustomed composure in the face of insidious complications created by the happy-go-lucky theatrical entity personified by Delia De Leon. Her memoirs become briefly realistic in the admission that "there had been differences between us on the Committee" (*ibid.*, p. 183), which is an understatement. When Meher Baba visited London in 1956, he was not greeted by a harmonious Spiritual League but by a faction locked in internal combat who requested him to preside at a special meeting. Baba assumed his guise of President with due aplomb and heard out the various grievances. De Leon reports that "Will blamed Charles and myself and said that we had tried to usurp his position, which had made him ill" (*ibid.*, pp. 183–4). Backett had at last become critical, rivalling even Purdom's sense of discrepancies (Purdom was never theatrical, and himself was wary of De Leon's devotionalism in the Kimco style). De Leon confesses: "I did feel that perhaps I should have given way more and I was relieved to get it all out in the open" (*ibid.*, p. 184). We are not told very much about "it," though sources attest that Backett never fully recovered his health for the rest of his life. He knew that his secretarial duties meant relatively little in theatre. He no longer wanted to be the Secretary (which De Leon neglects to state), and the President tactfully reorganized the Committee, allocating the disillusioned role to Dorothy Hopkinson. The role of Chairman was revised in terms of a triangular situation that involved a rota of six-month offices held by Backett, Purdom, and De Leon. The secretarial output was never the same again. Backett's detailed newsletters were replaced by the skeletal offerings from Hopkinson, Adi S. Irani (briefly), De Leon (briefly), and finally Molly Eve. Backett's paperwork had been unique amongst Western devotees since the early 1930s. He had made it his task to inform others of what was happening in India, but now he had given up. He had learnt that devotion does not necessarily produce wisdom, and can even cause illness. The only chance of sanity was in private meetings held at his home, where he could screen out problematic elements. The Christmas Social preferred by De Leon and others was not high on his list of engagements. He may well have reflected as follows: Baba had wanted a replacement for the Charing Cross Office he (Backett) had relinquished during the war, and he and Mary had accordingly moved to an accessible position in Acton despite the fact that they detested city life and preferred peaceful Old Oak Cottage, which they had sold. Yet De Leon had failed in her task of finding a self-contained and central building to use as a Centre. "Baba was informed that the failure was principally due to lack of funds" (Shepherd, *Life of Meher Baba Vol. 3*, p. 391). Yet De Leon's memoirs exhibit a suspicious lack of detail in relation to this episode. She merely states "we had been planning to open a center in London" (*Ocean of Love*, p. 168). That is really too much of an understatement and can be accused of being evasive. She appears to have contrived the excuse that Baba's New Life announcements in 1949 meant that the new Committee should discard the plan for a Centre. "We discussed scrapping this idea as Baba had told us to cancel all plans, but Will had already found a suitable property in Ealing and he was committed to buying it" (*ibid.*). What details does that statement conceal, the reader may wonder. De Leon does not mention her appointed role as a fund-raiser, and one may deduce that Meher Baba had given up waiting for his "dearest Leyla" to do something dedicated. Backett (and Purdom) knew that Baba had been in earnest, and that he had only vacated his role as President in Leyla's squeamish mind that wished to ignore funds. Backett furthered Baba's directive by selling his cottage in Sevenoaks. De Leon did not sell her assets, be it carefully noted. No changes occurred in her life; the New Life upheaval was a convenient face-saver. Backett knew that Meher Baba was walking into homelessness, but devotees like Leyla did not want extra worries and commitments. It seems that there are various ways of testing the "nearest," even if they do not recognize the gestures. The situation left Will and Mary Backett with a difficult move to Ealing, where quarters proved unsatisfactory. That was in 1949–50, and they maintained the spirit of the New Life of "hopelessness and helplessness." By early 1951 they had sold the house in Ealing and moved to the more peaceful bungalow in Acton. De Leon manages to mention that the Acton house became a mecca for British devotees and overseas visitors (*ibid.*), but has none of the details in a book that glorifies her own role instead. Quite apart from rumours about undeclared assets, there had been other failures in concerted activity, including the oft-aired conviction of De Leon that she was one of the "nearest and dearest" to Baba, a claim which supposedly justified her actions. The Backetts never described themselves in such eulogistic terms, preferring humble self-effacement. Too prim and proper for theatrical tastes? The ailing Will Backett was not well enough to go to America in 1958 for the *sahavas* at Myrtle Beach. De Leon did manage to be present, but was dismayed that Baba treated her more aloofly than in former years, which "was a little hard to bear" (*Ocean of Love*, p. 189). Backett may even have wondered whether, if Baba had not sent Delia such encouraging letters via Chanji in the 1930s, she would have continued to be a gushing devotee desirous of the limelight. When Backett died in 1963, leadership of the London group fell to Purdom, but he now had to struggle with illness; he tried to encourage a sense of comparative religion amongst the relatively small number his talks could attract. After Purdom's death in 1965, attendance further waned. There was nothing to draw interested persons except for the films of Meher Baba. De Leon became the Chairman, and emerged as the leader of the flagging Friends after an initial rivalry with Adi S. Irani, who had long since left the Committee and who subsequently dropped out in a dissident mood. See note 467 *supra*. De Leon eventually favoured the new identity of the Friends as Meher Baba Association, though Meher Baba Spiritual League was another of the rather pretentious labels in vogue. In 1967, at one meeting held at the rented room in the Poetry Society, the number of Friends had dwindled to only four. Yet "in the summer of 1967, there was a sudden influx of young people" (*ibid.*, p. 199). There followed much jubilation as the expiring Friends gained a new lease of life. A critical attitude is advisable, as history is not always favoured. In the summer of 1967 the social fashion changed to the hippy "summer of love" and a casual interest in Eastern religions that accompanied pot and LSD. It was not at first clear whether Pete Townshend was another casual, but he did eventually make plain that he was serious. Meanwhile, the Indian contingent had tended to evaporate, and the new recruits had changed what was left of the Backett-Purdom orientation and altered the terminology. It was now Baba's love game and Baba's umbrella. De Leon became the patron saint of the new generation, and received much adulation of an uncritical nature. The American devotee Don Stevens of Sufism Reoriented was also triumphant in this situation, being regarded as a master expositor of the *Discourses* and regularly lecturing to the neo-hippy audience who assumed that he was a Sufi and a "close disciple" of Meher Baba, which is the self-image he promoted. Purdom had not presented himself as a close disciple, and Backett had never aired himself as a Sufi, even being mistaken for a Methodist by the undiscerning De Leon. The latter now conducted summer garden parties and made the innovation of "holding informal weekly meetings using Mani's *Family Letters* as a focal point" (*ibid.*, p. 210). The veneration for Mani offput some analysts. A British literary critic had described a few of Mani's newsletters (the later ones) as "sentimental gush," though he was attracted to Meher Baba and was puzzled at the discrepancies in evidence. De Leon's version of events was very influential, and her role as one of the "nearest and dearest" was now unquestioned within the movement. Her version of events is contained in one of the "myself and Baba" books, a genre which frequently distorts Meher Baba. (I was able to obtain some additional information from her in 1966 and 1973, using a form of request that negotiated her favoured 1930s correspondence). In her book, she describes how the Association gained charity status in 1976, and then asserts: "The Meher Baba Association, organized on the democratic lines that Baba deemed best and with Meher Baba still as president, became the main organization and focus for Baba's work in Britain" (*ibid.*, p. 212). There are two points in that statement which can be repudiated. The idea that Meher Baba is still the President of the Association is surely an extreme devotional concept, and an equivalent exaggeration to the belief that the Association does "Baba's work" (a belief attested in other documents also). Meher Baba himself stated that his work was finished in 1968. The conceit of some devotees that they sequel his work is surely remarkable. Baba ends his work, and then devotees start it again in a charity status organization. Some devotees have defined their version of "Baba's work" as that of conveying his message, though they should surely qualify this in terms of their own activity and not Baba's. The confusions are many. There are glosses and missing details in *The Ocean of Love*, as is, for instance, evidenced in the glowing account of the 1970s Centre known as Meher Baba Oceanic which was established by Pete Townshend. De Leon's bland account totally omits reference to Townshend's lapse from codes associated with Meher Baba. Cf. *ibid.*, p. 215. Cf. note 466 *supra*. In other words, it does not matter in Association lore if the truth is not told. Devotees claim to do Baba's work, he is the presiding genius, and so forth. The sense of evasion can be quite formidable, as I found in 1988 when I contacted the new leader of the Association, namely Tom Hopkinson (sometimes described as Sir Tom Hopkinson). I had never met him or his wife, and as they were such senior and respected devotees, I felt that I ought to ascertain their views. Hopkinson had been a devotee since the 1950s and was the author of the book *Much Silence: Meher Baba, his life and work* (London, 1974), in which he and his wife stressed the subject's emphasis against mounting a new religion (*ibid.*, p. 42). I therefore hoped for a sane and rational response, if pessimistically. I sent a letter notifying Hopkinson of my new book *Meher Baba, an Iranian Liberal* and also my other books about closely related figures (including Baba's father and Hazrat Babajan). I gave the information that I had attended the London meetings in 1965–6, and subsequently made three visits to the Association that were relatively disappointing. Hopkinson replied very briefly and dismissively, saying that he and his Association did not want to see or read books on comparative religion, which was the category in which he placed all my books. The sole reason he gave for this uncompromising attitude was: "we are only interested in Meher Baba." My conclusion is that the pervasive devotional belief "Baba is always with us" leads to deception, delusions, superiority complexes, and unwarranted dismissal of alternative views. That devotional belief fluently condones the thoughts and actions of subscribers, leading them to assume that they are right and that others are wrong, and that they are beyond criticism as the representatives of a divine presence.

469. A belief attaches to the recital of the Universal Prayer he had dictated. Eruch Jessawala reported Baba to have said at the end of his life: "So every time anybody repeats the Prayer, I am there with him, my presence is there." The context was that "because of my participation now, it will help the one who repeats this prayer" (*Meher Baba Association Newsletter*, November 1991, p. 5). The mechanics of that process are not explained, but the affirmation does not amount to the same theme promoted by devotees after his death. Another statement sometimes quoted is: "When I drop my body [i.e., expire], I will remain in all who love me; I can never die." That contention is capable of different interpretations.

470. The strongest statement I have seen on this subject, doubtfully attributed to Meher Baba, reads: "Anyone seeking help at the tomb of the *avatar* is assured of help, because the devotee who approaches the tomb of the God-man has directly approached God for help." This was quoted in a letter dated 20th July 1993 from John Grant, a senior devotee of Australia, who was writing to a British enquirer. Grant does not cite the source for his quotation, and does not state which interpreter or editorial hand was involved (these are relevant factors, despite the orthodox facility in deeming such considerations to be unjustified). The elevation of Meher Baba's tomb has to be viewed in context. Throughout his life he consistently opposed popular ideas about tomb cults. He credited a "spiritual atmosphere" around saintly tombs, but sometimes said that this was largely created by the many pilgrims who had been visiting the shrine for centuries. One of his early comments about such tombs occurred in 1933 during his visit to Avila in Spain. A diarist recorded: "Baba explained that it is the spiritual atmosphere, the quickened vibrations, that give value to the shrines of saints; the saints themselves are not present in some more subtle body, nor is there any special virtue in the dry dust and bones of their physical bodies" (Duce, *How a Master Works*, p. 171, citing the report of Herbert Davy). In 1958, Baba said of his own tomb: "After seventy years, this hill will turn into a place of world pilgrimage where lovers of God, philosophers, and celebrities will come to pay homage to the tomb. How fortunate you all are that you are here in my living presence and that you could come up the hill with me." See H. P. Bharucha, *Meher Baba's Last Sahavas* (1969), p. 3, which is a more reliable document than many later reports. The gist of Baba's statements in this category is that his living presence was far more important than anything which might happen at his tomb after his death.

471. He is reported to have said that effects of his "work" would linger strongly for about a hundred years, and thereafter less strongly for another century. There is no reference in any of his messages to any personal guidance in the after-death phase. That topic was supplied by the *mandali* and has been greatly elaborated. In the late 1980s, Bal Natu was reported to have told Western visitors to Meherabad that "for 100 years after his passing, being at the tomb is the same as being in Baba's living presence." See D. Hastilow, "Journey of a Lifetime," *Meher Baba Association Newsletter* (London) Nov. 1989, p. 6, reporting a recent event. Bal Natu was a Hindu devotee who first met Baba in 1944, and who became a resident at Meherazad after the latter's death. Meher Baba might not have been flattered at his living presence being considered equal to tomb veneration, and the concept may be ascribed to sectarian hindsight.

472. This statement comes from the paperback cover of J. A. Grant, *Practical Spirituality with Meher Baba* (Sydney: Merwan Press, 1987).

473. Murshida Ivy Duce was one of those who were adamant that Meher Baba could not have a "chargeman," a term generally considered as interchangeable with successor. It is necessary to state the technicalities here for the benefit of those who find such arguments difficult to fathom. Supporting the dogmatic interpretation of Adi K. Irani, Duce argued that the *avatar* "could not possibly have a chargeman, since he overhauls everything and blueprints the entire 700 or 1400 years ahead and all he needs are executors of his will" (*How a Master Works*, p. 431). This claim sounds fantastic to many readers, though it has become a devotional doctrine, and one which makes outsiders feel like running for cover. One has to investigate the train of logic underlying these declarations. Ivy Duce and others were faced with the problem of how to explain away the statement of Upasni Maharaj that he had given Merwanji his "key." Duce makes no reference to Upasni's statement that he had given his "charge" to Merwanji (cf. note 231 *supra*). She states that Upasni's reference to the "key" was "symbolic of the five stewards of God surrendering their stewardship as custodians of God's world and the Divine Plan to the Avatar" (*How a Master Works*, p. 431). She introduces a rather superficial facesaver about Jesus giving Peter "certain assignments" (*ibid.*). Leaving aside the matter of Gospel references, it is possible to take the view that Murshida Duce was not being fair to the "five stewards of God" if the themes in Baba's cosmology are credited. If we follow and extend here the basic logic of the devotional argument, it is evident that the *avatar* must give back to the stewards the elusive charge or charges he has been given, and thus he would necessarily minister to one or more chargemen. According to Meher Baba's own teaching, there are always five *sadguru/qutub* entities in the world (see *God Speaks*, second edn, pp. 271ff.). Therefore the mysterious "key" would have been passed on to those able to use it, one may logically construe in this rather abstruse field. Otherwise Meher Baba's teachings about a "spiritual hierarchy" make no sense at all. To come to the point, it is evident that Murshida Duce and other prestigious devotees preferred to claim Avatar-related profiles while relegating the "symbolism" of *sadgurus/qutubs*. The devotees of the Avatar were thus empowered by their paradigm to pronounce upon, or against, anything that rivalled them, while favouring themes conducive to their own status roles. As Murshida of the organization called Sufism Reoriented (based in California), Ivy Duce surely had a lot to lose if she had admitted to a more inferior role in events. The devotional paradigm awarded her a role as a close disciple of the Avatar, meaning that she did not have to look elsewhere for guidance. This was in contrast to her predecessor Rabia Martin (d. 1947), who had so honestly confronted her own situation at the end of her career by recognizing that she needed a living teacher instead of believing herself to have all the answers. Of Rabia Martin, it has been said: "She did not meet Meher Baba, but she released her senior pupils from their vows to the Sufi Society and advised them to investigate and seek to accept, as she had, Meher Baba as the God-Man" (Le Page, *The Turning of the Key*, p. 5). Cf. Shepherd, *Iranian Liberal*, pp. 211ff. See also note 462 *supra*. There is a parallel with Rabia Martin in that when Ivy Duce had first met Baba in 1948, she admitted that she was not illumined, and he had responded by saying that he would take responsibility for her students for as long as she remained honest (this information is found in the video entitled *Murshida*). To what extent Murshida Duce remained honest after Baba's death is perhaps questionable. As Meher Baba mentioned to the leader of the British contingent of devotees that he would have a successor, one may conclude that it is additionally superfluous for Avatar dogmatists to dismiss such an issue. As that issue is impossible to verify in terms of any specific entity, I will here withdraw from the subject after having stated the obvious logical points generally avoided by attitudes of convenience.

474. A significant point for scholarly consideration is that Mani committed to writing the statement: "Baba books contradict each other in the matter of dates and things, and even the *mandali* do so when telling stories in Mandali Hall. You may notice that some dates and details given by me in this book differ from the ones I gave some time ago while recounting these same stories on tape or videotape." See Mani S. Irani, *God-Brother: Stories from my Childhood with Meher Baba* (Myrtle Beach, S.C.: Sheriar Foundation, 1993), p. viii. Many of the orally repeated stories told by various members of the *mandali* have found their way into print, adding to the confusions that exist in the literature. The present writer has seen some extreme instances where much of the context of an event is completely missing from the report. The storytellers are usually concerned with promoting "love and obedience" themes in the popular idiom. Statements attributed to Meher Baba are also dependent upon the memory of the *mandali*, though devotees deny that there is any problem with various unofficial communications from their figurehead. My only claim to some assessment of these matters is that I once spent several years of my life collecting and sifting numerous reports relating to Meher Baba's biography. That project, which I do not press as being of any importance, did teach me caution in relation to devotional literature.

475. The late Mani S. Irani (d. 1996) referred in her fading years to "my universal family in Meher Baba's timeless love" (*God-Brother*, p. viii). She was not always very generous to people outside her extended kin. Mani was the ashram official mentioned anonymously in *Minds and Sociocultures Vol. 1*, p. 202 n.276, relevant to the date of December 1993.

476. A graphic profile was afforded this situation by an Australian investigator in Brisbane, who wrote: "I am told that, by entitlement, as one of the early close followers, Bill (Le Page) stays in different quarters from his wife whilst at Ahmednagar. She, not qualifying for that perquisite, stays in the pilgrim's quarters at Meherabad, while Bill stays at Meherazad. This seems a charming example of the subtle inexorable system of little ways in which the *mandali* continuously contrive to enhance and consolidate their own status." This observation comes from a letter dated 23rd November 1993. The same writer adds with regard to the *mandali* etiquette and certain of their "practices which separately are quite justifiable on other grounds, but which collectively make up an unmistakeable network of ruses, all of which militate single-mindedly, pushing in concert towards the unspoken but clearly understood and organized purpose of feathering their own nest." The writer was a professional analyst who was well disposed towards Meher Baba, but who was clearly critical of organizational developments occurring after his death.

477. "Baba's world-wide family has the opportunity to participate in this effort in a significant way through donations" (*Avatar Meher Baba Trust Archives and Museum Project Circular No. 2*, Nov. 1996, p. 6). This refers to the objective of 240,000 dollars stipulated for a large conservation building proposed for Meherabad. The officials concerned, headed by two members of the *mandali* (including Bhau Kalchuri), state: "This is a Baba-given opportunity in which one and all are encouraged to participate" (*ibid.*, p. 7). The project is further referred to as "this momentous work in the service of the Avatar of the age" (*ibid.*). It is not based on any plan of Meher Baba, but on the plan of his sister Mani, who prior to her recent death was Chairman of the Avatar Meher Baba Trust officially based at Ahmednagar (see *Museum Project Circular No. 1*, May 1996). As Baba's "work" ended in 1968, according to his own statement, other projects should not be attributed to him, especially fund-raising projects of the kind he is known to have discouraged in places like Andhra Pradesh. Devotees cannot be blamed for wishing to provide museum facilities, but to credit such enterprises as a "Baba-given opportunity" is surely misleading to the gullible. It is a relatively minor point that some readers wonder why "a central computer room" (*Circular No. 2*, p. 3) is necessary in an ashram that was noted for simplicity and austere standards of living over several decades. When relics accumulate, the spirit can be lost, one might conjecture.

478. Of the Sakori situation, one Western commentator deduced: "For them (the devotees) he (Upasni Maharaj) is not really gone, for he had promised them 'I am never absent from Sakori' " (Harper, *Gurus, Swamis, and Avatars*, p. 51). One might argue that Upasni meant this in relation to his lifetime and was not undertaking any permanent posthumous presence.

479. A pointed version of the sectarian outlook has been expressed by an American devotee of Meher Baba, writing under the influence of the *mandali*. Don E. Stevens asserts of the *avatar*: "It is not just during the period of his physical presence that the guidance and grace of the Avatar are available. He is not only for contemporary humanity during his advent but for posterity as well. His grace and his guidance toward the Truth are constantly accessible to one and all." See D. E. Stevens, intro. to *Meher Baba: Discourses* (Myrtle Beach, S.C.: Sheriar Press, 1987),

p. xvii. In rather extreme terms, Stevens adds a description of the Avatar (i.e., Meher Baba) as "the eternal living Perfect Master" (*ibid.*), a phrase which stands bold in capital letters. This adventure in terminology was clearly devised to offset any rival contributions from living "perfect masters" in the physical world. Stevens gives the information that this treatment of "the unique availability of the Avatar at all times is from one of Meher Baba's *mandali*" (*ibid.*). It is obvious that this treatment amounts to an attempt to improvise a religious doctrine, despite the contradictory emphases in the literature that Meher Baba did not want to create another religion. The innovated phrase "Eternal Living Perfect Master" did not appear in the sixth edition of the *Discourses* (1967), but emerges in an editorial footnote to the seventh edition (p. 268) cited in this note. It seems possible that the phrase originated with Eruch Jessawala, who is one of the editors named in the seventh edition of 1987 (see note 423 *supra*). The exegesis is awkward for sectarian exponents, as Meher Baba conveyed that "the God-Man (i.e., Avatar) is the foremost Sadguru" (seventh edn, p. 275). Cf. the different wording in the sixth edn (Vol. 3, p. 27). Cf. the wording in the second edn (1947), which states: "The Sadguru who first emerged through evolution as the God-man, and helped and helps other souls in bondage, is known as the Avatar" (Vol. 4, p. 6). That reflects the original wording in the *Meher Baba Jnl*, the discourses of which later appeared in four bound volumes, together with an extra volume. The phrase at issue also did not appear in a provocative explanation entitled "Avatar as the first Master" which Baba dictated to Dr. Deshmukh in the 1950s. See *Beams from Meher Baba on the Spiritual Panorama* (San Francisco: Sufism Reoriented, 1958), pp. 27ff. The introduction by Ivy Duce informed that Deshmukh had "woven the material into its present form" as *Beams*, though Deshmukh's name does not appear on the title page as editor. Whatever Baba's precise dictation was, we might respect the theme that "the Avatar himself is the least concerned about whether or not he comes to be recognized as Avatar by large numbers" (*ibid.*, p. 31). Devotees seem to compensate for that restraint, and in the process alienate so many persons unable to digest metaphysical excesses. The present writer gratefully retires from the scenario in which Meher Baba says that he does not want to establish any religion and in which his devotees quickly set about doing just that.

480. One could argue that, as Hazrat Babajan was the initial inspirer of Merwan Irani, then she could be bracketed with Shirdi Sai as Sufi intermediary figures in the impacts which diversely passed to the Irani mystic eulogized as *avatar*. Meher Baba did award some importance to Shirdi Sai through their solitary encounter in 1915, and thus the reasoning suggested would not be superfluous by the standards of the more popular "Sai Baba movement." Further, it was Babajan who advised Merwan Irani to visit Shirdi Sai in 1915. That detail is recorded in Kalchuri, *Lord Meher Vol. 1*, pp. 216–17; second edn (1997), p. 216. The new edition, which combines volumes 1 and 2, is disappointing. Very little has been added, and the biographies of Sai Baba and Upasni Maharaj have not been duly improved. In these notes I have cited throughout the first edition, which was ignored by some writers. The second edition ignores the work of Antonio Rigopoulos and other researchers. A due revision has been applied in the second edition to the "first photograph as Meher Baba," now correctly dated to 1920 on p. 218 and frontispiece. See note 404 *supra*. Yet other descriptions are less satisfactory. For instance, on page 698 a photo has been inserted which is not chronologically applicable and in which the subject appears dressed as Krishna, while Mehera J. Irani appears in Radha costume. The footnote states that this photo was taken by Rano Gayley at Meherabad "during a Krishna feast in 1937," with no other qualification. The devotional appetite for such theatrical photographs is rather offputting. The present writer acquired a more reliable explanation of origin from Delia De Leon, who was a participant in the 1937 event. In 1966 she showed me a set of the "Krishna and gopis" photos that were in her collection, and in response to my puzzlement she explained that they were taken on a private occasion at Meherabad Hill when some of the Western women pressed Meher Baba to pose as Krishna, while they dressed up as the gopis. The Eastern women were amenable to this idea. Meher Baba may be criticized for the costume indulgence, though the event has to be viewed as an extension of the fad for charades that was typical of 1930s middle class Britain. The sober American Elizabeth Patterson declined to wear costume, to her credit. Mary Backett also did not change garb, though her accustomed "Biblical" apparel was colourful enough. The Western gopis were Princess Norina Matchabelli and the Kimco trio of British women nicknamed "the frivolous three." De Leon made no reference to a Krishna feast, which was certainly not the reason for the extravagance. See also *Kalchuri, Vol. 6*, pp. 2076ff., in which one of the captions almost tells the truth: "Meher Baba dressed by women mandali as Krishna" (p. 2076). The Western women staying at Nasik had a strong say in the charade. This was not a public event, but one limited to a visit made by the Western women to the women's ashram on Meherabad Hill, where the code was one of seclusion. Yet the erratic descriptions have led some readers to believe that a public event was in process. American presentations of photographic archives extend to some early photographs that were included in an album compiled by Meher Baba's brother Behram in 1965, two copies of which went to England via another relation, Adi S. Irani, from whom I acquired one along with the assurance that the details given were correct. Some date captions in that album differ from those given by L. Reiter.

For instance, the "cricket team photo" dated 1910 in the second edn of *Lord Meher*, p. 189, is dated 1907 in the 1965 album. Further, the family photo dated 1915–16 in the second edn, p. 198, bears the date 1912 in the earlier source. The entry dated 1916 in second edn, p. 203, is at variance with inscriptions of 1913 sponsored by the brothers Behram and Jal Irani in the 1960s. These discrepancies are further indicators of the need for caution in accepting dates and details as accurate. One can observe that the American editor of the second edition of *Lord Meher Vols 1 and 2* has made a strong claim in his prefatory remarks. According to Lawrence Reiter, "this Biography is one of the most extensive and detailed in history, because it is essentially one book eventually meant to be read by men and women everywhere for centuries to come." The Gospel stature of the project thus emerges. Though the vaunted Biography is undoubtedly lengthy, it need not be regarded as infallible or as comprising the whole truth about the data incorporated. The new Gospel of Kalchuri and Reiter leaves much scope for improvements and critical analysis. Kalchuri's biography is now fully published, the last instalment appearing as Vols 19 and 20 (Asheville, North Carolina: Manifestation, 2001). Some readers feel that the description as comprising 20 volumes is superfluous to the actual 13 volumes published. Nevertheless, it is still a lengthy work by any standards, and has some merits in the photographic documentation afforded. Yet Reiter has contributed a series of prefaces which exhibit a sectarian rhetoric that is rather more objectionable than the devotional stylisms of Kalchuri. Such factors, in combination with the activity known as Sufism Reoriented, tend to make the outlook for the Meher Baba movement a clouded prospect in the eyes of critics (who include the present writer). Some find more compelling Reiter's apology for error in Vol. 17 (preliminary Erratum). Here he says that "errors have inadvertently occurred in the collecting and retelling of stories" (*ibid.*). He also says that "in translation there will be errors, not only in content but also in meaning" (*ibid.*). He observes the flaw in the process of translation and retranslation at work in *Lord Meher*. More explicitly, from "Marathi or Gujarati into Hindi then into English" (*ibid.*). This evident problem perturbed the present analyst in the early volumes of *Lord Meher*, and not merely in the collecting and retelling of stories. Reiter's attitude is quite reasonable on basic points, and so one can hope that more discrepancies will receive attention in future. He has observed that Kalchuri has compiled and edited in the Hindi language sources that were written in other languages. Those sources include Behli J. Irani's unpublished biography in Gujarati, and the diaries of Dr. Ghani, Ramju Abdulla, F. H. Dadachanji, and Kishan Singh. Kalchuri's Hindi was subsequently translated into English by an Indian hand (Feram Workingboxwala), and afterwards edited by Reiter (*ibid.*). It is obvious that accuracy in wording can be adversely affected by such transliteration. Perhaps a minor point in such considerations is the tendency of *Lord Meher* to emphasize the word *avatar*, even in Paul Brunton's erratic commentary. See Brunton, *A Search in Secret India*, pp. 49–50. Cf. *Lord Meher*, Vol. 20, pp. 6758–9, which twice substitutes *avatar* for the words "founder" and "prophet" in Brunton's original. Although Meher Baba might have used the word *avatar* instead of prophet, the transcription process is clearly imposing post-New Life conventions upon an earlier source here. The sources need to be quoted verbatim to satisfy scholarly scruples, even when sources are in question for reliability (as Brunton's work definitely is). A due scholarly project is now the critical analysis of *Lord Meher*, and one serving to establish the precise content of the diverse sources incorporated.

Meanwhile, Bhau Kalchuri has claimed to represent Meher Baba in a questionable series of "awakening" messages (not in *Lord Meher*). Those messages attribute statements to an incorporeal Meher Baba. Whereas the American devotee Don Stevens has argued that Baba's published books are the true repositories of Baba's statements rather than personal interpretations. This disagreement arose in 2001, becoming available on the Internet. Cf. J.S. Rathore, "Baba's Words", http://members.tripod.com/-meherbhopal/babaswords.html. Prof. Rathore is in clear support of Kalchuri's subjectivity. Kalchuri is here described as one of Baba's "inner circle" (*ibid.*, p. 6), a theme which has become subject to speculation. 122 members are mentioned, and yet "there is no account found that Baba divulged their names" (*Lord Meher* Vol. 20, note to p. 6681). The ten circles denoted appear to have become identified with the *mandali*. Kalchuri's most dramatic message is that Meher Baba spoke two words aloud to him in Hindi shortly before dying. Those words were *Yad rakh* ("Remember this"), part of a sentence ending with "I am not this body". Kalchuri did not make his disclosure on this subject until 2001. His explanation is that Baba made the utterance to prove that his vocal chords had not become defunct, and that *Yad rakh* did not amount to the "Word of Words". Cf. D. Stevens, "Preserving Baba's Word", an Internet item dated 2001 which complains of a large body of inspirational messages that risk major confusion, messages occurring in the sect after "accounts of conversations which, on closer examination, are seen as almost certainly never having occurred". Correspondence between Stevens and Kalchuri dated 2004 further attests disagreement. "There might be some degree of uneasiness in the reader to see two of Baba's close companions disagreeing, vehemently at times." (M. Applebaum, *Mandali Email* Review, 2005, at http://www.yadrakh.org.) See also *Friends of Meher Baba* (Spring 2005), pp. 3-7, for Kalchuri's admission that he gave his own interpretation of the "world destruction" statement of Meher Baba, though he formerly failed to make this clear. *Mandali* exegesis should be critically regarded.

Appendix One

Satya Sai Baba of Puttaparthi – an Abuser of Devotees

The claims of Satya Sai Baba to possess miraculous powers have been contested for many years, notably by a former devotee, B. Premanand. This man is now a well known Indian rationalist and sceptic. Premanand has conclusively demonstrated that Satya Sai's "miracles" are just conjuring tricks of the type used by many magicians. Satya Sai's uncle was a magician, and was the person who taught him magical tricks. Satya Sai early performed sleight of hand tricks when he was a schoolboy, surprising his classmates and teachers. Not long after, he gained much more fame and scope for manipulation when he claimed to be the reincarnation of Shirdi Sai Baba. The grounds were very nebulous, being merely the supposed ability to perform miracles. The young magician, still in his teens, used a very simple trick as proof of his sensational claim. He would throw flowers on the ground which formed into the Telegu letters for the name Sai Baba. This trick impressed the gullible spectators, but was very easy to perform. The deception was achieved by marking the words on the floor beforehand with adhesive, and then by using a fan to blow jasmine flowers onto the sticky surface.[1]

Such ruses became habitual to the young Satya Sai Baba in his new career as a holy man. There had been no spiritual transformation, only a resort to tricks which gained him the limelight. The purported "miracles" became important in his creating a wealthy following which supported his ashram at Puttaparthi. Another typical trick of his was to produce *vibhuti* or *udi* (sacred ash) from a supposedly empty vessel; this deception was the more obnoxious because he would employ a statue of Shirdi Sai in the ignoble rite. The trick was so easy to expose that Satya Sai stopped doing this in 1978.[2] However, by then he had many other deceptions to fall back on as part of his showman's role. The word *satya* means truth, and it was extremely inappropriate for him to style himself a name with this term. He was the embodiment of constant lies, not truth.

One of his most well known, and also repulsive, gimmicks was to apparently produce a Shiva *linga* (made of gold or stone) from his mouth. This trick involved elaborate contortions and the semblance of a painful labour prior to "giving birth." A towel (or handkerchief) was used to wipe the sweat of the deceiver, the Shiva *linga* being concealed within it. When the towel was applied to the mouth, sleight of hand finished the deception that beguiled devotees. Again, Satya Sai stopped performing this trick after Premanand and others exposed it.[3]

The "materialization" of *lingas* has also been described less feasibly in terms of a regurgitation technique of Hatha Yoga, which involves swallowing water and the small object beforehand. That is still very far from the enthusiastic explanation supplied by Satya Sai's biographer: "This producing of the *lingams* is indeed a unique and mysterious manifestation of the Divine Will."[4]

A rather amusing episode occurred when another hoax was exposed. In 1968 Satya Sai visited Kerala, and at one venue a critic went up to the platform and removed the thumbtip from the vaunted holy man. The thumbtip is a standard item of magical apparatus, which Satya Sai used in some tricks of manifesting sacred ash. Some spectators thought that Satya Sai had lost his thumb, which they believed must have been mutilated by the interferer.[5] Satya Sai actually retained his thumb intact, but stopped using the thumbtip thereafter.

Subsequently, high profile publicity attached in 1992 to a deceit of Satya Sai which emerged on a video depicting his supposed materialization of a gold necklace in the presence of the Indian political leader P. V. Narasimha Rao. The video became famous for revealing the ruse of a necklace being stealthily passed to Satya Sai by his personal assistant prior to "materialization." Furthermore, a Dutch cameraman, working for the newspaper *De Volkskraant*, filmed Satya Sai at Puttaparthi with some rather negative consequences. Piet Vroon and his partner reported that they saw this guru stealthily remove rings, necklaces, and watches from behind flower vases and from pillows placed on his chair. Also employed in deceits was the popular *vibhuti* (sacred ash), allegedly hidden in his mouth and removed while wiping his face. In December 1992, Vroon concluded: "We just think that he's a trickster and a cheat."[6]

Over the decades, Satya Sai gained an extensive following, aiming at wealthy sectors of the population. His insidious propaganda tactics perpetuated the myth of the miracleworker despite the exposures. A person who habitually resorts to deceits and trickery will not necessarily stop at sleight of hand. There are further glaring holes in his career that his propaganda has not been able to conceal.

Fifteen years ago, it was stated that he had acquired ten million dollars in fixed assets,[7] and the scope for subterfuge has been prodigious in relation to economic projects, despite the role of humanitarian that he has cultivated. We have to deal with facts, not the hagiology as found in the four-volume work by his secretary, Professor N. Kasturi, who wanted readers to believe that Satya Sai was born "of immaculate conception." One cannot always rely upon academics to report accurately, and they are sometimes far worse than amateurs. We can treat as fact that in 1950 Satya Sai established a small ashram known as Prashanthi Nilayam ("abode of peace") at the village of Puttaparthi. The ashram swelled to the size of a small town, capable of accommodating tens of thousands of visitors in numerous hotels adjacent. An airstrip was constructed nearby to cater for the influx of devotees. Much was made of the schools and colleges which he established. The propaganda stressed that he was a great social benefactor. Yet what were the motives involved in all this promotion and expansion?

Some devotees were disconcerted when UNESCO withdrew from an international conference on education scheduled at Puttaparthi in September 2000. One of the reasons given was deep concern about widely reported allegations of sexual abuse involving youths and children that had been made against Satya Sai Baba.[8]

The bombshell dropped on Satya Sai's movement. *India Today* produced a cover story entitled "A God Accused." The millennium had brought a revelation of a most unexpected kind to some partisans. "A small but growing number of devotees — both foreign and Indian — all settled abroad, are rallying in anger, alleging that their divine avatar is nothing more than a sexual abuser of boys and young men."[9] Satya Sai was now in his seventy-fifth year. Just how many had he abused?

UNESCO backtracked because of the shocking nature of the reports that were surfacing amongst disillusioned devotees. Those reports were authentic and encouraged many people to come forward with similar data that had been suppressed or neglected for years. This data is now extensive and dispels forever any notion of Satya Sai as a proficient spiritual teacher. He was instead a deceiver in the paranormal, a paedophile, and an unscrupulous manipulator of funds. Many reports from young male victims contain sordid details of the guru's homosexual appetite, which had been seeking outlet for many years. Satya Sai Baba had started his career as a deceiver, and had never been any different. How he managed to dupe so many people (esti-

271

mated in the millions) is the only notable phenomenon existing in his exploitative career.

Satya Sai centres experienced many defections, and sought to justify their figurehead at all costs (certainly to their credibility). In Sweden the major Satya Sai group closed down, recognizing that their existence had been wrongly founded. The Internet became a major vehicle for the powerful allegations that were shaking a cult to the roots. Information became widely known that Satya Sai frequently molested young male students attending the schools and college of his ashram. The supposed educational venture was another hoax, is an attendant conclusion. The guru had a perverse inclination for oral sex. The sordid details have a horror quality in that many of the young boys were traumatised because they did not dare to tell their parents what was happening, as the latter were indoctrinated devotees who had too much to lose from confronting the truth.

The degree of Satya Sai's intimacy with his victims evidently varied. He would coerce a response, which was frequently not as enthusiastic as he wanted. Actual sodomy did not occur in many reported cases of molestation, but that would appear to have been the outcome he desired. His strategy was to select victims during the periods of daily *darshan* at his ashram, luring them into private interviews. What occurred at one of these "interviews" shocked even one of his hardened sensual colleagues, Dr. Naresh Bhatia, who had been participating in sexual activity with Satya Sai for six years. A young boy student emerged from the interview room crying — he did not stop crying for two days, and was unable to eat or study. Dr. Bhatia examined the child and found that he had been sexually penetrated via his anus. The victim was taken to Bangalore and re-examined; a second medical opinion confirmed sexual abuse. Bhatia complained to the guru: "Why do you do this to such a young child when you have all of us adults and the older students to play with?"[10]

The reply from the heartless paedophile known as Satya Sai Baba is reported to have been "Don't bargain with God."[11]

This episode was not over. Soon afterwards, five men went to the home of Dr. Bhatia, threatening him with knives. He managed to escape by car, fleeing to Delhi. The terrorist aspect of Satya Sai here emerges. Bhatia could not practise medicine because he left all his personal papers behind at Puttaparthi. The ashram would not give those papers to him unless he agreed to certain conditions, which included a promise on his part to keep quiet about the episode of the abused boy and also to keep his sexual relationship with Satya Sai a secret. Various false rumours were circulated at the ashram to explain Dr. Bhatia's disappearance from the scene.[12] This was part of the general situation of suppression and misrepresentation which occurred in that corrupt ashram of Puttaparthi.

Dr. Bhatia left the ashram in December 1999. When contacted on the telephone by other critics, he said that he had become a devotee of Satya Sai in 1971 at the age of twenty. He said that he had participated in sexual relations with the guru for a total of 15 or 16 years (a longer period than is stated by another source). Further, during that time he was aware that Satya Sai had sexual relations with "many, many" students from the ashram college and school, and with overseas devotees.[13] The total number of victims and willing partners is evidently a large one, and the whole sordid activity was concealed beneath the guise of spirituality and philanthropy. Readers can forget the propaganda image of the "man of miracles" avatar supplied in the Satya Sai commercial literature. Even willing sexual partners could find themselves in danger of their lives.

Two American university presses failed to set Indian mystical matters in due perspective during the 1990s. SUNY Press supplied a confusing validation of Satya Sai in a book about Shirdi Sai. Chicago University Press ignored Satya Sai and chose instead to slander Ramakrishna of Dakshineswar as a homoerotic. There was a very big difference between these two entities. While Ramakrishna was bearing the brunt of Christian bias,[14] Satya Sai was abusing many young men, confident after his many years of propaganda, which had been endorsed by SUNY Press.

A young American, who supplied one of the reports of abuse, was sixteen when he gained his first private interview with Satya Sai. That was in 1995. Sam Young had been born into a family of Satya Sai devotees, and had been reared to believe that the paedophile was divine. Young found that Satya Sai "materialized" oil in his left hand and rubbed this on his (Young's) genital area. Afterwards the advances became "progressively more abusive and forceful."[15] The sex-obsessed entity tried to coerce him into performing oral sex, blandly explaining that this was for purification. The victim was constantly lured with gifts of watches, rings, and cash. Young was told to say nothing to his parents. There was the incitement expressed to the boy that he was a special devotee. When Young attempted to resist, Satya Sai would threaten not to call his parents for any more interviews. In 1998, the

273

hypocrite attempted to rape him.[16] In the endeavour to gain willing partners, the debauched holy man was evidently prepared to take some time before making his full advances.

The true stature of Satya Sai Baba is not that of an omniscient avatar, but that of an obsessive sexual molester. This conclusion is in consonance with the contents of a document known as *The Findings*, which quickly achieved notice on the Internet at the end of the 1990s. This contribution is a 46-page report on Satya Sai's misdemeanours compiled by David Bailey, a British ex-devotee whose link with that guru dates from 1994. Bailey would visit the ashram three or four times a year, teaching music to students at the Satya Sai Baba College. Over four years, this concert pianist from Llandudno gained more than a hundred interviews with the obnoxious celebrity claiming to be an avatar. Bailey edited a magazine with his wife to propagate the guru's teachings. Yet the more he learned about Satya Sai, the more Bailey doubted. He concluded that the purported miracles were cheap conjuring tricks, that Satya Sai's proclaimed healings were a myth, and furthermore, that the guru was a dissolute charlatan. His unsteady faith was shattered when students from the College begged him to help them in their plight of being sexually abused by the avatar of Puttaparthi. These young men feared for their personal safety, being scared to inform their parents, who were totally brainwashed by the Satya Sai conditioning syndrome. Deeply shocked by this final revelation, Bailey ended his association with Satya Sai in 1998 and began to assemble a dossier that included verbatim reports of abuse from ex-devotees in Holland, Germany, Sweden, Australia, and India. Bailey felt a special obligation to counter the Satya Sai propaganda, because he and his wife had formerly supported the fake avatar so strongly and in print. Now his disillusioned wife described Satya Sai in terms of "his chicanery, illusion, fraud, embezzlement, implication with murders, ongoing paedophile activities, and the almost impenetrable fortress of lies creating his 'divinity.' "[17]

Faye Bailey was formerly an indoctrinated devotee, typically suspending all the critical faculties in admiration of the guru at Puttaparthi. When her husband began to question Satya Sai's validity, she at first refused to listen. For six months she resisted any negative statement about the man who had so succeeded in duping millions like her. Yet her husband eventually overcame this screen-out mentality. When they next visited the ashram, Faye Bailey altered her habit of looking adoringly at the face of Satya Sai. At her husband's insis-

274

tence, she instead began to notice the guru's very stealthy hands. She experienced horror at witnessing the deceptions thus emerging. The interminable rings, watches, and trinkets were blithely plucked from the side of chair cushions or palmed. The famous "materializations" of *vibhuti* were clearly derived from *vibhuti* tablets that the deceiver held between his fingers.[18] Seeing was believing in a quite different way; Satya Sai Baba was not a god but a scheming and incredibly selfish fraud.

Crushing *vibhuti* tablets in his right hand, and with spare tablets concealed in the hand holding up his robe, the trick magician was perpetually deceiving. He must often have thought that his ruses were invisible, that he was too clever for the audience. In general this was true. David Bailey was more alert and also discovered that Satya Sai's "jewellery," so facilely dispensed, merely comprised worthless trinkets. He was told by the guru that the ring "materialized" for him was "a sixty-four faceted diamond of great commercial value."[19] Bailey took this ring to a jeweller, who immediately recognized it as a typical "Sai Baba" ring of cheap manufacture. The metal was not gold, and the stone was a valueless zircon backed by a piece of silver paper. Bailey learned that these worthless rings were specially manufactured for Satya Sai, who was well aware of their nil rating.

Instead of finding that Satya Sai was a great healer as he claimed, Faye Bailey discovered that his advice on health nearly caused permanent damage to her before she instead resorted to Western medical treatment for her ailment.[20] Satya Sai Baba should be a legend of wrong advice, not of curative benefits.

This guru claimed to live on a simple diet of rice and *chapattis*. Do not believe this, because it was discovered that his evening meal consisted of six to eight different dishes prepared for him every night.[21] In other words, he was a lying glutton, and quite remote from ascetic privations. His tastes were inclined to be opulent in that he acquired several luxury cars supposedly "gifted" to him. His heaven was that of fondling male genitals, though he did not neglect to have the ceiling of his temple (*mandir*) covered in gold leaf.[22] He was not concerned with feeding the poor, but with dispensing fake jewellery to rich devotees as an encouragement to keep patronising his decadent ashram. Large donations were very welcome in return for worthless trinkets.

One of the means devised to gain donations at Satya Sai's ashram was the project known as the Super Speciality Hospital. Bailey reports that one wing of this had never been opened, supposedly through lack of funds. Yet the names of many heavyweight benefactors are on view in the hospital reception area. One of the many donations given for this building is stated as forty-nine million dollars. The total amount of the donations is remarked upon by Bailey as being "absolutely mind-boggling."[23] Were the figures exaggerated to excite competition amongst donors, or is it that so many gifts were appropriated by stealthy hands for personal aggrandisement? In this particular hospital, even donated kidneys were stolen in 1997, an event that was suspected of being part of a kidney racket in Bangalore.[24] We may correlate here the information that "large scale economical frauds and misuse of donated means exist in Prashanthi Nilayam,"[25] i.e. Satya Sai's ashram. That observation appeared in a circular letter to harrowing members of the Sai organization in Sweden when this body decided to close down because of the discoveries about exploitative activities. That observation doubtless explains why the sanitation in the Super Speciality Hospital was so disgusting that one of the doctors who worked there told Bailey never to let anyone he cared about become an inmate.[26] Everything is handicapped in a situation where a predator like Satya Sai Baba can be left alone in an interview room with a young boy.

The Findings document relates how, as the Baileys travelled around the world speaking to Satya Sai Baba groups, they found that "after almost every meeting people would come to us asking for help because of the financial trickery they had experienced at the ashram."[27] This trickery did not stop at small amounts of money. Trusting devotees would give thousands of pounds or dollars (or the equivalent) for a living space at the ashram. All in vain, and no receipt for the money. When the people concerned tried to get back their funds, they were told that there were no records of the transaction.

In the midst of such criminal tactics, Satya Sai spread the lie that he did not need donations. This measure doubtless looked "good" at the retreats and meetings where it was emphasized.[28] The hypocrisy shows up very sourly in the episode of the water project for which Satya Sai is notorious. This project apparently arose because the ashram had an inadequate water supply (through wells) which caused problems like gastric disturbances. The government refused permission for a water pipeline unless villages along that line could also be supplied. The ashram then instigated a "huge global fund-raising" which facilitated a new pipeline to the ashram and a selection of villages (no number is specified). Then the work stopped. Yet it was claimed that all 750 villages in the Sai Baba Water Project were now receiving water. David Bailey was one of those who believed this until he was shown a Telegu newspaper that showed photos of relevant Project villages "with no water, broken pipes, no pipes, pipes and no tanks, and many with nothing at all."[29] The newspaper accused Satya Sai of being a cheat. Bailey subsequently visited some of these villages and found that the adverse report was true.

The humanitarian reputation cultivated by Satya Sai does not stand up to close scrutiny. Bailey, like many others, was led to believe that the schools and colleges at Puttaparthi and the Whitefield colony had been created to give free education. In reality only the village school charged no fees, the reason being that this was run by the government, like other village schools throughout India. The other institutions of Satya Sai charged fees. Bailey specifies an annual figure of 20,000 rupees per child, plus extras if required.[30] The college boys were enrolled from all over India. Many of them regretted the homosexual attentions which they received from their corrupt patron.

The reaction of some prominent devotees was at first to deny David Bailey's discovery of the sexual abuse. Two of them eventually telephoned him to admit that they had known for years of these matters, "but he is God, and God can do anything he likes."[31] The indoctrination was acute, even in the face of perversion. Bailey also found another excuse being maintained that *kundalini* was raised by such sexual preoccupations. The accurate diagnosis of Satya Sai Baba is not that of an avatar or *kundalini* raiser. He is instead a singularly unscrupulous paedophile and sex maniac. Only that consideration need be read into the recurring situation described in *The Findings*. Satya Sai "would take these young men and boys into the private interview room alone with him, then insist that they take their trousers down and he would massage them, often masturbating them, and/or insisting on oral sex and sometimes collecting their semen in his handkerchief."[32]

The first report of Satya Sai's sexual abuse appeared in a book published in 1970 called *Lord of the Air* by Tal Brooke, a young American ex-devotee. This was dismissed by devotees at large. One of those who subscribed to the dismissal was a young German who visited Puttaparthi for the first time in 1989. In 1993 he (Jens Sethu) became suspicious about Satya Sai's lifestyle and the costly new buildings appearing every year at the ashram. He was married, and though an annual visitor, did not gain an interview until January 1996. At the second interview that month, the guru expressed annoyance at the presence of the devotee's wife, took him alone into the interview room, told him that his wife was diseased and that they should separate, and then started to kiss the new victim on the lips for some time. There followed the dubious ritual of anointing with oil. The victim was unhappy, but still trusted the guru. Satya Sai afterwards called this man's wife alone into the interview room. He told her rather nastily that if she did not separate from her husband, he would throw her out of the ashram. "He (Satya Sai) appeared wild and furious and she shivered all over."[33]

Some days afterwards, the young German again encountered the guru at the time of *darshan*, i.e., in the collective situation of audience. Satya Sai wanted to know if the enjoined marital separation had occurred. He was told not yet. The guru turned away and shouted, "Bad, bad boy." The recipient of his wrath remarks that "he was so aggressive and seemed to radiate such an aura of evil that I was really shocked."[34]

Sethu and his wife departed immediately, but he decided to return at the end of that year. The guru with the aura of evil was still oppressively sensual in the interview room, being concerned to massage the visitor's genitals in anticipation of an erection. This time Sethu at last understood the truth about Satya Sai Baba and was very shocked. The guru was disappointed with the emotional response and lack of an erection. The visitor returned to Germany, where he researched the Internet and traced another man who had encountered a similar experience of abuse at the same ashram. However, he decided to return to Puttaparthi in 1999 in order to collect some luggage. Yet he regretted this visit, as he came into collision with ashram surveillance officers who objected to his being in possession of two pages from the Internet. Satya Sai was noted for his opposition to the Internet, for very suspect reasons. Sethu received a warning that his life was in danger, and that he should leave immediately.[35] He escaped to Delhi and the German Embassy, who said that they knew of similar cases. Meanwhile, Satya Sai suffered two heart attacks in November 1999.

Sethu improves upon the hagiological fare by describing Satya Sai as "a mighty demon who came in the guise of a spurious saint,"[36] and urges that from the beginning of his career, Satya Sai was a liar. The guru was not born in Puttaparthi as he said, but in a nearby village. A friend of Satya Sai's youth is on record for having stated that "even in those days (Satya) Sai Baba was more like a politician or chieftain of a feudal system," lacking compassion.[37]

The propaganda of this deceitful guru about being the reincarnation of Shirdi Sai Baba may be dismissed as rank opportunism. If people believe in reincarnation, it seems that they should instead conceive of Satya Sai as a reincarnation of some feudal "left hand" potentate who exploited his subjects in a reign of terror and subterfuge. Alternatively, he can be viewed as a sinister paederast who betrayed the trust of many donors to his ashram. His sexual appetites are said to have extended to males between the ages of seven and thirty, though some older men are also implicated.

While some ex-devotees have carefully analysed what sort of error they made, many others are said to have turned to another proclaimed avatar, namely Bala Sai Baba of Andhra. "Bala Sai claims to be the real Sai avatar.... he dresses like Satya Sai Baba, performs the same kind of 'miracles' and has been successful in attracting a large number of devotees."[38] Satya Sai clones also feed on superstition and showmanship.

Notes to Appendix One

1.   B. Premanand, *Science Versus Miracles Vol. 1* (Podanur, Tamil Nadu: B. Premanand, 1994), pp. 58–9.

2.   *Ibid.*, pp. 61–2.

3.   *Ibid.*, p. 62. Cf. D. Bailey, *The Findings*, p. 22, the informant mentioning handkerchiefs.

4.   This quotation from N. Kasturi is given in D. Bayerstein, ed., *Sai Baba Miracles: An Overview* (Podanur, Tamil Nadu: B. Premanand). The complete text of the latter work is available on the Internet, where it is known as *Sathya Sai Baba's Miracles*. The Internet reference is http://www.psg.com/-ted/bcskeptics/sbmir/contents.html.

5.   Bayerstein, *op. cit.*, section 86, citing a lecture by B. Premanand that was sponsored by *Science World*, Vancouver, in December 1988.

6.   L. Hughes, "Who is Satya Sai Baba" (Dialog Center International). The Internet reference is http://www.dci.dk/engelsk/elefant/saibabaeng.html.

7.   L. Siegel, *Net of Magic: Wonders and Deceptions in India* (Chicago: University of Chicago Press, 1991), p. 344.

8.   *Indian Skeptic Vol. 13 no. 8* (Dec. 2000), pp. 3–4. The editorial comments in this periodical, published by B. Premanand, unfortunately generalize in relation to celibate populations, using such blanket stigmas as: "it is natural that when one tries to suppress the biological need of sex the person becomes a sex maniac" (*ibid.*, p. 4). The rationalist cause will not gain additional credence through such sweeping generalizations. It is not scientific to conclude that all celibates become undisciplined or hysterical sex maniacs. One might just as well believe that all married people become bisexuals. The Indian rationalists have gained a reputation for materialist philosophy, which is not necessarily the best yardstick for assessing social and "mystical" events.

9.   "A God Accused," *India Today*, Dec. 4th, 2000, reproduced on the Internet. See http://www.india-today.com/itoday/20001204/cover-4.shtml.

10.   D. and F. Bailey, *The Findings*, p. 19. This document is salient amongst the Internet sources as http://www.npi-news.dk/htm.

11.   *Ibid.*

12.   *Ibid.*, pp. 19–20.

13.   M. Brown, "Divine Downfall," *Electronic Telegraph*, 28th October 2000, p. 6. See www.telegraph.co.uk.

14.   On the misinterpretation of Ramakrishna, see part 4 of Shepherd, *Minds and Sociocultures Vol. 2* (in press).

15.   Brown, *art. cit.*, p. 5.

16.   *Ibid.* Cf. "A God Accused," p. 1, which graphically describes how the paederast was successful in eliciting by force a two-way oral sex in this instance.

17.   Bailey, *The Findings*, p. 3.

18.   *Ibid.*, p. 2.

19.   *Ibid.*, p. 5.

20.   *Ibid.*, p. 6.

21.   *Ibid.*

22.   *Ibid.*

23.   *Ibid.*, p. 7.

24.   *Ibid.*, pp. 35–6.

25.   *Ibid.*, p. 33.

26.   *Ibid.*, p. 7.

27.   *Ibid.*, p. 8.

28.   *Ibid.* See also note 2 above in the notes to the main text. Satya Sai's bank account number was no secret and was frequently given to new devotees.

29.   *The Findings*, p. 8.

30.   *Ibid.*, p. 11.

31.   *Ibid.*, p. 10.

32.   *Ibid.*, p. 9.

33.   *Ibid.*, p. 28.

34.   *Ibid.*

35.   *Ibid.*, p. 29.

36.   *Ibid.*, p. 30

37.   *Ibid.*

38.   L. Hughes, *art. cit.*, p. 2.

Appendix Two

The International Cause to Expose Satya Sai Baba

The ongoing exposé of the miracle guru has increased substantially in only a few years, since 1999. In that year, the international magazine *Nexus* published three influential articles concerning his sexual molestations and other misdemeanours.

Some critics of Satya Sai have long suspected his real profile. In 1970 was published the book *Lord of the Air* by Tal Brooke. That author lived with the guru for over a year, and reported sexual activities of a disturbing nature. Very few readers believed the contents at that time, and the book was banned in India. Over thirty years later, the new version of that book, known as *Avatar of Night* (1999), is now acceptable in Western countries as an early testimony to burgeoning data which reveals Satya Sai Baba as a malpractitioner in "spirituality."

Some reports now freely use the words paedophile and paedophilia as descriptions for certain activities of Satya Sai. It is clear that tendencies to underage seduction have been part of Satya Sai's psychology, in addition to his seduction of older age-groups. Satya Sai is sometimes defined as a serial sexual molester of young males, different nationalities being involved. Some ex-devotees were formerly in the category of those who vociferously denied reports by victims and parents of Satya Sai's molestations. Yet when they investigated more closely, they changed their attitude. Other devotees still deny the evidence and strong allegations.

Some writers have referred to the cause of opposing Satya Sai as the Exposé. This cause seems to deserve a capital letter, owing to the scope of the project and the gravity of the allegations and emerging data. The Exposé activities are mainly conducted by former devotees of Satya Sai. There are many of them, and their industry is impressive. The year 1999 saw Exposé activists commence dedicated campaigns to alert the media, the police, and government personnel to the dangers of decadent guruism. Prominent amongst them was an American ex-devotee named Glen Meloy, a retired management consultant. They had to face a counter-attack from the guru, who called them demons and traitors, and who continued to boast of his philanthropic works. Yet the Exposé knew that these activities had been "over-

283

whelmingly those of his devotees."[1] One accusation is that Satya Sai has been using the social work as camouflage for something very selfish.

The International Humanist and Ethical Union has complained of "the personal danger to its activists from fanatical followers of the guru, especially in India."[2] The spectre of terrorism exists because of the relative freedom enjoyed in India by Satya Sai. The IHEU is based in London and has NGO Special Consultative status with the United Nations and the Council of Europe. In March 2003, an executive director confirmed that officers of this organisation "have many times voiced their concern at the impunity with which Sathya Sai operates, untouched by the Indian criminal justice system."[3]

This factor of immunity sometimes puzzles Westerners who hear of the anomaly. How can such a situation possibly exist? An Exposé writer supplies us with the answer:

"The Indian power structure, including most sections of the media, constantly obstructs legal and other efforts by the Exposé.... Several of us, including those with excellent credentials, have written to the Indian President, Prime Minister and hundreds of parliamentarians, embassies, high commissions, and media. Reflecting shamefully on their country, they remain mute, showing rank irresponsibility and failure of courtesy. Some Indians who could help a lot do not, being afraid to offend the status quo."[4]

The level of legal action in India, in respect of Satya Sai, is not impressive. Some idea of the ideational problem may be gleaned from the episode in which B. Premanand, a leading critic of the guru, mounted a court action in Andhra Pradesh (the home state of Satya Sai). The High Court Judge was a devotee of the miracle guru, and obstructively "ruled that the law requiring a license to produce gold does not apply to Sathya Sai Baba, who, he determined, materialises his gold from a divine realm."[5]

Premanand was more successful in his appearance on the *Guru Busters* tv programme (of the 1990s), which spotlighted the Indian Rationalists in confrontation with deceiving holy men. The former party demonstrated that the same tricks and feats could be performed by ordinary men, and that no miracles or supernatural abilities are involved. Premanand is also the author of a lengthy book entitled *Murders in Sai Baba's Bedroom*. The title is a reference to the notorious events of June 1993, sometimes described as the "police killings." A major issue is here decoded, i.e., "Sai Baba's complicity in police executions in his private apartments at Puttaparthi on June 6th, 1993."[6]

Certain websites giving realistic information about the guru have been "repeatedly spammed and destroyed" by Satya Sai partisans.[7] This setback seems to have been influenced by the guru's policy of forbidding his devotees to view allegations on the Internet. "Some devotees have acknowledged seeing Sai Baba cheat, but say that it is his test of their faith."[8] The psychological stranglehold is formidable. Many officials in the Satya Sai organization are notorious for "totally disregarding the complaints by parents, boys and young men about sexual molestation."[9]

A strong challenge to the cult discrepancies is imperative. Otherwise, Satya Sai Baba "is all too likely to pass into history hailed as a world teacher and saviour. His devotees are legion in all the top Indian power structures. Slavishly, they, and millions of Indians, sink at his feet, declaring him a national treasure – the greatest divine incarnation ever – and believe him when he says that he will save the entire world, with India leading the rest of us. Heavily armed state and federal police forces, and his own security and intelligence force (some of them specially trained in Israel and the USA), guard him with a protection tighter than a drum. Why would they not? In the form of foreign currency, he brings billions into India."[10]

The propaganda of this guru began in 1943,[11] when he claimed to be the reincarnation of Shirdi Sai, who was remote in terms of both lifestyle and personal inclination. Hindu critics have emphasised the errors of Satya Sai in relation to Hindu scripture, errors that have often been removed by his translators.[12] The Australian researcher Brian Steel has shown that this guru's version of Christianity is very muddled.[13] Satya Sai seems to have mistaken Luther as a contemporary of Jesus.

Attempts have been made to place due information at the disposal of influential New Age writers who refer with approval to Satya Sai. Such writers are generally misleading sources who cause much confusion, and who need to go back to school rather than achieve celebrity. The New Age myth of Satya Sai as an educator and philanthropist should be dispensed with if the truth is desired. That myth was in vogue at places like the Findhorn Foundation for many years.

A strong pocket of the Satya Sai sect has existed in Australia, though combated by the Exposé in concert with experts on sexual abuse and an internationally eminent legal authority. The cult has percolated universities, and was paying big dollars to set up the Sai National Conference at Adelaide University in April 2003.[14] This was cancelled because of the increasing information about what the Conference would be glossing as unproven allegations about Satya Sai. It is also reported that "strong national parliamentary action is being prepared in the UK and Australia."[15] Due to the intervention of Exposé leaders, the British Prime Minister Tony Blair has stated in a letter that he will not meet Satya Sai.[16] Both the University of Manchester and University College (London) are reported to have prevented meetings of the problem organization.[17]

Yet the Indian Prime Minister proved a serious complication. Together with three high profile co-signatories, he said in a public letter that the Exposé data comprised "wild, reckless and concocted allegations made by certain vested interests and people against Bhagwan Shri Sathya Sai Baba."[18]

Ex-devotees who free themselves from vested interests, and who instead pursue a rational tactic of improved education, are not so much making allegations as telling the truth. Governments which support cults are in a more unenviable category.

Fortunately, UNESCO possessed stronger ethical priorities than could be found in some other directions. UNESCO was booked to co-sponsor an education conference in human values in September 2000 at the Puttaparthi ashram. The other co-sponsor was the University of Flinders, South Australia. (Some say that the cult gesture towards secular human values was calculated to attract auspicious attention.) The Exposé informed those parties of relevant details, and both of the sponsors withdrew from the conference. UNESCO did not make their decision until after obtaining reports from the French National Police (the Sureté). The Media Advisory posted by UNESCO on September 15th, 2000, included the statement:

"The Organisation [UNESCO] is deeply concerned about widely reported allegations of sexual abuse involving youths and children that have been levelled at the leader of the movement in question, Sathya Sai Baba."[19]

The Exposé has representatives from many countries, and has produced well-researched articles for the press on an international scale, from Canada and Chile to India and Australia. National broadcasters took up the cause in Holland, Denmark, Norway, Argentina, and Australia. Denmark and Norway were keen to promote the 54-minute documentary *Seduced*, a film which details the Exposé. Desperate attempts were made by Satya Sai devotees to press litigation action against Danish Broadcasting in 2002, but Danish scruple was not curtailed. The municipal authorities rescinded the sale to Satya Sai devotees of a prestigious castle in Copenhagen which was intended for use as a "Sai international school." Resistance came from a Danish businessman who was chairman of the fund board promoting this school. The courts of Denmark remained resolute in the face of risks discernible in such a project.[20]

"Major tv interests in the world have now purchased *Seduced*."[21] Other media exposures were also planned. Recently, BBC2 featured the documentary entitled *The Secret Swami* on June 17th, 2004. This footage interviewed some of the accusers and supporters of the Satya Sai sect, and also showed partisan reactions of Indian government officials.[22] It may be only a matter of time before Western countries jettison the myth of the miracle guru. The problem then will be to re-educate some sectors in India as to what comprises spirituality and social health.

Yet the scale of the Satya Sai movement is daunting. The BBC supply a high estimate of up to thirty million devotees worldwide from many countries. Most of these seem to be in India. The degree to which Satya Sai is unquestioned in these ranks is attested by the uncritical deference to his "education, health, and water projects." This has become a doctrine. In reality, the guru is more coercive and manipulative than popular beliefs have allowed for. The BBC has documented an ex-devotee (who claims that he was sexually abused) recollecting Satya Sai as enjoining "If you don't do what I say, your life will be filled with pain and suffering."[23]

A salient objector has been Basava Premanand, who was duly profiled by the BBC. He is described as founder of the Federation of Indian Rationalist Associations. The campaign of Premanand against Satya Sai is well known in Andhra. However, not everyone has been aware that Premanand "survived four murder attempts and bears the scars from several savage beatings." The assessment of this courageous objector is that Satya Sai is "nothing but a mafia man, conning the people and making himself rich"[24]

The BBC have won applause for their programme, though even they were confused by the popular assessment of Shirdi Sai that has gained such vogue in India over the years. The BBC state that Satya Sai "professes to be the reincarnation of a Hindu God-man from the nineteenth century"[25] Although that is doubtless the view of Satya Sai, the identity of Shirdi Sai was in reality less convenient to the "caste and miracle" platform.

Notes to Appendix Two

1.	B. Pittard, "Sathya Sai Baba Exposé: An Update," p. 1. This is an Internet item dated September 25th, 2003. The reference is bpittard-@beachaccess.com.au. Barry Pittard of Australia reports the guru's threat that his betrayal by ex-devotees "will not be atoned no matter how many births are experienced." This vengeful remark came from Satya Sai's discourse on Christmas Day, 2000. The guru interpreted the motives of his critics in terms of jealousy and receipt of money. Pittard counters that Satya Sai was "clearly losing his nerve." The unforgiving discourse was featured in *The Times of India,* December 26th, 2000, under the headline of "Sai Baba Lashes Out at His Detractors."

2.	Pittard, *art.cit.,* p. 2, who says that the IHEU has member organizations who wish to stage an international conference on the guru of Puttaparthi in a leading city.

3.	*Ibid.,* quoting an email from Babu Gogineni.

4.	*Ibid.,* p. 3, who adds that "the instrument of the subpoena may need to be used in cases such as that of Dr. Naresh Bhatia" (*ibid.,* p. 4). See also Appendix One. Dr. Bhatia was formerly in charge of a unit at the Super Speciality Hospital at Puttaparthi. Dr. Bhatia has stated that he still regards Satya Sai as his guru, and has chosen to remain silent about important matters.

5.	*Ibid.,* p. 2. In 1986 Premanand pressed court charges against the guru for violating the Gold Control Act by producing gold necklaces without the permission of a Gold Control Administrator.

6.	*Ibid.,* p. 7. The grim scenario of four boys murdered by a strategy of alleged guru complicity is deeply shocking. See also R. Priddy, "Faith-shaking events – the 1993 murders." This is another Internet article, the reference for which is http://home.no.net/anir/Sai/enigma/VKN1.htm. Four young male devotees broke into the private quarters of Satya Sai late at night and armed with knives. Their motives are not clear. They were stopped by the guru's personal attendants, and in the struggle two attendants were killed. The guru escaped, and the four intruders were found in his bedroom when the police arrived. The intruders were shot dead, the police stating self-defence as the reason. The government did not proceed with a due investigation. B. Premanand took up court action against the guru, but was defeated. The BBC has reported his discontent with officials, "because if the investigation takes place, a lot of things will come out like economic offences and sex offences." See also note 24 *infra*

289

and Appendix Three.

7.   Pittard, *art. cit.*, p. 5, and referring to the case of a woman "who for the sake of her own psychological wellbeing withdrew from the persistent outpourings of pro-Sathya Sai Baba vitriol."

8.   *Ibid.* p. 6, and also mentioning that "videos shot by well-known devotees show him, on careful analysis, faking materialisations."

9.   *Ibid.*, and relating what happened to one of the partisan leaders when he changed his attitude. Stephen Carthew was a prominent Australian devotee who was shocked after confronting first-hand reports of sexual molestation. He called a meeting of devotees in Adelaide, but was made an outcast by the officious ex-lawyer from Ceylon "who now works for the Law faculties of both the University of Sydney and the University of New South Wales" (*ibid.*, p. 7).

10.   *Ibid.*, p. 3.

11.   The revised dating (formerly 1940) has been advanced by Brian Steel in his researches available on the Internet. See Steel, *The Guru from Puttaparthi: An Alternative View of Sathya Sai Baba*, http://bd-steel.tripod.com. I borrowed from this useful source in my *Pointed Observations* (Dorchester, Dorset: Citizen Initiative, 2005), pp. 94ff.

12.   Pittard, *art. cit.*, p. 12, and who adds that Hindus active in the Exposé, "assisted by distinguished scholars, are now taking these matters to the leading Hindu councils in the world."

13.   *Ibid.*, p. 11; B. Steel, "Sai Baba and Christianity," http://bd-steel.tripod.com/More/Jesus1.htm.

14.   Pittard, *art. cit.*, p. 10, and informing that Satya Sai partisans were offering to pay the student union 30,000 dollars to hold the event.

15.   *Ibid.*, p. 9.

16.   *Ibid.*, and specifying that the letter of Tony Blair was written to the Hon. Tony Colman MP.

17.   *Ibid.* Other British institutions which have screened out Satya Sai sectarian meetings are Downey House public school and Lord Wandsworth College. At Glastonbury the popular Ramala Centre, run by two devotees of Satya Sai, has received disapproving attention from the Christian Church. Glastonbury is a place that has increasingly become a focus for occultism and New Age interests.

18.   *Ibid.*

19.   *Ibid.*, p. 8.

20.   *Ibid.* The sale of the castle Arresodal is linked to the sum of six million dollars, which Pittard associates with a key American devotee of the Satya Sai sect.

21.   *Ibid.*, p. 7. Pittard refers to a number of websites associated with the Exposé, which are constantly being updated. One should include here http://www.exbaba.com and http://www.saiguru.net. Several languages are involved, but English features on both these websites.

22.   The BBC documentary included Isaac Tigrett, a co-founder of Hard Rock Café whose support for Satya Sai extended to a promotion of the guru's "Love All Serve All" mantra. That phrase became the corporate slogan of Tigrett's restaurant empire. The mantra has since gained a sense of inherent contradiction and inverse emotion. Yet Tigrett seems contented at the financial benefits he derived from the serial sexual molester. See also the references in Appendix Three.

23.   For the testimony of Alaya Rahm, see *Secret Swami*, http://news.bbc.co.uk/go/pr/fr/-/1/hi/programmes/this world/3791921.stm.

24.   T. Datta, *Sai Baba: God-man or con man?* See http://news.bbc.co.uk/go/pr/fr/-/1/hi/programmes/this world/3813469.stm. Premanand has been campaigning against Satya Sai since 1976. He says that there are many Indians who claim to have been abused but who are too afraid to speak out.

25.   *Secret Swami.* See the reference in note 23 *supra*.

Appendix Three

The Extent of Abuse achieved by Satya Sai Baba

Recent contributions on the Internet by Robert Priddy underline the scale of Satya Sai's misdemeanours. Priddy is another ex-devotee. He and his wife were the leaders of the Satya Sai Organisation in Norway for some eighteen years. He wrote the pro-Satya book *Source of the Dream* (Bangalore 1994), and contributed over 25 eulogistic articles to the Satya Sai journal known as *Sanathana Sarathi*. During his visits to the guru's ashram since 1984, Priddy had encountered suspicious details, though he had explained these away according to the method of exegesis favoured within the sect. The crunch came in 1996, when his respected friend V. K. Narasimhan told him in secret some key facts about the notorious murders at the ashram in 1993. The shock caused Priddy to investigate further, a move which led to his increasing disillusionment. The evidence finally convinced him that Satya Sai was an accomplice to murder,[1] amongst other grave allegations. His doubts were accentuated by the world-wide reports emerging about the sexual abuse of young men and boys.

The "new" reports about the abuse were initially associated with David Bailey, whose *Findings* appeared on the Internet in 1999 (see Appendix One). Bailey encountered abusive and defamatory reactions and threats from those who were still devotees. A wealthy Australian devotee sent an email which derisively claimed that Bailey was merely an instrument of the all-powerful will of the guru. Devotee reasoning is sometimes extremely irrational, and fortunately could not prevent the resultant "chain-reaction among those who describe how they have been abused, defrauded and otherwise seriously maltreated by Satya Sai Baba."[2]

There were earlier testimonies of abuse long ignored and explained away. The expanding Internet permitted an increase of testimonies encouraged by the Exposé. These reports are too strong and consistent to be ignored. They afford proof of a serious malfunction in a popular and influential sect. The conclusion of Priddy is that Satya Sai "is a narcissist and uses many methods or tricks to attract and control people."[3] The intensive acquaintance of Priddy with the guru's discourses (which are numerous) tends to underline his judgement. He refers to "the many discrepancies and inaccuracies, sweeping generalisations and wild ideas"[4] expressed by Satya Sai.

The voluminous discourses of this guru have been analysed in terms of "any number of factually incorrect assertions on almost any subject that can be counter-checked."[5] Priddy here emphasizes the deficient references to Christian scripture, the life of Jesus, the lives and sayings of various famous people, the subject of health, geology, history, social movements, and also the size and prowess of Satya Sai's sect. Indeed, it seems that the guru's computation of his following has influenced more official versions. Though the BBC has generously stated up to 30 million followers, the more cautious estimates speak in terms of a million or more,[6] or ten million.

"Satya Sai discourses are packed with self-praise to the highest degree ever seen in world literature."[7] Even this drawback is a minor failing by comparison with other features of the guru's career. It is important to grasp that the Exposé "has laid out thousands of separate web pages which document most of the whole gamut of this fraudulent person's failings in such detail and with such credibility that not one devotee has been able to deal with it."[8]

The general difficulties in communication prior to the 1990s Internet boom assisted the internal censorship operating in the sect at issue. Scandals remained local and did not become widely known, and were also glossed and misrepresented by partisans. Reports of Satya Sai as "a homosexual and paedophile have circulated in diverse circles in India during the 1970s."[9] Well known at Puttaparthi was the guru's early relationship with a young man called Krishna, with whom he shared his rooms as a teenager in the 1940s. The guru is reported to have been much inclined to masturbation at that early period.[10] The family of Satya Sai were not converts, but at first believed him to be "possessed by a 'Muslim spirit,'"[11] a reference to their perception of Shirdi Sai as a non-Hindu. Satya Sai relied heavily upon his claim to be a reincarnation. A celibate role was lacking. Only later did the family begin to worship him; they also benefited from his increasing fame and wealth bestowed by the contrived Sai Baba image.

The guru's younger brother Janakiram became a multi-millionaire in local property speculation, and has since been implicated as "chief conspirator in blackmailing the police"[12] who shot dead the young men armed with knives in the notorious 1993 episode of the "bedroom murders." Some say that the young men were here seeking vengeance for the fate of so many molested victims. Certainly, there is the fact to confront of an "underage male student,"[13] a fourteen-year-old who was present in the bedroom on that dire occasion, and who was part of Satya Sai's alleged regular habit of sleeping with young males.

The important document by Robert Priddy on the Satya Sai sex scandal runs to over fifty pages. The detail is graphic and alarming, and annuls the partisan complacencies which are encouraged by secrecy and doubletalk. By no means the earliest problem was occurring at *circa* 1980, when the Malaysian branch of the sect experienced resignations due to the sexual abuse of young Malaysians at Puttaparthi and the closely related Whitefield colony. The Satya Sai College at Whitefield became notorious to Malaysian students, and a cassette tape circulated about sexual molestation. There was also a scandal in Greece about the sexual abuse of a Greek boy at the Satya Sai College, and similar accounts emerged in Yugoslavia during the 1980s. These scandals remained localised. Yet a major scandal arose independently in America during the early 1980s. However, the leading American devotee, Dr. John Hislop, wrote influential letters urging that the facts be suppressed as unconfirmed.[14]

Some partisan reactions to the subsequent exposure of the late 1990s were bizarre. "So-called 'Sai devotees' have tried to drag [David] Bailey's name through the mud as a condemned paedophile in prison and [they have] even spread the story that he hanged himself in his cell."[15] In reality Bailey has never been in jail and is alive with an updated website. Devotee lore is one of the biggest obstructions to justice and clear thinking. Bailey was told by a victim of sexual abuse that Satya Sai had for years been demanding oral sex and group sex amongst his college students. The same informant posed the pointed question: "Why do you think ex-students tried to kill him in 1993?"[16]

The most well known of the sexual abuse victims are Westerners, namely Conny Larsson of Sweden and Alaya Rahm (Sam Young) of America. The former has campaigned on tv around the world against his abuser, and Alaya Rahm has been featured by the BBC in *The Secret Swami*. The latter was an underage victim of the 90s mentioned by Bailey in *The Findings*. Further lurid detail is afforded in Priddy's excerpt from the Danish film documentary *Seduced* shown in 2002:

"One time he (Satya Sai) had his robe almost completely off and he tried to have anal sex with me, because he came from behind me and started climbing on top of me."[17] This seduction was relatively easy to accomplish with indoctrinated boys who were scared of parental displeasure if they told the truth. "And he was constantly having me take out my penis and he would hold it, sometimes put it in his mouth and look at me, and then ask me to do the same thing."[18] Yet worse still, the same boy was threatened with having his penis cut off if he did not do as he was told.[19] The anguish experienced by many Indian boys in the Satya Sai College would surely have been quite enough to send the four armed ex-students into the hated quarters of the miracle guru in 1993.

"Most of the allegations that have been levied at Satya Sai Baba by victims of sexual abuse are written statements open to a considerable degree of factual checking of details."[20] The problem of identity is much greater with Indian victims, who fear personal danger in view of the guru's control of the legal system and some government figureheads. Even in relatively free Europe, prominent Danish devotees maligned one of the prominent victims as a paedophile, namely Conny Larsson. These charges have been strongly refuted by the Danish journalist Ojvind Kyro (who also made *Seduced*). Such obstructive devotees have been promoting Satya Sai's purported Education in Human Values, accompanied by the dubious slogan "love in action."[21] The values are nil in realistic assessment.

An American named Timothy Conway has stated: "We now have trustworthy reports from over two dozen credible eyewitnesses (and sworn affidavits from many of them) indicating that probably hundreds of young men and boys have been molested and/or forced to perform oral sex and masturbation on Satya Sai Baba over the last thirty years or more."[22]

The intensity of these seductive activities may be gauged from the report of another American that it is "common knowledge that several students stay with Satya Sai Baba all night on an ongoing basis."[23]

Attention from this decadent guru has led to some harrowing consequences, including suicide. An Indian ex-Satya Sai College student (whose credentials were checked by the BBC) has stated that "he [Satya Sai] is a menace to teenage boys who are too afraid and ashamed to speak up.... he is a paedophile who blankets himself with the reputation of a god/living saint."[24]

There were also some older men involved, such as the American who was 26 or 27 years old when he was a recipient of the "oil ceremony" which so frequently inaugurated sexual molestation. Perhaps because of his age, this man escaped with a prolonged embrace and a slap across the face. He was one of the many who were given a finger ring with a purported diamond that transpired to be a fake.[25]

Robert Priddy was given a fake diamond ring in expectation of a substantial donation which he had offered to the duplicit guru.[26] He observes that Satya Sai had a habit of selecting for "very frequent interviews certain young men from 16 to 20 years old from Scandinavia, the USA, and Germany."[27] They all received gifts like rings and watches, and would always get private interviews. These young men tended to quickly disappear from the scene, never again visiting the ashram.

A significant report comes from Meenakshi Shrikanth, a Tamil and an ex-student at Whitefield who published a lengthy article on the abuse. "Many of these students were made gay by Swami (Satya Sai), who himself is a gay."[28] Another problem was involved here, as testified by another Satya Sai College student, who stated that there were at least three seniors who were themselves molesters. The excuse of these predators was that "Swami likes it," i.e., homosexual indulgence. They are said to have molested more than fifty boys at that period. The victims could do nothing about their situation in the sordid trend established by the key exploiter. One of the worst instances of molestation is described and named. "He must have molested hundreds of young boys/men, but lives scot free in Whitefield."[29]

There are also alarming reports of murders occurring prior to the bedroom incident of 1993. "A Tamil friend of mine was murdered in Satya Sai Baba's backyard.... He had his stomach cut out while he was sleeping and they found him still alive in the morning. Satya Sai Baba did not do a thing to assist anybody in the investigation."[30]

Another bizarre detail is as follows: "Several alleged victims report that Satya Sai Baba actually collected their sperm in a handkerchief."[31] Priddy offers the explanation that sperm is known to have been employed in some Tantric rituals. This is true, and may indicate a psychological affinity. Some think that Satya Sai should be described as an obscene left hand Tantric rather than a Swami, the latter word generally having the association of a celibate life. The word Swami is a misnomer in this instance. Satya Sai was of a homosexual inclination from his early years, and was a masturbator and improviser of deceitful miracles, not a renunciate.

"He has his 'male harem' in the colleges over which he rules like a despot, a reserve of thousands of boys to draw upon who cannot stand up against him."[32]

In 1980 an American female devotee was told by her teenage son that Satya Sai was a homosexual who wanted him to participate in oral sex. This boy had been unwisely placed in the Satya Sai College at Whitefield. The mother had heard stories about the guru's relations with the college boys, but did not believe them because of the propaganda. "I actually saw Satya Sai Baba grab at my son's crotch as he walked ahead of me into the interview room one time."[33] She had been a devotee for ten years. Now in desperation she asked American officials of the sect for an explanation. Their response was to say that she and her son were lying. She herself had previously dismissed the book by Tal Brooke (assigned various dates of publication) which had referred to sexual activities. In 1975 she had even hung up her phone on an Indian ex-devotee who warned her by saying that he had caught the guru in bed with his son.[34]

Dr. M. Goldstein has been described as "the top leader of the international Satya Sai movement." He is now well known for having uncritically accepted the guru's unlikely claim to purity. Goldstein is stated to have "returned unopened all mail from all former leaders" of the sect in America. Those letters were complaining about the reports of sexual abuse. Goldstein displayed an overbearing attitude in *The Secret Swami*, an approach which has earned him the designation of "doctor from hell."[35]

Devotee myopia is also associated with Isaac Tigrett, a wealthy and long-term supporter who is said to have donated all the funds for the Super Speciality Hospital (contrary to the report of Bailey, which mentions many benefactors). A BBC documentary has reported Tigrett's belief that the allegations of sexual abuse are true, but that this factor makes no difference to his faith in the guru. "He even opines that, were Satya Sai Baba to murder a person, it could not alter his opinion."[36] Priddy describes this as a "kind of derangement that affects such long-term devotees,"[37] and also affirms that the term "brainwash" is relevant in such instances.

Many devotees have interpreted the sexual abuse in terms of a suggestion "that the victims could themselves have been sexual abusers in a previous lifetime, and required this experience to put them on the straight and narrow."[38] This gravely flawed form of argument does indeed sound more like brainwashing than sane reflections about reincarnation.

Some spectators have despaired at the situation in which former Indian Prime Ministers Narasimha Rao and Atal Vihari Vajpayee "have denied in very public ways that Satya Sai Baba is, or ever could be, guilty."[39] The BBC revealed the rather inflexible attitude of another Indian Minister, namely Murali Manohar Joshi. Priddy says that this man was removed from his post as Minister of Human Resource Development by the Indian electorate, and implies a strong reliance in this case upon astrology and Satya Sai's teaching.[40]

What are the supporters of propaganda actually doing? They are masking a nightmare scenario in which "there have been numerous suicides among devotees and unexplained and uninvestigated deaths of students at the Satya Sai College."[41] One suspicious death (or murder) of a student at Puttaparthi was covered up by the Satya Sai Central Trust, causing a demonstration by local villagers who were in revolt over the issue. Some young "devotees" have killed themselves by jumping off high buildings.[42] The sight of the Satyan phallus does not confer bliss, one could construe in a mood of scepticism.

What is the truth about "miracles" and "love in action" and "social work" and "educational benefits"? Robert Priddy has supplied a useful gauge for future research:

"Satya Sai Baba schools and colleges, especially in India, are inevitably under the gravest suspicion of supplying a steady stream of under-age boys for sexual purposes, not only to Satya Sai Baba but to those masters and higher students who have been themselves turned into sexual abusers by Satya Sai Baba himself, or to those homosexuals and even paedophiles who have come there attracted by the precedence of Sai Baba's sexual activities."[43]

Some observers call this the vice ring,[44] and though late in the day, it is imperative for all universities and claimants to higher education or government efficiency to be duly discerning in matters of published data and sponsorship.

Notes to Appendix Three

1.   R. Priddy, "End of the Dream – My Credo as to Sathya Sai Baba," pp. 2–3. The reference is http://home.no.net/anir/Sai/enigma/credo.-htm. Elsewhere, Narasimhan is reported to have been under pressure from Satya Sai to lie to the press. A basic theme is that the police chief involved in the murders was blackmailed by Satya Sai's younger brother Janakiram and other Satya officials.

2.   R. Priddy, "World-Wide Exposure of Sexual Abuse and Sathya Sai Baba," pp. 6, 8. The reference is http://home.no.net/anir/Sai/enigma/Sai sex.htm.

3.   Priddy, "End of the Dream," p. 7.

4.   *Ibid.*, p. 8, where he also allocates to Satya Sai "too many of the characteristics of a psychopath and sociopath."

5.   *Ibid.*, p. 12.

6.   Priddy, "Sathya Sai Baba – The Enigma Reconsidered," p. 1, which states "perhaps a million followers or more." The reference is http-://home.no.net/anir/Sai/enigma.

7.   Priddy, "End of the Dream," p. 12, and stressing the frequent "absurdly excessive claims and proven-wrong predictions."

8.   *Ibid.*, pp. 13–14.

9.   Priddy, "World-Wide Exposure of Sexual Abuse,"p. 3.

10.   *Ibid.*, p. 47. After leaving Satya Sai, Krishna became a Christian and lived in Madras. Satya Sai went about with him "everywhere hand in hand," and the two intimates were called "Radha-Krishna." Priddy indicates that such details became suppressed, though many villagers were aware of the anomaly and "none of whom dare say a word about it" (*ibid.*, p. 3).

11.   *Ibid.*, p. 48.

12.   *Ibid.*

13.   *Ibid.*, pp. 1, 30.

14.   *Ibid.*, p. 4.

15.   *Ibid.*, p. 7. Priddy adds details of what Dr. Bhatia divulged, including his report of the "physically injurious anal rape of a minor, a boy student." This report was included in Bailey's *Findings*, though with the error of stating the boy to be seven years of age instead of in the seventh Standard. The boy was nevertheless underage, and was gravely abused.

16.   *Ibid.*

17.   *Ibid.*, p. 17.

18.   *Ibid.*
19.   *Ibid.*, p. 35, and repeating the guru's injunction to the same victim that "if you don't do what I say, your life will be filled with pain and suffering."
20.   *Ibid.*, p. 10.
21.   *Ibid.*, pp. 11–12.
22.   *Ibid.*, p. 17. Conway is described as having been an official of the Satya Sai Baba Centre of San Francisco in the early 1980s.
23.   *Ibid.*, p. 19, and reporting Jed Geyerhahn.
24.   *Ibid.*, p. 21.
25.   *Ibid.*, p. 23, from the report by Greg Gerson from Houston.
26.   *Ibid.*, p. 9. The ring is elsewhere described as a gold ring with a "green diamond."
27.   *Ibid.*, p. 25.
28.   *Ibid.*, p. 27.
29.   *Ibid.*, p. 35.
30.   *Ibid.*
31.   *Ibid.*, p. 37.
32.   *Ibid.*, p. 39.
33.   *Ibid.*, p. 33.
34.   *Ibid.*, p. 34.
35.   *Ibid.*, p. 16.
36.   *Ibid.*, p. 38.
37.   *Ibid.*
38.   *Ibid.*, p. 45.
39.   *Ibid.*, p. 44.
40.   *Ibid.*
41.   *Ibid.*, p. 40.
42.   *Ibid.*
43.   *Ibid.*, p. 46.
44.   See Shepherd, *Pointed Observations* (Dorchester, Dorset: Citizen Initiative, 2005), p. 373 note 98, and warning of the failure in certain academic works to penetrate the hagiology invented by the sect and vice ring.

Photographic Credits

The famous photograph of Shirdi Sai Baba is copyrighted by the Shirdi shrine; the precise date is elusive. The photographs of Upasni Maharaj are copyrighted by Sakori ashram. The copyright to many photos of Meher Baba is held by Lawrence Reiter of America. The copyright holder of some photos has also been named as the Avatar Meher Baba Perpetual Public Charitable Trust of Ahmednagar. The present writer purchased a large number of photos from Meher Baba's brother Beheram Irani in the 1960s. Those photos had to be ordered via Beryl Williams of New York, who collaborated with Mani S. Irani in commissioning Behram to process them. Meher Baba had given his permission for their project, and Beheram seems to have been the copyright holder. The photo of Hazrat Babajan was at that time included in Beheram's set, with the permission of Meelan Studio (Poona), whose stamp it bore. Nobody seemed to know the date that photo was taken. Beryl Williams also gifted me with some other photos not included in Beheram's selection. In addition, I was bequeathed a number of other photos by the British devotee Ann Powell in 1965. In the mid-1960s I also gained photos from Douglas Eve in London, who had access to negatives inherited by the London devotees from Will Backett. I was also sent yet other photos of ashrams and related places by the American devotee Lenny Willoughby, who was the photographer in this instance at the time of the East-West Gathering in 1962. I have used all these sources in compiling the illustrations for this book. I have found that dates (and even locations) have differed in a number of ascriptions. The photo of Sheriar Mundegar Irani was salvaged by Behram and offered in a special "family" packet in 1965 and distributed in Britain by Adi S. Irani, which is how I got mine. Most devotees knew very little about the ex-dervish parent of Meher Baba. Cf. Shepherd, *From Oppression to Freedom*, Part One. The jacket photo of Satya Sai Baba is a well known Internet picture and is apparently copyrighted by the Satya Sai Baba Central Trust.

INDEX

Aurobindo Ghose, Shri, 1, 99, 103, 109, 215 n.348, 234 n.424

Australia, 149

avadhuta, 44, 57, 68

avatar, 2, 4, 20, 29, 43, 44, 48, 57, 67, 108, 110, 139, 140, 142, 146, 158, 159, 163 n.2, 196 n.238, 205 n.307, 214 n.342, 215 n.348, 217 n.359, 220 n.372, 223 n.396, 226 n.396, 229 n.399, 237 n.436, 246 n.462, 260 n.470, 261 n.473, 262 n.473, 264 n.477, 264–5 n.479, 268 n.480, 279

Avatar Meher Baba cult, 239 n.445, 249 n.464

Avatar Meher Baba Poona Centre, 55

Avatar's Abode (Kiel Mountain), 238 n.445, 239 n.447

Avila, 123, 206 n.310, 261 n.470

Awarif al-Maarif (Suhrawardi), 238 n.442

awliya, 12

Ayurveda, 64

Ayurvedic medicine, 63

Bab (Mirza Ali Muhammad), 109, 206 n.313

Baba (Meher Baba) Centres, 139, 142, 143–4, 145, 158, 223 n.396, 238 n.445, 248 n.463,

Babb, L. A., 163–5 n.2

Babis, 117, 206 n.313, 211 n.331

Backett, Mary, 225ff. n.396, 250 n.467, 255 n.468, 256 n.468, 258 n.468, 266 n.480

Backett, William A., 225ff. n.396, 241 n.456, 250 n.467, 253ff. n.468

Bade Baba, 40, 184 n.155

Bahais, 117, 118, 119, 211 n.331

Bahaullah, 211 n.331

Baidul (R. B. Irani), 117, 240 n.453, 244–5 n.460

Bailey, David, 274ff., 293, 295, 298

Bailey, Faye, 274ff.

Bala Sai Baba of Andhra, 279

Balakrishna Govind Shastri (brother of Upasni), 63, 67, 68, 183 n.141

Bam, 119, 120

Bandra, 39

Bangalore, 272, 276

Banne Mian (Banemiyan), 40, 184–5 n.156

Bappa Baba, 185 n.164

baqa, 52

baraka, 45, 47

Baria, Ardeshir Shapurji (Kaka), 199–200 n.259, 240 n.453, 244–5 n.460, 256 n.468

Baron Von Frankenburg, 235 n.432

Barton, Minta, 212 n.339

ba-shar, 48

batini, 248 n.464

Bayaji (bai) Kote, 185 n.158, 185 n.162

BBC, 287, 294, 295, 298

Be in the world but not of it, 111

Benares, 37, 78–80

Bengal, 140

Bhagavad-Gita, 10, 18, 24, 103, 179 n.106, 203 n.297

bhagavata, 42

Bhagubai, 75

bhajans, 37, 143

bhakta, 27, 28, 60, 87

Bhaktalilamrita (Das Ganu), 169 n.23

bhakti, 7, 15, 34, 102, 146, 188 n.179

bhakti tradition of Maharashtra, 45, 173 n.36

bhang, 51, 56, 182 n.135

bhangi, 75

Bharucha, H. P., 154, 241 n.455
Bharucha, Minoo, 219 n.364
Bharucha, P. S., 183 n.137
Bhatia, Dr. Naresh, 272–3, 289 n.4,
    300 n.15
Bhorawke (Borawke), Yeshwantrao, 87,
    88, 132, 133, 194 n.231, 195 n.233
Bhorgad cave, 188 n.184
Bhorgad mountain, 62
bhramishtavasta, 69
Bidkar Maharaj, 11
Bijapur, 47, 49, 50, 51, 52, 53
bi-shar, 48
Bistami, Abu Yazid, 109
blacksmiths, 75
Blair, Tony, 286, 290 n.16
Bombay, 7, 23, 44, 80, 86, 88, 116, 124
Bombay Presidency, 45
Borkar, Chandrabai, 71
Brabazon, Francis, 149, 151, 235–6
    n.432, 240 n.453, 244 n.460
Brahma, 25, 71
Brahma vivaha, 97, 98, 201 n.273
brahman, 6, 8, 9, 12, 15, 16, 18, 22, 24,
    27, 28, 29, 30, 31, 37, 38, 41, 44, 57,
    59, 72, 75, 88, 89, 90, 125, 166 n.12,
    181 n.125, 193 n.226
Brahman, 58
brahman caste, 103
Brahmanda, 191 n.206
brahmanical demotion of female rights,
    129
brahmanical food taboos, 31
brahmans, 5, 6, 7, 9, 10, 22, 29, 35, 40,
    41, 47, 66, 74, 76, 77, 78, 79, 83, 88,
    91, 96, 98, 99, 106, 107, 108, 113,
    124, 128, 131, 133, 195 n.233, 199
    n.259
brahmarandhra, 71
Brieseman, Dr., 155

Brisbane, 149, 263 n.476
British army, 9, 105
British Raj, 45, 53
Brooke, Tal, 277, 283, 298
Brunton, Paul, 123, 214 n.342, 215–16
    n.349, 244 n.460, 268 n.480
Buddhism, 96, 141
Buddhists, 145
Bushire, 115
Buti, Gopalrao, 37, 38, 39, 40
Buti wada, 39, 40, 41
buzurg, 117

cage (*pinjra*) at Sakori, 91, 92, 103, 134,
    202–3 n.285
cannabis, 51
carpenters, 75
Carter, L. F., 208 n.320
Carthew, Stephen, 290 n.9
caste issue, 94ff., 107–8
celibacy, 46, 111, 248 n.463
Ceylon, 140
Chand Bodhale, 15
chandalas, 75
Chandorkar, Narayan Govind
    (Nanasaheb), 24, 32, 179 n.106
Charters and Sayings
    (Narasimhaswami), 38, 40, 167 n.16
chavadi, 28, 180 n.121
Chhagan Sitaram Dattatrey, 193 n.226
Chhota Baba, 229 n.398
Chhota Khan, 40
Chicago University Press, 273
child marriage, 61, 103
chilim, 31, 182 n.135
chilla(s), 146, 235 n.429
China, 126
Chinnaswami, 75

311

206 n.316, 207 n.318, 208–9 n.320,
209 n.322, 211 n.331, 212 n.339, 213
n.340, 215 n.348, 215 n.349, 216
n.350, 216 n.354, 218 n.361, 218
n.362, 219 n.364, 220 n.372, 221
n.388, 222 n.393, 223 n.395, 229
n.399, 230 n.401, 231 n.403, 235–6
n.432, 238 n.442, 239 n.447, 239
n.448, 240–1 n.453, 241 n.454, 245
n.462, 248–9 n.464, 261 n.470, 261
n.471, 262–3 n.473, 264 n.477, 265ff.
n.480
Meher Baba, an Iranian Liberal
(Shepherd), 209 n.322, 210 n.325,
223 n.396, 232 n.417, 237 n.437, 238
n.445, 248 n.463, 248–9 n.464, 260
n.468
Meher Baba Association (London), 158,
249ff. n.467, 253ff. n.468
Meher Baba Oceanic (London), 249
n.466, 259 n.468
Meher Baba sect, viii, ix, 157, 194 n.229
Meher Baba's Call (1954), 142
Meher Center-on-the-Lakes (Myrtle
Beach, South Carolina), 143, 148,
149, 153, 213 n.340, 213 n.341, 223
n.396, 224ff., 228 n.397, 229 n.398,
232 n.417, 237 n.437, 248 n.463, 258
n.468
Meher Prabhu (Kalchuri), 168 n.21, 240
n.453
Mehera J. Irani, 130, 139, 156, 197
n.245, 217 n.357, 222 n.391, 223
n.395, 245 n.461, 266 n.480
Meherabad, 100, 105ff., 135, 158, 160,
208 n.320, 263 n.476, 264 n.477
Meherabad Hill, 105, 108, 138, 156, 266
n.480
Meherabad tomb, 152, 154, 155, 158,
204 n.305, 261 n.470

Meherazad, 138–9, 141, 144, 150, 151,
158, 159, 263 n.476
Melanie (pop star), 153
Meloy, Glen, 283
Merwan S. Irani (Meher Baba), 76, 79,
81, 82, 83, 84, 85, 86, 87–8, 130,
192 n.221, 194 n.231, 195 n.234, 206
n.313
mescaline, 240 n.450
mihrab, 210 n.325
miracle hoaxes, 269–70
miracle lore, vii, 2ff., 6–7, 19, 29, 31,
43, 55, 136–7, 186 n.171
miracle lore repudiated, 110, 136–7
miracle mentality, viii, 21
Miraj, 77
moha, 102, 203 n.293
monism, 52
monistic beliefs, 50
Mubaraka, 118
Muhammad (prophet), 26, 47, 192
n.220
mukti, 91
Mule Shastri, 37, 38
mulla, 13, 46
Mundegar the *salar*, 118
murid, 15, 46
murshid, 12, 149
Muslim caste, 7
Muslim *faqirs*, 19
Muslim Sufi influences, 15
Muslims, 7, 8, 9, 11, 18, 23, 28, 40, 41,
47, 53, 57, 76, 89, 105, 108, 115ff.,
113, 158, 192 n.220, 197 n.241, 204
n.304

naga sadhus, 50, 93
Nagpur, 39, 53, 65, 74, 76

Rajahmundry, 142, 143, 235 n.427

Rajneesh, Bhagwan Shree, 1, 3, 111, 146, 157, 208–9 n.320, 238 n.442

Rajneesh Neo-Tantra, 111

Rama, 37

Rama Ashram, 188 n.186

Ramadasis, 37

Ramakrishna of Dakshineswar, 246 n.462, 273, 281 n.14

Ramalingaswami, 39, 181 n.132

Ramana Maharshi, 1, 6, 77, 181 n.127

Rama-Navami festival, 27, 180 n.118

Ramju (Abdul Karim) Abdulla, 113, 125, 127, 210 n.324, 210 n.325, 214 n.342, 219 n.369, 267 n.480

rasul, 120

reincarnation, 53

reincarnation (Meher Baba), 145

Reiter, Lawrence, 231 n.404, 266–7 n.480, 302

Reza Shah, 120

Rigopoulos, Antonio, viii, 4, 10, 17, 19, 40, 50, 55, 56, 165 n.3, 166 n.13, 168 n.17, 169 n.23, 170 n.25, 172 n.30, 172 n.36, 173 n.36, 173–4 n.37, 176 n.79, 177 n.86, 177 n.89, 178 n.104, 181 n.128, 181 n.129, 181 n.132, 182 n.136, 183 n.138, 184 n.150, 184 n.153, 185 n.167, 186 n.171, 186 n.173, 186–7 n.174, 190 n.201, 192 n.213, 221 n.388, 230 n.402, 231 n.403, 266 n.480

ritualism demoted, 145

Rizvi, S. A. A., 55

Roshan, 11

Roshan Shah Mian, 11, 12, 13, 15, 30, 58

Ross, Sir Denison, 121–2

Round Table Conference (London), 95, 121

Rumi, Jalal al-Din, 45, 56, 109

sadguru, 85, 88, 94, 133, 146, 159, 191 n.212, 195 n.231, 206 n.309

sadguru/qutub entities, 262 n.473

sadhana, 34, 59, 60, 65, 68, 83, 98, 101, 102, 145, 146

sadhus, 3, 20, 24, 34, 51, 93, 150

sadra, 111

Sage of Sakori (Narasimhaswami), 133, 137, 187 n.175

sahaj samadhi, 69

sahaja, 93

sahavas, 149, 156, 238 n.441

saheb-e-zaman, 139

Sahukar, Mani, 102, 186 n.173, 188 n.184

Sai Baba movement, vii, viii, 1, 6, 42, 44, 110, 136, 137, 160, 165 n.3, 206 n.316, 210 n.325, 221 n.388, 231 n.403

Sai Baba of Shirdi (Shirdi Sai), vii, viii, 1, 2ff.,, 69, 72, 76, 77, 79, 80, 81, 86, 90, 98, 108, 112, 138, 142, 147, 160, 165 n.6, 166 n.12, 166 n.13, 167 n.14, 167 n.16, 168 n.17, 168–9 n.21, 169 n.23, 169 n.24, 170 n.24, 171 n.25, 171 n.26, 172 n.36, 174 n.37, 175 n.62, 176 n.77, 179 n.106, 180 n.122, 182 n.135, 183 n.149, 184 n.153, 184 n.155, 185 n.167, 186 n.171, 186 n.174, 192 n.221, 199 n.259, 206 n.316, 219 n.369, 221 n.388, 265 n.480, 279, 287–8, 294

Sai devotionalism, 16

Sai Sharan Anand, Swami (Vaman Prangovind Patel), 11, 22, 30, 57–8, 183 n.149

Sai Vak Sudha, 92

Sainath (Hindu name for Shirdi Sai Baba), 28

Sakori ashram, 77ff., 100, 109, 129, 131,